European Modernity
and the Arab Mediterranean

# European Modernity
# and the Arab Mediterranean

Toward a New Philology
and a Counter-Orientalism

Karla Mallette

**PENN**

UNIVERSITY OF PENNSYLVANIA PRESS

PHILADELPHIA · OXFORD

Published by
University of Pennsylvania Press
Philadelphia, Pennsylvania 19104-4112

Printed in the United States of America on acid-free paper

10   9   8   7   6   5   4   3   2   1

Library of Congress Cataloging-in-Publication Data
Mallette, Karla.
    European modernity and the Arab Mediterranean : toward
a new philology and a counter-orientalism / Karla Mallette.
        p. cm.
    Includes bibliographical references and index.
    ISBN 978-0-8122-4241-6 (hardcover : alk. paper)
    1. Arabic philology—History—19th century.   2. Arabic
philology—History—20th century.   3. Islamic civilization.
4. Europe—Civilization—Arab influences.   5. Scheherazade
(Legendary character).   I. Title.
PJ6057.M35   2010
492.709—dc22
                                                    2009049134

*Once again, this book is for Evangeline*

CONTENTS

*Chapter 1*

# Scheherazade among the Philologists
# (Paris, 1704)

Il giudizio sopra facilità o difficoltà di una lezione sarà tanto più sicura, quanto meglio il giudice conoscerà le consuetudini di linguaggio e di pensiero delle età che l'hanno trasmessa, che può averla coniata. Il miglior critico di un testo greco di tradizione bizantina sarà quello che, oltre a essere un perfetto grecista, sia anche perfetto bizantinista. Il miglior editore di un autore latino trasmesso in codici medievali o postmedievali sarà colui che, quanto il suo autore e la sua lingua e i suoi tempi e la lingua dei suoi tempi, altrettanto bene conosca il Medioevo o l'umanesimo. Un critico siffatto è un ideale che nessuno può incarnare in sè perfettamente, ma al quale ognuno ha il dovere di cercare di avvicinarsi.

   —Giorgio Pasquali, *Storia della tradizione e critica del testo*

[A judgment concerning the facility or difficulty of a reading will be that much surer if the one judging knows the habits of language and of thought of the age that has transmitted the reading, and that may have created it. The best critic of a Greek text transmitted through the Byzantine tradition will be the one who, besides being a perfect Greek scholar, is also a perfect Byzantinist. The best editor of a Latin author transmitted in medieval or postmedieval codices will be the one who, along with his author and his author's language and times and the language of his own times, will know just as well the Middle Ages and humanism. Such a critic is an ideal that no one can incarnate perfectly in himself, but which each has the obligation to try to approach.]

I BEGIN THIS book by posing a series of questions that I will not attempt to answer until the final chapters. In these pages I will describe the stages by which modern scholars proposed and defended a historical narrative that contradicts accepted histories of the origins of the European nations. The Orientalists whose work I survey traced a modern European national genius to a spark kindled by the Arabs who occupied the territory of the modern nation during the medieval past. They argued that European modernity, in all its splendor, emerged when Christian Europe coaxed this spark into a roaring bonfire: when Christians acquired a rational science from Islamic translations of Aristotle, for instance, or when they learned from the Arabs to sing poetry about the spirit of love between men and women and its carnal celebration. This version of medieval history contains a germ of truth, to be sure; the scholars whose work I read here did a good job of substantiating it, and elements of it are widely accepted today by historians. Yet because it challenges the standard genealogy of the intellectual patrimony of modern Europe—from Greek and Roman antiquity, by way of the Italian Renaissance—it has not won universal acceptance.

The scholars who argued the centrality of the Arab Mediterranean to European modernity used a scholarly methodology that, although it is of ancient vintage, was decanted into sparkling new bottles during the nineteenth century. They produced philology-powered readings of national history—the history of a modern European nation as written by Orientalists, a story that lay unread for centuries because it was hidden in Arabic texts. And their narratives acquired an unprecedented power from the startling claims that philologists began to make about the *scientism* of their reading practice during the nineteenth century, as philology absorbed the deductive methodologies and the self-assurance of the modern sciences. The philological reading asserted that its scientific standards granted it a unique authority: it and it alone could interpret the truths concealed in historical texts. At the same time, during the nineteenth century, philology came to support and to rely upon historicism. It no longer saw itself as a primarily aesthetic strategy of reading whose purpose was to untangle the linguistic difficulties of the great books of antiquity and reveal their literary genius. Rather it became both handmaiden to and mistress of the science of history. It assumed that only detailed and precise historical knowledge about the era when a text was produced would allow the scholar to interpret the text accurately. And it asserted (with somewhat brazen tautology) that dependable knowledge about the past could be derived only from patient study of the texts that the philologists themselves taught the world to interpret.

In this book I will sketch the outlines of scholarship produced (roughly) between 1850 and 1950 that transformed the way we understand the intellectual history of the medieval Mediterranean and insisted on the relevance of that history to the contemporary actualities and the future of modern Europe. Despite the undeniable brilliance, importance, and beauty of this scholarship, it raises crucial questions about the methods we use to read a history whose extant record is primarily textual: Does the hermeneutic circle compromise the value of the historical conclusions we derive by studying premodern texts? Philologists have long recognized that in the most insightful readings of texts made difficult by their historic or linguistic distance from us, understanding frequently precedes analysis. Brilliant philology begins with a spark of intuition and picks its way through the text seeking confirmation (or refutation) of that insight. This is true of the Orientalist philology I will discuss in this book—the work of historians who traced European modernity to the Arab Mediterranean—as it is of more normative scholarship on textual history. Does the philologist's willingness at times to beg the question, to suspend deductive analysis and advance understanding of the text by means of the inductive leap, undermine the contribution that the philological reading can make to our understanding of history?

This conundrum, of course, calls into play disciplinary distinctions and niceties that we as scholars use to position ourselves professionally within the academy. What has literary scholarship to do with the discipline of history, or Arabic literature to do with the literary history of Europe, or the methodology of comparative literature to do with philology? The three questions may at first blush seem unrelated. Yet the scholarship I examine in this book will reveal their interrelatedness. The scholars whose work I will read and (in most cases) celebrate negotiated a series of conversion experiences in order to articulate the decisive contributions that the nations of Mediterranean Europe made to European modernity. First, and most dramatically, they learned Arabic in order to read the past of a European nation. And their scholarship was informed by the presupposition that Arabic and Western letters were not alien each to the other, but rather sibling branches of the same parent stock (to jumble the genealogical and botanical metaphors used by nineteenth-century philologists). Thus at times their pursuit of knowledge about the nation's history required them to trample the finer distinctions between the academic disciplines and to produce readings of the textual past that some of their peers denounced as unmotivated (that is, *unscientific*) or simply outré.

I begin in this first chapter by surveying the developments in philological scholarship most relevant to my concerns, using the peculiar textual history of the work of Arabic literature that has become more familiar than any other to Western audiences—the *Thousand and One Nights*—to explore the evolution of Orientalism and philology in Europe in general over the last three centuries. And in the next I will move to southern Europe, examining the use of philology to articulate a national history in a region characterized by late development and a local history complicated by medieval Arab occupation. Thus these first two chapters serve as co-introductions, sketching a broad overview of the three terms central to the argument of the book: Orientalism, philology, and nationalism.

The bulk of the book examines the work of philologists and historians who depicted the European Middle Ages as a drama starring not only Christian kings and queens, theologians and minstrels, but also Arab sultans, philosophers and poets, Berber warriors, and an Arab maiden with a Persian name who has had an inordinate influence on European letters over the last millennium and more. The book began (as philological readings frequently do) with a perception that matured into an intuition and inspired the investigation of a textual puzzle. While researching the history of the Arabs in Sicily, I was startled by the unique importance that the Normans held in the work of Sicilian scholar Michele Amari. Amari depicted the Normans of Sicily as antecedents of the Renaissance and thus the inventors of modernity. While this assertion might appear grasping to a casual reader, a medievalist would find it unsurprising; nineteenth-century European scholars frequently made such claims on behalf of the medieval fathers of their respective nations. What made Amari's scholarship striking was the relation between his *Normans* and the *Arabs* from whom they won their Sicilian kingdom (and who were the focus of his monumental history, the *Storia dei musulmani di Sicilia*). The Normans, in his telling, channeled the learning and culture of the Arabs; by translating Arab scholarship and cultural practice into the languages of Europe, they planted the seeds of the Renaissance. That is, Amari implicitly made the *Arabs* of Sicily into the progenitors of modernity. (On Amari, see Chapter 3 below.) And I found a similar embrace of Arab culture as the origin of a modern sensibility in other scholarship on the history of Arab Sicily and Spain and on parallel questions such as the influence of Islamic culture on Dante or Petrarch. Enrico Cerulli affirmed the formative importance of Arab depictions of the afterworld to Dante's vision (see Chapter 5). In so doing he picked up a thread first unspooled by Miguel Asín Palacios, who wrote a bold book arguing the influence on Dante of Ibn 'Arabi—"a Spaniard," according to Asín, "though a Muslim" (see Chapter 2). The nineteenth-century eccentric Pietro Valerga proposed that the soul of medieval Arab poet Ibn al-Farid was reincarnated in the poet who single-handedly invented literary modernity, Petrarch (see Chapter 2); Emilio García Gómez wrote that the genius of Spanish verse was first sung by Arab poets (see Chapter 6). In the most startling version of this narrative I found, a nation negotiating the difficult and intricate process of standardizing its national tongue, Malta, used the Arabic language as a template in order to turn a spoken vernacular into a literary medium (see Chapter 4).

There were, of course, other scholars who scoffed at the theses these men presented, historians who maintained the exteriority and irrelevance of Arab culture to European modernity (they are discussed especially in Chapter 2). It seemed to me, however, that the story of scholarship on the Arab origins of European culture was one that should be told for two reasons in particular. In the first place, despite expanding interest in the history of Orientalism, too little still is known about the Orientalism of southern Europe. And yet it is in many ways the most interesting of the various schools of Orientalist thought, for southern European Orientalists frequently are writing national history: they often describe the Arab past of their nation. And in the second place the story of this scholarship is an extraordinarily hopeful one. It is the tale of a peculiarly Mediterranean modernity, a model of modernity created by Arabs and Europeans in concert and to which Arabs and Europeans both continue to contribute.

## Philology and European Intellectual History

The story begins (as philological stories so often do) with a definition. What precisely does the term *philology* connote? Edward Said, in a late essay entitled "The Return to Philology," made a bid to revamp philology and burnish the philologist's somewhat dusty reputation. The essay begins by evoking two figures whom Said situates as gatekeepers of the philological tradition. One of them embodies the image of philology as (in Said's words) "sterile, ineffectual, and hopelessly irrelevant to life": he is the Reverend Casaubon, from George Eliot's *Middlemarch*—the creaky, paradigm-obsessed scholar whom the well-intentioned but misguided Dorothea marries. Said plays Casaubon against a contemporary figure who could be called the poster boy for a fertile, effective, and relevant philology. Nietzsche began as a philologist, and he retained a philological passion for language throughout his life. In "The Return to Philology" Said celebrates the philology symbolized by Nietzsche as a peculiarly engaged and committed reading practice. He defines the philological project as "a detailed, patient scrutiny of and a lifelong attentiveness to the words and rhetorics by which language is used by human beings who exist in history."[1] And Said calls for a return to this Nietzschean philological tradition.

Said's discussion illuminates a tension central to the history of philological practice. *Philology* can connote the pursuit of knowledge of the text in isolation from—even as distinct from—lived history (this is the branch of philology symbolized, in Said's discussion, by Casaubon). At the same time it can suggest the network of links that bind lived and written reality (represented by Nietzsche). Anthony Grafton, in his elegant scholarship on the philology of the humanists, has identified a similar tension in the work of the Italian intellectuals of the sixteenth century. "One set of humanists," Grafton writes, "seeks to make the ancient world live again, assuming its undimmed relevance and unproblematic accessibility; another set seeks to put the ancient texts back into their own time, admitting that reconstruction of the past is difficult and that success may reveal the irrelevance of ancient experience and precept to modern problems."[2] Grafton depicts the competition as pragmatic: the ends of the scholar's research—in the first case the text as literary model, in the second the text as historical record—will determine to which camp he belongs. Said suggests that the distinction is a measure of personal commitment and personal engagement. Both, however, describe the same paradox: philology can denote a reading strategy that either distances the reader from the text or annuls the distance between text and reader.

Or it might perform both of these operations at once. Grafton writes that certain philologists (both humanists and nineteenth-century European intellectuals) strove "at once to read their texts historically and to treat them as ahistorical classics," and thereby "made their texts yield a meaning directly useful to modern readers," despite the antiquity of those texts. Arguably, this tendency—what Grafton calls an "interpretive schizophrenia"—has been present but marginal throughout the long history of philology.[3] During the nineteenth century it was elevated from scholarly pathology to become the modus operandi of an empowered philology—a transformation that marks the point of departure for this book.[4] Herman Melville began *Moby-Dick* (first published in 1851) with a philological investigation of the word *whale:* a handful of dictionary definitions lifted from "old lexicons and grammars"; a short list of the words for "whale" in languages from Hebrew, Greek, Latin, and Anglo-Saxon to the Romance languages and the tongues of the South Seas; eighty brief descriptions of whales gleaned from various texts, from the Bible to Rabelais and Shakespeare to Darwin and the popular whaling songs of Melville's own day (compiled, according to the text, by a sub-sub-librarian—stand down, Nietzsche!). The prelude renders the whale visceral and real in the reader's mind—or rather the transhistorical traces that the Leviathan has left in language, a crystalline portrait of literary and linguistic *whaleness.* And it demonstrates to the twenty-first-century reader the visceral power that philology acquired during the course of the nineteenth century.

Philology, briefly stated, attained the ability to create intimacy between an object located at a limitless distance from the reader—the whales of the open sea; the persons and events described in the texts of scriptural antiquity—and the reading subject, through the medium of textuality. It did not deny the distance of the phenomena described in the text in order to achieve this. On the contrary, philologists affirmed and even emphasized the historical and/or geographical space that separated the composition of the text from its modern, Western readers. However, at the same time the philologist confidently asserted the capacity of modern scientific methods to allow specialists to adjust for historical or geographical difference: to reconstruct the historical and linguistic conditions that would reveal the meaning of the text.

The philological revolution began with the German hermeneutists who in the closing years of the eighteenth century and the opening decades of the nineteenth devised new strategies for studying the texts (both scriptural and secular) of antiquity. The hermeneutists modeled rigorous methods of scrutinizing the letter of the text, drawing on a profound understanding of historical linguistics, grammar, and literary practice. And their readings promised to generate a more dynamic insight into the spirit of the text. The philological revolution would have a profound influence on nineteenth-century scholarship in the humanities, influencing disciplines from literary studies to religious history to social and political history. In this book I am interested in one philological trend in particular: the genesis of a technology of reading designed to describe the formative affiliations that linked modern communities to premodern documents of foundation. There are a thousand and one ways to tell the story of the regenerative philology of the nineteenth century. I have chosen one of the most visible advances (and controversies) of the period, also one of the driest aspects of the philologist's job and most suggestive of the clichéd derogatory descriptions of the philologist: the dispute over appropriate standards for the production of modern editions of premodern texts.

The first technological advance in the science of textual criticism—the first philological *discovery*—of the nineteenth century came from Italian Jesuit and Orientalist Angelo Mai (1782–1854). Mai pioneered a technique for reading the earlier and nearly eradicated script of medieval palimpsests, which he used in 1814 to reveal a Ciceronian text previously thought lost. Giacomo Leopardi wrote one of his most ardent *canzoni* in praise of Mai and his marvelous capacity to "svegliar dalle tombe i nostri padri" (or "awaken our fathers from their tombs").[5] More recent historians of philology—in particular Helmut Müller-Sievers and Sebastiano Timpanaro—have looked on Mai's activities with a more critical eye.[6] The technique that Mai used to expose the lower, earlier hand—bathing the manuscript pages in a noxious chemical bath—brought hidden script to light, but only temporarily, long enough for the philologist to transcribe it. After that not only the earlier writing but also the subsequent hand would be destroyed. And because he typically disassembled manuscripts in order to submit them to this process, Mai sometimes damaged other works as well, or at least made it impossible for subsequent scholars to reconstruct their collation.

There is something ghastly but also enormously suggestive about Mai's contribution to the history of textual criticism. Müller-Sievers has pointed out the parallels between Mai's method and contemporary Romantic notions of artistic creation. The philologist read the text by achieving a spontaneous and temporary union with the manuscript; once this moment passed, no one would read it again. Add the chemical bath in which he submerged the manuscript and the image of the fathers rising from their tombs, and a portrait emerges of Angelo Mai as the Dr. Frankenstein of the Ambrosian Library. That is, more than a Romantic artist, Mai resembled—and, in fact, was—a *scientist* of the Romantic era. Mai pioneered philology as textual conflagration; he ignited the text and read its meaning by the light of the flames that licked the edge of the page. He produced the results he sought, and by those standards his contemporaries judged him: the intense, almost sacred interaction between philologist and text allowed the dead fathers to speak again, mediating between the present and a distant moment of origin. And once he discovered how to reveal the lower hand in the palimpsests he abandoned his training in the Oriental languages—Hebrew, Aramaic, Syriac, Arabic, Amharic—so tangential to the discovery that allowed him to channel the voices of the Greek and Latin fathers.

As the nineteenth century advanced, scholars made substantial improvements in the methods they used to reconstruct medieval and ancient texts. The "Lachmannian method"—typically evoked today in quotation marks because it didn't really begin with the philologist for whom it was named, Karl Lachmann (1793–1851), and because Lachmann himself didn't consistently practice it—was based on an implicit understanding of the text as an organic phenomenon and therefore subject to the laws of nature. Lachmannian strategies of textual criticism were tooled to reconstruct a literary text produced in a manuscript environment. The vicissitudes (or the felicities) of nonmechanical reproduction generate variance. Because of scribal error and scribal intervention no two copies of the same manuscript are identical. How should the modern editor select between manuscript variants in order to reconstitute the text as the author wrote it? In the Lachmannian model of textual criticism the scholar begins by constructing a stemma codicum: a plausible history of textual transmission, the family tree or genealogy of the text as it has come down to us in its surviving manuscript copies. The textual critic identifies variants that entered the tradition through scribal innovation, each generation producing a new crop of variants and thus marking its increasing distance from the Ur-text—the oldest and purest version of the text. By systematically removing all detected errors the scholar aims to recreate that originary text.

The Lachmannian revolution was decisive in a number of ways, and Lachmannian method is still highly regarded by textual critics. It serves as a superb standard for producing the critical edition: it accounts for the diversity of textual witnesses while not allowing manuscript diversity to threaten the intelligibility of the text. But Lachmannian method is significant in its form no less than its content, in medium as much as in message. Lachmannian textual critics used the language of science to describe what had been seen largely in terms of aesthetics: the textual critic's understanding of the meaning of the text and the intentions of its author. They devised a technical vocabulary, a chorus of plummy Latin words designating phenomena and activities peculiar to the textual critic's work: stemma codicum, textus receptus, editio princeps, recensio. And they applied rigid standards that allowed the textual critic to reconstruct a work as close to the Platonic ideal that existed in the author's mind as humanly possible. Of course, many of the methods adopted by Lachmannian editors during the nineteenth century were not new.[7] However, a sense of furious industry arises from their introductions to their editions and their textual controversies, as if they labored under a terrible urgency, a commandment to fill some Noah's ark with all the literary harvest of antiquity and the Middle Ages before the flood.

The "Lachmannian method" engaged in an emphatic and sincere dialogue with evolving scientific models and therefore possessed at least a veneer of the inductive methods of which Angelo Mai was wholly innocent. For this reason, it is a useful register of the scientific ambitions of philological practice during the nineteenth century. And scientism proved a compelling model for scholars engaged in the "lower criticism" (as textual criticism with the aim of producing the modern edition was known in the English-speaking world) as well as the "higher criticism" (hermeneutics, or textual interpretation). Philologists perceived their discipline as (in the words of Ernest Renan) "an organized science with a serious and elevated object; it is the *science of the products of the human spirit*."[8] At the same time, some nineteenth-century philological practice combined scientism and sacralization of the text. Philologists used emerging scientific models of reading to charge historically distant texts with dynamic contemporary relevance or to produce revitalized readings of texts already deemed sacred. This *philologie engagée* was directed at two types of texts in particular: works depicted as founding documents of national identity (for instance, the *Chanson de Roland*, the *Divine Comedy*, or *El Cid*) and religious scripture.[9] It asserted its scientific precision and vaunted the greater accuracy of its readings because of the scientific methodology it used. At the same time it used the lens of a science-assisted reading practice to examine (or, more accurately, to create) the intimate bonds that linked contemporary communities to a distant medieval or ancient moment of origin.

Obviously, such motivated readings of medieval texts might have (and most usually did have) a pressing contemporary relevance. See, for instance, Gaston Paris's reading of the *Chanson de Roland* at the Collège de France during the 1870 Prussian siege of Paris. It is not remotely surprising to a twenty-first-century reader that Paris evokes the *Roland* at such a moment as a banner of French identity and French pride: such is the staying power of the engaged philological reading of medieval texts. What we find more startling is that he should pause precisely at such a moment to underscore the *scientism* of the philological method he uses to illuminate his reading of the medieval text. In a charged, dense, and poetic passage, Paris evokes the rigid discipline that science imposes on its practitioners, while at the same time visibly chafing against disciplinary limits:

> But—for all that it is foreign by its very nature to sentiments, even the most elevated, and to passions, even the noblest—science is not bound to restrict itself with a merciless narrowness to the domain of the facts it observes. It re-emerges from the domain of fact into the perspective of the laws that govern the development of humanity in general or nations in particular, of the consequences that it has not only the right but the need to bring to light. If one forbids it this, one reduces it to being nothing more than erudition, a blind and greedy seeker that does not enjoy its own riches and accumulates only for its heirs.

Paris will burst the bonds that science places on the philologist when he proclaims defiantly: "I will not resist the occasion to demonstrate those close ties that bind us to this poem;—that real solidarity that renders this ancient French poem still entirely alive to us, this ancient poem that we had forgotten so completely and that we believed to be good and dead."[10]

Nineteenth-century philologists saw the epics that stood like indestructible monuments at the origins of their national literary traditions as sublime expressions of national identity. At moments of national crisis—these, of course, came thick and fast during the European nineteenth century—the philologist could evoke the medieval epics as touchstones of national identity, national anthems *avant la lettre*. "Une littérature nationale," Paris would declare at the rousing conclusion of his address to the Collège de France, "est l'élément le plus indestructible de la vie d'un peuple."[11] And in 1844, Giuseppe Mazzini—not a philologist, but (like Paris) an ardent nationalist—wrote, a propos of another nation and another national epic: "The thought that was in Dante is the same as that which is now fermenting in the bosom of our own epoch, and we feel this instinctively; therefore it is that we press around him with fresh ardor. . . . [His] aim is the *national aim*—the same desire that vibrates instinctively in the bosoms of twenty-two millions of men, and which is the secret of the immense popularity Dante has in Italy."[12] These readings of medieval texts promoted a palpable and urgent sense of identity between medieval and modern Italians or between medieval and modern Frenchmen, and deployed that identification to an immediate political end. And when conducted by professional readers—by philologists—they frequently underscored at the same time the modernity of their reading methods and the superior precision that scientific reading methods granted their interpretations of the text.

Readers familiar with the contours of nineteenth-century philology will recognize that, mutatis mutandis, Mazzini's and Paris's readings of literary history differ not in nature but in rhetorical degree from typical contemporary philological readings. During the nineteenth century European intellectuals recognized the necessity to construct a horizon for the nations emerging in the foreground, the literary historical equivalent of the swathes of ravishing Tuscan countryside glimpsed through palace windows in Italian Renaissance paintings. This they found in the medieval literatures which expressed a national genius in its oldest and purest form. In Germany the *Niebelungenlied*; in Britain *Beowulf*; in France the *Chanson de Roland;* in Spain *El Cid;* in Italy the *Commedia* in the north and the lyrics of the "Scuola Siciliana" in the south: these works came to be recognized during the course of the nineteenth century as the ululations that celebrated the birth of a recognizable national character in a distant medieval terrain.[13]

Much, of course, distinguished this process nation by nation and literary work by literary work. For instance—and to name only one of many historical facts that differentiate one national context from another—*Beowulf* survives in a single manuscript and was published in a modern edition only in 1815; its language is incomprehensible to a speaker of modern English. Dante's *Commedia* was among the most-copied of medieval literary works, attested by more than seven hundred manuscript versions, and though it demands a thoughtful reading Dante's Italian is recognizably a grandmother to modern Italian. Yet both *Beowulf* and the *Commedia* became objects of scholarly attention during the nineteenth century, when literary historians came to realize the unique contemporary relevance of their scholarship: they gave national cultural identity a history—indeed, they identified its point of origin.

Furthermore, the process of adducing the medieval origins of the nation that began with the nineteenth century continued well into the twentieth. Joseph Bédier, for instance, contributed to it in the French context in the years following World War I; Enrico Cerulli and Emilio García Gómez, whose work I will discuss later in this book, produced scholarship in this spirit during the post–World War II period. Not all philological works produced during the period functioned in this way, of course. Many philologists discussed aspects of distant premodern texts without delineating their relevance to the present; these are the unengaged (and unengaging) studies of the dusty past represented in Edward Said's philological economy by the figure of the unfortunate Reverend Casaubon. (Of course philologists themselves will insist on the importance—indeed the necessity—of such philological research: the Reverend Casaubons of previous generations are the giants on whose shoulders we stand, and their insights provide the foundation for our analyses.) Some, however, used new technologies of reading to study premodern texts for the purpose (sometimes explicitly stated as such, sometimes not) of producing an archaeology of a modern community. By asserting its scientism such philology insists on the distance between the text and the modern reading, a gap that can be bridged only through the sustained effort of trained specialists. And by claiming identity between the sentiments expressed in the text and those felt *in the bosoms of modern men* it erases that distance.

A development parallel to the nationalist philology of the European nineteenth century occurred later in the century and chiefly on another continent—in North America, where religious scholars utilized philological method in order to revitalize readings of Christian scripture. Their readings stressed the intimate connections between ancient texts and modern communities defined not by political but by religious identity. German hermeneutists had kicked off the philological revolution during the late years of the eighteenth century in part by using new, rigorous, scientific strategies of reading to reassess Christian scripture. Hermeneutical research made fantastic progress in revolutionizing the interpretation of scriptural texts and the sorts of information that could be gleaned by studying them in the Christian West. However, by the closing decades of the nineteenth century some Christian scholars decided that the hermeneutists had gone too far. Historians generally point to an article entitled "Inspiration," written by Princeton Theological Seminary professors A. A. Hodge (1823–86) and B. B. Warfield (1851–1921) and published in 1881, as the point of departure for this revolution.[14] Hodge and Warfield wrote out of and in response to the hermeneutical tradition, and they acknowledged that scriptural texts had been authored by human beings and in conditions defined by human history. However, they simultaneously asserted the divine inspiration and inerrancy of Christian scripture, arguing that divine guidance more than human foibles determined the content of scripture. They believed that corruption of the texts was minimal. And they believed that the task of philological criticism was to resolve the few interpretive doubts that still shrouded the meaning of scripture. "Believing criticism," Hodge wrote elsewhere, "by the discovery and collation of more ancient and accurate copies, is constantly advancing the Church to the possession of a more perfect text of the original Scriptures than she has enjoyed since the apostolic age."[15]

The fundamentalist movement would acquire its name from a series of pamphlets published in the United States between 1910 and 1915, *The Fundamentals: A Testimony to the Truth*. These publications promoted the foundational doctrines articulated by conservative Protestant Christians during the second half of the nineteenth century; early issues include articles on the virgin birth and divinity of Jesus, the nature of the Holy Spirit, and the inerrancy of the Bible. Most relevant to the current argument, *The Fundamentals* accepted the hermeneutists' historical analysis of scripture (or, as it is called in the pages of the publication, the Higher Criticism or simply *philology*) as the gold standard of biblical analysis. At the same time, the scholars who wrote for the pamphlets (and they were scholars, their names followed by thickets of initials demonstrating their academic credentials) argued forcefully that Bible criticism must approach the text from the perspective of belief. Professor J. J. Reeve states the situation this way, in a testimonial entitled "My Personal Experience with the Higher Criticism":

> [The Higher Criticism] is destined to stay and render invaluable aid. To the scholarly mind its appeal is irresistible. Only in the light of the historical occasion upon which it was produced, can the Old Testament be properly understood. A flood of light has already been poured in upon these writings. The scientific spirit which gave rise to it is one of the noblest instincts in the intellectual life of man. It is a thirst for the real and the true, that will be satisfied with nothing else. But, noble as is this scientific spirit, and invaluable as is the historical method, there are subtle dangers in connection with them. Everything depends upon the presuppositions with which we use the method.

Reeve argued that the philological revolution had inaugurated a revolution in the reading habits of *believing* scholars: "Conservative scholarship is rapidly awakening, and, while it will retain the legitimate use of the invaluable historical method, will sweep from the field most of the speculations of the critics."[16]

From an outsider's perspective, it appears that the first fundamentalists exhibit a remarkable insouciance in the face of the hermeneutic circle. Belief in divine guidance of the authors of the Old and New Testaments is (to use Reeve's terminology) a *presupposition* for textual criticism. The fundamentalists argue the inerrancy of scripture by citing scripture itself, by citing the practice of the early church, or simply as an article of faith. Doubts concerning the divine inspiration of the Bible, according to Charles Hodge, "have their origin in the state of the heart. The most important of all the evidences of Christianity can never be properly appreciated unless the heart be right in the sight of God."[17]

But it must be said, in defense of the fundamentalists, that in this blithe deployment of a circular argument to establish the legitimacy of its primary thesis, fundamentalist philology does not differ appreciably from nationalist philology. In his address to the Collège de France, Gaston Paris did not pause to prove the "solidarity" that linked the warriors of medieval Gaul to the Parisians of 1870. He might defend the scientism of his method in general; he might defend his reading of difficult lexical or historical points in the text in particular. But he did not turn the bright light of positivism on the kernel of his argument, the fundamental identity of medieval and modern "Frenchmen": for Paris, one senses, that was an article of faith. In each of the arguments I will discuss in this book—scholarly studies that argue an Arab origin for a modern European national identity—we find a similar combination of apparently inimical elements: scientism rubbing shoulders with an intuitive perception that looks unmotivated or misbegotten only to an outsider. Each of the Orientalist philologists whose work I will discuss spoke out of a profound personal conviction that created its own gravitational field. Their scholarship took its point of departure from an "inner click" (to borrow a term used by Leo Spitzer to describe a parallel phenomenon[18]): their perception of their nations' debt to the Arabs who occupied the territory of the nation during the Middle Ages.

The next document I offer in this galloping history of the philological art appeared eighteen years after the first of the *Fundamentals* pamphlets. It is one of the most extraordinary testimonies in the history of philology; and it turned literary scholars' complacent faith in the efficacy of Lachmannian textual criticism on its head. In 1928 Joseph Bédier (1864–1938) published an article that was in essence a manifesto attacking the "Lachmannian method." Bédier argued that the most fruitful response to the complexities of medieval textuality was a modern edition that did not claim to mediate between variant manuscript versions, as the Lachmannian edition did. Rather the textual critic ought to reproduce a single manuscript in its particularity and peculiarity—leaving intact, that is, its medieval alterity. Bédier's article remains one of the most frequently discussed philological essays of the twentieth century, in part because its provocations remain cogent and in part because of the startling beauty of Bédier's prose.[19] "Il en est," Bédier writes in the opening sentence, "de l'art d'éditer les anciens textes comme de tous les autres arts : il a évolué au gré de modes qui meurent et renaissent."[20] Thus in two lines of text Bédier both summons the shade of Ibn Khaldun (suggesting that human history, like the natural world, obeys an inescapable cyclical rhythm) and evokes the organic metaphors that he will consistently use in this article to describe (and to mock) Lachmannian method.

*La Tradition manuscrite du* Lai de l'ombre: *Réflexions sur l'art d'éditer les anciens textes* is an extraordinarily rich text; I will summarize only a couple of points that are directly relevant to the current argument. The story that Bédier tells takes the form of a conversion narrative. Thus he, like so many twentieth- and twenty-first-century philologists, uses biographical data relating to the life of the scholar to elucidate the scholarship (in this case using *autobiography* to gloss the evolution of his own scholarly practice). Bédier apologizes on the opening page for the necessity to speak of his own life, excusing himself by explaining that he has had a lifelong engagement with the *Lai de l'Ombre*. In this article, he will present the conclusions of his work on the *Lai*. His awareness of the complexity and corruption of the manuscript tradition of the *Lai* brought him to the point of despair when he came to believe that the Lachmannian critical method (applied by his teacher Gaston Paris to the manuscript history of the *Lai* in an article critical of Bédier's work on the text) could not clarify the convolutions of the manuscript tradition. Lachmannian method requires the scholar to sift manuscript variants, produce a stemma codicum to chart a manuscript genealogy that can account for variant readings, cancel those readings introduced through scribal error, make judgment calls where interpolation is suspected but cannot be positively identified, and use his own understanding of linguistic and literary history to propose readings where the text has been mangled beyond hope of reconstruction. At each of these junctures, however, the scholar's intellectual arrogance might steer him wrong. Bédier mockingly lists the technical vocabulary that is the Lachmannian editor's armor (in French rather than Latin, in deference to twentieth-century sensibilities): "faute," "bonne leçon," "'leçon moins bonne,' ou 'suspecte,' ou 'altérée,' ou 'refaite.'" How can the modern textual critic question the authority of the manuscript on medieval literary or linguistic usage? To do so is to beg the question: to step into the vertiginous eye of the hermeneutic circle.[21]

Bédier argues that rather than seek to reconstruct a lost text, the modern editor ought to reproduce a single manuscript witness. This did not mean that the editor relinquished all intellectual control over the edition, of course. Editorial expertise guided the scholar in selecting the manuscript to be reproduced: he should base the edition on the medieval manuscript that his scholarship reveals to be exemplary. Nor did it suggest that Bédier had relinquished the grand promise of the positivism of the Romantic era—the notion that current scientific scholarship granted the textual critic a substantially more accurate understanding of textual history than the methodologies that predated it. Rather, in the closing lines of the article, Bédier makes a familiar statement: if textual critics will only follow his method, the past will speak for itself, truthfully and accurately, *for the first time.*[22]

Subsequent scholars have revealed the extent to which Bédier's political commitments informed his scholarly work. Alain Corbellari has argued that anti-German sentiment led Bédier to resist the tendency of German scholars (who were also, of course, *Lachmannian* text editors) to claim the French literary tradition as their own. Per Nykrog has suggested that what motivated Bédier was less anti-German contrarianism (or oedipal competition with his German-trained mentor, Gaston Paris) than the impulse simply to be aggressively, quintessentially, chauvinistically French. Michele Warren saw Bédier's intervention in the context of his colonial origins (Bédier was born and grew up in Réunion, a French possession in the Indian Ocean).[23] The political investments of Bédier's thought alert us to the location of his Achilles' heel, the political presuppositions that inform his scholarship. At the same time the practitioners of a North American "New Philology" consistently use Bédier's scholarship as a touchstone (perhaps inspired by his stylistic brilliance and his suggestive biography as much as the intellectual content of his scholarship). Indeed Bédier's passionate attentiveness to the material peculiarity of the individual manuscript meshes well with the materialism of the New Philology.[24] Thus subsequent investigations of Bédier's contribution to the discipline have acknowledged both the elegance of his argument and its political and historical interestedness.[25]

It is interesting to note that in the seminal essay on the *Lai de l'Ombre*, Bédier consistently uses the word *philologue* with a visible curl of the lip.[26] It is a term of contempt for him; *philologues* are those who read with no sensitivity to the text, who do violence to textual traditions by imposing their own modern sensibilities on premodern manuscript history. Late twentieth-century scholarship has to some extent rehabilitated the image of the philologist (particularly in the United States). Now philological scholarship frequently connotes what might be termed *thick* philology: reading with an eye to the historical constitution of the text, but also with an awareness of the tradition of scholarship on the text. The finest contemporary philology is a textured history of the readings that have (in the case of many, if not most, medieval texts) become fused with the substance of the text itself, like the iridescent layers that form the pearl.

Nowhere is this more true, it seems, than in the field of *Orientalist philology*. Of course the word *Orientalism* is not any longer used, for excellent reasons. Scholars in the field (as distinct from medievalists and classicists) also avoid the word *philologist* except in a pejorative sense: it has been tainted by association.[27] For this reason it seems inappropriate to apply the term *philology* to the investigations of disciplinary history that have become so important in the field of Arabic and Islamic studies in particular. Yet to some extent the impulse that guides scholarship in both cases is roughly equivalent: scholars have looked back at the history of their discipline in order to diagnose intellectual errors and, in some notable cases, to redress historical misjudgments of earlier scholars.[28] The Orientalist philologist is one who willfully chooses to stand outside of the culture which generated the texts that he studies for his livelihood (perhaps with the aim of manipulating that culture for personal gain). The *good* scholar of the Islamic "Orient," however—and the most powerful insight of recent studies of disciplinary history is that there *is* such a thing as a good "Orientalist"—pays close attention to the historical and cultural constitution of the texts which are our witness to the past and in large part to contemporary history.

Of course, one stark difference distinguishes Orientalist philology from medieval philology: its perceived incapacity to generate *philologies engagées* like the nationalist and fundamentalist scholarship discussed above. The familiar Saidian definition of the Orientalist describes a scholar whose object of analysis could not be more distant from himself (and in Said's work the scholar most emphatically is a *him*). The dis-identity of the Orient with the West and the constitution of the Orient as an object of colonial interest characterize Saidian Orientalism. More recent scholarship has pushed gently at the Manichean boundaries of this theoretical formulation. Todd Kontje's work on German Orientalism, Billie Melman's on women travelers in the Orient, and Lisa Lowe's on French and German Orientalism—for all their disciplinary breadth—have a common denominator: they argue the rich diversity of northern European Orientalisms between the eighteenth and twentieth centuries and the central importance of Orientalist formations to the intellectual history of the period in general.[29]

However, the radical identification of a modern community with a distant textual history brought close to the present through the modern technology of philological reading—the foundation of an engaged philology—seems altogether lacking in the field of Orientalist philology. The Orientalist does not identify himself with a community that traces its origin to the texts he studies. At best he appropriates Oriental culture for Western use (think of the manipulations of Sanskrit described by Percy Schwab, or Goethe's *West-östlicher Divan*); at worst he reveals another community's destiny to be dominated by his own in the pages of Oriental texts (think of Renan's famous cry, "L'avenir, Messieurs, est donc à l'Europe et à l'Europe seule"[30]). The disidentification of the scholar with the texts he studies may allow Orientalism to escape the most embarrassing excesses of an aggressively nationalizing reading of the premodern past, for instance, but it may also vitiate the Orientalist reading—if one allows that the identification of a modern community with a premodern text grants the philological reading a palpable power.

Yet recent scholarship has sensitized Western scholars to two truisms—the one historical, the other geographical—that have typically flown under the radar not only of the general public but also of professional observers of the past. Even though Westerners may not in general identify personally with the Orient, still communication and exchange (sometimes, but not always, hostile) between the Islamic East and the Christian West have remained a historical constant for the last millennium and a half. And this engagement has not always and not merely taken the form of an asymmetrical aggression on the one side and passivity on the other. From the Middle Ages through early modernity and into the late modern period, the Mediterranean has served as a lens that has focused attentive glances from one shore to the other.[31] This engagement may pass through periods of intensification and abatement; the Mediterranean at times functions less as a conductive mechanism and more as a barrier.[32] But at no time has communication across it ceased. Furthermore scholars outside the region have not generally acknowledged developments in the European south, where a history of Arab occupation has produced a starkly different intellectual terrain. Here modern Orientalist scholarship has had to accommodate a fact of regional history: the object of the (distancing) Orientalist gaze is the history of the nation.

## Orientalism and European Intellectual History

It might be possible to find a better text to compare the relative strengths of the various models of textual criticism and to trace the development of academic and popular Orientalism during the modern period than the *Thousand and One Nights*. But one would be hard pressed to find one more engaging, more central to both popular and intellectual history and, in all honesty, more fun. The *Thousand and One Nights* is among the most famous examples of a framed narrative in world literature. In framed narratives, stories are captured within stories, when a character in a tale begins relating another tale. The frame story typically has a hermeneutic function: it serves as a key to interpreting the stories within the frame. Edgar Allan Poe—in his extraordinary and outrageously mendacious essay, "The Philosophy of Composition"—describes such literary devices thus: "it has the force of a frame to a picture. It has an indisputable moral power in keeping concentrated the attention."[33] So does the tale of Scheherazade in the case of the *Thousand and One Nights*. The story of the valiant vizier's daughter become sultaness, who saves her city by enmeshing the murderous sultan in a net of tales, insinuates itself into the fabric of the stories within the frame. They are seen by modern readers (and modern writers) as celebrations of the capacity of narrative to vanquish abuses of power in the sphere of politics or of psychology. Scheherazade has been canonized as the patron saint of literary invention in successive generations of Western works that riff on the *Nights*, from novels to movies to even translations of the *Nights*, which in a handful of noteworthy cases depart from the text so radically as to constitute independent literary works themselves.

The *Nights*, that is, is itself enmeshed in the Western tradition in a meta-literary frame. We see it irresistibly within the context of the European and, later, American riffs on the text. Furthermore, recent philological research has shown that the work as it has become known in the West, a groaning board of fantastic tales from the most various sources, is largely the product of Western Orientalists (and Arab philologists living in the West). For this reason—because the *Nights*, a framed tale, has itself been captured within an interpretive frame which has become perversely difficult to separate from the text itself—the work suggests a series of hermeneutic questions that scholarship has only recently begun to address: Where do we draw the line between the provinces of the premodern author and the modern textual critic, particularly in the case of a work whose proximity to the oral tradition makes it peculiarly fluid and therefore peculiarly vulnerable to modern manipulation? Is it possible to filter the Western interventions out of the text and to see it as a work of Arabic literature, in the context of the Arabic literary tradition? If not, can the Western imitations serve as an interpretive lens for the text? Should they serve a hermeneutic function, or would that denature and desta- bilize the text? Is it possible to produce a coherent reading—using either the Lachmannian or the Bédierist method—of a text so radically contaminated (to use the technical philological term) by innovations and exterior interpola- tions?

So embedded is the *Nights* in the Western tradition that it is hard to imagine Western literature without it. Yet Scheherazade entered Western let- ters at a precise moment, and not in the foggy distance of the Middle Ages but at the cusp of modernity: in the translation produced by Antoine Gal- land, an editor of the *Bibliothèque Orientale*, and published in serial volumes between 1704 and 1717. The tale of Galland's translation and manipulation of the text, and the influence that this publication history had on both West- ern and Arabic letters, is among the most familiar stories in the history of Orientalism. I will merely sketch it here and refer the interested reader to the superb, detailed accounts of an extraordinarily convoluted history available elsewhere.[34] Galland's translation took as its point of departure a Syrian manuscript produced some time between the fourteenth century and the second half of the fifteenth century C.E.[35] This manuscript was incom- plete—it ended in the middle of a story, and less than a third of the way to the promised thousand and first night. Between 1704 and 1706 Galland trans- lated and published the core manuscript, inserting into it the tales of Sindbad the sailor, which he believed formed part of the *Nights* tradition (although we now know that the Sindbad stories existed as an independent cycle and had not historically been associated with the *Thousand and One Nights*). He then stopped, having run out of stories to translate. In 1709, without alerting Galland, his unscrupulous publisher released the next volume of the *Nights*. This volume included a tale ("Ghanim") that Galland either had translated earlier or invented himself—no manuscript has ever been found—and two that a colleague of his had translated from the Turkish (the tales of Prince Zeyn Alasnam and Codadad). In that same year, at a dinner party, Galland met a skilled storyteller from Syria by the name of Hanna. Ultimately he would overcome his reluctance to publish tales without a legitimate affiliation with the *Nights* and would fill out the balance of required nights by develop- ing the brief notes he received from Hanna into full-length tales. This is the source of Aladdin and Ali Baba and indeed of a full one-third of the pages of the *Thousand and One Nights*; only nine of the twenty-one story cycles in Galland's translation come from the Syrian manuscript that provided the seed of his *Nights*. The tales that Galland heard from Hanna have no known manuscript versions that predate Galland's "translation" of them; even the notes that Hanna provided have disappeared. And because Galland's extant notes on the progress of the text are sketchy, it has proved difficult or impossible for scholars to reconstruct the tales Hanna told him (and hence to understand the extent of Galland's embroidering).

Galland's translation made an extraordinary splash, in part because it responded neatly to a number of discrete popular and intellectual interests. It served as an antidote to the Enlightenment: Galland's Baghdad—where genies popped from bottles, willow-waisted maidens were transformed into moon-faced cows, and monarchs in disguise went on nocturnal rambles to get acquainted with the populace—was a wonderland marvelously exterior to the chill light of reason that suffused the eighteenth century. Historians generally point out the similarity in spirit between Galland's *Nuits* and the *contes des fées*, or fairy tales, that enjoyed an immense vogue in the salon culture of late seventeenth-century France.[36] Galland's translation of the *Nights* was addressed to and first circulated among the same crowd that had eagerly consumed those homegrown tales of the fantastic. At the same time, it made a substantial contribution to the Orientalist vogue that arose roughly at the moment when the Ottoman threat to European shipping interests and European cities abated (Vienna had successfully repelled the last Ottoman siege in 1683). A Grub Street English translation of Galland's French version appeared almost instantly and was in its fourth edition by 1713; by the end of the eighteenth century, retranslations of Galland's translation had appeared in German, Italian, Dutch, Danish, Russian, Flemish, and Yiddish.[37] And Galland's translation inspired a cottage industry of independent pseudo-Oriental tales, sold by the yard in English and French.

In addition, the elusiveness of manuscripts acted as a tease to scholars and collectors whose appetite for manuscripts of all kinds grew exponentially through the course of the century. Galland was never entirely forthcoming about his manuscript sources; after his death scholars sought the manuscript he had translated among his books, without success. The search expanded as collectors sent word to their Middle East contacts to scour the book markets for manuscripts of the work. Here too they found little; for the *Thousand and One Nights*, so warmly received in the West, had enjoyed scant popularity in the Arab world. Or more precisely it seems to have been enjoyed as *oral* literature but did not generate a substantial textual tradition. This is why Galland's efforts to find a "complete" manuscript of the *Nights* failed (and why he was obliged to write his way to the thousand and first night himself); this is why, when Western Orientalists sought manuscripts of the work for the public and private libraries of Europe, they came up empty-handed. And so the *Nights* gave occasion for another activity to which eighteenth-century scholars devoted prodigious amounts of energy: literary forgery. Two independent transcripts of "complete" manuscripts of the *Nights* were produced between 1780 and 1810, both by scholars with access to the Bibliothèque du Roi, to which Galland had left his papers and manuscripts (including the Syrian manuscript of the *Nights*).[38] In both cases the scholars claimed that they worked from a newly discovered manuscript; in fact they simply transcribed from Galland's papers. When the craftsmen faced the task of producing an Arabic version of the stories known in Western criticism as "orphan tales"—those for which no Arabic originals predating Galland's "translation" have been found—they found an expedient way around the difficulty: they translated Galland's French into Arabic.

By the last decade of the eighteenth century a new kind of interest in the *Nights* emerged: a technical or philological interest on the part of scholars who had expertise in the Arabic language or simply a broadly defined interest in Oriental and/or ancient literatures. A series of letters in the British *Gentleman's Magazine* which appeared between 1794 and 1799 posed questions about manuscripts of tales found in Galland's *Nights* that had recently surfaced in England: are they *genuine?* If they indeed are authentic witnesses to the *Thousand and One Nights* tradition, how do they compare to Galland's translation? Can they *authenticate* Galland's work—now almost a century old? Patrick Russell (co-author of the *Natural History of Aleppo*) mentions that he has compared manuscript versions of the work—in Aleppo and at the Vatican—with Galland's translation and found a number of differences, chief among them the absence of the Sindbad cycle from the manuscripts he has inspected. He notes, with consummate discernment (and gentlemanly disdain), that "M. Galland is sometimes exuberant far beyond the original, and inserts in the narrative what is rather a commentary for the European reader than suitable to the characters of the drama."[39] We are at the dawn of European Orientalism: study of the Arabic language, Arabic literature, and Arab customs allows specialists to begin to question the authority of the Galland translation.

Others who discussed the Arabian tales did not have the capacity to read them in the original; a vivid interest in the use and value of fantastic tales in general compensated for the lack. Thus James Beattie, a Scottish scholar and author of many moral, religious, and poetic works, expressed his general distrust of Galland's translation on the basis not of his inspection of manuscripts or consideration of Arabic stylistics (he notes that the *Thousand and One Nights* is "the greatest, indeed the only, collection, that I am acquainted with, of Oriental fables"), but rather of his impression of the Oriental tale: "whether the tales be really Arabick, or invented by Mons. Galland, I have never been able to learn with certainty. If they be Oriental, they are translated with unwarrantable latitude; for the whole tenor of the style is in the French mode." Beattie draws a stern judgment of the work as literature: "There is in it great luxury of description, without any elegance; and great variety of invention, but nothing that elevates the mind, or touches the heart. All is wonderful and incredible; and the astonishment of the reader is more aimed at, than his improvement either in morality, or in the knowledge of nature." But he allows that the work does offer something of moral value (a "pretty just idea" of the government and the customs of "those eastern nations") and of pleasure. As an example of the latter—astonishingly, given the lofty moral tenor of his discussion—he cites the outstanding example of the story of the barber and his brothers, a tale that reads like a particularly frenetic Monty Python sketch.[40]

Finally, Western readers studied the *Nights* in order to learn about the history of the Arabs, and in particular about a period of Arab history that would prove to have an irresistible hold on the Western imagination: Abbasid Baghdad. Nathan Drake, in a work that recollects and reflects on his extensive readings, castigated the Galland translation—the only translation available to Europeans, since it still constituted the basis for all translations into European languages—for its historical infidelities.

> To the *Arabian Nights' Entertainment,* though in general merely considered as a work of extravagant fiction, their reader will be indebted for much genuine information relative to the domestic habits of the court and people of Baghdad, as they are now fully ascertained to convey a just picture of the manners and customs of the Caliphate during this splendid portion of its existence; and had the translation been more faithful to the idiom of the original, had better supported its peculiar spirit and strong features, and not mutilated a production of undoubted genius,

these tales had still further merited the attention of the philosopher and historian.[41]

During the course of the nineteenth century general dissatisfaction with Galland's translation was answered by three new retranslations of the mammoth whole of the text, as defined by Galland's translation, from Arabic into English. Edward Lane, Victorian adventurer par excellence, produced the first of these translations, published in 1839–40. John Payne's translation appeared next, in 1884–85, followed swiftly by Richard Burton's (1885–88, taking in the translation of the *Nights* proper as well as the *Supplemental Nights*). Each of these productions had its own distinct character. Lane introduced a more scholarly element to translations of the *Nights*; his notes on the text would be republished in an independent volume, *Arabian Society in the Middle Ages*. At the same time he expurgated the racy passages from the text, the erotic scenes that might fluster a Victorian readership. Payne included notes on the customs of the Arabs as illuminated by the text (as Lane had done); he didn't translate the poetry, fearing that it would weary his readers. However, he did not excise the erotic episodes. His decision not to expurgate the text obliged him to publish it through a private subscription society. Burton, finally, relied extensively (most observers would say *unscrupulously*) on Payne's translation. He not only included but exaggerated the erotic content of the text (his translation, like Payne's, was sold by subscription). His remains the most popular of the nineteenth-century translations, in part because of the rambunctious lexical quality of the translation itself (he seems to have looked upon the thesaurus somewhat as pirates of yore did the Spanish galleon), and in part because of the quirky, kinky, at times surreal nature of his annotations. If Lane and Payne viewed the notes that accompanied their text as an occasion to educate the reading public on the customs of the Oriental nations, Burton took the notes to another level, including not only accounts of Arab customs but also autobiographical anecdotes and moral and speculative reflections. John Barth, an ardent fan of the *Nights*, wrote: "It would be a more splendid destiny to have cooked up *Burton's* version of *The Thousand and One Nights*—footnotes, Terminal Essay, and all—than to have written the original."[42] By the end of the nineteenth century the *Nights* had traveled a long way from their Western invention by Galland, whose salon-ready fairies and princesses look quaint in comparison to Burton's rampaging blackamoors and glowering genies. In the English-speaking world the text had now become more than an *entertainment* (as its original English title,

*Arabian Nights Entertainments*, advertised it): it both entertained and educated the reading public in the customs and manners of the Arab and greater Islamic world.

The retranslations from the Arabic had been made possible by a series of printed editions of the text that appeared during the first half of the century: four versions were published between 1814 and 1842. These editions, rather than correcting the difficulties introduced into the manuscript tradition by the Galland translation, rather aided and abetted them. Each of them (with the exception of the 1835 Bulaq edition, printed in Cairo) was initiated and financed by Europeans, and each accepted the contours of the work as established by Galland's translation. The nineteenth-century printed editions also continued the theme of forgery. The Habicht or Breslau edition (published in 1825–28), which claimed to reproduce a nonexistent Tunisian manuscript, was in fact a compilation of stories from a variety of sources. And the last of the nineteenth-century editions to be produced (Calcutta II, or MacNaghten, which appeared in 1839–42) was supposedly based on an Egyptian manuscript; again, the manuscript was never found. Subsequent scholarship has shown that the text incorporates details that appeared first in the Habicht edition (which itself claimed to reproduce a phantom manuscript).[43]

If the new editions of the text made the new translations possible, the new translations in turn informed an explosion of literary and cinematic works inspired by the *Nights* during the nineteenth and twentieth centuries. Filmmakers celebrated the *Nights* as a bottomless well of narrative: some of the earliest films of the new century drew on narratives from the *Nights* (a French Aladdin appeared in 1906, a French Ali Baba in 1908); the work inspired the famous Ray Harryhausen Sinbad films and a delightful Bollywood version of Ali Baba, along with such notable works as a World War II-era film that makes Ali Baba into a freedom fighter, and the recent Dream-Works version of Sinbad in which the lead character appears, unaccountably, to be Greek.[44]

At the same time, writers of serious literary fiction depicted Scheherazade as a patroness of creativity and literary invention. Already during the nineteenth century a number of writers had honored the *Nights* as a fountain of narrative invention and paid due homage to Scheherazade. Edgar Allan Poe wrote the mischievous "Thousand-and-Second Tale of Scheherazade," in which Scheherazade relates wonders that are no fictions but recountings of recent scientific advances and discoveries; the sultan becomes so exasperated at her preposterous inventions that he orders her execution at last. Charlotte

Brontë's Jane Eyre modeled her behavior toward the brute Rochester on Scheherazade's toward her sultan; Tennyson composed the "Recollections of the Arabian Nights"; and Robert Louis Stevenson wrote the *New Arabian Nights*. During the twentieth century Western writers widely recognized Scheherazade as a symbol of the power of the literary imagination: see not only John Barth but also Proust, E. M. Forster, Jorge Luis Borges, A. S. Byatt, and Salman Rushdie. "Never in any other book, perhaps," wrote G. K. Chesterton, "has such a splendid tribute been offered to the pride and omnipotence of art."[45]

And at last, following her long Babylonian captivity in the West, Scheherazade would return to the lands of her birth. With the nineteenth-century renaissance of Arabic imaginative fiction, Arab writers turned to the *Nights* as a homegrown source of inspiration to set against their myriad Western models.[46] The *Nights*, not surprisingly, has proved particularly useful to Arab expatriate writers who live in the West: Rafik Schami, a Syrian who lives in Berlin, wrote a modern riff on the *Nights*, *Erzähler der Nacht* (which appeared in English as *Damascus Nights*). Assia Djebar's *Ombre sultan* (translated into English as *A Sister to Scheherazade*) presents a feminist reading of Scheherazade's gambit. Most interesting, a recent novel by Libyan British author Hisham Matar, *In the Country of Men*, emphasizes the sinister undercurrents of Scheherazade's tale. The main character's grandmother is a devotee of Scheherazade, but his mother isn't so sure; living under Qaddafi, she finds much to distrust in the story of a woman who manipulates narrative in order to survive a life under occupation.

Finally, during the twentieth century and into the opening years of the twenty-first scholarly Orientalists would engage in the painstaking project of sorting out the origins and development of the text. This process, of course, began with the first eighteenth-century attempts to understand what Antoine Galland had translated, what he interpolated, and what the text would look like once Western interventions were teased out. Given the complications of the tradition, of course—the translations of texts that don't exist and counterfeit transcriptions of phantom manuscripts that characterize the history of the work—the task has not been a particularly easy one. In 1984 Muhsin Mahdi, a professor of Arabic literature at Harvard University, published a scholarly edition of the *Nights* which will shape the course of subsequent scholarship on the Arabic text. It is one of the ironies of the manuscript history of the *Nights* that the Syrian manuscript with which Galland began his translation remained for three centuries following his translation both the oldest manuscript we possess and the only substantial version of it that pre-dates his translation.[47] A single page from a ninth-century manuscript and two earlier references to it in Arabic bibliographical sources demonstrate the antiquity of the tradition.[48] But because the *Nights* is a popular rather than a learned work of literature, it did not generate a significant manuscript tradition. Mahdi, judging the Galland manuscript to be the most authoritative exemplar of the tradition, based his edition on it, introducing corrections from eight other manuscripts. His work makes it possible for the first time for scholars to study one manifestation of the *Nights* tradition as it existed in the Arab world before the European interventions of the early modern period. Of course modern audiences are reluctant to relinquish the *Nights* as they have come to know and love it, including the fantastic geographies of Sindbad's voyages and Sindbad's merchant savvy; Aladdin's pluck and Ali Baba's sangfroid; and the whole portmanteau-esque plenitude of the work. Still, thanks to the exemplary quality of philological research into the manuscript tradition of the *Nights* like Mahdi's and the scholarship on which Mahdi's work built, we now understand the extent to which Western "readings" of the *Nights* have defined the constitution not only of Western variations on and appropriations of the work, but even of the Arabic text itself. As in quantum physics, though perhaps in a less disinterested way, in the case of the *Thousand and One Nights* the act of observing phenomena fundamentally alters the nature of the phenomena observed.

The *Thousand and One Nights* is often characterized as a literary work composed across the divide between the Arab world and the West; neither can claim sole authorship. The text as it has become familiar to Western readers—a complex web of tale that encompasses the compendious nineteenth-century English translations, themselves based on the nineteenth-century editions published (in most cases) under European supervision, emerging from the translation which Galland teased from the seed of a late medieval Syrian manuscript, laced with tales from the oral tradition, themselves novelized by a man immersed in the salon culture of early modern France—this complex manuscript tradition has become the scaffolding for both scholarship and new literary and cinematic composition in the East and the West. Both Payne and Burton based their English translations on the Calcutta II edition, selecting it in large part because of its rich detail and narrative abundance. The literary appeal of that edition is undeniable but is apparently of nineteenth-century vintage: it was one of the editions allegedly based on a manuscript that has never been retrieved. Nevertheless its literary qualities made it the text of choice for scholars as well as popularizers.

The decision to use this edition as a foundation for scholarship in particular implies a judgment about the polyvalence of the work that has sweeping implications. Such a reading assumes a robust *Lachmannian* understanding of the polygenesis of the text, its multiple births across a multitude of cultural boundaries. "The original author of the *Arabian Nights* is unknown," wrote an obscure literary observer of the early twentieth century, "but the book has become a household possession in every civilized country in the world."[49] It has no nation; its homeland is nowhere and everywhere. It is a vast, raucous, transnational celebration of the messy and exhilarating power of narrative. Under the sign of Galland's translation-without-originals, not only literary authors but also scholars have come to celebrate the *Nights* as a work that is equally "original" in each of its incarnations—the various modern and premodern manuscript versions, the modern editions, the translations, films, and literary imitations.

But despite the invigorating openness of the text seen through a Lachmannian lens, it remains possible to celebrate the philological insights that allow us to see the historical outlines of the text with more precision: to perceive the contours of the work at each stage in its development, and to understand the historical factors that shaped its evolution. The unique manuscript history of the text invites a Bédierist intervention. This was, indeed, Mahdi's accomplishment: to prune away the profusion of manuscript embellishments, the ramifications grafted onto the core manuscript tradition during the course of its history in the West, and to reconstruct the work as it existed at a single moment in its complex textual history. What can we say about the text as a work of Arabic literature, in the Arabic tradition? How does it respond to Arab history? The version of the work edited by Mahdi seems to have been written during the late Middle Ages, but it looks back with a particular urgency at the Abbasid past, and especially at the caliphate of Harun al-Rashid.[50] How does the text comment on the Abbasid past from the perspective of the late Middle Ages? Despite the limitations of our knowledge about the work—we still do not understand well the audience for whom the work was composed or the motivations of the authors who created the manuscripts we possess—scholars have begun to produce sophisticated, compelling, and important readings of it based on the evidence produced by philological scholarship. Thus the history of scholarship on the *Nights* demonstrates the efficaciousness and the ongoing relevance of philological analysis. Only the dogged pursuit of philological insights has enabled us to tease out the preposterously complex manuscript history of the work; today the fundamental milestones in the constitution of the text are understood with appreciably more clarity than they were in the past.

Finally, the curious tale of the *Nights* caught between its Eastern origin and its adopted home in the West serves as a useful gauge of interactions between the Arab-Islamic world and the West during the modern era. The story begins with a potent cocktail of naïve admiration and capitalist calculation at the beginning of the eighteenth century. A confluence of diverse interests accounts for the extraordinary success of the *Nights* in Europe. French *salonnières* seeking *divertissement*, manuscript bounty hunters trawling the book stalls of Levantine cities, Englishmen seeking an outlet for their lexical erudition: these compose only a small fraction of the public that contributed to the work's immense popularity during the eighteenth century. Western colonial interest in the Arab shores of the Mediterranean quickened at the dawn of the nineteenth century; the foundation for British rule in India was laid during the last quarter of the eighteenth century, but the British Raj was consolidated and expanded during the nineteenth. The new tenor of relations between Europe and the Arab and Islamic world helps to account for the existence of the multiple printed editions of the work: the first of the nineteenth-century editions (Calcutta I, 1814–18) was published in British India and intended as a primer for British colonial officials. And colonial interests explain in part the curiosity concerning the customs of the Arab and Islamic world on the part of Western readers that was answered by the copiously annotated nineteenth-century English translations of the *Thousand and One Nights* (although it is abundantly clear that to see Edward Lane, John Payne, and Richard Burton merely as fulfilling the interests of a colonizing state would oversimplify their lives and work unconscionably).

During the twentieth century and the opening years of the twenty-first Western and Arab writers have transfigured Scheherazade, illuminating her power and, in the most striking departure from traditional readings of the text, her ambiguity. It is perhaps unsurprising that Arab writers (and non-Arabs from Islamic nations) view the self-proclaimed sultaness with more ambivalence than Westerners. For every writer who celebrates her as a liberator (see, for instance, Azar Nafisi: "Scheherazade breaks the cycle of violence by choosing to embrace different terms of engagement") there are others who see something vaguely insidious in her ("Scheherazade," Hisham Matar's protagonist's mother tells her son, "was a coward who accepted slavery over death").[51] Westerners, whose distance from the tradition she represents allows them to make freer use of her, are more likely to see her as an undiluted heroine. Thus A. S. Byatt—explaining her choice of the *Thousand and One Nights* as the best book of the millennium—wrote that "Though it appears to be a story against women, it actually marks the creation of one of the strongest and cleverest heroines in world literature."[52] European and American writers have naturalized Scheherazade as a transnational symbol of the power of literary invention. Their affection for her, their familial embrace of her, says many things about the way that writers view their craft. In the current context, most importantly, it belies the notion that the divide between the Orient and the West constitutes a kind of harem wall that Westerners cannot breach. More striking is Westerners' passionate curiosity, their eagerness to embrace (albeit selectively) the artifacts that reach them from across the divide, their capacity to write their way to the world that produced Scheherazade and back again. This affective connection, of course, is not sufficient to undo all the harm done by rogues and politicians in the ongoing war, hot and cold, between East and West. Nevertheless it substantiates the perception that emerges from recent scholarship on communications between the Islamic Orient and the Christian West: the fates of East and West have never disentangled themselves the one from the other, and will remain locked in engagement with each other—whether a fruitful or a fatal embrace, only time will tell—for the foreseeable future.

The scholars whose work I will survey in this book provide another testimony to the continuing textual connections between Europe and the Arab-Islamic world. These historians use philological method to read textual history. Like the philologists who identify the origins of the French nation, for instance, in the Old French epic, they use the medieval past to evoke a distant, originary moment of cultural identity. However, they ground a European national culture in the *Arab* past. Such a narrative may startle readers who expect a more adversarial relation between Europe and its Arab "other." At the very least, the reader is likely to characterize such scholarship as *counterintuitive*. As will become apparent, however, this reading of European history is motivated by a number of factors. It accounts for the realities of regional history: the Arabs occupied Spain, Sicily, and Malta for extended periods of their medieval history; immigration and trade patterns have kept those regions in contact with the Arab world beyond that era of occupation.

At the same time, the narrative of Arab origins is to some extent a by-product of the power of the philological model. During the nineteenth century philology emerged as a technology for reading textual history as the origin of a modern sense of identity. Readers learned to view the relation between the *Chanson de Roland* and modern France or between *Beowulf* and modern England in terms of consanguinity: Frenchmen wrote the *Roland* and Englishmen wrote *Beowulf*, despite the fact that the language they used in the text would not be comprehensible to a speaker of modern French or modern English. They owed this belief to the labor of philologists who articulated nationalist readings of the epics, who catalogued the differences but at the same time stressed the continuities between a distant historical age and the present.

That is, considerable mental effort must be expended to produce a reading of an "Old French" or "Old English" text like the *Roland* or *Beowulf* as the origin of a modern national linguistic and literary tradition. Scholarship that seeks in medieval *Arabic* texts the gleam in a distant father's eye marking the origin of a national cultural identity differs not in kind but in degree from these readings. The medieval Arabic literary tradition poses considerable challenges for a Western scholar. Once the languages have been mastered, however, philological technique seems almost to generate narratives of filiation of its own accord. Like the Romance philologist, the Orientalist—while not denying the alterity of the Arab past—yet might stress the identity of past and present, at once acknowledging the difference and distance of the world witnessed by medieval textuality and asserting its proximity and identity. Most intriguingly, we will see that some narratives of Arab origins are informed by a sense of Mediterranean exceptionalism. In some cases scholars offer a regional history as a way to challenge northern European primacy, to situate their nation not at the fringe of the grand adventure of modernity but rather at its center.

In the next chapter, I will present an overview of two dominant threads in scholarship exploring the relation between the European nations and the Arab past—investigations conducted both by scholars who denied and others who affirmed the links between European modernity and the Arab past. Then I will introduce a gallery of southern European scholars who identify the Arab past as constitutive of a European modernity. I aim to write the history of an idea, not a comprehensive survey of southern European Orientalism: this book has been conceptualized as a picaresque rather than an epic. My readings emphasize the Italian contribution; I present a perspective that has had very little presence in European scholarship—the Maltese; I include a relatively small sliver of Spanish history. This emphasis reflects my own expertise and interests. At the same time, I am eager to present material that may be less familiar to an English-speaking audience. The Spanish context has received more attention than the Italian, because of the comparative length and intensity of its involvement with the Arab world and because of the relative familiarity of the Spanish language to readers both in Britain and in North America. Those who wish to learn about Spanish Orientalism in depth can refer to James Monroe's authoritative and compulsively readable monograph, *Islam and the Arabs in Spanish Scholarship* (or for those who read Spanish, Manuela Marín's more recent, article-length, lively summary, "Arabistas en España: Un asunto de familia"). About Malta the English-speaking world tends to know little or nothing, despite England's long involvement with the tiny nation. And while English readers might be familiar with certain chapters of Italian intellectual history—in particular humanism—Italian Orientalism has been underreported in English scholarship.

Finally, in the closing chapter of the book I will return to the Scheherazade perplex, tracing one of the circuitous paths the text followed from its medieval genesis to modernity. This coda is intended to demonstrate again the power of the philological reading, its capacity to produce answers to antique problems and to generate new readings of familiar texts. It articulates the ongoing, intimate links between the Arab world and the West. And it also responds to current literary styles. In the frenetic recycling of the modes of the past that we postmoderns have grown accustomed to, it seems that at the present moment the Gothic is in the ascendant. We feel most comfortable with chiaroscuro narratives that emphasize the *scuro*. Scheherazade herself, in my reading of her, is turned resolutely toward her own past; or perhaps she is herself the face of the past, staring down the present. She is a bit of a siren. Perched on the shoals of Abbasid Baghdad, enticing the latter-day Sinbad toward shipwreck in a city known both for its vibrant multilingual literary tradition and its frightful political history, she is as veritable a portrait of Philology in the twenty-first century as we could hope to find.

*Chapter 2*

# Metempsychosis: Dante, Petrarch, and the Arab Middle Ages

> It is difficult for people to understand each other through the medium of a foreign language.
> —Ugo Foscolo, *Edinburgh Review*, 1818[1]

PIETRO VALERGA, BORN in 1821 in Liguria, took his vows as a Carmelite in 1837 and left for the Holy Land in 1845. He would remain in the East serving in various offices for the Carmelites for more than two decades; by 1868 he had returned to Rome, where he advised the Vatican Council on the Oriental Christian churches. In 1871, following the suppression of the monasteries in the Papal States, he applied for and received secularization, taking a job as professor of the Arabic language in Florence. During this period Valerga also tried his hand at various literary projects. In 1874 he published an extraordinary translation (into Italian) and study of the diwan of the medieval poet Ibn al-Farid. There was nothing unusual in translating medieval Arabic poetry into the European languages during the nineteenth century, nor in choosing the poetry of Ibn al-Farid for translation. In fact a German rendering of Ibn al-Farid's "Ta'iyya al-kubra" (or "Long poem rhyming in T") had been published just twenty years earlier by the rather better known Orientalist Joseph von Hammer-Purgstall.[2] What made Valerga's translation noteworthy was the claim that he made in the opening sentence of his lengthy introduction:

> The spirit of the Muslim poet Ibn al-Farid, having passed away in Cairo, the chief city of Egypt, in the year of the Hegira 632 and the year of

Christ 1234, after he had for some seventy years animated the limbs of some other obscure mortal, and after wandering here and there—through populous cities and villages, through fields and deserted shores—reappeared, three centuries ago [*sic*], as Francesco Petrarch, born in Arezzo on July the 20th of 1304. . . . Thus reborn, having altogether forgotten the Arabic language, the one he had always spoken and written with perfection . . . he began to babble words like *babbo* [daddy] and *mamma* in the sweet Tuscan idiom, to drink with his first milk the customs of gentlefolk and to learn . . . the ever novel ways of the West.[3]

In the introduction and throughout the translation Valerga continued this conceit, citing Petrarch's *Canzoniere* to gloss Ibn al-Farid's rather more obscure Arabic inventions. He explained his motives for suggesting that Ibn al-Farid's soul was reincarnated in the flesh of Francesco Petrarch by pointing out that the genius of a language is not immediately apparent to those who don't know that language. So he set parallel passages from Petrarch alongside his translations of Ibn al-Farid in order to help an Italian readership appreciate the sentiments and the linguistic brilliance of Ibn al-Farid's work.[4]

It seems unsporting to spoil the fun, yet it must be done: Valerga's argument was philologically irresponsible. He made no attempt to adduce any means of transmission of Ibn al-Farid's poetry to Petrarch; he could not do so, for the simple reason that none existed. Ibn al-Farid's poetry was not translated into any of the European languages during the Middle Ages, and Petrarch could not read Arabic. However, if we disregard the sheer lunacy of his thesis, Valerga's description of the relation between Ibn al-Farid's poetry and Petrarch's can be read as an intriguing and even surprisingly sophisticated resolution of a stubborn literary historical problem. In this chapter I will survey some of the milestones in the evolution and articulation of the "Arabic thesis," the proposition that the poetry of the Arabs of al-Andalus influenced early Romance poetics, as they relate to the Italian poets of the fourteenth century, Petrarch in particular. A number of scholars have floated and defended theories of Arab influence, particularly during the last century. In general, however, they have found their opponents difficult to convince. In part the impasse stems from an old prejudice. For centuries Western scholars (as well as nonscholarly audiences) had little desire to acknowledge the cultural communications between Muslims and Christians in Mediterranean Europe during the Middle Ages. In part, too, the manifest differences between the languages and literary traditions of the Arab world and the Romance-speaking West account for the difficulty. How can one think *influence* between languages that seem to have so little cultural or lexical common ground?

Valerga responded to this difficulty by inventing a new way of representing influence: *metempsychosis*—the incorporeal migration of ideas from one human mind to another. He sketches what he intends by this idea in the introduction to the *Diwan:*

> I believe that those who wish to pursue the aforementioned comparison [that is, between Petrarch's and Ibn al-Farid's poetics], despite the diversity of race, religion and language and the distance in time and place that separate our two poets the one from the other, might recognize in them such analogies and similarities as would excite the curiosity of the erudite and the philosopher to investigate the causes. Setting aside the idea of metempsychosis, which was put into play until now to expel the tedium and monotony of the comparison, it remains to be said that the similarity, if it was not simply the result of chance, emerged either from spontaneous imitation, as the intended result of a deliberate effort [to imitate], or from a common inspiration and from similarity of genius. . . . Since one cannot doubt the veracity or the genius of Petrarch, of necessity we must reject (of the reasons we have outlined) not only plagiarism, but also the deliberate imitation of the thoughts and the words of Ibn al-Farid. And that is to say, pedantic imitation: for with regard to another sort of free and noble imitation, we will see shortly that such is not at all entirely impossible.[5]

The spontaneous imitation that Valerga alludes to in the closing sentence occurs when two minds, possessed of like genius, stumble independently upon the same felicitous solutions to given literary problems. In this manner, he suggests, Petrarch's wholly Italian verse duplicated the sentiments and rhetorical strategies of Ibn al-Farid's utterly Arabic poetry.

One regrets that the woeful clumsiness of his execution made Valerga's work so obscure. Were his literary style not so atrocious, had he hit upon a concept less silly than metempsychosis to express his notion of "free and noble imitation," his thesis might have become more widely known and discussed. For "metempsychosis" is nothing less than Valerga's reformulation of the problem of literary influence. Valerga proposes it, in effect, as a more sophisticated description of Arabic-Romance literary communications than

the "post hoc, ergo propter hoc" narrative that most literary historians produce (or strive to produce) to account for such data.

How do we explain the parallels between medieval Arabic and Romance
vernacular lyric: their emergence at roughly the same time (the eleventh and
twelfth century) and geographical location (the Iberian peninsula and the
Pyrenees), their similar thematic motifs (the highly stylized travails of adulter-
ous love) and formal devices (end rhyme and stress meter rather than the
quantitative measures of classical Arabic and Latin verse), most startling their
use of the spoken language rather than a formal literary language as a vehicle
for poetic composition? The "Arabic thesis"—or *thèse arabe*, as it is sometimes called in English language scholarship—proposed that the poetics of
the Arabs of al-Andalus influenced the earliest lyric poets to write in a Romance tongue. But the skeptics remained unconvinced, largely because proponents of the "Arabic thesis" had yet to produce convincing manuscript
evidence of literary communications between the two communities. Philologists use comparative analysis of linguistic structures with an evident genealogical relation to each other to build incremental arguments. When editing
texts they identify and track variants, individual manuscript divergences from
a (theoretical) exemplar; in linguistic analyses they seek cognate relations
between languages descended from the same mother tongue; in philology-
powered literary criticism they analyze points of identity (images, phrases, or
plot elements borrowed) generally between texts written in sibling tongues.
Philological method is not tooled for more robust comparative analysis. It
has not traditionally accommodated intuitive leaps between cultural systems
which its own historical narratives and interpretive metaphors have represented as unrelated: for instance, the Arabo-Islamic and the Latino-Christian.

But Valerga's metempsychosis thesis introduced another wrinkle as well,
pushing the *thèse arabe* deep into the territory of the outré. The earliest
proponents of the theory argued the influence of the Arabs on poets perceived
to be wholly medieval, and furthermore more popular than literary: the Occitan troubadours, whose poetry—with its occasionally bawdy or maudlin sentiments and the toothsome crudity of its language—occupied a midpoint
between the popular verses of the medieval court, tavern, or market and the
learned compositions of a Dante or a Petrarch. The terms of engagement
change once these writers are named both because of their prominence and
because European readers typically consider them to be not medieval—or not
*only* medieval—but rather the first breath of something new and recognizably
modern. In Spain historians sought to account for a looming Arab presence

in the premodern background, in the gloomy landscape of the Middle Ages, so distant and so different from modernity. But in Italy philologists, and in particular Orientalists, challenged the scholarly community to acknowledge Arab influence on Dante, a poet widely recognized as the father of the Italian language and the honorary godfather of the Italian nation—a man whose profile now appears on the Italian two-euro coin. And, in an obscure nineteenth-century translation of the poetry of Ibn al-Farid into a language approximating Italian, an obscure former Carmelite turned the presuppositions of the *thèse arabe* upside down, using the genius of the inventor of modern poetic sensibility, Petrarch, to elucidate the verses of a medieval Arab.

Valerga's metempsychosis theory appropriated the central argument of the "Arabic thesis"—that literary communications occurred between Arabic and Romance-speaking populations—and displaced it from twelfth-century Iberia (where the scholar could marshal historical facts to defend it) to fourteenth-century Italy (where it could only appear unmotivated and, frankly, eccentric). He situated the work of the most important poet of early modern Europe on the border between Europe and the Arab world, and in this he went too far. Yet at the same time he produced a startlingly original response to the standoff that frustrated many literary historians who tried to describe the operation of influence across the stark boundary that separates Arabic and Romance poetics. A truly philological argument in defense of the "Arabic thesis" would emerge gradually during the century that followed Valerga's translation of Ibn al-Farid. By the end of the twentieth century both the accumulation of data concerning Muslim-Christian cultural relations—the product of generations of research—and a new sensibility emphasizing the relevance of broader cultural evidence to readings of medieval literary history allowed scholars to make exciting progress in elucidating stubborn literary historical puzzles. To date, however, no eleventh-hour developments have confirmed Valerga's intuition of a metaphysical link between Petrarch and a thirteenth-century Egyptian poet.

Valerga's reading of Petrarch serves as a useful provocation in another sense as well, for Petrarch—mysteriously, somewhat perversely—did claim to know (and despise) the poetry of the Arabs. If this conundrum is in itself of compelling interest and has inspired important investigations into the dissemination of Islamic culture in the Christian communities of Mediterranean Europe, the historiography of the scholarship is no less intriguing and no less revealing. In this chapter, I will focus on that historiography since it is most relevant to the task at hand: surveying southern European Orientalists' readings of their nations' Arab past, and detailing some of the most significant differences between the Spanish and Italian readings of that history. But I cannot resist dipping into medieval literary history, if only briefly. I will look into one of the more tantalizing suggestions that has emerged from recent scholarship on Petrarch's knowledge of Arabic poetry in order to give the reader a sense of the richness of the materials these Orientalists study—texts which, in some cases, lay hidden for three or four centuries, between the end of the Middle Ages and the nineteenth century, because European intellectuals no longer found a use for them. To a great extent, the story that I am telling in this book is a group memoir of those scholars who have worked— from the various shores of the Mediterranean (and occasionally from the New World), from various disciplines, at different times and for diverse motives—to bring this secret history to light.

The chapter will close with a meditation on the difference between Spanish and Italian history and between the Spanish and Italian response to the philosophy, and the letters in general, of the Arabs. The Iberian and Italian peninsulas lay uniquely exposed, to an equal degree but in distinct ways, to the crosscurrents of cultural production during the millennia when the Mediterranean functioned as an engine of cultural transmission. The Iberian peninsula, geographically and historically peripheral to Mediterranean history, became a center for cultural production under Arab domination; when Christian forces conquered it they laid claim to a network of metropolises in some disarray, yet still furnished with the trappings of a cosmopolitan civilization: the libraries, the architectural monuments, the scholars and artisans. But the Italian peninsula, geographically and historically at the center of the Mediterranean, did not undergo the thorough erosion of Christian political and economic institutions seen in the Iberian peninsula. The Arabs did not dominate the Italian peninsula as they had the Iberian peninsula. During the late Middle Ages, the social and political structure of the Italian communes and their economic ambitions created a dynamic thoroughly different from contemporary Iberia. The Spaniards conquered the territory of the Arabs and laid claim to the libraries they left behind when they fled. But the Italians— merchants, diplomats, crusaders, pilgrims, and humble sailors—traveled out to the Arab ports of the Mediterranean and returned with tidal regularity through the long centuries; they haggled over, purchased, transported, picked apart, repackaged, and remarketed the intellectual products of the Islamic Mediterranean. The word *influence* betrays the manifest complexity of the cultural transactions of the Spanish and Italian Middle Ages in distinct ways.

It misrepresents the curiosity of the Christians who set out to possess the culture of the Muslims and the Muslims who agreed—for different reasons in different times and places—to supply their needs. It disavows the urgency of those cultural transactions and the revolutionary impact of the knowledge and technologies thus acquired. And it understates the banality of the transaction, the familiarity—by turns comforting, wearisome, or noxious—with which Muslims and Christians at times approached the other's culture.

## Petrarch and the Arabs

Each of the three great writers of the Italian Trecento—Dante (1265–1321), Petrarch (1304–74), and Boccaccio (1313–75)—poses the question of Arab influence in a distinct way. Boccaccio worked Arab figures and Arab tales into the tapestry of the *Decameron*, and he gave a short list of his tales Arab settings.[6] The classic study of the medieval cognates of Boccaccio's tales (A. C. Lee's *The Decameron: Its Sources and Analogues*) cites parallels from the *Arabian Nights* to six tales in the *Decameron*.[7] Of these, only one (II, vii) has retained an Arab stage dressing as well: its central character, the maiden Alatiel, is an Arab princess. Interestingly, the Arab origin in this case is a variant on the frame tale of the *Thousand and One Nights*, a meditation on a theme that never fails to fascinate: the insatiability of the feminine sexual appetite. Boccaccio's version, of course, ends well. The fabulous Alatiel— whose name is an anagram of *La Lieta*, "the happy one"—"marries" nine men in nine Mediterranean ports. She is finally handed over to the man she was on her way to marry when a storm blew her ship off course and her Mediterranean adventures began; they live happily ever after.

Of course the presence of Arab characters and settings and even the use of Arab tales as source texts is something of an inevitability given the Mediterranean milieu in which the tales of the *Decameron* are for the most part set and given the environment in which their author lived. As a young man Boccaccio apprenticed at the Naples office of the bank that employed his father, the Compagnia dei Bardi. There he moved in a Mediterranean milieu and would have had easy—indeed, inescapable—access to the popular culture (presumably including the tales and songs) of the Arabs with whom the Italian merchants did business, who manned the ships that sailed between the Mediterranean ports. Scholars have shown relatively little interest in Boccaccio's manipulations of Arab culture, perhaps because he does not hide away his references.[8] Arab characters and settings appear in a matter-of-fact way, not as objects of particular interest or attention.

Dante's masterpiece, in contrast to Boccaccio's, has proved an irresistible challenge for Arabic theorists—the rough equivalent, in the world of comparative medieval philology, of the Paris-Dakar rally. In scholarship on Dante and Islam scholars have formulated the question of Arab influence, simply stated, as follows: How can we imagine that Dante *did not* know what the Arabs had to say about the afterlife, given the nature of Dante's own work, the importance and penetration of Arab ideas about the afterlife in Christian Europe in Dante's day, and Dante's intellectual ambition? Dante was a fiercely proud writer, a man who aimed explicitly to compete with the great literary works of antiquity and the Middle Ages. It makes sense that he would have sought to learn what the Muslims—who, after all, had made something of a literary industry of describing the afterlife—said about the condition and progress of the soul following death.

Two magisterial monograph-length studies of the question appeared during the first half of the twentieth century. In 1919, in a book entitled *La escatología musulmana en la* Divina Comedia (*Muslim Eschatology in the* Divine Comedy), Miguel Asín Palacios (1871–1944) argued that Dante drew on two sources of knowledge about the Islamic afterlife: popular legends about the *mi'raj*, Muhammad's nighttime journey to heaven and hell—an episode based on two fleeting references in the Qur'an, lovingly elaborated in the medieval popular and philosophical traditions—and a more learned account of the afterlife produced by Andalusian mystic and poet Ibn 'Arabi (1165–1240). Asín's erudite analysis of the points of contact between Dante's description of the afterworld and those found in the Islamic sources drew the admiration of members of the international community of scholars. Others, however, posed a legitimate objection to Asín's argument: Asín had not bothered to demonstrate the means of transmission of either the Islamic legends or the Arabic poetry to Dante. The philologist might point out intriguing points of similarity by the bushel; but if he cannot show that Dante had the opportunity to read and understand the works in question, his argument of influence must fail. But Asín did not pause to ask the crucial question of transmission. He plunged into a comparative reading of the mi'raj material and the *Commedia* like a diver picking his way through a particularly rich shipwreck—in reach of all, yet still unplundered—without suggesting how Dante himself might have learned about either the popular or the learned poetry of the Arabs. He believed confidently that the glorious parade of parallel details from Ibn 'Arabi and the *Commedia* that he marshaled effectively made his case. On the closing page of the book he celebrated his discovery in triumphant tones: "It is no longer possible to ignore the glory due to this thinker—a Spaniard, although a Muslim; that is to say: this Murcian, Ibn 'Arabi—in the deed of literary genius that Dante Alighieri carried to glorious completion in his immortal poem."⁹

Because *La escatología musulmana en la* Divina Comedia was a book written by a Spanish Orientalist about a great work of Italian literature, it represented a decisive intervention in two discrete fields of intellectual history: scholarship on Dante and Islam and Spanish Orientalism. Since the days when Spaniards could learn Arabic from their Muslim neighbors were far in the past, by the middle of the nineteenth century Spanish students had begun to make the pilgrimage to the European center of Orientalist studies—Paris—in order to write the history of their own country.¹⁰ And Asín's teacher, Julián Ribera y Tarrago (1858–1934), was the first Spanish Orientalist to study in the Arab world.¹¹ Ribera brought back texts from Cairo (al-Ghazali, in addition to the Andalusians Averroes, Ibn Hazm and Ibn 'Arabi) that Asín read closely. Thus—although Asín himself did not study in Paris or Cairo—an unbroken chain of tutelage (what Arabs call a *silsila*) connected him to the capital of European Orientalist studies on the one hand and of Arab intellectual life on the other, infusing his thought with a robust cosmopolitanism. In addition to being a scholar, Asín was a cleric. His work on Dante (and on Thomas Aquinas, about whom he wrote a study that appeared in 1904, fifteen years before his book on Dante) viewed Christian thought from the perspective of faith but also with a deep passion and respect for the syncretism of medieval Andalusian civilization. Finally, Asín brought to his work the perspective of the generation of 1898—the Spaniards who, after the loss of the last of the Spanish colonies, Cuba and the Philippines, turned to self-analysis and national soul-searching in an effort to understand the process by which the nation had lost its position of prominence in the modern world. So Asín approached a rich and complex body of material—on the one hand Dante's *Commedia*, on the other the poetry of Ibn 'Arabi and the medieval mi'raj accounts—from an equally complex position: he wrote as a Spaniard with a sophisticated perspective on European and Arab intellectual history, as a Catholic with strong ecumenical convictions, from a nation given over for the moment to navel-gazing. As we will see, Julián Ribera, Asín's teacher, had worked to demonstrate the Hispanicity of medieval Arab Andalusian history (see the passage from Ribera's response to

Asín's inaugural lecture at the Real Academia quoted later in this chapter). Asín took Ribera's thesis a step further. He argued the centrality of medieval Spain to Christian intellectual history by establishing the indebtedness of *non-Spanish* Christians to Arab cultural formations, in particular in the field of theology, and showing (as James Monroe wrote) "that if Spain was 'Arabized,' so were Dante, Thomas Aquinas, and a great part of medieval European thought."[12]

In the uniquely combative field of Dante studies, Asín's work did not receive unanimous praise. Dante had only relatively recently been rescued from the gloom into which the Enlightenment had plunged him. In 1818 the novelist and poet Ugo Foscolo (1778–1827) published two articles in the *Edinburgh Review* that provide a convenient point of departure for tracing the sudden, striking shift in Dante's fates. Foscolo talks about a Dante whom we don't know: Dante as a poet who is no longer read; for he had fallen definitively out of favor during the eighteenth century. Foscolo writes that Dante "conceived and executed the project of creating the Language and the Poetry of a nation—of exposing all the political wounds of his country—of teaching the Church and the States of Italy, that the imprudence of the Popes, and the civil wars of the cities, and the consequent introduction of foreign arms, must lead to the eternal slavery and disgrace of the Italians" (initial caps, tellingly, all Foscolo's).[13] In Foscolo's two articles we witness the emergence of a recognizable Dante: the father of the nation; an author who could create an unforgettable portrait of an individual in just a few lines.[14] And in these articles, as in so many of the philological manifestoes of the nineteenth century, Foscolo creates a vertiginous sense of identity between the medieval past and the present day. It is at times impossible to determine whether he is talking about the present, the past, or a powerful amalgam of the two, concocted by Foscolo acting as vatic poet rather than critic and historian.

The idea that this recently christened national poet might have been chummy enough with Islamic thought to borrow uncritically from it—such was Asín's suggestion—provoked a firestorm of critical response. In 1924 Asín would publish a pamphlet summarizing the controversy from 1919 to 1923 ("Historia y crítica de una polémica") that would be included, along with supplemental notes on the continuation of the polemic, in the 1943 edition of *La escatología musulmana*. There is something dismaying about thumbing through the pages of this document, as if the years between the European wars had been for these Europeans anything but a truce. Asín seems to find a certain comfort in a comment made by an English Dantista named Mac-Donald at the beginning of the controversy: Dante scholars are "no peaceful folk."[15] The book presented a peculiar difficulty to the scholarly community not only because it was perceived in some quarters to challenge the orthodoxy of the greatest poet of the Christian Middle Ages but also for a simple pragmatic reason. Asín's thesis mediated between Dante scholars—who were by disciplinary training Italianists or Romance philologists—and Orientalists. No single scholarly community could transcend linguistic parochialism to evaluate Asín's thesis cogently and comprehensively.

Yet evidence of the accessibility of Muslim beliefs about the afterworld to the Christian West would come to light—though not, sad to say, until after Asín's death. Over the course of the previous two centuries a trickle of evidence of the translation of the mi'raj narratives into the languages of Christian Europe had appeared.[16] But no scholar as yet had tracked down the extant manuscripts in European libraries and compared them to Dante's text. Finally, in 1949—six centuries after it was created, two centuries after a bibliographer noted the presence of a Latin translation in a French library, and six years after Miguel Asín Palacios's death—a modern edition of the medieval French and Latin translations of the "Book of the Ladder" (or "Liber Scalae," as it was known in Latin) appeared.

In fact, two editions of the work were published in 1949—the one, appropriately enough, edited by a Spanish scholar and the other by an Italian. Enrico Cerulli's edition has overshadowed José Muñoz Sendino's in part because of the dazzling erudition of Cerulli's work and in part because of the unfortunate rhetorical excesses of Muñoz's. The delicacy of the material demanded reserve; scholars had been quibbling bitterly over Asín's suggestions since his book appeared thirty years earlier. Muñoz's tone would not allay the anxieties of an international scholarly community. Here Muñoz describes the impact of Miguel Asín's book on critical understandings of the *Commedia*:

> When Asín Palacios's book pierced and shattered the vague reaches of those distant and unexplored horizons, explained his disconcerting theory with the dazzling parade and in the garb of the legend of the ascension of the Prophet, and established the solid resemblance of the architecture, conception and substance of episodes in the [mi'raj] legend and the *Divine Comedy*, the surprise had no limits. The dogma of the

semidivine genius of the poet was turned upside down and, what was worse, exaggerated nationalism was wounded to the marrow—the nobly exaggerated nationalism, if you wish, of the keenest defenders of the dogma. The heart and the joints of the poem had been revealed; and all the medieval antecedents (the Christian legends held to be precursors) were seen to derive from a single source, situated within Islam.[17]

Neither the tone nor the content of the book was likely to make Muñoz many friends among Dante scholars—who were, after all, "no peaceful folk."

Cerulli's book, on the other hand, is recognized as the crowning achievement in twentieth-century scholarship on Dante and Islam. Cerulli reproduced the text of the "Book of the Ladder" in the medieval Latin and French translations. In addition he included a lengthy compilation of references to the legend in Spanish and Italian literature, and witnesses to the general knowledge of Islamic eschatology in Spanish, Italian, and French between the ninth and the fifteenth century—with a chapter on the influence of Islamic depictions of the afterworld on the thirteenth-century philosophers of the Oxford school for good measure. The image that emerges from his painstaking philological detective work is one of a medieval Europe with disconcertingly porous boundaries. Medieval Christians may well have identified Muslims as exterior and alien to their own communities, and as military opponents. Yet Christian intellectuals eagerly gathered information about the beliefs and practices of the Muslims, collecting and tabulating the information for an audience deemed equally insatiable.[18] In a later chapter I will discuss the historical context in which Cerulli—who had the extraordinary ill fortune to live through two world wars and to be in the thick of Italy's colonial experiment in Ethiopia from its ignominious beginning to its ignominious end—produced this monumental work of scholarship.

To date, I am sorry to say, the discovery of the translations of the mi'raj tradition into the languages of Christian Europe has failed to satisfy the scholarly community as a whole. Scholars no longer discuss Dante's knowledge of Ibn 'Arabi—given the fact that no translations of Ibn 'Arabi's poetry into the languages of Christian Europe have been discovered, the idea is a nonstarter—but continue to debate the possibility that Dante knew and made use of the "Book of the Ladder." And critics have begun to ask other, intriguing questions about his knowledge of and response to the Arab philosophy of his age, his engagement with Averroism in particular.[19] Finally, a more sophisticated understanding of Dante's manipulation of his sources in general

(Christian and classical Roman in addition to Islamic) allows us to put his relation to the Islamic sciences into a more meaningful perspective. But despite the fact that I myself have published on the subject and feel that evidence in favor of influence is, if not incontrovertible, at least reasonably convincing, I would be remiss if I didn't report that scholarly consensus has not been reached.

The difficulty in tracing the influence of Islamic depictions of the afterlife on Dante's work can be attributed to the fact that Dante at no point gives positive evidence of his knowledge of those sources. But Petrarch poses a diametrically opposed problem. For Petrarch *did* claim to know the poetry of the Arabs; yet scholars have not been able to determine the source of that knowledge, and hence have not agreed whether his statement should be believed. And the question of the influence of Arabic poetics on Petrarch's poetic practice has not been broached by literary scholars—unless one accepts Pietro Valerga's metempsychosis thesis as a discussion of influence. Indeed, the nature of Petrarch's poetry makes the question extraordinarily difficult to frame. Petrarch—more than any other Italian poet; more than any other *European* poet—furnished a transnational and translinguistic model for the poets of Europe during the years of transition between the Middle Ages and modernity. European readers celebrate his *Canzoniere* as the dove sent out from the ark of the Middle Ages to seek the terra firma of the Renaissance. His emphasis on the significance and centrality of individual emotional truths and his strong feeling for the fragmentary, the transient, the *sparso* feel irrefutably modern. And he modeled a spirit of proximity to antiquity (and distance from the medieval) that would characterize the Renaissance. In a sensitive and compelling reading of a particularly charged passage from one of Petrarch's letters, Giuseppe Mazzotta argued that his articulation of this sense of intimacy with classical antiquity in effect announced the advent of the Renaissance—or at least sounded the death knell for the mongrel Middle Ages.[20]

Certainly not coincidentally, Petrarch also voiced some of the earliest expressions of full-blown Saidian Orientalism, anticipating the summary and facile denunciation of the Arabs that would be associated with modernity. In a notorious passage from a late letter he instructed Giovanni Dondi, a medical doctor, not to sing the praises of the Arabs to him: "I beseech you that these Arabs of yours be kept off, that they be exiled from all your advice to me. I hate the whole race." He reviled at some length the Arab physicians' stranglehold on contemporary medical science. And, curiously, he denounced their poetry: "The Arabs! You know them as doctors; I know them as poets.

Nothing more insipid, nothing softer, nothing more flaccid, nothing more obscene . . ."[21] Pietro Valerga acknowledged this comment in the introduction to his translation of Ibn al-Farid's diwan, although he did not explain how a reincarnated Arab might acquire upon his rebirth such a strong distaste for his former ethnicity.[22] And Julián Ribera, the great Spanish Orientalist who trained Miguel Asín Palacios, alluded to the passage when he wrote: "Petrarch was one of those who protested with great force [Christian reliance on the Arab sciences]; but for so long as the Arab works substituted for the Greek and Latin originals, such lamentations and complaints were quite vain."[23] Indeed the reference has excited a substantial amount of comment on the part of philologists, who have sought to understand how Petrarch could have known—as he claims to do here—the poetry of the Arabs.

Petrarch, of course, did not have access to Arabic poetry; no one (pace Valerga) has suggested that he could read Arabic. While Christians translated philosophical treatises from the Arabic in abundance, works of poetry were not in general translated during the Middle Ages—although we will encounter the most notable exception to this rule in a moment. Petrarch's curiosity about the culture of the Greeks is well known. His ardent interest in classical antiquity inspired his attempt to learn Greek (although he didn't get very far with the project). In this he anticipated the humanist enthusiasm for ancient Greek letters.[24] However, he never betrayed the vaguest curiosity about the culture of the Arabs; he seemed content to denounce it without knowing much about it.

As scholarly interest in cultural communications between medieval Christians and Muslims increased over the course of the last 150 years, Petrarch's denunciation of the poetry of the Arabs has solicited comments from scholars wondering what he knew about that poetry and where he learned it. Renan, in *Averroès et l'Averroïsme* (published in 1852), described with éclat Petrarch's position as the first of the moderns ("Petrarch deserves to be called the first modern man" because "Petrarch was truly an ancient"). He also signaled the passage in question in the course of his discussion of Petrarch's loathing for the Arabs. After citing the comment he asked in a footnote: "How could Petrarch have known Arabic poetry, of which the Middle Ages had not the slightest notion?"[25] In a work published in 1931, H. A. R. Gibb wrote that "Petrarch's violent nationalist outburst against the Arabs proves at least, if it proves anything, that the more popular kind of Arabic poetry was still known in Italy in his day"; of course few scholars today would agree that this passage constitutes convincing proof of knowledge of popular Arabic poetry in fourteenth-century Italy.[26] In 1965 Enrico Cerulli (who in 1949 had published the French and Latin translations of the miʿraj narrative) speculated that Petrarch had in mind classical Latin references to the ancient Arabs as *mollis, imbellis* and *effeminatus* (soft; unfit for war, flaccid or timid; and effeminate).[27] Finally in 1982 C. H. L. Bodenham identified a likely source not only for the final adjective that Petrarch used to describe the poetry of the Arabs, which bore no similarity to those that appeared in the classical sources cited by Cerulli—*turpis*, "base" or "obscene"—but also for his claim to know Arabic poetry: Hermannus Alemannus's Latin translation of Averroes' Arabic commentary on Aristotle's *Poetics*. And Bodenham argued that by condemning it as *obscene* Petrarch seconded Averroes' own critique of certain Arabic poetry that might incite lascivious behavior on the part of those who read it.[28]

In reviewing this scholarship one is impressed at how well the philological model works to advance our understanding of literary history. Each of the articles on Petrarch's knowledge of Arabic poetry builds on the evidence and insights provided by previous scholarship—from Renan's reference, which tagged the passage for future scholars, to Bodenham's suggestion of a plausible source for Petrarch's knowledge of Arabic poetry. And each takes advantage of the accumulation of data about the medieval past by painting an ever more detailed picture of the cultural and historical landscape in which Petrarch lived. The philology of the late twentieth and early twenty-first century in general seeks to read medieval texts in the context of the vibrant intellectual environment in which they were produced. Our picture of the Middle Ages is far from complete, of course. But in certain cases—especially around questions that have been scrutinized with particular intensity, such as Dante and Islam or Petrarch and the Arabs—we are able to produce an image with startling resolution. Not surprisingly, the more we know about the Middle Ages the more complex it becomes.[29]

Consider, for instance, the work that Bodenham identified as Petrarch's source of information about Arabic poetry: Hermannus Alemannus's thirteenth-century Latin translation of Averroes' twelfth-century Arabic commentary on Aristotle's *Poetics*. No other text that I am aware of encapsulates quite so perfectly the unique linguistic and literary complexity of the age of Dante, Petrarch, and Boccaccio; it is, simply stated, the medieval Mediterranean between cloth covers. Hermannus Alemannus translated Averroes' treatise on the *Poetics* in Toledo in 1256.[30] He produced translations of al-Farabi's and Averroes' commentaries on Aristotle's *Rhetoric* around the same time; the translation of the *Poetics* completed this small library of rhetorical works.[31] His translation of Averroes on the *Poetics* enjoyed a certain vogue during the Middle Ages. It survives in a respectable twenty-four manuscripts and a number of prominent authors—including Thomas Aquinas, Roger Bacon, Coluccio Salutati, and the Italian humanist Albertino Mussato—cited it.[32] Because the medieval philosophical tradition believed that Aristotle intended his treatise on poetics as part of the Organon—the works on logic—medieval philosophers and theologians treated the treatise as central to the Aristotelian corpus, albeit a difficult and somewhat eccentric component of the corpus.[33] Thus the work was taught at the great universities, and numerous florilegia excerpted important passages from it as cribs for instructors, students, and armchair philosophers. Jean de Fayt, a scholar and preacher who was in Avignon at the same time as Petrarch, produced one such florilegium, apparently for use at the University of Paris.[34] It is this florilegium that may have provided Petrarch with a crash course in Arabic poetics. Jean's selection of citations from Hermannus's translation includes Averroes' denunciation of the poetry of the Arabs: it is "a provocation to the coital act, disguised and prettified with the name of love."[35]

Hermannus's *Poetria* (as his treatise was generally known) is a palimpsest in which antiquity and the Muslim and Christian Middle Ages are layered, no layer quite successful in eradicating what preceded it. For the passage through time and languages had so thoroughly transformed Aristotle's treatise that the text on which Averroes commented bore little relation to the work that Aristotle wrote. Averroes reproduced the tradition that reached him when he divided poetry not into the dramatic genres of comedy and tragedy, but rather satire or vituperation (*hija'* in Arabic) and eulogy (*madih*). And Hermannus (who did not have access to the Greek original) duly translated Aristotle's words as transmitted by Averroes: "Omne itaque poema et omnis oratio poetica aut est vituperatio aut est laudatio" ("Every poem and every poetic oration is either vituperation or praise").[36] Averroes departed from previous commentary on the *Poetics*—and from Aristotle's own work—by including numerous excerpts of Arabic poetry (from the pre-Islamic poets to contemporary medieval poetry) and the Qur'an to illustrate the concepts he discussed. And Hermannus included in his version of the treatise Latin translations of forty-three citations of Arabic poetry, as well as those Qur'anic references that he could decipher from Averroes' telegraphically brief citations. Scholars have excavated a very small handful of other examples of Arabic poetry translated into Latin.[37] But this collection is unique both for the number of translations and the fact that in many cases Hermannus translated poetry into poetry: he gave some of his Latin versions of the Arabic verses end rhyme (if not poetic meter). Thus the *Poetria* presented a rare opportunity for the medieval Christian reader to study Arabic poetry in translation—to hear echoes of the verses the Arabs sang to condemn or praise each other (and to seduce each other's wives).

One of the loveliest passages that Hermannus translated comes from the large body of medieval verse attributed to a legendary poet known as al-Majnun, the "Madman" who lost his senses out of unrequited love for Layla. In Hermannus's translation, the verses—which Averroes cites to illustrate prosopopeia, a rhetorical figure that endows abstract concepts or inanimate objects with the capacity to reason and speak—do not have the rhythm of poetry. But note the care that Hermannus has given to creating end rhyme:

> O domus egregia, compungor ad lacrimas tuam intuens solitudinem;
> at illa contremuit compassa michi propter lacrimarum multitudinem,
> cui inquio: 'ubi queso sunt qui quondam in te habitaverunt,
> et iocundam vitam cum securitate et temporis amenitate duxerunt?'
> At illa 'temporales, inquit, existentes temporaliter cum tempore transierunt,
> et me quoque sub sorte temporis quandoque transituram dimiserunt;
> res nempe nulle stabiles, que cum fluxu huius temporis fluxibiles fuerunt.'[38]

[O noble house, I am moved to tears when I look upon your solitude; but she (i.e., the house) trembled, moved by my abundant tears, and I asked her: 'Where are those who once lived in you, and led a happy life of safety and sweet days?' And she replied: 'temporal things, being temporal, change with time, and they abandoned me; and I too am fated to disappear with time; for nothing is lasting which has changed with the flow of this temporal world.']

The fragment is a hauntingly evocative composition with a loose and flowing rhythm, held together by end rhyme and by the melancholy play on words having to do with time, transience, and decay in the final three lines. In translating Averroes' treatise Hermannus dropped or replaced some citations of Arabic poetry—brief passages that were too fragmentary to translate effectively, that contained proper names (which gave Hermannus, lacking cultural fluency, a great deal of difficulty), or that relied on wordplay for their significance.[39] However, he chose to embroider and elaborate this passage. He expanded it from three lines to seven and reproduced the end rhyme of the original in his Latin version.[40] The word play in this selection—*temporale, temporaliter,* and *tempore* in the fifth line; *temporis, fluxu,* and *fluxibiles* in the last*—*is the translator's interpolation. Although Arab poets in general love lexical tomfoolery, there is no parallel wordplay in the Arabic poem that Hermannus is translating. Likewise the sinuous rhythm and alliterations of the final line, so appropriate to the subject, do not reflect the relatively prosaic original.[41]

The thicket of words derived from the roots *tempus* and *fluxus* in the closing lines and the meditation on the quintessentially Petrarchan theme of instability make Hermannus's translation feel like a rough sketch for one of Petrarch's sonnets. It's easy to imagine Petrarch—if he did come across the *Poetria,* or Jean de Fayt's collection of excerpts from it—reading these lines and being struck at once by the mood of loss and longing and by the word-play in the closing lines, so crude by Petrarchan standards yet so redolent of what we think of as a Petrarchan sensibility. Certainly few words appear more frequently in the *Canzoniere* than *tempo.* And the word *fluxus,* used twice in the last line, has a peculiarly suggestive lexical range in the current context. It means flowing, like water; it also can mean *lax, dissolute, careless, effeminate; frail, weak, fleeting, transient, perishable.*[42] *Fluxus* may designate that which bends to pressure or flows, like a stream. At the same time its semantic range allows the reader to interpret it in a condemnatory mode, as a castigation of what is merely temporal and thus subject to decay:

res nempe nulle stabiles que cum fluxu huius temporis fluxibiles fuerunt

[for nothing is lasting which has proved frail and dissolute with the
   transience of this temporal world]

Hermannus's translation of a fragment of Arabic poetry—brief as it is, simple and unprepossessing as it is—rehearses themes central to Petrarch's poetics: instability, fragility, tenuous temporality; the moral peril of the un-stable, the fragile, the tenuous. Pietro Valerga's suggestion that Petrarch knew and was influenced by the poetry of Ibn al-Farid sounded like madness to his contemporaries (and still does today). Yet from the pages of a book that might well have been known to Petrarch, a book that he could have studied in his own language, Latin, comes a suggestion no less strange. Did the great poet of the cusp of modernity derive inspiration from the *nasib* (amorous introduction) of a medieval Arabic *qasida* (ode), in which the bereaved lover pantomimes a topos lifted from the classical poems of the pre-Islamic era— the Bedouin poet viewing the mournful traces of his beloved's abandoned desert encampment? Despite Valerga's cautionary example I cannot resist the temptation to cite an example of prosopopeia from Petrarch's *Canzoniere* to elucidate the sentiments and rhetorical strategies of the medieval Arabic poem, a passage in which hope personified speaks, offering the poet bitter-sweet comfort for the absence of his beloved:

> [. . .] Perché priva
> sia de l'amata vista,
> mantienti, anima trista;
> che sai s'a miglior tempo ancho ritorni
> et a piú lieti giorni,
> o se 'l perduto ben mai si racquista?
> Questa speranza mi sostenne un tempo:
> or vien mancando, et troppo in lei m'attempo.
>
> Il tempo passa . . .
> (Canzone 37, "Sí è debile il filo a cui s'attene," vv. 10–17)[43]

> [ . . . Although you are deprived
> of the beloved face
> endure, sad soul;
> do you know whether you will yet return to a better time
> and to happier days,
> or whether you will once again acquire the good you have lost?
> This hope sustained me for a time:
> now it dwindles, while I dwell (*m'attempo*) too much on it.
>
> Time passes . . . ]

I am tempted to suggest that Petrarch did indeed know and use Herman-nus's *Poetria*, though the evidence is circumstantial and my conclusion little more than a hunch. Or—to state the hypothesis more cautiously—if Petrarch happened upon Hermannus's treatise it seems likely that he put it to use, weaving the good and the bad of it into his own poetic practice as well as his judgment of Arabic poetics. This scarcely constitutes an argument in favor of influence, of course. Petrarch—recipient of so abundant a poetic gift—did not need to nourish his genius on the meager poetic banquet offered by Hermannus Alemannus, Averroes, and the Arab poets in Latin masquerade. At most the philologist could argue, on the basis of the evidence marshaled here, that Petrarch—who had a demonstrable professional interest in the poetry of the Arabs: "you know them as doctors, I know them as poets"— could have derived double value from Hermannus's treatise. If he did en-counter it, he would indeed have found there grounds to criticize the Arab poets in Averroes' own criticism of the moral peril posed by certain poetry. And he could have taken away from it as well a lingering sense that behind the screen of Hermannus's Latin renderings there lay a poetry of dazzling lexical opulence, redolent of melancholy for a mourned "double treasure" (as Petrarch would put it in a sonnet) whose loss "neither earth nor empire, neither Oriental gem nor the power of gold can restore."[44]

Petrarch—more than Boccaccio, who lived and worked in a port city open to the vibrant multifaceted culture of the medieval Mediterranean, and more than Dante, who studied and reworked the philosophy of the Arabs— perceived the Arabs as alien and rejected them as exterior to his interests at best, inimical at worst. Petrarch, of course, expressed a deep antipathy to Dante's poetry as well. In a notorious letter to Boccaccio he vehemently denied feeling envy for the poet whom he could not bring himself to name (though he confessed to meeting him as a young man), whose work he could not avoid knowing although he stated emphatically that he had never read it. He told Boccaccio that he hadn't sought out Dante's books, yet he claimed familiarity with Dante's writing. His description of Dante's poetry suggested that he knew the *Commedia* because he had heard it recited in public. He speaks of poems that "charm the ears"; he speaks of the "illiterates in the taverns and squares" who know Dante's poem; he mentions "ignoramuses . . . at the street corners" declaiming his poetry.[45] Petrarch knew the *Commedia* as poetry that one en-counters in the mouths of common people, not that one studies in the pages of books.

For Petrarch, Dante's poetry is what one always already knows, without having sought it out and studied it. Petrarch made himself modern by creat-ing difference between himself and the vestiges of the medieval past that surrounded him, like Dante's inescapable *Commedia* and the unavoidable culture of the Arabs. He called for the Arabs to be *exiled* (see note 21 to this chapter), as Dante had been from their mutual native city; and he chafed against their cultural dominance, as he did against the cultural currency of the *Commedia*. In the letter to Giovanni Dondi discussed above he repeated with scorn a comment he had heard at a lecture before an audience of doctors: "A Latin doctor, if he were the equal even to Hippocrates, might be able to speak; but unless he were Greek or Arab he would not dare to write, and if he wrote he would be scorned." After the Greek philosophers, Petrarch pointed out, the Romans had written philosophy; after Homer came Virgil; after the Greek historians and lawgivers and theologians the Romans still dared to create works of history and laws and meditations on the divine. Yet "after the Arabs, no one will be allowed to write!"[46]

Petrarch created a literary modernity by consigning Dante and the Arabs equally to the ungainly, mongrel, medieval past and moving into the wide literary and intellectual space he had thus created. Of course, even for those born long before Freud, the repressed sometimes returns. It is tempting to wonder whether Petrarch—if indeed he read Hermannus's *Poetria*, if indeed he read it carefully—thought of Dante when he heard from Averroes' mouth the quintessentially Dantean warning against poetry that incites the reader to lust. If so, it would count as one more reason to distance himself from Dante (even as he anxiously replicated Averroes' and Dante's gesture of condemnation): as Asín described him, a man who from the promontory of genius overlooked the complexity of his age.

## The Problem of Influence

During the nineteenth century, as Valerga worked on his translation of Ibn al-Farid, philologists throughout Europe became intimately involved in the sorts of questions discussed in the previous chapter: identifying the moment when a nation emerged, recognizably itself, from the premodern penumbra. Philologists working in Mediterranean Europe faced a thorny difficulty. How should the historian characterize the historical relation between an Arab past and a European modernity epitomized in the formation of the (Italian or Spanish) nation? The difficulty was particularly acute in the Spanish context. Arabs dominated medieval Spanish history; the Christian history of the age was defined by the presence or near proximity of the Arabs.[47] Arabs occupied portions of the Iberian peninsula from 711 until their expulsion in 1492 (and even beyond; the last Arab residents of the peninsula, descendents of Andalusian Muslims converted to Christianity, were not expelled until 1609–14). Muslim Spain produced literary figures of dominating importance: the philosopher and litterateur Ibn Hazm (994–1064); the vernacular poet Ibn Quzman (1078–1160); Ibn Tufayl (1109/10–1185/86), author of the remarkable treatise "Hayy Ibn Yaqzan"; the philosopher Ibn Rushd (1126–98), ultimately more important to medieval Christians—who knew him as Averroes—than to the medieval Islamic philosophical tradition; mystic, philosopher, and poet Ibn 'Arabi (1165–1240). Andalusian Jewish figures of major importance who used the Arabic language as poetic or philosophical lingua franca included the poet and philosopher Moses Ibn Ezra (ca. 1060–ca. 1039); Petrus Alfonsi (1062–1110), a convert to Christianity who wrote a framed narrative in Latin consisting largely of translations from Arabic wisdom literature, the *Disciplina clericalis*; and philosopher Maimonides (1135–1204), who fled al-Andalus in his youth with the advance of the Almohads. Remarkable Christian figures wrote across the border between the Arab and Christian worlds, including the translators hired by Alfonso el Sabio (1221–84) and the philosopher and evangelist Ramon Llull (ca. 1232–1316).

No responsible historian could think Spanish history without its Arab component. But how to write the historical relation of Muslims and Christians in the Iberian peninsula; how to write the contribution of Iberian Arabs to *Spanish* history? Some Spanish philologists resolved the knot of Spanish history by appropriating the vocabulary of origins and writing Andalusian Arabs as Spaniards *avant la lettre:* they asserted the Hispanicity of the culture of medieval Andalusian Arabs. The Muslims of medieval Spain, wrote Francisco Fernández y González (1833–1917) in a work published in 1866, "maintained a patriotic sentiment of attachment to their native country, like the sailor who prefers to ride out any danger rather than abandon his ship. Spaniards without doubt, the *moriscos*."[48] José Antonio Conde (1765–1820)—the first modern Spanish historian to use Arab sources—struck a particularly vivid image to evoke the ventriloquism whereby Arab patriots wrote the history of medieval Spain. In his *Historia de la dominación de los Árabes en España* (published in 1820–21) he invited the reader to enter a looking-glass land: "The readers who happen to pick up this book should imagine that it was written by an Arab author; for in effect it is an extract and a faithful translation of many of their works. . . . This book is like the reverse of our history; and just as in our history one says little or nothing about the succession and order of the Arab dynasties and of Moorish customs, here one finds little of the matters of Leon and Castile."[49] Curiouser and curiouser! The reader of Conde's history of Spain would encounter a national past written by an Arab and peopled with Arab warriors, statesmen, and poets—one where Spanish Arab philosophers and scientists brought illumination to a Europe slumbering through its Dark Ages and where Castilian poets learned to sing from Arab masters.[50]

Although Conde's narrative was lively and readable, his crude historical methods would make later historians cringe. Pascual de Gayangos (1809–97)—whose treatment of Conde was relatively amiable—pointed out, in the introduction to his *History of the Mohammedan Dynasties in Spain* (written in English and published in 1840), that Conde's work was "far from fulfilling the expectations of the scholar." At the same time Gayangos acknowledged the difficulties that Conde struggled against to write his history: the Spanish government's contempt for the Arab past, which left the Arab manuscripts in Spanish collections vulnerable to neglect; the general ignorance of the Arabic language in Spain—again, a result of Spaniards' hostility toward their own national history; and last but not least the political vicissitudes of the age. For Conde was a French appointee to the position of chief librarian at the Royal Library in Madrid. When the Spaniards drove the French out of the peninsula in 1814 Conde lost his position and his official protection. He wrote his history of the Arab past in a state of destitution and left the second volume unfinished. He died in 1820; and "his unfinished manuscript," Gayangos wrote, "fell into the hands of parties totally unacquainted with the subject, and who increased, instead of remedying, the confusion."[51]

Gayangos himself deplored the Spaniards' contempt for Arab civilization ("the Arabs," he wrote, "instead of being commended to the gratitude of modern ages, as they assuredly deserved to be, have been often charged with corrupting the infancy of modern literature"). And in his own work he strove to correct the imbalance of Spanish history, which he found to be, "notwithstanding the labors of modern critics, a tissue of fable and contradiction."[52] Gayangos embodied the new, scientific attitude toward philological research. He lived in France during his teen years, studied Arabic in Paris with Antoine Isaac Silvestre de Sacy as a young man, and brought modern philological method to Spain when he returned. And the time that he spent living outside of Spain—he married an Englishwoman and spent periods of residence in London throughout his life—gave his historical work a European perspective. The expansion and contraction of nineteenth-century continental liberalism infused his vision of national history with a particular urgency (as it would the nineteenth-century Sicilians whom we will meet in the next chapter).

Spanish historians argued the centrality of Iberian Arabs to Spanish history as early as the first half of the nineteenth century; by the turn of the twentieth century this argument was accepted by most historians and by the mid-twentieth (by the most conservative estimate) it had become normative. Scholarship on Spain's medieval history had, in effect, Hispanized the Arabs who peopled the Iberian peninsula during the Middle Ages. Julián Ribera—in his response to Miguel Asín Palacios's discourse on Dante and Islam on the occasion of his entry to the Real Academia Española (on January 26, 1919)—said:

> I repeat (and I will repeat until satiety, since justice requires it) that the Muslims of the Peninsula were Spaniards: Spaniards in race, Spaniards in tongue, Spaniards in character, taste, tendencies and genius. . . . And we should consider the merits of the Spanish Muslims to be our own national, Spanish wealth; by means of their civil virtues, they made southern Spain the best run country, the most powerful, the richest and most cultured of the first half of the Middle Ages, and by means of its natural gifts of genius they excelled to such an extent in the deeds of the spirit that they created a peculiarly Spanish scientific, literary and artistic culture, absolutely unique and without equal in any of the previous periods in the history of Spain.[53]

In Ribera's eyes, the history of the Muslims who inhabited the Iberian peninsula as much as a millennium before Spain became a nation was *Spanish* history, and indeed the glory of Spanish history. Thus during the course of the nineteenth century and the early decades of the twentieth Spanish historians created a reading of national history that posited identity between the dominant Muslim culture of Spain's medieval past and Christian modernity.

In Italy, however, historical differences caused the problem to be phrased differently. The Arab presence consisted chiefly of voices offstage; Arabs did not have a starring role in Italian history. The former Arab domain on Italian soil was limited to a marginal part of the nation: the south, in particular Sicily. Arab rule of Sicily lasted only for two centuries (compare more than seven hundred years in the case of al-Andalus). And Arab Sicily didn't produce literary giants as al-Andalus did, with the single exception of the great poet Ibn Hamdis (1055/56–1133). Furthermore the years of Arab rule in Sicily, from the mid-ninth until the mid-eleventh century, constituted only one of a series of conquests and dominations (albeit a crucially important one). The

Greeks, Romans, and Byzantine Greeks had ruled Sicily before the Arabs. And the centuries of Arab rule were followed by the Norman domination: an extraordinary period when Christian kings adapted Eastern Christian, Western Christian, and Islamic institutions to rule a kingdom of Muslim and Christian citizens. Finally, the years of Norman rule would culminate in the reign of Frederick II (1194–1250)—a figure who dominates not only Italian but indeed European history and is recognized as one of the most important monarchs of the Middle Ages. Spaniards have a rough equivalent in Frederick's contemporary Alfonso el Sabio, king of Galicia, Castile, and León, who commissioned a number of important translations of scientific works from the Arabic into the languages of Western Christianity. While Alfonso's interactions with Arabic letters would ultimately have decisive significance for European intellectual history, he does not have the charisma of Frederick: a man who traveled with a menagerie, battled popes, negotiated his way to possession of Jerusalem, and banished the Arabs of Sicily and Malta to a Muslim ghetto city on the Italian mainland where he maintained a palace (equipped with a private harem) for his personal use.

But the most striking differences in the arc of Spanish and Italian history would follow Arab occupation of national soil. Spanish Orientalists would come to see the caliphates of medieval al-Andalus as a pinnacle of cultural sophistication and enlightenment, followed by a period not nearly as distinguished as what preceded it. The Italian Middle Ages, however, would culminate in the glories of the Trecento, when three Italian writers brought the European Middle Ages to a conclusion and in effect invented modernity: Dante, Boccaccio, and Petrarch. The explanations outlined above account in large part for the vehemence of Italian scholars' reaction to Miguel Asín Palacios's proposal that Dante drew on Islamic sources in writing the *Commedia*: Asín's assertion (in his critics' view) that the most Christian poet of the Middle Ages had studied at the feet of imams; Dante's relatively recent anointment as the poet of the nation. But it is also useful, and historically suggestive, to read this scholarship in light of distinct understandings of the mechanics of influence.

Asín imposed a Spanish understanding of influence on the Italian poet. He assumed a Middle Ages of fluid boundaries and porous borders—indeed, with a singular lack of differentiation between one population and another. The word *influence* seems inadequate to describe the model of Muslim-Christian cultural communication proposed by Asín and other Spanish historians between the mid-nineteenth and mid-twentieth century. From their scholarship emerged the image of a thoroughly hybridized environment, where Muslim and Christian communities produced a culture of fusion without losing their individual cultural and religious identity. Asín's Dante could borrow freely from popular Islamic legends of the afterworld (or from Ibn 'Arabi, for that matter) in order to produce the Christian masterpiece of the Middle Ages. Asín's Thomas Aquinas and Averroes—"always judged to be irreconcilable enemies"—reveal themselves to be intellectual and spiritual soul mates, "to the extent that Averroes' theological doctrine of reconciliation of reason and faith coincides wholly with that of the Angelic Doctor."[54] In the best of this scholarship philological rigor prevented the historian from blurring the precision of the Christian or the Islamic traditions within which individual figures worked. Asín would not paint Thomas or Dante as crypto-Muslims. Yet meticulous sifting of a mountain of textual details would produce a dizzying number of points of convergence. In order to make sense of this evidence the Spanish Orientalist learned to celebrate the vibrant syncretic culture of medieval al-Andalus (or, in Asín's more capacious vision, the medieval Mediterranean) as a Spanish phenomenon, and indeed as the origin of the phenomenon of Spain. Asín closed his study of Thomas Aquinas and Averroes by celebrating the glorious fusion of Scholastic philosophy, a theological chain reaction that spans the Mediterranean but is finally located, with a curious geographical precision, in Spain: "And thus entered the Scholastic synthesis, purified of its errors against the Christian faith, the copious wealth of philosophy up to the theology of Averroes; just as in its turn this theology was nothing other than an accommodation of Christian dogma from the Eastern church, adapted to Islam by means of a laborious and difficult gestation through the efforts of al-Ghazali in the East and of Ibn Tufayl and Averroes *in our Spain*."[55]

The Spaniards might imagine medieval Arabs contributing to the project of building a national character—tributary streams of genius feeding the reservoir that would, under the brilliant light of modernity, be recognized as the source of the genius of Spain. But such a leap of faith did not come easily to the Italians, who preferred to see their own modernity as a reinvention of the Roman miracle. As a gauge of Italian resistance to the suggestion that Dante had borrowed from the Muslims, it is telling to note that the Italian translation of Miguel Asín Palacios's *La escatología musulmana en la* Divina Comedia would not appear until 1994—seventy-five years after the first Spanish publication of the book. And it must be said that the perception of medieval Mediterranean history as a concert of civilizations did not win unanimous approval even in the Spanish context. While some Spanish Orientalists worked to reconstruct Spain's Arabo-Islamic history as part of its national heritage, others rejected the spirit of this historiography. Francisco Javier Simonet (1829–97), in a work published in 1888, argued vociferously against the "Arabic thesis"—even deploying in his defense the verses from Horace's "Ars Poetica" that have been for two millennia a balm from Gilead for conquered peoples. Medieval Iberian Christians did not learn from their Arab conquerors, he wrote, but rather taught the glories of early medieval Christian culture to the unlettered Arabs:

> it is appropriate to apply to the Spanish nation, in its relations with the Moors who subdued and ruled them, those verses of Horace:
>
> Græcia capta ferum victorem cepit, et artes
> Intulit agresti Latio.
>
> [Captive Greece herself captured the savage victor
> and brought the arts to wild Latium.][56]

Simonet proposed an alternate narrative of national history, one that posited a Christian continuity in Spanish history even when Christian Spaniards lived under Arab rule and themselves spoke Arabic. His *Glosario de voces ibéricas y latinas usadas entre los mozárabes* (*Glossary of Iberian and Latin Words Used among the Mozarabs*, 1888) traced Spanish identity not to the Arab inhabitants of medieval al-Andalus but to the Christians who spoke Arabic and lived under Arab rule (known in modern scholarship as Mozarabs). And he worked to construct the lost language of the people—that Romantic chimera—by removing the thin veil of Arabic to reveal the "national hispano-Latin language" spoken by "nuestros Mozarabes."[57]

In order to make such a claim, of course, Simonet must write against the tide of the philological evidence—lexical and literary data, as well as social and political history—that had surfaced by the last decades of the nineteenth century. And he bolstered his interpretation of history by asserting that the manuscript evidence to support his supposition of the survival of an Iberian Romance, the vehicle by means of which the Iberian Christians preserved their indigenous culture, would emerge in time.[58] But the manuscripts whose testimony he anticipated failed to materialize, and his intuition that Iberian Christians maintained their discrete identity even during the Babylonian cap-

tivity of Muslim rule would not withstand the scrutiny of philologists and
historians. His final work, the *Historia de los mozárabes de España* (1897–
1903)—which was informed by an intimate familiarity with the Arabic and
Latin sources, but at the same time denied that the Mozarabs ever absorbed
Islamic culture; affirmed their cultural autonomy, their Christianity, and
their Hispanicity; and indeed asserted that the glories of medieval Andalusian
civilization were no more than the treasures of medieval Christian civilization, taught to the Muslims by the indigenous Christian population—would
not appear until after his death, because members of the Real Academia de
la Historia opposed its publication.[59]

But Simonet's willingness to argue his perception of history in the absence of substantial material evidence to support it was far from unique. Asín,
after all, produced no evidence to demonstrate the validity of his proposition
that Dante had access to medieval Islamic legends of Muhammad's journey
to the next world. And in this passage from his 1919 response to Asín's presentation of that thesis to the Real Academia Española, Julián Ribera chafed
against the scientific standards that made it difficult for earlier generations of
scholars to defend the "Arabic thesis":

> No documentation was produced to demonstrate the influence of the
> Muslims on such matters. This was enough to refute it; and further it
> was made scientific dogma and fashion among the more prominent to
> reject any affirmation of influence in these matters, without thinking
> that there are phenomena of real and true imitation in which the influ-
> ence is carried out through hidden intermediaries, through unknown
> passageways, in a diffuse manner, whose tracks or traces are not easy to
> perceive or are not detectable without a more profound study or some
> other manner of demonstration—above all such acts as occur among
> dominated populations and do not find official expression in the lan-
> guage of the dominators. . . . [I]f indeed it is true that one ought not to
> affirm without proof, neither should we deny without it; and an attitude
> of indecision, or a confession of ignorance, ought to be the norm of
> scientific discretion in matters not well understood or unexplored.[60]

Ribera argued that the absence of proof did not refute the "Arabic thesis"
but rather marked areas where more research was necessary. Many of the
insights of scholars like Ribera and Asín would prove sound as years of diligent philological scholarship unearthed evidence—treatises translated, Arab

authorities cited—to support their hypotheses, as Simonet's thesis did not endure the Darwinian struggle for survival because the manuscript evidence to confirm his assertions has failed to materialize.[61]

Most of the philologists I have discussed in this chapter wrote in explicit support of (or, in the case of Simonet, resistance to) the "Arabic thesis." Others had little interest in literary history in particular and aimed simply to uncover the secret history of Arab Spain. In either case the narratives they spin undermine the modern perception of an eternal and absolute divide between the Islamic "Orient" and the Christian "West." Indeed, the evidence of cultural interpenetration amassed by philologists and historians does more than challenge the transhistorical validity of the woefully unsophisticated "Clash of Civilizations" model of Muslim-Christian relations. It also requires scholars to reconsider their definition of the mechanics of influence and the strategies and standards they use to determine when influence has occurred. Américo Castro—who coined the term "convivencia" to describe the co-existence of Muslims, Christians, and Jews in medieval Iberia—makes this point in his striking account of medieval Andalusian history:

> The term "influence" does little good here, because in reality it is a matter of the protective action of one interior disposition of life over another [on the part of a population] which ended up not converting itself to the beliefs of a powerful, fearsome and prestigious adversary, but rather using its own beliefs in a new and unanticipated way. . . . Christians did not suffice to themselves, neither when they occupied only the northern strip of the Peninsula, nor when their political dominion extended from Mallorca to Lisbon. Their life was like that of three Siamese twins (supposing that such a thing could exist), forced to live together as one, all the while anxious that they might be annihilated.[62]

In Castro's view, even when the Christian poets *didn't* model their literature, for instance, on the poetry of the Arabs, the historian must yet assume that cultural communication played a crucial role in literary history. The fact of co-existence made of Andalusian history (in the words of historian David Wacks) "an agonistic yet productive symbiotic relationship in which each participant is a *sine qua non* in the construction of the other's identity and cultural formation."[63] The historian simply cannot think Andalusian history without taking into account the cultural complexity that characterized that history before the wars and expulsions of the late medieval and early modern period.

During the early modern period—as the culture of Christian Europe gained confidence, as Europeans learned to hop the Middle Ages and trace their intellectual ancestry directly to the ancients—the divide between Arab and European cultures would come to seem increasingly absolute to European intellectuals. But we do well to remind ourselves of the time and industry required to generate and sustain the notion of the exteriority and irrelevance of Arabic letters to European modernity. The Greek text of Aristotle's *Poetics* came to Italy, along with a flood of other Greek manuscripts, following the fall of Constantinople to the Ottoman Turks in 1453. A Latin translation made directly from the Greek appeared in 1498, and a Greek edition of the text was published in 1508. During the course of the sixteenth century no fewer than eight retranslations (into Latin or Italian) or reprints of translations were made directly from the Greek. But during the same century, between 1481 and 1600, the Hermannus Alemannus translation—along with Latin translations of Hebrew translations of Averroes' commentary—appeared in *ten* editions and reprints.[64] It took a century of debate and negotiation for the notion that Aristotle's Greek should be viewed as the *correct* version of the *Poetics*—the most proximate and most relevant to European letters—to establish itself in the intellectual circles of Europe.

And once the Averroes-Hermannus treatise had been superceded, memory of it gradually faded. The text was apparently unknown to many of the philologists I have mentioned in this chapter: Julián Ribera, Miguel Asín Palacios, Enrico Cerulli. A thirteenth-century Latin translation of Aristotle's *Poetics* made directly from the Greek by William of Moerbeke was published in a modern edition before Hermannus's version, despite the fact that medieval readers seemed not much interested in that text: it lay uncopied on a library shelf, forgotten until its discovery by twentieth-century scholars.[65] Hermannus's translation from Averroes—judged a monstrous deformation of Aristotle's work by those modern scholars who knew it; Ernest Renan called it "tout à fait inintelligible"[66]—appeared in a modern edition only when the editors made the decision to append it to the second edition of William's translation. It is thanks to the diligence and prodigious efforts of the twentieth-century scholars cited above (Boggess, Bodenham, Burnett) that we now are able to reassess Hermannus's *Poetria*, to understand what it can teach us about our own literary history. And what a startling story that treatise tells: Averroes' commentary on Aristotle's *Poetics* embraced the tradi-

tion of translation and interpretation that preceded it; it worked through
Aristotle's words to try to reconstruct the vanished Greek poetry behind
them; and it moved forward from Aristotle to account for the Arab poets
using the universal structure of Aristotelian thought. And Hermannus followed Averroes step by step, gamely translating even Averroes' illustrations
from the Qur'an and from the Arab poets into Latin. Hermannus's and
Averroes' works on the *Poetics* were, in a word, radically comparatist treatises,
infused with an awareness of linguistic and historical depth of which Aristotle
himself was entirely innocent. Both versions were generated by, and themselves produced, an awareness that the literary tradition in which they participated was bounded by other traditions which lay beyond their own and
which were only partially perceptible to them. Thanks to the scholarship
discussed in this chapter, we can once again walk through the spacious rooms
of this philosophical pleasure palace, decorated with the spoils of Greece and
al-Andalus, whose galleries so many scholars and curious dilettantes have
strolled over the years—and wonder what Francesco Petrarch, in his labori-
ously constructed Christian and continental keep, might have made of it all.

## Chapter 3

# I nostri Saracini: Writing the History of the Arabs of Sicily

HISTORIANS TYPICALLY PREFACE the story of the rediscovery of Sicily's Arab past by relating an episode in late eighteenth-century Sicilian history so notorious that it has earned not one but two epithets. Giuseppe Vella's forgery of documents relating to the Muslim history of Sicily is regularly referred to as "l'arabica impostura," the *Arabic imposture*, or—borrowing a phrase from a contemporary poem by Sicilian Giovanni Meli—the "minzogna Saracina," or *Saracen lie*. The events in this oft-told tale can be summarized in few sentences: in 1783 Giuseppe Vella, a Maltese cleric living in Sicily, began to circulate curious historical documents among intellectual circles in Palermo, purported to be the letters exchanged by the Muslim emirs of Sicily and the caliphs of North Africa. His Latin translation of the letters was published in 1788 (as *Codex diplomaticus Siciliae sub Saracenorum imperio*); the Arabic text of the same letters appeared between 1789 and 1792 (as *Codice diplomatico di Sicilia sotto il governo degli Arabi*). Subsequently Vella would publish translations of a second series of letters, these exchanged by the early Norman rulers of Sicily and the North African caliphs (the *Libro del Consiglio di Egitto*, 1793).[1] In 1795 he would be tried and convicted of counterfeiting all the documents. His manufacture of the Arabic manuscripts and Latin translations, along with a number of coins to support the historical inventions in the letters, is one of the most audacious hoaxes of a century known for historical counterfeits (witness also the eighteenth-century production of the false transcriptions and translations of the *Thousand and One Nights*).[2]

Subsequent research has shown that Vella was largely a victim of competing interests: on the one hand the Sicilian aristocracy angling for greater autonomy from the Naples-based Bourbon monarchs of the Kingdom of the Two Sicilies, on the other Sicilians loyal to the Bourbons. While Vella himself certainly set the game in motion—he casually let drop that he had turned up the manuscript containing the first letters and began to produce his "translations" in response to avid public demand—as events unfolded their content would increasingly be defined by the interests of the powerful men whose company he kept once he became the darling of Palermo society. Like an early modern Sicilian *Turn of the Screw*, Vella's tale poses a series of questions that historians have not quite answered concerning the guilt and innocence of the major players and indeed the intentionality of Vella's actions from beginning to end of the sorry episode.[3]

Vella's fraud stands as a watershed in the historiography of Arab Sicily and in Sicilian participation in the flowering of Orientalist studies in Europe. Vella was able to perpetrate his hoax in large part because no Sicilian had the linguistic capacity to challenge the legitimacy of his documents and his translations of them. Sicilians' ignorance of Arabic and of the Arab history of Sicily did not necessarily indicate a lack of interest in the island's Arab past. Indeed the Sicilian aristocrats' enthusiastic reception of Vella's revelations encouraged his increasingly bold inventions. Historians usually identify Monsignor Alfonso Airoldi, Vella's patron and the man who brought to Sicily the Arabic type that would allow the publication of his manuscripts, as something of a co-dependent in Vella's fraud. According to Vella's subsequent testimony, he plucked many of the ideas that turned up in the early letters from his conversations with Airoldi and his circle of friends. But Airoldi would also play a crucial role in unmasking Vella. As early as 1787 he sought the opinion of continental authorities, sending copies of fragments of Vella's manuscript to European Orientalists (worried, it seems, more about Vella's capacity to interpret the documents than about the legitimacy of the documents themselves). And he held up publication of the *Codice diplomatico* (the Arabic text of the first batch of letters that Vella cooked up) to give the scholars a chance to complete their examination. Two of these experts refused to draw any conclusions concerning the documents without seeing more evidence. Remarkably, the one specialist who would take a stand—Danish Orientalist Olaus Gerard Tychsen—far from questioning the authenticity of the manuscripts responded by addressing a series of questions concerning their linguistic peculiarities to Vella, whom he recognized as an authority on Siculo-Arabic. The most generous conclusion one can draw is that the science of Orientalism was still in its infancy.

Others, however, proved more difficult to convince. Rosario Gregorio (1753–1809) distrusted Vella's fabulations from the beginning. Gregorio knew nothing about the Arabs—their history, their language, or their rites—but was a passionate student of Sicilian history: "he loved," according to Domenico Scinà, "as virtuous men do, his homeland and his nation, and from his earliest childhood focused his mind on the task of elaborating the affairs of Sicily."[4] Gregorio noted that Vella's Arabs measured time by the dates of the Christian calendar and observed no Muslim rites, and he smelled a rat. Popular tradition holds that he wrote a letter published, in extremely bad French, in Malta in 1788 denouncing Vella's manuscripts as counterfeits, though there is no firm proof of his authorship. Ultimately, however, Gregorio would—out of patriotic passion to unmask Vella and do justice to Sicilian history—teach himself Arabic and produce two scholarly works that did a great deal to unravel Vella's web of inventions. In 1788 he published an article in which he demonstrated that Sicilian Arabs did indeed use the Islamic calendar. And in 1790 a collection of Sicilian Arabic documents, edited by him, appeared in print: the *Rerum arabicarum quae ad historiam Siculam spectant ampla collectio* (*Ample Collection of Arabic Materials Relating to the History of Sicily*). For both of these publications Monsignor Airoldi allowed Gregorio to use the Arabic type that he had brought to Sicily for the purpose of printing Vella's manuscripts.

When Vella was tried publicly, in 1795, a continental Orientalist—the Viennese Joseph Hager—came to Sicily, questioned Vella, examined his manuscripts, and denounced them as spurious. Following the trial the Bourbon authorities brought others to Sicily to inspect Vella's work: Monsignor Germano Adami, bishop of Aleppo, and his secretary Antonio Dakur. With combined Sicilian, continental, and Levantine expertise on their side, the Sicilian authorities finally put an end to Vella's con; he lived under house arrest until his death in 1814.

It is difficult to isolate the most remarkable or most telling facts in this improbable and event-crammed narrative. Sicilian historians regularly read Vella's story in the context of Sicily's long struggle for autonomy and independence from the Bourbon rulers in Naples. It seems (though the record is sketchy and the series of events not always easy to reconstruct) that Vella first served as the mouthpiece of the anti-Bourbon Sicilian nobility who sought to prove that the island possessed its own distinct legal tradition in order to underscore its history of autonomy from the mainland half of the Kingdom of the Two Sicilies. He then switched tack and reproduced the views of a pro-Bourbon functionary particularly close to him during the months leading up to his denunciation, stressing the *continuity* between mainland and insular legal practice in the second volume of his "translations."[5] Though that story is undeniably important, I confess a partiality to another perspective. Vella's story reveals in almost excruciating detail the linguistic contingency of public life in Sicily (and to some extent in Malta as well) at the beginning of the nineteenth century.

Vella exploited contemporary Sicilians' incapacity to read the fragmentary remnants of Sicily's years of Muslim domination: the weathered Arabic inscriptions on Sicilian buildings and moldering Arabic documents in Sicilian libraries. Seven decades after Vella's trial—more than halfway through the century during which, through long and diligent labors, Sicilians would disinter their buried Muslim history—Orientalist Salvatore Cusa published a collection of Greek and Arabic records from the years of Norman rule in Sicily. In his introduction to that collection, justly remembered as one of the literary monuments of the Sicilian nineteenth century, he described the fate of the Arabic documents still buried in provincial archives centuries after Arabic literacy was lost in Sicily:

> It must be acknowledged that the ignorance itself which in ancient times caused these pages to be scattered was the motive which later caused them to be saved from total ruin. Written in a language and in characters more or less unknown, they had value simply for that; they were guarded jealously by archivists, shielded even from the view of the vulgar crowd. The word *Greek* evoked something of deep mysteries; and that of *Saracen* remained in the prejudiced mind of the people something altogether arcane and fabulous, relating to the days when the enemies of God governed this island.[6]

As we will see in this chapter, it fell to the enlightened few who could see that the Arabs were no enemies of God but bearers of a new science to blow the cobwebs from the archives and bring that lost history to light.

Vella himself knew no Arabic when his Sicilian adventure began. His spoken Italian was approximate enough. Sicilian literary historian Domenico Scinà wrote, with his typical scorn for all things Vella, that "though he believed that he was speaking Tuscan, in fact with a Maltese accent he pronounced a bastardization of the Sicilian tongue, or rather a language all his own."[7] And it seems that he used his native Maltese dialect—an Arabic colloquial—to entertain a visiting Moroccan dignitary in 1782; that first social success planted the notion of the Arabic imposture in his mind. He did over time acquire a smattering of Arabic, enough to forge the Arabic "originals" of the documents he had already "translated."[8] But he certainly knew little more than the Semitic core of his native language when, in 1785, a chair in Arabic at the University of Palermo was created for him. A twentieth-century American Orientalist examined the manuscript that was Vella's final creation—he was at work on it when his trial commenced in 1795, ten years after he assumed the chair in Arabic—and wrote, "What adjectives were fit to qualify the language it expressed? None that I could find. It was quite evidently Arabic—or was intended to be—but it was the most impossible Arabic that I had ever seen. Very soon certain peculiarities which were easily recognized as Maltese and Tunisian came to view, but most of the sentences could not be construed even upon the very liberal basis laid down by Arab grammarians. Through some of them shimmered an Italian construction or an Italian word composition. This was too much even for a willing believer."[9] The Vella caper illustrates the immaturity of late eighteenth-century European Orientalist studies. Antoine Isaac Silvestre de Sacy, the man who trained a generation of European scholars in the languages and research methods of Orientalist philology and is generally called the father of nineteenth-century academic Orientalism, began to teach Arabic in Paris in 1795—the year when Vella was convicted and imprisoned. Vella managed to pull off his hoax largely because European specialists lacked the expertise to see through it (and lacked the resources or the initiative to ask Arab scholars for assistance).

Sicilian Orientalism would establish itself in the wake of and initially in response to Vella's fraud, as historians used new philological methods (and a genuine knowledge of Arabic) to study Sicily's Muslim past. Salvatore Cusa celebrated the role played by Vella's first patron, Monsignor Airoldi, in promoting the study of Arabic in Sicily. After Vella's disgrace Airoldi used his influence to see that "serious and truthful studies cast light among the shadows in which the memories of the Saracens were enveloped, and to promote at the University of Palermo the institution of a chair in Arabic for this sole purpose."[10] Rosario Gregorio—the first to respond to Vella's challenge by learning Arabic and venturing into the unknown territory of Sicily's Muslim history—would not, however, be considered for that position. He continued to write about Sicilian history (and remains one of the most honored Sicilian historians of the late Bourbon era). But once he published his collection of

Siculo-Arabic documents he gave up his Arabic studies and did not return to Sicily's Arab history again.[11]

The letter composed in poor French and published in Malta denouncing Vella's fraud—which Gregorio may or may not have written—indicates Sicilians' sense that their Arab history had brought the island to the attention of a broader European audience.[12] Europeans did not generally deem debates between the Sicilian aristocracy and the Bourbon rulers of Sicily worthy of continental attention. But when Arabs of the tenth century discussed affairs suspiciously similar to contemporary squabbles over local legal traditions, Europe listened. It seems odd that the author of the letter would choose French over Latin, still at the end of the eighteenth century the international language of European scholarship and of Orientalism in particular, especially considering that he lacked the rhetorical skill to make his case in French. It's likely that the language was chosen in deference to the perceived audience of Vella's fabricated letters: not Orientalists first but nationalists, the Sicilian aristocracy who sought autonomy and independence from the Naples-based Bourbon rulers of the island and the growing European audience sympathetic to the liberal cause. An author hoping to engage this audience would choose to write in French, not Latin or Italian, even absent a firm command of the language.

Both in Sicily and to a much greater extent in Vella's native Malta the question of language could touch off an explosive chain reaction of related questions concerning cultural and ultimately national identity. In the next chapter I will discuss the formation of a national language on the European model in Malta during the nineteenth and early twentieth centuries. Because of its proximity to Italy, Sicily responded more emphatically than Malta to the gravitational pull that the Italian language exerted on the Mediterranean in general during the late medieval and early modern period. Italian was the language of cultural life in Sicily. But it was neither the language of the people, nor even cultured Sicilians' mother tongue. Note, in the passage cited above, Domenico Scinà's distinction between "Tuscan" and the "Sicilian tongue." Giovanni Meli—the poet who coined the epithet "minzogna Saracina," arguably the most popular writer in early modern Sicily—wrote in Sicilian. In standard Italian his epithet for Vella's fraud would read "menzogna Saracena": what a difference a vowel makes!

Sicilians received Vella's mock-Arabic letters with ardent enthusiasm because they answered one of the most insistent questions of contemporary Sicilian public life: What were the origins of the Sicilian legal tradition? The

Bourbon rulers in Naples used a legal code with a Norman provenance and imposed the same legislative system on the island and mainland halves of their kingdom. But the first letters translated by Vella proposed an alternate origin for Sicilian legal institutions and insisted on the autonomy of Sicily's legal system. The pronouncements of Vella's medieval Arabs suggested to Sicilian aristocrats that "the Arabs," in the words of historian Giuseppe Giarrizzo, "had inaugurated the modern history of Sicily."[13] Although Sicilian Orientalists would ultimately replace Vella's historical whimsies with narratives that had some grounding in historical fact, in this sense Vella's intervention seems remarkably prescient. During the nineteenth century Sicilian Orientalists deciphered the Arabic documents that gave expression to Sicily's difference from an Italian standard, the distinct origin of its cultural traditions. As it turned out, no archives dating to the years of Muslim domination remained on the island. The documents in Arabic that lay unread in Sicilian libraries were produced during the years of Norman rule on the island; the medieval works that held information about Muslim Sicily were in the collections of continental libraries (or in the Arab world—but Sicilians of the nineteenth century did no work in Arab libraries). Sicilian historians who learned Arabic—particularly during the second half of the century, as philologists developed more sophisticated methods for extracting information from medieval documentary sources—often focused on the Norman period, not the years of Muslim domination. Thus during the nineteenth century historians cracked the code that allowed them to tell one of the most remarkable stories in medieval European history: the tale of a Christian kingdom that participated as a full partner in the dominant, vibrant Arabic-language culture of the medieval Mediterranean. And in the "arcane and fabulous" history of the Norman era, Sicilian Orientalists found a medieval past with compelling contemporary relevance.

In this chapter I will trace the emergence of a Sicilian Arabic historiography, the stages by which Sicilian historians discovered the island's Arab history and framed the narrative that gave it shape and meaning. As always in the production of historical narratives, the tale that Sicilian scholars articulated during the nineteenth century responded both to the objective data that form our record of the past—medieval documents, the architectural and toponymic traces left on the Sicilian landscape—and to contemporary exigencies. Nineteenth-century Sicilian historiography cannot be understood without reference to the political history of that tumultuous century. At the beginning of the century Sicilian intellectuals resisted the rule of the Bourbons; by its end the island would be integrated into a unified Italy. And smack in the middle of the century the Sicilians had their 1848. In fact the European *moti* of 1848 were felt first in Sicily; an armed uprising began during the celebration of the Bourbon king's birthday in Palermo on January 12. Sicily became modern by acknowledging the failures of European liberalism in 1848 and (in the works of the Sicilian Orientalists, at any rate) compensating for the collapse of its dreams of autonomy and ultimately its absorption into a unified Italy by asserting its Mediterranean difference. Sicily's centuries of participation in Mediterranean Arabic culture, according to Sicilian Orientalists, granted the island a unique historical primacy: in European exposure to the Arab sciences through the conduit of Sicily, in particular in Norman translation of the Arab sciences, European modernity was born.

My examination of Siculo-Arabic historiography will focus on three men born in the *anni mirabiles* of 1806–7, students of Sicily's Arab history whose paths crossed in Palermo in 1848: Michele Amari, Pietro Lanza, and Vincenzo Mortillaro. And I will consider more briefly a handful of scholars who contributed to the excavation of that lost history, in particular two historians whose work merits greater recognition than it has received outside Sicily: Salvatore Morso, who used Arabic-language sources to write a recollection of Norman-era Palermo, and Salvatore Cusa, the alter ego of the much better known Michele Amari. The historians discussed in this chapter shared a sense of the urgency of their work: they were (to use a metaphor and an epithet that appear repeatedly in their writings) shining a light into the shadows of Sicily's Arab past in order to illuminate the forgotten history of "i nostri Saracini," *our Saracens*. By the dawn of the nineteenth century, Sicilians had long since lost touch with their Arab past. But with the discovery of new scientific methods of investigating the textual past, "at last a happier age has shed its light upon Siculo-Arabic Literature."[14] The "new, pure, and copious light" of modern philological method would allow Sicilian historians for the first time to write "our Saracen history"; the story of "our Arab memories"; the history of "our ancestors," the Arabs—with such locutions did the Sicilian historians of the nineteenth century describe their project.[15] As was the case throughout Europe, the formation of philology as a humanistic discipline with a scientific methodology informed these historians' work. And the demands of an *engaged* philology—the imperative to produce a narrative of national history that would define and exalt the national character—gave their work a sense of urgency and moment, as Orientalists shined the brilliant lamp of empirical investigation into the dark corners of Sicily's oddly modern Saracen past.

In the aftermath of Vella's forgeries, during the first third of the nineteenth century, two scholars—neither of whom read Arabic—wrote surveys of the history of Arab Sicily. Their linguistic incompetence, though not in keeping with the spirit of the new century and the new scholarship, was not atypical of previous Sicilian historiography. Before Rosario Gregorio crammed enough Arabic to translate an anthology's worth of documents, only Francesco Tardia (1732–78)—who died young and devoted the mature years of his short life to the reconstruction of that Mediterranean chimera, Phoenician—had gone to the trouble of acquiring Arabic. Other historians simply relied on sources available in translation.[16]

Saverio Scrofani (1756–1835), in a work entitled *Della dominazione degli stranieri in Sicilia* (*On Foreign Domination in Sicily;* 1824), proposed a startling argument, a thesis that "will not," he stated hopefully in the preface, "fail to edify my fellow Sicilians or the foreigners who aspire to rule this land." Of the many foreign powers that occupied Sicily through the centuries, he argued, almost none "breached its coastlines unless the Sicilians themselves first requested or aided their entrance."[17] Scrofani argued throughout the work that no imperial state had imposed itself on Sicily; the Sicilians themselves had opened their doors to each of the states that colonized the island.

Scrofani arrived at this thesis purely through political interestedness. Though it was published only in 1824, the book was written between 1810 and 1814. During this period Sicily saw occupation by both the British (who had come to repel Napoleon's troops from the mainland) and the extravagantly corrupt Bourbon court, seeking refuge from threatened Naples. Order would be restored—the Napoleonic threat would recede, the British would move on, and the Bourbon monarch Ferdinand I would abrogate the liberal constitution drafted during the British occupation—by 1816. In what seems not the most disinterested response, an English reviewer celebrated Scrofani's work: "Every nation ought to have a book similar to this work of signor Scrofani's, to remove from the minds of all any pretext of occupying with impunity the kingdoms of others. The author merits for this the recognition of his government and of his fatherland."[18] When it appeared in print, although the moment when he could gain from flattering British sensibilities had passed, Scrofani's thesis still had currency as an anti-Napoleonic brief.

Scrofani (not unlike Vella) was a scam artist of the first water. Chased out of Sicily in 1787 for forging signatures on official state documents, he would be jailed in Paris for theft (from the estate of a recently deceased friend); he was released in order to spy for an Italian ambassador in Paris, Marzio Mastrilli. After he left Paris he would live in Greece, Venice, Trieste, and Florence before returning to Sicily in 1822. He managed to keep his public reputation above reproach (this was still possible in the days before paparazzi and tabloids) but after he died the seamy truth gradually emerged— starting with an 1835 obituary that dropped a casual reference to Scrofani's opium addiction, a habit that he had acquired, the author speculates, "perhaps on his voyages to the Levant."[19]

When he writes the history of the Arabs of Sicily—despite the brevity and vagueness of his account—Scrofani tells a story that will become familiar. He must part the clouds and shine light into the darkness in order to tell his tale of Sicily's decline under Byzantine rule and resurgence under the Arabs. "It is known," he wrote, "what shadows (for lack of writers) engulf the long and bloody history of the Caliphs in Sicily; still it pleases me to add to what I have said my findings from the few Arab and Sicilian annals that have survived the fury of ignorance and flames."[20] In the narrative that he pieced together from the paltry sources available to him, the Saracens saved the island from its Byzantine rulers—so weakened by their decadence and incapacity that the Arabs settled in Sicily "as in a land without a lord."[21] And in Sicily the Arabs "made the beauty of studies flourish again, and by translating into their tongue the exemplars already lost elsewhere of the greatest Greeks they advanced those studies beyond anything before accomplished."[22]

But Scrofani has a failure of the imagination when attempting to imagine the Saracens as lords of Sicily; his pages on those centuries are few and bland. And he has particular difficulty squaring the fact of Arab rule with his master narrative. "Who would have said," he wrote, "that the Sicilians could have pushed themselves to such a perilous pass, calling impetuously upon this other foreign race and bidding them to penetrate among themselves without hindrance? This part of history is so remarkable and strange that I do not believe it forbidden me to narrate it, nor injurious to others to read it."[23] Nor, apparently, did Scrofani feel disinclined to perform Procrustean edits in order to squeeze Sicilian history into the narrative he had fashioned for it. Remembering the historians of Arab Sicily, Michele Amari wrote (with somewhat atypical generosity) that Scrofani dealt "lightly" with the topic of Arab rule in Sicily; Vincenzo Mortillaro described Scrofani's book as "a story that one reads with pleasure, but without profit, rather with gravest damage to the truth . . . For these reasons it would seem to merit the name of historical novel rather than history . . . but such a novel and composed in such a way that it delights you until it would cause pain to chop off a part or to change any of its conceits."[24]

Scrofani's histrionic and skewed account would be answered by the publication of Carmelo Martorana's *Notizie storiche dei Saraceni siciliani*, which appeared in 1832. Martorana (late eighteenth century–ca. 1870)—who did not read Arabic—gathered the material for his history of "i nostri Saracini" from Arabic accounts that had been translated as well as the Greek and Latin writers who commented on the history of Muslim Sicily.[25] Despite his lack of access to Arabic-language records, he aimed to redeem the years of Muslim domination in the perception of the Sicilians. With a touching faith in the values of the Enlightenment, he believed that the days when baseless prejudice defined Sicilians' view of their history were in the past.

> Although the remains of Saracenic history gave us clear witness that our island enjoyed certain good conditions under the Muslim domination, still the Arabic records of Sicily suffered so much damage for the frenzy of arms and of religion, and those that remain lay so thoroughly unknown since that time that historians in general had no idea of those Sicilian Saracens other than as barbarian peoples and destroyers. And there are many among the moderns themselves, ignorant to such an extent of Arab civilization and literature that they would like to believe that the Saracens of Sicily were all savages, like those of the first human race, who nested in the trees. . . . Today however, when the human spirit, exalted by the loftiest movements, has wished to hurl itself against every limit not only of space but also of time and has called to its review even the most remote centuries, it has made wondrous efforts to slash the obstinate veil in order to reveal the ancient marvels of the Orient.[26]

Martorana perhaps overestimated his own enlightenment. He spends an entire chapter of the second volume castigating the Islamic faith for its falsehoods and absurdities. However, he ends the work on an upbeat note: in the next volumes he promises to show the reader how Sicilian culture flowered under the Arabs, until "it seemed that the qualities of the ancient times of the Hieros had returned to Sicily, in the guise of another language, other customs and legislation."[27] Martorana's intention to peer into the "extremely dense darkness that cloaked this part of our history" would be thwarted by the events of 1848.[28] The library in his Palermo home was destroyed; only the first two volumes of a projected four-volume study would see publication.

Neither Martorana nor Scrofani used the scientific methods of textual analysis pioneered by modern philologists to tell the story of Sicily's Muslim past. Before the 1840s, the historians who discussed that shadowy period of Sicilian history—and they were few—still relied largely on a received bare-bones narrative, a short list of facts culled from sources available in the European languages: the island's decadence under Byzantine rule, its fall to the Arab warriors invited to sort out a local dispute, its eventual flowering under Arab command and fall to Norman warriors. In one of the most interesting documents from the Vella scandal to see publication, Vella himself under-scored the temptation that this dark chapter in Sicilian history presented to modern historians. After his trial and conviction, while he was living under house arrest, Vella was apparently approached by a Viennese editor assembling a volume of Arabic literature in translation who asked him to contribute selections from his own collection of Sicilian Arabic letters. Neither the editor's letter nor the fair copy of Vella's response survive, but in 1905 scholar Pietro Varvaro published a draft of Vella's response found among his papers. In a sublime passage—discussing in the abstract the authenticity of his Arabic codices; it is impossible to tell whether he is replying to a direct question or voicing his own anxious internal debate—Vella affirms the value of his documents. The personality of each individual writer stands out clearly in the letters of his Sicilian emirs, he says; the sequence of events is depicted with clarity and precision; the engines of history are plainly visible. "One must therefore admit that if I had done nothing other than guess, I could not have guessed more accurately; and that the inventor of such a singular production would be—allow me to say it—of indeed another order of merit than the modest translator of a collection of Arabic letters gathered in the Chancery at the time when the Arabs dominated Sicily."[29] Vella's state-ment—which effectively renders much of Jorge Luis Borges's oeuvre redun-dant—demonstrates with uncanny and uncomfortable precision Vella's own historical position. Vella sat astride the fence that divided the eighteenth century, with its cunning counterfeiters and dilettantes who repackaged myth as historical fact, from the nineteenth century, when scientific techniques of verifying historical sources allowed historians to celebrate prodigious ad-vances in the accuracy of their narratives of premodern history.

The generation of Pietro Lanza, Vincenzo Mortillaro, and Michele Amari—all three born within a year of each other, in 1806 and 1807—would decisively transform Sicilian historiography, as Orientalists trained (however crudely by twentieth-century standards) in Arabic letters and philological methodology brought Sicily's Muslim past to light. The drama of excavating the lost centuries of Sicilian history took place against a vivid historical backdrop, a half-century of resistance to Bourbon rule. After an anti-Bourbon uprising in 1812, after the parenthesis of occupation by the Bourbon court and the British anti-Napoleonic forces, following the restoration of Bourbon rule in 1816 and another anti-Bourbon revolution in 1820, Sicily saw the eruption of the first of the European revolutions of 1848. At the time Sicilian aristocrats dreamed of independence from the Bourbons and autonomy or imagined that Sicily might become an autonomous member of a still vaguely defined Italian federation. Sicilians even believed—briefly but, one imagines, intoxicatingly—that they could export their revolution to the continent: at the height of the 1848 revolution one hundred Sicilian militia departed to help liberate Lombardy from the Austrians. The Sicilian 1848, of course, ended in disaster for the liberals. The core revolutionary figures went into exile or were punished—with torture, interminable imprisonment, or death— by the Bourbon regime. The Bourbon repressions would ultimately end in a kind of victory for the people, in Sicily as throughout the Italian peninsula. In 1860 Garibaldi would lead the march of I Mille from Palermo. He eventually reached Naples and overthrew the Bourbon government; Sicily—which a short time earlier aspired to independence and autonomy—would become part of a new pan-Italian state.

Three of the most prominent nineteenth-century historians of Muslim Sicily were in Palermo and played an active role in the events of 1848. Pietro Lanza (1807–55), a member of one of Sicily's oldest aristocratic families, didn't read Arabic; he was not indeed a professional scholar, but a passionately devoted student of Sicilian history and contemporary political thought and (first and foremost) a patriot. He wrote a detailed history of Arab Sicily, relying on sources available in translation, which he read in 1832 at the Accademia di Scienze e Belle-lettere in Palermo and later published with the full complement of scholarly notes. He played a central role in the administration of the revolutionary government in 1848–49 and was forced into exile with the collapse of the revolution. He would die not long after in Paris in 1855.[30]

Michele Amari (1806–89), an ardent patriot and the most prominent scholar of Muslim Sicily of the nineteenth century, was already in exile in Paris when the Sicilian revolution began in January 1848. In 1842 he had published a book on an event in Sicilian history subsequent to the years of

Arab rule—the 1282 Vespers uprising, when a popular resistance movement overthrew a foreign monarch. The book was informed by sophisticated archival scholarship. The Bourbon government, suspecting Amari of seditious activities, had already exiled him from Sicily to Naples, and he used the government archives there to research the work. At the same time his account of a medieval rebellion functioned as a thinly veiled revolutionary manifesto, a blueprint for the successful overthrow of an unpopular monarchy. The Neapolitan censors allowed the publication of the book, realizing its revolutionary subtext only after it appeared in print. Rather than stand trial in Naples Amari escaped to Paris. There he would learn Arabic (studying with Joseph Toussaint Reinaud, a student of Silvestre de Sacy) in order to write the history of Muslim Sicily. On the continent he had access to the great libraries that held the Arabic manuscripts required to write a truly modern history of medieval Sicily. In Paris he worked at the library that was the depository for Antoine Galland's papers and the Latin translation of the story of the prophet Muhammad's journey to the next world (known during the nineteenth century, depending on which way the wind blew, as the Bibliothèque du roi, Bibliothèque impériale, and finally Bibliothèque nationale). And he traveled to other European libraries in order to consult their collections. Already in 1845—three short years after he arrived in Paris and started his study of Arabic—he published the first fruits of his investigation of Sicily's Muslim past: the Arabic text of an account of Sicily by the medieval traveler and geographer Ibn Hawqal, with his own translation into French. When revolution broke out in Palermo in 1848 Amari rushed back and, like Lanza, played a key role in the revolutionary government. And he too would flee to Paris after the failure of the revolution. He would continue his work on Muslim Sicily, writing a history (published in multiple volumes between 1854 and 1872) that remains to this day the authoritative work on the subject. He returned to Italy in 1859 and, converted to the dream of Italian unification, played an active role in the Risorgimento; he taught Arabic (chiefly in Florence), and never again lived in Sicily.[31]

Vincenzo Mortillaro (1806–88), a member of the petty aristocracy, was a Sicilian-trained Arabist. He had studied with Salvatore Morso (himself trained by Rosario Gregorio), whose luminous work on medieval Palermo I will discuss later in this chapter. Mortillaro inherited the duties that were the legacy of Vella's intervention in Sicily's Muslim history. He wrote, for instance, on Siculo-Arabic coinage. Numismatics was a topic of pressing (and, to the twenty-first-century sensibility, unaccountable) interest for nineteenth-century historians. In Sicily the matter had a peculiar urgency: Vella, who made a cottage industry of manufacturing Siculo-Arab history, had minted counterfeit coins as well as manuscripts. Subsequent Sicilian historians worked diligently to separate authentic medieval Sicilian coinage from Vella's inventions, as they had to unmask his manuscript forgeries. Mortillaro published a history of Muslim Sicily in 1846. And he too was in Palermo during 1848. But whereas Amari and Lanza participated in the events of 1848 as passionate liberals and as committed members of the revolutionary core, Mortillaro—a conservative—kept his distance from the revolutionists during that anarchic year and was a vocal critic of the revolution subsequently.[32]

Mortillaro, indeed, would become Amari's mortal enemy during the years following 1848 and would not miss an opportunity to criticize Lanza either—though because he published little and died young Lanza presented a narrower target. In his history of Arab Sicily, published shortly before the events of 1848, Mortillaro had produced a compendious *catalogue raisonné* of the historians of Sicily's Arab past. There he noted simply that Lanza's work on Arab Sicily "was the first of those patriotic studies in which Lanza subsequently had worthy success." And he lauded Amari for the two translations of Arabic texts relevant to Sicilian history which he had at that point published.[33] The subsequent transformation of his opinion of the two men is remarkable even for a man whose temperament a sympathetic biographer termed "bilious and choleric."[34] In 1861—after the *moti* of 1848, after Garibaldi's march from Palermo to Naples, and following the publication of the first two volumes of Amari's *Storia dei musulmani di Sicilia* (which appeared in 1854 and 1858)—Mortillaro would write toxic assessments of both Amari's *Storia* ("the author ought not to have called it a *History*, because it has neither the content nor the style of a history") and Lanza's work on Muslim Sicily—published, in all fairness, three decades earlier ("he repeated the very same tales narrated and repeated by all those who do not know the works of the Arab writers").[35] And in the first volume of his interminable *Reminiscenze* (published in 1865) Mortillaro would write that Amari's book on the Vespers was guilty of "the vice of fantasizing about history for the purpose of sacrificing it to a preconceived notion (which others had arrived at before him) . . . using, as he himself admits, an uneven style, feverish, stammering like the words of one being tortured."[36]

Amari, however, gave as good as he got. In the opening pages of the *Storia dei musulmani di Sicilia* Amari provides an abundant and lively history of previous scholarship on Sicily's Muslim past. In this context he mentions

Mortillaro's contributions to Sicilian historiography. But he writes at much greater length about the role that Mortillaro played in Palermo in 1848–49:

> I will perhaps have occasion to correct here and there a few of signor Mortillaro's errors, among those that do violence to historical truth; it is not necessary to detail all the errors in the work of a man who has not had the opportunity to study the language well. And I will do it with regret, because literary gossip disturbs me profoundly, and because I fear that my criticism will be imputed to hostility. But, whatever my attitude may be toward the author, I hold that the political conduct of a man has nothing to do with the merits of his scholarship; and I would be the first to applaud as a writer such or such a one whom I would punish as a citizen with all the severity of the law, if ever events called me again to the execution of the law. Thus, writing a few pages above of Martorana, I, impenitent revolutionary of 1848, have forgotten that he was then prefect of police in Palermo and that he imprisoned my friends.

Martorana, of course, was the historian manqué who began a history of Muslim Sicily left unfinished when his library burned in the flames of 1848. In a footnote Amari reviews more of the information that his conscience will not allow him to include in the pages of his scholarship: "To whomever might ask me why I saw fit to remember in this place the affairs of 1848 I will respond that I wrote and published these words during my second exile, while the marquis Mortillaro governed an important branch of the public administration in Sicily. And in point of fact I alluded to his conduct during the spring of 1849, when he was a warm promoter of the Bourbon and clerical reaction in Palermo."[37]

At moments like this, it's easy to forget (as Amari himself seems to have done) the cast of characters who populate the pages of medieval history that follow: the sons of Qayrawan who crossed the sea to Mazara del Vallo, led by the *qadi* Asad ibn al-Furat and at the invitation of the Byzantine insurrectionist Euphemius, in 827; the Muslim troops who entered Palermo in 831 under the command of Berber general Asbagh ibn Wakil; the penetration of Muslim armies through the Italian peninsula as far as the Garigliano River, the border between Latium and Campania, in 882. We are in Palermo in the spring of 1849; Mortillaro, from the safety of his bureaucrat's desk, forwards the Bourbon cause, while Amari is running for the docks.

It is illuminating, having reviewed the bitter disputes between these men, to turn to the pages of their histories of Sicily. Their inequalities are substantial. Amari's passion and probity, and his considerable skills as a stylist, are such that they elevate him not only above Mortillaro and Lanza but indeed above most historians of the nineteenth century. Yet for all their political, scholarly, and literary differences the three men tell a strikingly similar tale. They—like previous historians approaching the same material—see these centuries as a secret history to be discovered; they are shining the light of historical inquiry into the dark corners of the past. Mortillaro sings the praises of his predecessor Rosario Gregorio, who "dissipated the darkness in which the Saracen epoch was cloaked." Lanza promises to "dissipate the shadows that cover that age." And Amari undertakes his history of Muslim Sicily "moved by an irresistible desire to look into the shadows that shroud the history of Sicily before the Normans."[38]

When they cleared the cobwebs from the past, the three historians found a strange new history that belonged unmistakably to the distant past, yet spoke to the present. They would see Sicily's history of serial conquest—in the hands of other historians, evidence of Sicily's abjection throughout history—as a source of its glory. Lanza makes a particularly lovely story of this heritage. The Greeks and Romans left traces of their culture on the island; even the depredations of the Byzantines and the occasional barbarian incursion couldn't erase that glorious past entirely. Thus when the Arabs arrived in Sicily they did not find a cultural void, as other armies of the Arab expansion did in Africa, Asia, and Spain. Rather they nourished the sparks of cultural life surviving here and there until a flourishing culture emerged.

> They gathered the most beautiful [remnants of previous civilizations], and they gave us the seeds of their own letters and their own sciences, which bloomed among us. Nor could it have happened differently: for having done the same among other peoples they certainly could not do other than diffuse these seeds in a land revered by all, whose inhabitants were endowed with a swift intelligence and given to innovations, and who had, to the benefit of civilization, received, nourished and promoted every branch of learning. And to me it seems certain that as the Saracens, in the shadow of peace, made agriculture and commerce flourish among us, so with their example they awakened slumbering spirits—chasing away their inertia, inviting them to literary emulation, and propagating civilization.[39]

Amari tells a similar story of serial conquest as a source of strength for Sicily, contrasting Sicily's past with the distinct history of that other Arab state in Mediterranean Europe, Spain. And in this passage from his first publication on Muslim Sicily, his edition and translation of Ibn Hawqal's account of his visit to the island, he combines a summary of Sicily's conquests with the familiar motif of the hidden history that must be brought to light.

> Spain, occupied by the Visigoths, already had the characteristics of a Romano-Germanic society at the epoch of the Muslim conquest. Sicily, on the other hand—pillaged rather than conquered by the barbarians of the North—was still Greek and Roman when the Saracens invaded. The Germanic element penetrated only after the Muslim element, when a handful of the Norman nobility, whom one could regard as already French, came to found there a realm half Christian and half Muslim.
>
> That glorious Norman government which soon enough extended throughout southern Italy took its substance from the Arab civilization which dominated in Sicily. . . . What indeed was this Muslim population of Sicily during its most beautiful days? What did it borrow from Greco-Roman Sicily? What were its resources, its vicissitudes, its deeds? These are the questions to which the Muslim and Christian chronicles that we possess fail to respond; incomplete chronicles, written for the most part during the twelfth and thirteenth centuries.
>
> The history of Muslim Sicily is indeed still to be written; more than that, we must yet find the materials [to write it].[40]

Amari, of course, would hunt down and publish the necessary materials and write that history himself. This 1845 publication was his first contribution to Siculo-Arabic historiography. In addition to his multivolume history of Muslim Sicily he would ultimately publish two volumes of a *Biblioteca arabo-sicula*, an anthology of medieval texts relevant to Sicily history, first in the Arabic original and then in Italian translation.[41]

In this passage Amari alludes to a third theme that would inspire some of the most pyrotechnical passages in his history and in the works of Mortillaro and Lanza as well. The culture of the Arabs of Sicily would expand beyond the island. Transferred to the Italian peninsula, it would awaken the Italians from their medieval slumbers. Here Lanza extols the civilizing effect that Sicilian Arabs had on Sicily, on Italy, and indeed on the modern world:

Thanks to the illumination of our age, and thanks to the wholesome critical attitude that now guides every sort of study, not only are the Normans praised—because they are worthy of praise, since they are numbered among the first peoples who with their chivalry brought civility to the Middle Ages, and because among us they created, in the manner of their age, one of the most beautiful kingdoms of that epoch; but the Saracens are not slandered, but rather venerated, because far from being barbarous and ignorant, it was they who gave the world modern civilization.[42]

Lanza's praise for Arab civilization (and for the enlightenment of his own age) may seem excessive. Yet it was not immoderate by contemporary standards. Here Mortillaro extends himself on the Saracens of Sicily—painted as fathers of the Sicilians and as bringers of enlightenment to the Italians:

Now let those men who call us Saracens and think they mock us know that our fathers were not brigands, living only by pillage and united by love of booty, but illustrious Saracens, warriors and adventurers, full of life, emotion, intelligence; and that from that promontory upon which, through all the changes of fortune, the spark of genius was never extinguished, they granted laws to those close to them and granted laws to those distant; and dominating with their arms by land and by sea, and with the intelligence in their breasts, they awakened the valor that slumbered in the chests of the Italians, and opened the heavy lids of their eyes.[43]

Even Amari would be tempted to rhetorical excess by the achievements of the Arabs and the effect their civilization had on Italians—although in his work, tellingly, it is the Norman continuation of Arab culture rather than the inventions of the Arabs themselves that worked the cultural miracle on the mainland. Under the Normans, he wrote, "that labor had been accomplished, under the aegis of a new people, which had been begun by the Arabs 400 years earlier: Sicily, returned to power and splendor, predominated for the rest of the twelfth century among the Italian provinces; it mastered the southern regions of the Peninsula; it occupied temporarily some African cities, and scattered on the continent many of the seeds of that wondrous civilization of our common fatherland, which within a few centuries dispersed in Europe the shadows of the Middle Ages."[44]

Indeed as the work of the Sicilian Orientalists advanced, the line between Norman Sicily and Arab Sicily became increasingly blurred. Few historians of Muslim Sicily could resist the temptation to advance into the years of Norman control, particularly when treasures like al-Idrisi's geography (produced under the patronage of Norman king Roger II) and the Arabic poetry written in honor of the Norman monarchs awaited them on the other side. Lanza ends his account by summarizing the Arabic-language achievements of the years of Norman rule; Mortillaro and Amari close their histories with the death of Frederick II, the great Norman-Hohenstaufen king of Sicily, in 1250. In fact about 46 percent of Amari's two-thousand-page history of *Muslim Sicily* deals with the years of Norman, not Arab, rule.[45] So too did Salvatore Cusa and Salvatore Morso, whose work I will discuss later in this chapter, concentrate their own research on the Normans.

Two motives account for the appeal of the years of Norman domination. First, for Sicilian Orientalists who remained in Sicily, a pragmatic consideration agitated in favor of emphasis on the Normans. No records of Muslim Sicily remained on the island. The Arabic-language works preserved in Sicilian archives belonged to the Norman period. The history of the Muslim era must be traced in the compendious Arabic-language histories available only to those who, like Michele Amari, left Sicily and had access to continental libraries. Thus, ironically, it was the case that Sicily's Arab history could best be written by those outside Sicily. At the same time, however, Amari would discover that the history of Norman Sicily was difficult to write *without* access to the Arabic language records that remained in Sicily. The records in Greek, Latin, and Arabic which could be studied in continental libraries gave a limited account of the Norman administration; crucial documentation—tax records, legal records, and epigraphy—were preserved in Sicily.

And second, the years of Norman rule had been previously and became to an even greater extent during the nineteenth century a source of enormous pride for Sicilians. Under the Normans Sicily dominated the central Mediterranean and indeed, in the hands of the Sicilian historians, became the major maritime power throughout the Mediterranean. If the scientific culture or the legal institutions of European modernity came from the Arabs, it was the Normans who first recognized the potential of that Arab seed, nourished it, and transplanted it to the European mainland. To recognize the triumphs of Norman civilization, to detail in particular Norman reception and manipulation of Arab civilization, was to demonstrate Sicily's centrality to European history and to European modernity in particular. This task became more acute as Sicily's dreams of autonomy faded and Sicily found its place not, once again, as an independent island state, but as an insular coda to unified Italy.

So it comes as no surprise that, when Vincenzo Mortillaro wanted to attack Amari, he would impute to Amari a desire to deny Sicily's difference, the Mediterranean peculiarity of Sicily's compound Arab-European culture under the Normans. In 1868 Mortillaro wrote an open letter to Amari that he published as a pamphlet; in it he savaged Amari in a tone surprising even to those familiar with the often toxic language of academic quarrels. Mortillaro fills the bulk of the letter with a detailed and eminently forgettable criticism of Amari's discussion of medieval coinage. As tiresome as Mortillaro's enthusiasm about the topic may seem to us, we do well to remember that by stressing his superior familiarity with medieval Sicilian numismatics Mortillaro emphasizes his advantage over Amari: he, unlike Amari, is not an exile. Unlike Amari, he was and remains a *Sicilian*. For this reason he has access to the insular numismatic collections which Amari is not able to study. Most interesting from our perspective, however, is a passage in which Mortillaro responds to a chapter of the final volume of Amari's *Storia dei musulmani*, which is still in press but which Mortillaro has seen in galleys: "We will speak at greater length at another time, once you have finished the publication of your work, in which you, Sicilian, wish to teach us, Sicilians [voi siciliano ammaestrar volete noi siciliani] to believe (something that you alone believe) that nothing less than our civilization was imported by Italians from *upper Italy* [*Italia di sopra*; emphasis in the original], Piedmontese, Genoese, Lombards, at the times of the Normans."[46] In this pregnant paralipsis Mortillaro aims to scandalize his Sicilian readers (*noi siciliani*) by telling them that in his new book—the first of the three volumes that he will publish on the Norman period of the history of Muslim Sicily—Amari will claim that the culture of the Norman era was an Italian import.

Unsurprisingly, this is not at all what Amari wrote. In the specific chapter to which Mortillaro refers, Amari argues from literary and linguistic evidence that the indigenous non-Arab population in Sicily was either not particularly numerous or not particularly important during the years of the Norman domination. And he points out that an influx of population came to Sicily from "Italia di sopra," correcting earlier historians who argued the influence of indigenous Sicilians or immigrants from the southern part of the peninsula on the administration of the Norman regime and the culture of the Norman age. He twice uses the term *Italia di sopra* to refer to the links that bind Sicily to Lombardy and Piedmont. Perhaps most galling to a Sicilian audience—and in particular to a historian whose interpretation of historical sources he has corrected—Amari tells the story of a Sicily intimately bound to the peninsula, affirming that those bonds will become ever clearer as historians use the philological method developed by continental historians to read the historical record more accurately: "Today the felicitous political events that tighten the links that bind and multiply commerce between all the Italian peoples, and the progress of linguistic studies in Europe, give us the ability to derive much more precise conclusions."[47]

However, as his history of Norman Sicily progressed, when the second and third volumes on the Normans appeared, Amari's perception of the Sicilian contribution to Norman culture would become clear. European encounters with Arab culture in Sicily generated the cultural miracle of Norman Sicily. But the Normans did not passively accept an Arab culture they found in situ. More important were the cultural institutions they sought out and imported from the Arab ports of the Mediterranean and the Arabic-language works produced under their rule. Sicily, in a sense, is not a noun but a verb in Amari's *Storia dei musulmani di Sicilia*. It denotes the capacity to mediate between European and Arab cultures and in particular the Normans' capable manipulation of the Arab culture of the contemporary Mediterranean.

The dispute between Mortillaro and Amari illuminates the differences in their perceptions of Sicily's relations with the continent and of Sicily's Mediterranean particularism. Amari's emphasis on Sicily's links with peninsular Italy is not all that surprising in the work of a Sicilian historian who had been converted to the dream of Italian unification. Amari locates Sicily's Arab history in the past. He insists that Sicilians need the new methodologies developed by continental historians to bring that distant history to light. And he suggests that the gradual progress of understanding Sicily's past achieved by means of those new research methods will in turn strengthen the ties between Sicily and the continent.

Mortillaro, however, viewed Sicily's Arab history as something transhistorical and indigenous—indeed, immanent—and accessible only to those who had direct access to the soil of Sicily. Continental methods of research might help to clarify specifics. The essential thing, however, was contact with Sicily itself; for Sicily's Arab history was inscribed in its very landscape. In a letter to philologist and Orientalist Angelo Mai written around the same time as his history of Muslim Sicily, Mortillaro bemoans continental ignorance of

Sicily's Arab history.[48] And he evokes a Sicily that holds the record of its Muslim past not in its libraries but in its very mountains, fields and rivers:

> Since I read the first letter of that oracle of German Orientalists, the most eminent de Hammer, on Oriental manuscripts and particularly Arabic manuscripts that are preserved in the various libraries of Italy, I have felt a secret displeasure that Sicily was not mentioned. I have been pained ever since, I confess, that that gentleman—having undertaken a journey throughout all of Italy, as far as Naples—did not make the passage to Sicily, being so close; for it is a land respectable in the eyes of Orientalists, who cannot be ignorant that this island for more than two centuries was dominated by Saracens. Here Arab productions, and stones, and money, and monuments of every sort are found, and not only the names of the cities, but also the mountains, the fields, the rivers, witness the long sojourn of the Muslims in this region.[49]

This letter—which predates 1848, and hence predates Mortillaro's bitter dispute with Amari—anticipates the core of Mortillaro's argument with Amari. Sicily's libraries do not hold the key to her Muslim history; the splendid new philological methods pioneered by European Orientalists will not suffice to bring the past to light. Sicily's Arab civilization, the kernel of Sicilian history and the key to Sicily's contributions to modern European history, can be understood and written only through direct access to the physical reality of Sicily. Exiles cannot write it, but only those Sicilians who have remained *Sicilians.*[50]

On balance one is relieved that history remembers Amari's name and his contribution to Sicilian history, while Mortillaro's has been largely forgotten. Mortillaro's essentialist understanding of national history would not prevail; Amari's careful philological analysis of the historical records of Muslim Sicily has, if anything, appreciated in value over the years. Yet the substance of Mortillaro's argument—that Sicily's fields and rivers, and the tangled streets of the older quarters of its cities, record an essential element of the history of Muslim Sicily—holds a certain amount of truth. Amari, for all the sophistication of his continental training, at times found himself at a disadvantage because of his distance from the archives and monuments of Sicily. And Sicilian historians—that is, those who remained in Sicily—might press their own advantaged access to Sicily as resource. I am thinking in particular of two Sicilian historians whose names have not been remembered outside Sicily (although they remain familiar to Sicilians who know their nineteenth-century history) and who deserve to be much better known for the scientific, historical and literary value of their work. Salvatore Morso wrote a magnificent account of the Palermo of the Norman era—something of a historical travel guide—drawing on the Arabic sources that no historian of Norman Palermo before him had used. And Salvatore Cusa (1822–93) is best known for his anthology of documentary sources from the Norman era in Greek and Arabic, with an introduction that is justly remembered by Sicilian historians as one of the most beautiful historical essays of the nineteenth century.[51]

Following the monographs published by Lanza, Mortillaro, and Amari in the 1830s, 1840s, and 1850s, the next important work to be published on Sicilian Muslim history would be Cusa's edition of Greek and Arabic documents relating to Norman history: *I diplomi greci ed arabi di Sicilia*. Due to the meticulous care with which he edited the documents, Cusa's work had a long gestation period—unconscionably long, in the opinion of the rather more impetuous Amari.[52] Amari urged Cusa to publish *I diplomi greci ed arabi di Sicilia*, doing so both out of his desire to use the materials for his own pages on Norman Sicily and a sense of decency: if Cusa edited the documents Amari would not have to scoop Cusa (or go to the trouble of editing them himself). Amari himself had edited the sources on the history of Muslim Sicily which he found in European libraries; the first volume of his *Biblioteca arabo-sicula* appeared in 1857. However, he did not have access to the documentary sources held in Sicilian libraries and archives—sources dating to the Norman period, and therefore necessary for the three-part third volume of his history on Muslim Sicily, which dealt with the Normans. Amari fumed over Cusa's hesitations and the interminable delays in publication of his work. In 1867 he wrote in exasperation to a mutual friend that the publication of the documents was crucial "1. for science 2. for Italy 3. for the homeland [i.e., Sicily; "per Campanile"] 4. for Cusa himself who knows Arabic well."[53] At the same time, Amari would collaborate with Cusa from a distance by looking over documents that Cusa sent him for his opinion; and he would, of course, benefit from the opportunity to review the documents before publication. *I diplomi greci ed arabi di Sicilia* would finally appear in 1875, though the first volume was backdated—"with transparent cunning," wrote Amari—to 1868.[54]

Amari's and Cusa's work on Sicily's history had a strangely symbiotic relationship. Amari published sources found only in the great libraries of Europe; Cusa provided the texts accessible only in Sicily. Cusa edited documents largely without interpreting them: he did not produce a great work of historical synthesis, as Amari did. But his introduction to his edition—the *Dizionario dei Siciliani illustri* calls this essay "a prominent monument of profound, vast, and sure erudition"[55]—is written with an eloquence and a passion which even Amari, one of the greatest historical stylists of the nineteenth century, can scarce match. Taken in broad strokes, Cusa's argument is by now familiar. The Normans represented the apex of Sicilian history; they would export the magnificent achievements of their civilization to the Italian mainland; the historian cannot understand the years of their domination without access to their Arabic archives. But he adds a new element to this narrative. In the past the historians of Europe had their go at Sicilian history, and in general they took charge of those periods that they could claim as their own: continental classicists have written the ancient Greek history, the Italians have written the Roman history, the Spaniards have written the Aragonese history, and so on. "But one period has always been the preferred study of our own historians. It is that which is called the Norman-Swabian period, that upon which the Sicilian of every age has fixed his gaze, as on a white point against a black horizon. The foreigner, moved by respect, has left it to us untouched, because it is our property; and the sources from which its history is drawn are in good part ours, and are studied only by us."[56] Now, however, the situation is changing. Now the Norman history of Sicily is not a matter for Sicilians alone. Sicily, no longer the subject of a colonizing power nor sovereign herself, pulls closer to the continent. And this era of Sicily's past—when the nations of Europe, for all their differences of culture and language, were united through Latinity, feudal law, and the Roman rite—has a new resonance in contemporary Europe.

> It is for this reason that the memories which concern the history of one [nation] are held to be useful for clarifying that of another; and while we, to better understand our own affairs, profit from those published in other countries, we consider our own to be not a matter of indifference for them; so that from the common fund the history of civilization of all peoples advances, and at the same time that of each individual people.
>
> To this end, today, no effort is spared; even the peace of the dead is disturbed, from whose ashes it is hoped that the materials of a new and different life might be extracted; ruins are laid bare, antiquities, marbles, medals and coins discovered, archives are rifled and papers of every sort are rummaged through.[57]

Cusa sees the new European order emerging around him as a shadow cast by the European order of the Norman age. That past speaks to the present, and to all Europeans—not just to Sicilians.

Yet Cusa's vision of Sicilian history does not flatten its difference, the Mediterranean particularity that Sicilian historians had learned to celebrate during the course of the nineteenth century. On the contrary he insists on the relevance and the centrality of the Arabic-language (and Greek) witnesses to medieval Sicilian history. This, of course, is the motive for his anthology of Greek and Arabic documents. But the sophistication of his treatment of historical sources is most evident in his lovely essay on the Sicilian palm tree, first published in 1873. Throughout history the palm tree has been used as a symbol of existential and mystical truths: Cusa begins the article by meditating on the palm as symbol of God, of man, and of love, citing passages from scripture, the Qur'an, Arabic literature, and Dante. At the same time it is the most useful of plants. Cusa discusses scientific writings on the palm and its management in Arabic, Latin, and Greek. Cusa would know the palm first, however, as a familiar part of the Sicilian landscape. In the final section of the article he quotes poetic and documentary references to the palm from Sicilian sources: the Arabic poetry and the Greek and Latin documents of the Norman period, as well as modern vernacular poetry. He closes his article with a striking nominalist statement and a final mystical gesture: "The Saracens taught us how to make use of [the palm]; or better, the abundant use that they themselves made of it was passed on to us with the thing itself, and with the names that they had attached to it. The utility of this plant does not end even with death, and as from the noble date-palm man harvests wood for construction and materials to burn, so from the most humble varieties he draws the oil that is so useful for agriculture, and he uses its ash to fertilize the land [*a debbiare la terra*]."[58] Cusa's "us," of course, signifies *Sicilians*: he refers to the lexical and scientific legacy that the Arabs left behind in Sicily.

Throughout the article Cusa cites Arabic, Greek, Latin, and Romance sources alongside each other, giving equal weight to each. In a footnote to the closing sentence he discusses the peculiar word *debbiare*, a word of uncertain etymology which here means "to burn the stubble in a field then turn the ashes under, in order to increase the fertility of the soil." He traces the word to both Latin and Arabic sources. But he does not suggest that it appeared first in the one language or the other, or that one language acquired the word from the other. Rather he leaves the two etymologies dangling as if the word had sprung fully armed from the foreheads of both languages, a bizarre case of parentage as co-monogenesis. Indeed throughout his article on the Sicilian palm he cites parallel linguistic traditions without heed to questions of precedence and influence: he poises the languages beside each other and admires the composition they form. In so doing he celebrates the Sicilian past as a history of co-existence on the Andalusian model, a history that can't be known without reference to the multiplicity of populations that inhabited Sicily and Sicily's plural literary-linguistic tradition. The presence of the three languages—Arabic, Latin and Greek—on Sicilian soil is an irreducible fact of Sicilian history. And in his treatment of Sicilian linguistic complexity—the intellectual and historical balancing act whereby Cusa parallels them without resolving his discussion into a "post hoc, ergo propter hoc" discussion of cause and effect, of *influence*—Cusa Mediterraneanizes Sicilian history.

Amari and Cusa together represent the culmination of nineteenth-century Sicilian historiography. Both men made their separate peace with Sicily's integration into a unified Italy by finding a way to express Sicilian particularity not as mere historical quirk but rather as crucible: as the origin of an Italian modernity. Amari and Cusa were sophisticated philologists. They documented their arguments with painstaking care, citing detailed historical records in a bouquet of Mediterranean languages as the foundation for their narratives. And those narratives had crucial relevance to the history unfolding around them in contemporary Europe. In Sicily, some seven centuries earlier, a dynasty of rulers translated the knowledge of the Arabs into the languages of Europe, and hence a new age of enlightenment was born. It was the task of philologists and historians such as Amari and Cusa to identify the origins of a recognizable modern identity in the gloaming of the distant past, and to teach their co-nationals what the nation's past had to say to the present.

It is illuminating to turn back from their works to an earlier chapter in Sicilian historiography, to observe a perceptive historian working with the cruder philological instruments of an earlier age. Salvatore Morso (1766–1828) took over the chair in Arabic created for Giuseppe Vella after Vella's fraud was exposed, in 1797.[59] Domenico Scinà, the historian who chronicled most closely the Vella affair, wrote that Morso "was the first—after the corrupt Maltese dialect had been chased out—to make the halls of our university ring with the sound of the pure Arabic language."[60] Morso wrote a grammar and dictionary of Arabic for use in the university. But he is best remembered for his *Descrizione di Palermo antico ricavata sugli autori sincroni e i monumenti de' tempi* (*Description of old Palermo based on the contemporary authors and the monuments of the age*; 1827). Mortillaro, Morso's student, wrote a memorial essay in which he sang his teacher's praises with due rhetorical flourishes: Morso, he says,

> was convinced of the utility that he drew . . . from his knowledge of the language of a nation that preserved some of the splendor of the sciences through the centuries of ignorance, and that quickened the first sparks of the felicitous renaissance of modern literature in Europe . . . persuaded of the necessity of cultivating such studies on our Island, a region ruled by the Saracens for a good two centuries, and enriched with valuable Arabic documents, inscriptions, products and medals; and where the names of the cities, the fields, the mountains, the lakes, the rivers, the beaches everywhere recall the Arabs and their domination.[61]

Amari, however, sniffed a bit in his account of Morso's contribution to Sicilian historiography: "he knew that language [i.e., Arabic] a bit better than Gregorio; . . . but it seems to me that he erred in his topographic plan [in the *Description of Palermo*]."[62]

If Mortillaro exaggerated Morso's significance, perhaps Amari—in his pride at the European pedigree of his Orientalist learning—is not entirely fair to him. For Morso's *Description of Palermo* is most certainly not without merit: it is a curious and compelling attempt to recreate Norman Palermo on the page, to reanimate it from the descriptions of the medieval witnesses who walked its streets in its most glorious years. Because he read Arabic, Morso had access to a source that previous Sicilian historians had not used in their discussions of medieval Palermo: he referred regularly to the compendious geography produced under the patronage of Norman king Roger II, al-Idrisi's "Book of Roger," the greatest geographical treatise of the late Middle Ages. Roger, according to the story that al-Idrisi tells, required representatives from the merchant ships that called at Sicilian ports to state their accounts of all the lands they knew from personal experience. He culled the information thus collected, tested it through comparative analysis, and used it to produce a silver globe representing the known world. Roger then commissioned al-Idrisi to write his geography as a descriptive accompaniment to the globe. Al-Idrisi's account naturally placed Sicily at the center of the known world. He described Sicily with special care and sang the praises of Palermo in particular as the seat of the Sicilian monarch.

Morso drew on al-Idrisi's description of Norman Palermo to describe in lavish detail a short list of Palermitan monuments, mostly lying within the medieval city walls. However, he included reference to two extramural monuments, pleasure palaces which, at the time that Morso wrote, were in a state of ramshackle disrepair: the Cuba and La Zisa. Sicilians of the age generally assumed both palaces to be remnants of the years of Muslim domination because of their architectural style and their Arabic inscriptions, which no scholar had yet accurately transcribed or translated. Morso had a run at copying out and translating the inscription on La Zisa, but the peculiarities and difficulties of the text confounded him. In his modesty he sent a transcription to two of the greatest Orientalists of the age: the omnipresent Antoine Isaac Silvestre de Sacy and Joseph von Hammer-Purgstall. In a postscript to his chapter on La Zisa in the *Description of Palermo* he reprinted his letter of inquiry and the replies he received from both men. "I have undertaken a difficult task," he wrote in his initial letter, "since neither verses from the Qur'an, nor the names of Mohammedan people, nor the year of the Hegira, which can be of help in interpreting Kufic inscriptions in general, are to be found" in the inscription. And he speculated that this explained why Rosario Gregorio neglected to include the inscription in his own collection of Siculo-Arabic texts. Morso proposed a translation for the text but admitted his lack of confidence in his resolution of its linguistic difficulties and invited the more experienced Orientalists' advice. However, he was quite sure of one thing: the contemporary popular name for the quarter in which the palace is found, La Zisa, must derive from the Arabic word al-'Aziz, which means *mighty, powerful,* or *noble,* and which appeared as the final word in the inscription, where it referred to the building itself.[63]

Morso also speculated tentatively that he had found the name of a Norman king, Roger, in the inscription—thus suggesting that the palace had been built not by the Arabs but during the Norman era, for a Norman patron. Both Silvestre de Sacy and Hammer disagreed with this suggestion. Silvestre in particular pointed out extremely sensible linguistic reasons why it was impossible that Roger's name should appear where Morso saw it. And he added a postscript to his letter, having mulled the inscription and noticed the verbs that directed the viewer's gaze from the vantage point of the palace to the surrounding countryside: "I suspect that this inscription was inscribed near that part of the royal chambers where the King revealed himself to his court, and where he was accustomed to sit when he wished to display himself to his subjects. With this in mind we understand immediately why no mention of any particular ruler is made in the inscription: it referred to all those who might be King of Sicily in future."[64]

Having considered the evidence—his initial transcription and translation of the text and the responses of the continental Orientalists regarding its ambiguities—Morso presented a revised version of the inscription and his conclusions concerning La Zisa. He made no pronouncement on the intriguing question he had raised concerning the patronage of the palace. He pointed out that although the Arabic inscriptions and architectural style suggested that the building was a remnant of the Muslim rulers of Sicily, some speculated that La Zisa dated to the years of Norman rule. And he himself adduced evidence in favor of Norman authorship: the images of palms and peacocks, both Christian symbols; human representations, proscribed in the Islamic tradition; the recessed fountain in the form of a Greek cross. He reviewed again the difficulty he had in deciphering the inscription: "The Qur'anic formulas which abound in all Cufic inscriptions could give me no help, because none was to be found here; there was no indication of a date; all was obscure and equivocal." But he was obliged to abandon his most convincing evidence of Norman construction. He recalled that "I thought I had found the name of King Roger" in the inscription but was now convinced by Silvestre de Sacy and Hammer's arguments that he had been mistaken.[65]

Silvestre de Sacy and Hammer were absolutely correct in their interpretation of the inscription: Roger's name did not appear where Morso saw it. But it is one of the most delicious ironies of nineteenth-century Siculo-Arabic historiography that Morso, in a way, was also right. Michele Amari, in his work on the Arabic epigraphy of Sicily, would demonstrate that a Norman king did build La Zisa and that the inscription did name him. The king, however, was Roger's grandson, William II, and the inscription gave his Arabic 'alama (or honorific royal title) rather than his Christian name. Amari translated the inscription from a rubbing made for him by a Parisian friend who was able to visit Sicily (as Amari himself, persona non grata, could not). The inscription reads:

> Whenever you wish, you may regard the best kingdom
> the most exalted realm in the world . . .
>
> You may see the king of the age in an excellent habitation
> which merits haughtiness and delight
>
> This is the earthly paradise which comes into sight
> That is the *Musta'izz*, and this is the *'Aziz*[66]

William II used *al-Musta'izz,* "the exalted one," as his honorific title. The word is derived from the same etymological root as the name of the palace—*al-'Aziz,* "the mighty." The inscription identifies the king of Sicily with his palace and exalts the power and strength of both. In his analysis of the inscription Amari had great fun with the bumbling efforts of previous Orientalists to decipher it. While discussing their Keystone Kops–like stabs at interpretation he referred the reader to Morso for a full description of "the history of the interpretation of this epigraph, which would be a long and tedious account," and spoke graciously of the "admirable clarity" of Morso's transcription.[67] But he did not acknowledge that Morso had himself attempted to link the palace to a Norman monarch half a century earlier.

Amari is remembered today as the greatest of the nineteenth-century Sicilian Orientalists who labored to unearth Sicily's Muslim history. And so he should be: he not only reconstructed the history of those forgotten centuries through painstaking analysis of obscure and difficult records, but also demonstrated the relevance of Sicily's past to the present day. Atto Vannucci, a Florentine patriot who traveled to Paris for medical reasons and met Amari there, published a review in 1856 of the first volume of the *Storia dei musulmani di Sicilia,* which had appeared two years earlier. In it he demonstrated clearly the contemporary relevance of Amari's historical work. In his history, Vannucci wrote, Amari

> narrated in swift and splendid pages the ancient upheavals of the Arabs, their nature and customs, laws, military orders, arts and commerce, and the cause and development and consequences of their civilization; and with new documents he demonstrated that Muhammad was the greatest religious and legislative reformer of his age, *and was the founder of a social democracy based on the equality and brotherhood that the practice of Islam called for among believers:* an order that infused a new life in the Arabs, and made them capable of portentous works; a simple and vast religious and political system that met the test: for, says the author, it regenerated a people more swiftly than any other law would have done, it contributed not a little to civilizing a great part of the human race, and it endures still, nor does it seem inclined to die.[68]

Neither the Americans nor the French can take credit for the invention of modern democracy, Vannucci suggests. Rather Amari's history of medieval Sicily identifies the origin of European democracy in the very substance of

Islamic revelation—the "social democracy" that Islam demanded of believers—and finds democracy in practice in the Islamic states established in Mediterranean Europe (although Vannucci, like Amari, is interested only in the Sicilian example).

It seems, however, more than mere sentiment to call attention to the other remarkable historians of the Sicilian nineteenth century, Salvatore Cusa and Salvatore Morso. Cusa should be remembered for his introductory essay to his edition of Norman-era documents and for his essay on the palm. While subsequent scholarship has superseded some of his work, his analysis remains erudite and cogent. By moving between the Arabic, Latin, Greek, and Romance traditions without imposing the causal hierarchy of origins on his material—that is, without reference to a narrative of influence—Cusa models a comparatist reading of Mediterranean literary traditions. And Morso's work is memorable if only because scholars no longer attempt such things: a vivid recreation of a current capital in an earlier stage of its development. Because Morso describes a lost Palermo with reference to another Palermo equally lost to us—he recalls twelfth-century Palermo with nineteenth-century eyes—the work possesses a particularly rich historical veneer. It is twice removed from reality and twice lost to nostalgia.

But modern philologists might come to appreciate and value Cusa's and Morso's work not only for their insights but also for their shortsightedness, for their subjectivities as well as the objective accuracy of their observations and analysis. Cusa's reading of the contemporary relevance of the Norman era—*it shows Europeans what we are now becoming*—tells us a great deal about how Europeans understood their past and how philologists viewed their project at a given moment during the consolidation of the European nationalisms. And I must confess a particular affection for Morso's anecdote about his misinterpretation of La Zisa. Amari does not give us stories like this. He recounts a lovely tale about the Cuba, the other extramural pleasure palace built by the Normans. At a party in Paris, at the house of the same Sicilian aristocrat who would later send him the rubbings of the epigraphs from La Zisa, Amari heard his host argue with a French historian of architecture about the provenance of the Cuba. The Sicilian aristocrat argued that the Arabs built it; the French historian gave the Normans credit for it. Two years after this overheard conversation, Amari himself would take rubbings of the inscriptions on the Cuba—making them in a rush, on the day before he fled Sicily in 1849. His interpretation of the inscription would prove the French historian right: the Normans had built the Cuba too.[69] This story embodies the qualities for which we love Amari—he was at once an adventurer, a revolutionist, and a careful scholar. His account of Muslim Sicily remains current today for its historical accuracy (C. A. Nallino corrected some of the inevitable omissions for the twentieth-century edition) as well as its moral grandeur.[70] Yet Morso's modest story about an intuition that the specialists proved wrong is equally memorable: it possesses a tender beauty, a startling denouement, and an element of truth. Morso got the details wrong but the story right. He argued a hunch and withdrew it when the documentary record contradicted him. Yet in time the philologists would find evidence to support Morso's intuition: La Zisa, like the Cuba, was a product of Norman ventriloquism of Arab architectural conventions.

At the end of his review of the *Storia dei musulmani di Sicilia*, Atto Vannucci expresses an ardent hope that Amari will untangle one of the pressing questions of the age: that voiced by proponents of the "Arabic thesis." "It has been repeated," Vannucci wrote, "up to our own day, by many scholars, that the poetic and chivalric influences of the Arabs on Provençal and Italian literature were profound." Of course other scholars disagree; Vannucci cites Ernest Renan sneering at the notion. But he holds out the hope that "Amari, who knows better than anyone the language and the literature of the Arabs of Sicily, will be able to answer definitively such a question with the history and with the facts, and say what Italian civilization does or does not owe to the Arabs."[71] Amari and Renan, critic of the "Arabic thesis," were good friends. They worked together at the Bibliothèque impériale and exchanged letters after Amari moved to Italy. One can scarcely imagine two more different sensibilities than Amari's and Renan's. Amari was an avowed agnostic, Renan a former priest; Amari was a revolutionary while Renan had an outspoken revulsion for public violence; Amari was a meticulous philologist while Renan's philological method was (to put it kindly) approximate at best. So, too, on the question of Arab influence on European culture the two men must have agreed to disagree. Renan insisted on the absolute, irreconcilable difference between Arab and European culture. For good reason Edward Said used Renan as the model of his Orientalist: Renan held that Semitic culture in general and Arab culture in particular possessed an essential element that was alien and inimical to European modernity. Amari, however, believed that when the Arab sciences met a European sensibility in medieval Sicily, an alchemical transformation occurred. Norman manipulation of Arab civilization allowed Sicily to dominate the Mediterranean; passed to the peninsula, this Sicilian innovation sparked the Renaissance. On the question of literary history in particular Amari could not produce manuscript evidence of Arabic influence; indeed, if he had, subsequent philologists would have sainted him. Still he insisted that the Arabs influenced the evolution of European literary history: "The manner alone—I believe—of the splendid Muslim courts of Spain carried into the Christian castles of the West, along with other luxurious notions, the pleasing habit of listening to poetry in the local vernacular tongue: prizes and honors encouraged national poets to recite at princely gatherings those verses that one heard before in the obscure street-songs of the cities and the countryside; so that vernacular poetry, rather than *born*, one should say was *emancipated* and *ennobled* during that period."[72] Under Muslim rule, according to Amari, Sicily became Arab. Sicilians absorbed the culture of the Arab Mediterranean. During the Norman years rulers from the north and immigrants from *Italia di sopra* would tease the potential of Muslim culture from the soul of Sicily, "emancipating and ennobling" the Arab seed gone native in Sicilian soil.

Of course Amari's discipline as a historian saves his work from the imprecisions and excesses of a Scrofani, a Martorana, or a Mortillaro. When he does allow personal sentiment to color his work—as, for instance, when he tells us the motives for his disagreement with Mortillaro—we read it as evidence of his moral strength. It helps us to understand the environment in which Amari worked; we are grateful for the window onto the passions of the era. Mortillaro's insistent return to his grievance against Amari, however, is unlikely to inspire gratitude, but rather makes him appear to our eyes captious and peevish. This in part is because Mortillaro was on the wrong side of the disputes of his age, from our perspective. A conservative, he fought against the causes that (for all the failings of the Sicilian revolutionaries of 1848, and they were many and considerable) we would defend, shoulder to shoulder with Amari: autonomy and self-rule, the end of the corrupt royalist regimes of early modernity. I have discussed his work in such depth here in part in the interests of thoroughness and in part to demonstrate how powerful the narrative of Arab origin was to nineteenth-century Sicilians, irrespective of their stance with regard to the pressing political questions of the age.

By the same token, *all* the historians whose work I have discussed in this chapter argued a position that, although it is accepted in broad outlines by most medieval historians, has yet to win over a nonscholarly public (or even an academic public among those who do not specialize in the Middle Ages). By insisting on the European debt to the Arab civilization of the medieval Mediterranean they distinguished the story they told from standard, normative perceptions of European history. Amari, far and away the most familiar of the names I have mentioned in this chapter, is remembered today because his history of Muslim Sicily remains invaluable (but again, that history has not been superseded in part because European historians perceive it as marginal and largely irrelevant to European history). Although he founded a school of Arabic in Florence he is not typically named among the fathers of Italian Orientalism. He trained a student, Celestino Schiaparelli, who carried on his work in Siculo-Arabic studies but did not have any successors himself. The great Italian Orientalists of the twentieth century would come from the universities that trained missionaries and colonial functionaries in Naples and Rome. It seems likely that stripped of his romantic biography—the early manifesto on the Sicilian Vespers; the Parisian exile; the triumphant return to Palermo in 1848 and noble defeat in 1849—Amari's work on Muslim Sicily would be more obscure today. And if he had not supported the right causes—Sicilian autonomy in 1848 and Italian unification in 1860—his reputation would be more tenuous still. Given all that distances them from us, it requires a prodigious intellectual effort indeed to reconstruct the more radical elements of Amari's, Morso's, and Cusa's historiography: their capacity to think a Mediterranean philology that encompasses and mediates between Latin, Greek, and Arabic; and their commitment to the futurity of their philology, their belief that the Mediterranean past has something to teach Europeans about their future.

*Chapter 4*

# The Ramparts of Europe: The Invention of the Maltese Language

Glaubst Du mit mir, dass die Religion von einer göttlichen Offen-
barung ausgegangen ist, dass die Sprache einen eben so wundervollen
Ursprung hat und nicht durch Menschenerfindung zuwege gebracht
worden ist, so must Du schon darum glauben und fühlen, dass die
alte Poesie und ihre Formen, die Quelle des Reims und der Alliteration ebenso in einem Ganzen ausgegangen ist, und gar keine Werks-
tätten oder Ueberlegungen einzelner Dichter in Betracht kommen
können.
　　—Jacob Grimm, 1811[1]

[If you believe with me that religion originated in a divine revelation,
that language too has a miraculous origin and does not come from
human invention, for that very reason must you believe and feel that
so too did the old poetry and its forms, the origin of rhyme and of
alliteration, emerge fully formed, and it is out of the question that
they came from some workshop or from the reflection of some individual poet.]

Among his signs are the creation of the heavens and the earth and
the differences in your languages and your colors; indeed, here are
signs for those who know.
　　—Qur'an, al-Rum (sura 30), 22

WE TEND TO think of the division of the Mediterranean into Muslim shores on the one hand and Christian on the other as a timeless organization of that contested space, or at least as old as the revelation that brought Islam into being. In fact, as medievalists well know, it took some centuries to hammer out this division of property that rulers, generals, and ambitious corsairs had sparred over since the emergence of Islam. Only during the sixteenth century did the Ottoman Turks assert authoritative control over the full sweep of the southern and eastern Mediterranean, soon after Christian kings eradicated the last Muslim settlement on the Iberian peninsula. Philologists may appreciate the irony that, while an exacting but inequitable hand parted the inland sea to create Muslim and Christian shores, Italian intellectuals quibbled over which was the true version of Aristotle's *Poetics* and the most useful to European poets—Aristotle's Greek version or Averroes' Arabic (see Chapter 2). So too, during this watershed century at the cusp of modernity, did another grand project of the Middle Ages generate a mannerist sequel: while Torquato Tasso (1544–95), in his epic poem *Gerusalemme Liberata*, codified the crusades as Europe's archetypal battle against the barbarians at the gates, the conflict between Christianity and Islam devolved into piracy.

By the end of the fourteenth century the heroic era of the crusades had long ended. Christians contented themselves with a series of petty crusades against Ottoman cities in the Mediterranean, the Baltic, and the Balkans, and the Ottomans responded by seizing virtually all the territory remaining to the Byzantine Empire (and Constantinople would fall to Ottoman armies in 1453). In 1492, with the Spanish conquest of Muslim Granada, Christian expansion eradicated the last of the Muslim colonies in southern Europe. And over the course of the sixteenth century a series of conquests and concessions set the stage for a face-off between Muslim and Christian forces which most commonly took the form of predation, as corsairs sailing from Malta and the Barbary Regencies each attacked their opponents' merchant vessels in the shipping lanes of the Mediterranean. In 1530 Charles V, the Holy Roman Emperor, handed the Maltese archipelago (including Malta, the inhabited islands Gozo and Comino, and two minute, uninhabited atolls) to the Order of Saint John; in return the Knights of Malta agreed to pay in yearly rent the famous Maltese falcon. In 1565, a short thirty-five years after receiving the keys of Malta, the knights proved themselves worthy of European confidence when they defeated the redoubtable Ottoman naval forces in the battle known as the Great Siege of Malta. Following that engagement and the Christians' victory at Lepanto in 1571 the Ottoman navy posed no credible threat to Christian sovereignty on the northern shores of the Mediterranean. During the same period, however, the Ottomans steadily consolidated their hold on the southern Mediterranean: Ottoman generals seized Algiers in 1529 and Tripoli in 1551; the Turkish conquest of Hafsid Tunis in 1574 put the entirety of the southern and eastern shores under Ottoman control. The European states focused their attention elsewhere—the Atlantic and beyond—and the inland sea was no longer the theater for large-scale, state-supported battles. But the stage was set for the golden age of Mediterranean piracy.[2] The Barbary and Maltese corsairs recast piracy by solidifying its ideological underpinnings as a variety of holy war that set believers against infidels and offered the victor religious glory and booty to boot.[3]

Thus during the sixteenth century Malta found itself on the front lines of the battle between Christianity and Islam, and the Knights of Saint John—who once ran the hospitals that treated pilgrims and crusaders in the Holy Land—served as warriors and admirals in that war. The grand master of the Order of Saint John granted privateering licenses to independent captains who sailed from the harbors of Malta to attack Muslim ships. And the knights themselves, generally young men who served a turn in Malta then returned to secular careers in Europe, manned caravans that looted the ships sailing from the Barbary coast and the Levant. During the seventeenth century even the Protestant families of northern Europe might send their sons to Malta; a turn on a Maltese caravan came to be seen as the young aristocrat's finishing school. But by the mid-eighteenth century shifting trade and travel patterns had transformed the Maltese caravan into a pro forma exercise, something like a Disneyland version of the real experience. The knights communicated their planned itineraries to the Barbary states before departure so that they would not interrupt trade; they collected sums from the families who sent their scions to Malta, rather than prizes, for their trouble.[4] Privateering ships manned by Maltese sailors, meanwhile, still worked around the limitations imposed by papal edicts and treaties. Their activities were suspended altogether only once—when Napoleon arrived on the island in 1798—and then only briefly. Under British rule, at the beginning of the nineteenth century, the privateering would resume.

The arrival of the Knights of Saint John made Malta into something of a premodern United Nations. During the sixteenth century the island became a linguistic melting pot, or perhaps more appropriately a mosaic of Mediterranean tongues. Malta—perched at the midpoint of the Mediterranean, 58 miles south of Sicily, 180 miles north of Libya, and 180 miles east of

Tunisia—had, like nearby Sicily, been occupied by Arabs during the ninth century and by Normans during the eleventh. It been ruled by the Swabians (1194–1266), the Angevins (1266–83), and the Aragonese (1283–1530). Before the arrival of the Order of Saint John, Malta functioned as a de facto extension of Sicily, and the Maltese used the Sicilian dialect as the language of bureaucracy and business. The residence of the order would complicate the linguistic scene substantially. Organized into eight *Langues*—Auvergne, Provence, France, Aragon, Castile, England, Germany, and Italy—the knights lived in separate *auberges* along with their co-nationals. Italian remained the language of business on the island—now, in recognition of the transnational nature of the business conducted there, Tuscan rather than Sicilian. In their *auberges* the knights communicated in their native tongues. And with the Maltese—the men who sold them bread and the women who mothered their children—they spoke Maltese.[5]

The Maltese language is one of the great linguistic mysteries of the Mediterranean. Maltese is an Arabic colloquial. It is closely related to the Maghrebi dialects spoken on the African shores nearest the Maltese archipelago, though it also shows evidence of Levantine influence. Over time the language acquired lexical accretions from the Romance tongues, in particular Italian; and during the twentieth century the quantity of Romance vocabulary in general use increased substantially. However, its morphology and grammar have remained substantially Arabic. In Maltese, Romance words can be reduced to three (or four) radical consonants and can generate derived forms, as Semitic lexemes do.

That such a language should have evolved on a small island with Malta's history is not surprising; more remarkable is its survival through the eventful centuries. The Arabs occupied Malta for a relatively brief historical parenthesis. Yet despite subsequent rule by a series of Romance-speaking kingdoms, despite the strong affinity that the Maltese—staunch Catholics—feel for the Romance-speaking nations of southern Europe that governed the islands, and despite their history of antagonism with the Arabic-speaking Muslims of the Mediterranean, they have displayed a remarkable linguistic conservatism. They have preserved a microlanguage spoken only in the Maltese archipelago, at the cost of maintaining diglossia (or triglossia) in order to do business with the greater Mediterranean world. Most strikingly, the Maltese have created a colloquial Arabic literary tradition on a modern European national model. Malta today is the only country in the European Union in which a Semitic language is spoken. And Maltese is the only colloquial Arabic dialect that has generated a standard written form with its own literary tradition.

In this chapter I will survey some of the things that observers, both Maltese and foreign, have said about the Maltese language over the course of the last five centuries. The decades of debate that led to the acceptance of Maltese as a national language—in particular the years between 1880 and 1936—constitute one of the most heroic chapters in the history of the European nationalisms. Maltese had competition for the role of national language. During the nineteenth century and the first decades of the twentieth Maltese nationalists might support either English or Italian, depending on their political affiliations, as the language of culture in Malta. Indeed during the nineteenth century most nationalists attacked the Maltese language as a liability to the nation—a fact that will surprise those who have read their Herder (as these men themselves most probably had). Nineteenth-century Maltese nationalists generally believed that the Maltese should use Italian, the lingua franca of the late medieval and early modern Mediterranean, as a language of culture. It was only during the early twentieth century that Maltese found widespread support as a language of culture and as the national language of Malta.

Some of the stories I tell in this book have heroes, though most would be unlikely to be elected idol by any but an audience of philologists: Pietro Valerga, the garrulous eccentric; Amari, the gun-toting, verb-crunching revolutionary; Cerulli, a Heathcliff among the paladins; Scheherazade, at once heroine of the resistance and ambiguous—possibly malevolent—temptress. In this chapter, a language plays the role of hero. Maltese is not striking for its athletic excesses or freakish oddities; unlike other languages that have attracted the attention of linguists or the general public it does not have one hundred words for snow or a single verb that means "to fall into a well that one did not know was there."[6] Rather it astonishes us with its fluent negotiation between the Semitic and the Romance, and with its historical capacity to demonstrate at once remarkable fluidity and resilience. It has resisted change over the centuries, preserving even elements of archaic Arabic, while at the same time absorbing Romance (and, more recently, English) vocabulary into an essentially Semitic grammatical structure. Maltese speakers are said to be able to select between the Arabic and Romance lexemes in the language with relative ease—a fact that seems more astonishing if one imagines an English speaker distinguishing between the Romance and Germanic etymons in our language in conversation. The Maltese language has achieved a synthesis that the casual observer might think impossible. Like the lingua franca of the early modern Mediterranean, a hybrid tongue spoken by merchants, pilgrims, and pirates, the Maltese language knits together Italian and Arabic. However, Maltese has not disappeared beneath the waters of the Mediterranean, as the lingua franca did with the decline of trans-Mediterranean commerce, but has survived and even thrived, becoming a fully fledged modern language used for communication at every linguistic range and for literary invention. Maltese, like a gemstone of exceptional quality, demands a setting graceful in proportion to its beauty: the Mediterranean itself.

Malta first attracted the attention of a broad European audience when the Knights of the Order of Saint John settled on the island.[7] The earliest formal description of the island in a European language (that is, excluding the medieval Arab geographers' references to it) was written by a Frenchman who came to Malta as a hospitaller during the 1530s, soon after the island was handed over to the knights. Jean Quintin d'Autun modeled what would become a literary fashion when he included, in his overview of the island, a thumbnail description of its language:

> Our island of Malta is separated from Sicily by sixty miles of quite dangerous sea, in the direction of Africa. It once was under Phoenician rule; still now an African language is used there. Even now some stones inscribed with Phoenician letters remain; in their shape and with the dots added to them, they almost resemble Hebrew. Indeed the language they speak now differs in little or nothing from the old language. The Maltese can understand the Phoenician character Hanno in Plautus, Avicenna, and many Phoenician words similar to these—although their language is such that it cannot be accurately written in Latin letters, much less pronounced by the mouth of anyone who is not of their race.[8]

D'Autun's description of the Maltese language as *Phoenician* and his confusion concerning the relation between the various Semitic tongues—Phoenician (extinct for centuries), Arabic (written by Avicenna), and Hebrew—became a leitmotiv for descriptions of Maltese. D'Autun's tics were repeated in the most extensive early description of the Maltese language. Hieronymus Megiser, a linguistic tourist who traveled in order to gain firsthand knowledge of languages, visited Malta in 1588. In 1606 he published a pamphlet on the Maltese language entitled *Propugnaculum Europae: Wahrhaffte, eigentliche und*

*ausführliche Beschreibung der viel und weitberühmten africanischen Insul Malta*
(*The Ramparts of Europe: A true, actual and detailed description of the very well
known African island Malta*). The first (Latin) section of this wordy, macaronic, and revealing title referred to the Knights of Malta's heroic resistance
to the Ottoman navy in the Great Siege of 1565. The German subtitle slyly
shifted Malta's location; no longer the *ramparts of Europe*, it became an outpost of Africa. Here is Megiser's description of Maltese in the brief essay
introducing his Maltese-German glossary: "Although they are Christians,
they make use of a language which is Saracen, Moorish, or Carthaginian or
'lingua punica,' which is a kind of Arabic and which has its origin in Hebrew.
A number of words representing a 'Specimen' of this language are listed
below, even though these words can hardly be written with our letters, and a
foreigner can hardly pronounce them."[9] Like Jean Quintin d'Autun, Megiser
connects the language spoken by the Maltese to the extinct language of the
Phoenicians (or Carthaginians). But he goes further than d'Autun both in
his attempts to analyze Maltese and in the confusion that results. He parallels
"Saracen," "Moorish," "Carthaginian," and "Phoenician" in a vexingly
vague way: does he lay the adjectives beside one another because they are
distinct or because they represent diverse names for the same tongue? He is
quite vague on the relation between these Semitic tongues and Arabic and,
of course, has no notion of the genetic relation between Arabic and Hebrew.
It is clear that Megiser writes long before the nineteenth-century philologists
refashioned linguistics on a scientific model.

European interest in the language would die down after the flurry of
descriptions occasioned by the knights' arrival in Malta. During the eighteenth century an uncertain number of Maltese produced grammars and dictionaries of their language; the exact number is hard to determine, because
of their deplorable rate of survival to the present day.[10] The disinterest of
European observers during the century of the *lumières*—despite Europeans'
contemporary efforts to compile and categorize their knowledge of practically
everything—may be attributed to the Enlightenment prejudice in favor of
ancient, monolithic, and unified linguistic traditions and parallel contempt
for dialects and regional tongues. In his article on Malta for Diderot's and
d'Alembert's *Encyclopédie ou Dictionnaire raisonné des sciences, des arts et de
métiers,* Louis de Jaucourt referred to the language of the Maltese en passant
as "a patois which resembles a corrupt Arabic." The authors of the *Encyclopédie* dwelt on language in Malta only when referring to the Phoenician

inscriptions found on the island and when citing scholarly opinions that the language retained elements of Punic.[11]

At the end of the eighteenth century Maltese had not yet been used as a literary language. Historians would later discover a poem in Maltese copied into a notarial register which they dated to the fifteenth century. And a poetic tribute to the grand master of the Knights of Malta was published in the late seventeenth century.[12] But during the early modern period Maltese with literary ambitions wrote in Italian.

With the intervention of Mikiel Anton Vassalli (1764–1829), however, Maltese abruptly encountered modernity.[13] Between 1790 and 1796, Vassalli—regularly referred to as the father of the Maltese language—crafted a new alphabet, based on Latin letters, that would allow the language to be written and understood by Europeans as well as Maltese, and he produced a grammar and a dictionary of Maltese. Vassalli studied Arabic in order to elucidate the grammatical and lexical constitution of Maltese. At the same time he drew on nascent Romantic conceptions of the mother tongue as the Ursprung of the national character; a presupposition of the unbridgeable gap between the Maltese and the Muslim population of the northern shores of Africa caused him during the 1790s to deny the similarities between Arabic and Maltese. Later in his career, however, Vassalli would recognize the relation between the two languages. But, like too many scholars and artists, Vassalli's career was cut short by ill health, endemic poverty, and the political vicissitudes of his age. Had he lived, had he completed his study on the ties between Maltese and Arabic, he might have carried his early scholarship to its logical conclusion by writing the Romantic manifesto of a Catholic nation that spoke a sibling tongue to the language of its Mediterranean rivals, the Arabs.

The introduction to his dictionary of Maltese, published in 1796, suggests the power that such a document might have had. Vassalli was a magnificent literary stylist, an ardent nationalist, and an erudite grammarian, born in a time and place that demanded precisely this constellation of skills in order to complete its transition to modern statehood. The introduction to the dictionary—justly celebrated in Malta as the most important early document in the evolution of the Maltese language and of Maltese national identity—expressed his patriotic ardor for his language and his people in a passionate Italian that both evoked and transcended the acute difficulties of the moment in which he lived. Vassalli dedicated his dictionary "alla Nazione Maltese." And he opened it with a dedicatory letter to his "Concittadini" (or

Fellow Citizens). "A niun altro che a Voi consacro la presente opera," he began, "To none other than You I consecrate this work, because it belongs first and foremost to you. To You alone must I dedicate it, because it describes and illustrates the praiseworthy monument of the ancient tongue [favella] that you have preserved to the present day."[14] Like other writers of his age Vassalli used the initial capital liberally to emphasize words of importance: You, Fellow Citizens; la Nazione; la Patria. He would also spell another set of words with the initial capital of gravitas: Alphabet, Orthography, Grammar, *la Lingua Maltese*.[15] In part this was because the alphabet, orthography, and grammar to which he referred were not common nouns. He spoke about a literary language that scarcely existed independent of his own treatment of it in his earlier works of the 1790s: the Alphabet and Orthography to which he referred were his own (published in 1790) as was the Grammar (1791).[16] Previous scholars had struggled with the task of forging an alphabet to write the language—which, as both d'Autun and Megiser had pointed out, "can hardly be written with our [Latin] letters"—and, as we will see, the debate over the Maltese alphabet would continue until the twentieth century.[17] It is not an exaggeration to say that Vassalli called the Maltese language into being in this unlikely manifesto. In the dictionary, he would infuse the skeletal Alphabet and Grammar he had created with its lifeblood, the words he had culled from long study with the people of Malta and Gozo.

In this brief citation from the dedicatory letter Vassalli demonstrates another literary habit typical of the dedication and introduction to the dictionary: he refers to the Maltese language as a *monument*. Later in the introduction, describing his methods in compiling his lexicon, he writes that he gathered the words of the Maltese and Gozitans (residents of the adjacent island, Gozo), "the pure guardians [ingenui depositarij] of this monument." And he refers to the language as "the rarest monument of antiquity."[18] For Vassalli the Maltese tongue constitutes the core of Maltese identity by conserving the essential details of Maltese history: it is a monument to the path the Maltese have traveled toward nationhood. In this he is clearly inspired by Herder and the German Romantics who perceived national tongues in general as both the medium and the most programmatic statement of the national character. National history is embedded in the very substance of the national tongue.

But Vassalli used a potent and precise tool to examine this powerful but imprecise perception of the national language as a repository of national history: the new scientific instruments of linguistic and literary analysis, *philol-*

*ogy*. In particular he used comparative linguistics to investigate the structure of the tongue. Vassalli had begun the study of Arabic in Malta; in 1785 he registered at La Sapienza in Rome in order to continue his studies. In the introduction to the dictionary he told his readers that he had learned Arabic in order to better understand Maltese, "by which means I learned that the essence of our tongue [nostra idioma] is altogether Oriental."[19] But he agreed with those who, like Jean Quintin d'Autun, believed that the Maltese had preserved an ancient Phoenician dialect. Indeed for Vassalli the language—with its essentially Phoenician identity—reveals the tenaciousness with which the Maltese have always safeguarded their autonomy, their liberty, and their distinct identity. In particular it is a measure of the Maltese people's resistance to the Arabs, whose religion and customs they abhorred. Rather than accept the Arabs as their masters by speaking the Arabic language, the Maltese preserved their proud heritage in their own, distinct Phoenician tongue. Those who see an intimate relation between Maltese and the Arabic dialects of the North African littoral are mistaken; any resemblances between spoken Arabic and Maltese are due to their common Phoenician ancestry.[20] In the same spirit did Francisco Javier Simonet insist that medieval "Spaniards" resisted their Arab conquerors by tenaciously preserving their Christian tongue (and with it their proto-Spanish identity; see above, Chapter 2).

It is easy to scoff at Vassalli's historical naïveté. However, the views he expresses in this lexical manifesto are, despite his occasional accommodation of the prejudices of his age, remarkably complex. He inserts the Maltese language into the pantheon of Oriental tongues and argues that by studying Maltese, scholars will discover lexical clues regarding the etymology not only of Phoenician and Punic words—"so longed for and sought after in the republic of letters"—but also Chaldean, Syriac, Hebrew, "a very great number of literary and poetic Arabic words, and even a few Persian."[21] And in a brief discussion of poetry he states that in its vivacity of expression Maltese can provide a magnificent vehicle for poets; but he warns them that "in order to succeed one ought to stay away from the poetic customs of those nations of heterogeneous language with regard to our own, which I do not believe an ancient Oriental language may adapt."[22] He does not, however, state which models the aspiring poet should emulate: does he imagine Maltese poets writing *qasidas*, or (more likely) basing their national epics on the Psalms? The lacuna indicates one of the difficulties the nascent Maltese literary tradition would face: finding models for poetic composition from an uneasy linguistic perch between Sicily and Libya, fitting the rhythms of a Semitic language to the measures forged by Romance poets.

Toward the end of his life, his health undermined by hard work and the rigors of poverty, Vassalli would publish a second edition of his grammar of Maltese. In the introduction to that work he would acknowledge the genetic relation between Maltese and Arabic, and he promised a more detailed study of the ties between the two languages.[23] As fate would have it this work would remain unwritten. The revised grammar appeared in 1827; Vassalli died less than two years later, in early 1829. The difficulties of his life prevented him from publishing any further considerations of the nature of the national history revealed by the national tongue and presumably made it difficult for him even to meditate deeply on that legacy.

Vassalli's life spanned the first crisis of the eventful Maltese nineteenth century. At the age of twenty-one, in 1785, he left Malta for Rome. Following his return to Malta, in 1797, he would be sentenced to life imprisonment for his criticism of the Order of Saint John.[24] Napoleon invaded Malta on his way to Egypt in 1798; he cast the Knights of Malta off the island, and his government freed Vassalli from the life sentence to which the knights had condemned him. If Vassalli's intervention marked the beginning of Maltese linguistic modernity, Napoleon's abrupt and brutal arrival on the island—and the events that incursion set in motion—marked the inauguration of the bureaucratic institutions of modernity in Malta.

Later, Sir Walter Scott would write that the Maltese put up no resistance to Napoleon's army when it arrived in 1798:

> The 10th June brought the armament before Malta, once the citadel of Christendom, and garrisoned by those intrepid knights, who, half war-riors and half priests, opposed the infidels with the enthusiasm at once of religion and of chivalry. But those by whom the order was now maintained were disunited among themselves, lazy and debauched voluptuaries, who consumed the revenues destined to fit out expeditions against the Turks in cruizes for pleasure, not war, and giving balls and entertainments in the seaports of Italy. Buonaparte treated these degenerate knights with a want of ceremony, which, however little it accorded with the extreme strength of their island, and with the glorious defense which it had formerly made against the infidels, was perfectly suited to their present condition. Secure of a party among the French knights, with whom he had been tampering, he landed troops, and took possession of

these almost impregnable fortresses with so little opposition, that Caffar-
elli said to Napoleon, as they passed through the most formidable de-
fenses, "It is well, general, that there was some one within to open the
gates to us. We should have had more trouble in entering, if the place
had been altogether empty."[25]

Scott's account reveals more about subsequent English perceptions of Malta
than about the events of 1798. There is undoubtedly some truth in his evocation of the decadence of the Knights of Malta. However, his contrast of their
glorious deportment in the 1565 Siege of Malta and their current decadence,
his suggestion that Napoleon merely gave the knights what they had coming
to them, and his disregard for the residents of the island beyond the Order
of Saint John are informed largely by subsequent British colonial attitudes
toward the island.

It is true that when Napoleon arrived the Maltese initially received him
without resistance (and seemed not overly dejected when he expelled the
Order of Saint John from the island). However, the depredations of the
French troops soon drove the Maltese to insurrection. The leaders of the
Maltese resistance called upon the British navy to aid them; in 1800, after
two years of battle, the French army withdrew.[26] The 1802 Treaty of Amiens
gave Britain sovereignty over Malta but provided for both the return of the
Order of Saint John and a power-sharing arrangement with the order, grant-
ing the Maltese themselves a share of sovereignty in the government of the
island. In the event—and despite consistent and passionate resistance from
the Maltese—the British would remain in Malta until 1964. The island's
strategic location at the center of the Mediterranean made it too valuable to
British interests to relinquish.

Thus Malta—a small Mediterranean island whose residents spoke a language incomprehensible to outsiders and used Italian to communicate with
the larger Mediterranean world—became an outpost of the British Empire.
English travelers called at the island for motives of diplomacy, tourism, or
health. They seldom expressed enthusiasm for its scenery, its residents, or its
culture. Coleridge—who lived there during 1804–5, quite early in the British
colonial period, for reasons of health—called it "the dreariest of all dreary
islands." And he, like earlier visitors, remarked on the local language: "The
Maltese talk Arabic mixed with Italian."[27] A short time later, in 1809, Byron
would stop by on his way to Greece, and again on his return trip from Greece
in 1811. In Malta he took up the study of Arabic (and soon abandoned it), and

he fell in love—not for the first time, certainly, but with his first adventuress, Constance Spencer Smith, who herself pursued a wearying itinerary fleeing from her Russian husband and had been imprisoned by Napoleon's army. He too had little affection for the island:

> And now, O Malta! since thou'st got us,
> Thou little military hothouse!
> I'll not offend with words uncivil,
> And wish thee rudely at the Devil,
> But only stare from out my casement,
> And ask, for what is such a place meant?[28]

Byron's epithet for Malta—"military hothouse"—is indicative of a prevailing British perception of the island. Like Gibraltar, Britain's other Mediterranean possession, Malta was viewed as little more than a warship defending British interests in the region. During the opening years of the nineteenth century—in an oft-cited quip—the duke of Wellington is said to have remarked, in response to Maltese demands for increased sovereignty and for a clear articulation of the British role in Malta, that "one might as well give a constitution to a man-of-war as give it to Malta."[29] Given the withering impressions of Malta and its residents expressed by British visitors, the Maltese people's contempt for their new overlords is not surprising.

In no area was the hostility between Britain and the Maltese more outspoken than on the topic of language. When the British arrived the language of culture on Malta was Italian. Thus Mikiel Anton Vassalli had written his grammatical manifesto not in the spoken tongue he sought to elevate to a literary language, but in Italian. Italian granted Maltese authors a broader audience (and, of course, there was as yet no substantial tradition of literary composition in Maltese). The British, for strategic reasons—in order to resist the centripetal force that at times threatened to sweep Malta into an Italian republic—opposed Italian cultural influence and Italian literacy in Malta. They promoted early education for the children of Malta in their native tongue. And they sought to underscore—and even, in the opinion of many Maltese, to exaggerate—the similarity between Maltese and Arabic. This, too, served British interests. As Britain's colonial involvements in the Arab and Islamic world grew, they stepped up their efforts to educate colonial subjects as functionaries to support the administration of the Empire. And they viewed fluency in Maltese as a stepping stone to Arabic.

Thus it was that the Maltese language bore the brunt of the contentious debates over sovereignty in Malta between the 1830s and the 1930s. At times, particularly during the early stages of the dispute, the battle took the form of alphabet wars. What alphabet should be used to write a language whose phonological distinctness from Latinate standards observers had noted for centuries? After chatting with a Maltese priest, Gerard Manley Hopkins would write a lovely note in his diary about the phonetic curiosities of the language: "Newspapers are published in it in European 'script': an Oriental character would have been better, because some sounds cannot be expressed in our letters except by a convention. Rather to my humiliation I found great difficulty in hearing the gutturals (*gh*, *kh*, and another there is). . . . It is clear how differently quickened the ear must be to meaning and unmeaning sounds."[30] Arguably, no English poet after Shakespeare possessed Hopkins's fine Anglo-Saxon feel for the physicality of language. His comment confirms (with the elegance and modesty typical of him) what others had said before him: the alphabets of Europe could not do justice to the "meaning sounds" of Maltese. And to this day Maltese orthography continues to reflect the presence of some letters that are no longer pronounced in order to indicate semantic provenance—a convenience that makes it possible, among other things, to look up words in the dictionary under the three-consonant root (as one does with Semitic languages). At the same time Maltese uses sounds that don't exist in Arabic: the consonants *p, v,* and *ch;* the five vowels of the Romance languages rather than the three vowels of Arabic.

An Arabo-Persian alphabet was proposed in 1829.[31] But few participants in the debate would advocate such an extreme philo-Arabic position; it found little support. Most pro-arabicizing observers argued for a modified Latin alphabet that integrated a discrete number of Arabic letters to represent sounds that did not exist in the European languages. Others, finally, resisted the use of any Arabic letters and sought a way to represent the sounds of the languages using only the letters of the Latin alphabet.[32] Thus Francesco Vella argued that the Semitic nature of the language should be recognized. However, he abhorred the hybrid alphabets that blended Arabic and Latin letters, which he termed "hermaphrodite letters."[33] And in 1836 he published a polemical poem in opposition to them, printing the poem in two distinct orthographies: the proposed alphabet blending Arabic and Latin letters and his own modified Latin alphabet. The second and final stanza of the poem runs:

In-Nofs-Gharab xikkel
B'dak xaghrek kollu nari;

Mill-alfabet imfixkel
Ehles it-tfal skular;
Iddew ehles kmieni![34]

[Fetter the half-Arabs
With your hair all aflame;
From the confused alphabet
Free the schoolchildren;
Free them soon!]

Without judging the work on its literary merits—some of its simple charm and polemical power, after all, has evaporated in translation and with time—Vella's poem is useful as an illustration of the passionate tenor of debate over the Maltese language: how it should be written, and indeed *whether* it should be written; whether it should be used as a language of instruction for schoolchildren; whether it should be promoted, beyond its use in early education, as a literary language. During the nineteenth century two government hearings were held on education in Malta and on the use of Maltese as an official language on the island, in 1837–38 and again during the early 1880s. During these meetings a striking dynamic unfolded. The British officials consistently promoted the use of Maltese in early education (and beyond) and asked probing questions about the structure and historical origin of the language, its literary potential, and its significance as a symbol of national identity. Most Maltese patriots (or the most vocal Maltese patriots) opposed the elevation of Maltese and English to official status; they argued fervently that Italian should remain the language of culture in Malta. They saw British advocacy of Maltese as cynical self-interest. They believed that the British promoted Maltese as part of their program to prop up English, thus encouraging Maltese dependence on Britain and marginalizing Italian influence. And the patriots attacked the Maltese language as aberrant and incapable of expressing the sentiments and aspirations of a modern European nation.

The first of the government hearings on language was held in support of the British policy of using Maltese in early education as a bridge to fluency in spoken and written English. In these hearings, British officials underscored the necessity of creating a standardized alphabet and imposing grammatical standards on the language—which they defined as "a corrupt dialect of the Arabic"[35]—while the Maltese intelligentsia continued to argue the historical importance of Italian on the island and resisted the use of Maltese in the classroom and the imposition of English in both the schools and the law courts. Tensions over the language question (and over the terms of the British presence on the island in general) escalated. Finally Patrick Keenan, who had recently reformed the educational system in Britain's other linguistically troublesome island—Ireland—was called in to review the situation. In 1879 the Keenan Report appeared, outlining his assessment of Maltese education and his recommendations for reform.

Though the Keenan Report is remorselessly pragmatic, the thumbnail linguistic history of the Maltese archipelago which introduces the document is written with economy, urgency, and an almost swashbuckling flair. The Greek, Carthaginian, Roman, and Byzantine occupations of the island come and go in the blink of an eye. With the Arab conquest, "the foundation was laid of the Language, to which, with characteristic Saracenic pertinacity, the Maltese still cling." The Normans would conquer the island; the Maltese would adopt Sicilian and then Italian as a language of bureaucracy. But neither Italian administration nor their passionate adherence to Catholic Christianity could dislodge the Semitic tongue they had adopted. "The Maltese had, in fact, become Arabs in language."[36]

The report details the relative strength of Italian and English on the island. It is true that Italian literacy is dominant; more Maltese can speak, read, and write Italian than English. But with patent chauvinism Keenan points out the swift gains that English has made, while Italian literacy over the previous three decades has remained stagnant.[37] Keenan's brief was to design a program to encourage English fluency among the Maltese. He recommends the use of Maltese in early education as a bridge to English. And if the students' "intellects are equal to the acquisition of another language, which I very much doubt, they might, if it be deemed desirable, take up, AS AN EXTRA BRANCH, taught before or after the ordinary school hours, the study of the Italian language."[38] Keenan is eager to demonstrate that Italian literacy, though it is a historical fact on the island, will have little relevance to Malta's future.

Keenan seconded a number of opinions and practices that had become standard in British linguistic policy in Malta. He recommended the use of Maltese in early education as a bridge to English. He recognized that, because Maltese had not been used systematically for education, bureaucracy, or literary composition in the past, it must be augmented in order to function adequately in its new role. And he acknowledged the expert opinion of contemporary linguists who urged the Maltese (like their ancestors, the corsairs) to plunder the nearest relation to their tongue, Arabic: "the most rational process for reforming it and restoring it seems clearly to be to recur to the richer and more regular branch of the same family, and improve the Dictionary by borrowing their words, and the Grammar by following their analogies."[39]

Keenan's enthusiasm for the promotion of Maltese as a language of education provoked a mixed response in Malta. Certain topics were regularly taught in the Maltese language at Maltese schools: midwifery (because the students were women); religion (because the students were Catholic).[40] Some observers and experts felt that Maltese could not and should not be used in the classroom beyond these rudimentary subjects. Thus Sir Adrian Dingli, a prominent Maltese judge, in a letter solicited by Keenan and appended to his report, expressed the opinion that the Maltese language would do little to aid a community "whose intellectual condition is much more likely to be maintained and improved by its remaining at the tail of Europe, than by its placing itself at the head of Africa. Our interest is to have a language which enables us to participate in the progress of civilization in Europe. We have everything to learn from that part of the world, and nothing from the other."[41] The Società per la coltura della lingua maltese, however, advocated the use of Maltese in early education. The brutality of refusing children their native tongue, they argued, was "stupefying" to the intellect; "and the sole object for which this costly sacrifice of no less than the human reason was made, is not even attained by any material progress in the *philological crusade*."[42] While one appreciates the succinct and wholly Anglo-Saxon power of their rhetoric (the letter is appended to the report in English translation), their abject motives for defending the native tongue seem, even at the distance of a century and a half, rather heartbreaking.

The Keenan Report does record a titillated excitement about the Maltese language, but it comes from an unexpected source. In a letter solicited by Keenan, the Maltese collector of customs, F.V. Inglott, recalls a conversation with Nicholas Patrick Cardinal Wiseman. Wiseman taught Hebrew and Syriac at La Sapienza in Rome—the university where Mikiel Anton Vassalli had earlier studied Arabic—before being made archbishop of Westminster in 1850. When briefed on the development of a Latin alphabet for the writing of Maltese and the plan to enrich the language with borrowings from Arabic, Wiseman remarked:

The adoption of the plan . . . to improve the Maltese language, and the use of the Roman or Italian letters to write it, will be equal to giving to Europe the key of Oriental literature. Hitherto, the strange characters of the Arabic alphabet have deterred and dissuaded the studious from applying themselves to master the Arabic and explore the great Oriental literary works; but the method proposed of writing the Arabic by means of the Roman or Italian alphabet (simply modified by very few dots and accents) is *a very ingenious novelty*, which will prove powerfully attractive and highly useful in a literary point of view.[43]

When Thackeray visited Malta in 1844 he reported breathlessly that "[i]n the altar [of St. John's Co-Cathedral in Valletta] are said to lie three of the most gallant relics in the world: the keys of Acre, Rhodes and Jerusalem."[44] Now, in the altar of national identity, the Maltese tongue, an even more valiant relic has been discovered: the *key of Oriental literature.*

The Keenan Report (and the generally worsening relations between the British and their colonial subjects) provoked a series of government debates on the language question between 1880 and 1885. The transcripts of these encounters between Maltese intellectuals and colonial administrators make clear the acutely contentious role that the national language had come to play in understandings of national identity and sovereignty. The most pitched discussions—the most emotional and the most revealing—occur when Fortunato Mizzi (1844–1905), the single most important Maltese figure on the political horizon during the closing decades of the nineteenth century, responds to British statements about the nature and potential of the Maltese language and plans for its development. The macaronic linguistic structure of the published transcripts of these debates starkly reveals the linguistic contingency of public life in Malta during the period. Mizzi speaks in Italian; his British interlocutors reply in English. Maltese would not be spoken in government chambers until 1886, when a brothel keeper and a blacksmith— voted in as ministers by the Maltese public in an "infamous election" engineered by Mizzi to protest the trumpery of representative government under the British—addressed the government in their mother tongue; presumably they knew no other.[45]

But I get ahead of myself. The discussion between Mizzi and the British officials traces the major points of contention argued by opponents of the British policy of elevation of Maltese to the status of national language. In a debate that took place in 1881, Mizzi pointed out that the government advocated the "purification" of Maltese by forcibly removing from it its Italian lexemes and replacing them with Arabic. To the British claim that they were simply restoring the language to its pristine state, Mizzi replied that there is no record of Maltese to demonstrate its historical evolution; "thus to put Arabic words in the place of the Italian words we use is not to purify Maltese, but to create a new language. . . . The scope therefore is ruinous and destructive."[46] Mizzi's linguistic position is certainly defensible. Prevailing opinion held that languages ought to be true to their historic origins; but this was no easy matter in the case of Maltese, which had only the most exiguous of written records. Yet his interlocutors expressed surprise and dismay at the vehemence of his resistance to the promotion of Maltese, and in particular at the delicacy that obliged him to resist bolstering the language by introducing Arabic elements: "If the Arabic is to be introduced and its introduction will improve the Maltese language, why should we not introduce it out of respect to the Maltese language itself?—It strikes me as being far from patriotic to hear Maltese uttering so contemptuous an opinion of their own language. Literary men abroad speak of the Maltese language with the great interest, and say that it contains philological beauties of which we are not aware."[47] The response is certainly disingenuous. (As a pamphleteer wrote in 1880, "Something other than philanthropic sentiment must animate those who in spite of history would have us Saracens."[48]) Yet the legitimacy of most of the sentiments—despite the political weight they carried in the context—cannot be denied. The nineteenth-century patriot was expected to champion the national tongue. Yet here an activist used the rhetoric of patriotism to assault the language of his people, a language whose mysterious "philological beauties" outsiders celebrated, if not Maltese nationalists.

Mizzi would state his contempt for the Maltese language in even more direct terms in a debate held four years later, in 1885. Mizzi was no mean rhetorician; he made his points in fluid and forceful sentences—as when he referred to the Maltese tongue as "this national curse." The director of education responded in astonishment, "Does the honorable gentleman call 'maledizione' our own language?" "I repeat it," Mizzi replied, "and I prove it. The Maltese language is the nation's curse." The language not only isolates Malta from the rest of the world; it stands as a reminder of the Maltese subjection to the Arabs. "And I ask whoever has a Maltese heart whether the Arab domination, from which we have inherited this monument, was a blessing or a curse? And if it was a curse, I say with all emphasis, Maltese is nothing more than the monument of our most unfortunate age, the age of our slavery, which arrested progress in Malta."[49] How far we are from Mikiel Anton Vassalli's gentle affection for his native tongue! Vassalli had seen the language as the *monument* of national identity; for Mizzi, it is rather a monument of the Arab domination which (in Malta, as in certain accounts of Spanish history) explains the nation's developmental delay relative to the rest of Europe.[50]

Mizzi's words, as may be expected, provoked a flurry of comment. The lieutenant governor summarized the chamber's response:

> The honorable member surprised me much by saying that Maltese is the *maledizione del paese*. It is scarcely my duty to controvert it; but I certainly should like to point out that the statement coming from a Maltese is a very extraordinary one, and still more so, coming from a gentleman who is one of the party which he calls the "National Party." If a people have no national language where would be the distinction amongst neighboring nations? . . . The statement as coming from the honorable gentleman rather surprised me; and I should say that, unless I am much mistaken, his statement will be remembered in Malta.[51]

The British governor, though clearly motivated by political concerns, seems on this occasion less cynical than commonsensical. Maltese nationalists wrote pages and pages of invective against the Maltese language during the long years of linguistic debate in the nation, as "romantic philologists" and "improvised archeologists," to quote a particularly scurrilous editorial, debated the fate of the national language.[52] But there is something uniquely horrifying about Mizzi's statements to the 1881 Council of Government; the image of a nationalist intellectual spurning the national tongue with such fiery rhetoric does indeed, as the lieutenant governor foresaw, linger.

During the nineteenth century the prevailing attitude held that Maltese could not and should not serve as a literary language and as the national language of the Maltese. However, the language did acquire a growing base of support, from literary writers in general and poets in particular, from about the mid-nineteenth century on. The revolutionary spirit and national sentiment that swept the continent contributed to nascent interest in Maltese. The political upheavals that culminated in the Italian Risorgimento brought a large number of political exiles to Malta, and these revolutionaries modeled the use of the national tongue as a vehicle for expressing national aspirations (and, by all accounts, had a rowdy good time on the island).[53]

Gabriele Rossetti (Dante Gabriel's and Christina's father), deported from Bourbon Naples in 1821, spent two and a half years in Malta before moving on to England. He participated actively in public and intellectual life on the island (his capacity to extemporize verse was particularly appreciated by the Maltese) and remembered his time there with a guarded affection. He celebrated the Maltese for their "Italian character and Arab tongue." But he had been tormented by Bourbon spies there; at the end Malta seemed to him "a nest of corsairs."[54] Maltese literary historian Joseph Brincat reports that Rossetti was instrumental in awakening an appetite for literature in Malta, particularly for political poetry, both in the European languages and in Maltese.[55] And Walter Scott's visit to the island in 1831 (he came for reasons of health and by all accounts was expected to die in Malta) inspired a number of swashbuckling historical novels in both Italian and Maltese. The capture of Maltese women by Turks supplied a particularly popular theme.[56]

Thus by the end of the nineteenth century, despite the strong opposition to Maltese as a language of culture voiced by influential public figures like Fortunato Mizzi, experimentation with the language as a literary medium had quietly begun. In his 1879 brief on language and education Patrick Keenan reported that one group of Maltese intellectuals—"pretty numerous, and highly influential also—is enthusiastic in the expression of its opinion that not only should the Maltese be cultivated in the Primary schools, but that philological attention should be devoted to the removal of its imperfections, so that it may be elevated from its position as a mere dialect to the dignity of a language."[57] His own political investments, of course, might lead him to exaggerate the enthusiasm for promoting Maltese as a literary vehicle. As evidence to support his optimism, however, the late nineteenth century saw two Maltese translations of that most unlikely of political manifestoes, a text which (for reasons that remain mysterious from this distance) inspired nationalists throughout Europe during the nineteenth century: the Ugolino canto from Dante's *Inferno*.[58]

Of course as was the case with any new literary language, poets and intellectuals must refine the spoken tongue in order to use it as a vehicle of linguistic expression. Thus it happened that the Maltese language internalized the central cultural competition of the Maltese nineteenth century. The hybrid nature of the language and its plasticity—because of the absence of preexisting literary standards—made it into something of a cultural Rorschach blot. During the mid- to late nineteenth century, Maltese intellectuals were of two minds concerning the ideal form of literary Maltese. Some of them—generally speaking, those who argued that Malta was culturally an extension of Italy—believed that Maltese should be recognized as an Italian dialect and exaggerated its Romance content. Their Maltese used a high percentage of Romance cognates and new coinages from the Italian. Others, however, "purified" the Maltese language by arabicizing it. They avoided words with a Romance provenance and chose words with Semitic roots whenever possible. The nineteenth-century debate would continue into the twentieth century. But as a mature literary tradition emerged during the opening decades of the twentieth century the question would be settled by default: literary Maltese would be defined as an aggressively semiticizing koinê that left Romance etymons on the cutting-room floor.

Consider, as an example of the romanticizing position, a statement from a 1922 article by patriot and scholar Giovanni Vella entitled "Religion, Patria, Lingua u Bandiera": "Avvanza o lingua Maltija. Ixhet dauc l'ghajnejn tighec intelligenti lejn l'energica, gharfa u Cattolica Europe u mhux lejn l'ghazziena, ignoranta u Pagana Asia"[59] ("Advance, O Maltese language! Cast those intelligent eyes of yours towards energetic, learned, and Catholic Europe, and not towards indolent, ignorant, and pagan Asia"). The whole of the title and much of the citation is Romance. To translate the first sentence cited into Italian one would simply need to change the ending of the adjective: "Avvanza, o lingua *Maltese*." The author's intention in this passage is to deliver a body blow to those who attempted to emphasize the Semitic content of the language. He urges Maltese writers rather to embrace and to deepen the Romance content of the language. Only by building on the Romance foundations already present in the language, these intellectuals would say, may Maltese become a language capable of serving as national tongue for a modern *European* nation. They would assert that the Semitic lexical pool of the language is incapable of expressing the abstract notions at the heart of modern intellectual life. Indeed in the brief passage cited above the author uses nine Romance nouns or verbs.[60] Other Maltese intellectuals would object that such an extensive injection of Romance words would render the language incomprehensible to the average Maltese. It would produce not a popular tongue that might serve as a banner of national identity, but rather a Frankenstein's monster of a language, stranded between Europe and Africa.

The word that Vella uses for *language* in this passage is an Italian cognate, *lingua*. It is of some interest in the current context to note the word for *language* used by Dun Karm (1871–1961), the most famous Maltese poet of the twentieth century, in a poetic manifesto in celebration of the Maltese language. It is an Arabic cognate, *lsien*.

> Għaliex tarmih il-Lsien li tatek ommok,
> u titlef għaqlek wara Lsien barrani?
> Maltija kienet l-ewwel kelma f'fommok
> u bil-Malti tkellimt tifel daħkani . . .[61]

> [Why do you cast away the tongue your mother gave you,
> and waste your wits upon a foreign tongue?
> Maltese was the first word in your mouth,
> and you spoke in Maltese as a happy child . . . ]

"Love foreign tongues if they are of service to you," the poet instructs the reader in the closing lines, "but don't drive out what is within." Dun Karm models literary Maltese in this poem (and in his poetry in general) by using exclusively Semitic vocabulary. In the four lines of the poem cited (as in the remaining eight lines of the poem) there is not a single Romance cognate.

Carmelo Psaila, a Catholic priest known universally by the affectionate nickname Dun Karm, began his literary life in the first decade of the twentieth century by composing poetry (as did most Maltese with literary ambitions) in Italian.[62] In 1912 a friend—Ġuze Muscat Azzopardi, himself a figure of major importance in twentieth-century Maltese letters—invited him to write a poem in Maltese for a journal he edited. Dun Karm obliged his friend and would write primarily in Maltese for the rest of his life; he became the first poet of international stature to compose poetry in Maltese. His poetry is celebrated for the simplicity and vitality of its imagery and its language. Italian is a trained and experienced poetic medium, a language with a vast and intricate literary history. Writing in Maltese, a language almost virginal with regard to poetic composition, Dun Karm created a poetic voice that felt at once novel, intimate, and weighted with visceral memories.

Dun Karm's conversion to Maltese occurred as the movement known as "Malti Safi"—"Pure Maltese"—gained traction. These linguistic activists held that Maltese was a Semitic language and ought to look like one: they advocated pruning the Romance borrowings from the language and stripping it to its Semitic roots. The movement represented the final phase of the language wars initiated by the British colonial government a century earlier; proponents of Malti Safi tended to advocate a close alliance with

Britain and to resist Italian literacy and political alliance with Italy. But Dun Karm did not align himself with the Malti Safi movement. His poetic diction drew not on the political debates of the age but on a long-standing Maltese literary tradition. Literary Maltese, until very recently (and with the exception of certain genres), has regularly favored Semitic words over Romance. In newspaper reportage and in certain genres modeled closely on European exemplars—in the popular corsair novels of the nineteenth century, for instance—Maltese may use a relatively high percentage of words of Romance derivation.[63] Maltese poets, however, have historically and apparently instinctively gravitated toward the Semitic lexemes in the language, as if these gave their verses greater beauty, gravitas, simplicity, vitality, or simply felt more Maltese.

Consider, for instance, Pietro Caxaro's mysterious "Cantilena," the oldest known remnant of literary Maltese. The poet laments the destruction of his house; the house seems almost certainly a metaphor for something else—like the traces of the vanished Bedouin encampment in the fragment of a *nasib* translated by Hermannus Alemannus (discussed above, Chapter 2)—but the ambiguity of the language makes its significance impossible to pin down. The poem is composed almost entirely of words with Semitic roots, with a single exception.[64] Maltese literary historians have debated whether the Semitic vocabulary of the poem provides an accurate snapshot of the spoken Maltese of the era—that is, whether the language during the fifteenth century was much closer to Arabic than it would be three centuries later, when a more robust written tradition attests to the presence of Romance lexemes—or the author actively chose Semitic words, feeling that they were more appropriate for poetic composition. The question, of course, cannot be finally answered with regard to the fifteenth century. During the modern period, however, it seems evident that the choice of Semitic roots over Romance was motivated by aesthetic considerations.

Maltese provides the literary writer with a remarkably elastic medium, both because of its hybrid nature and its relative youth as a literary language. The language has traversed a "classicizing" period, modernism, and postmodernism in a single swift century. If writers of the first half or two-thirds of the century favored Semitic lexemes, the same is no longer uniformly true. Oliver Friggieri is one of the most important and popular Maltese writers of the present day. This stanza taken from his poem, "Jekk" ("If")—which appears today etched onto the glass of bus shelters throughout Valletta—uses a series of Romance-derived words doled out one per line (*numri, alfabett, teorema, kuncett*), most of them emphasized by end rhyme:

> jekk tgħodd in-numri kollha
> u taf kull alfabett,
> jekk tħott kull teorema
> u zħarma kull kuncett . . .

> [if you count all the numbers
> and recognize all alphabets,
> if you unlock every theorem
> and dismantle every concept . . . ]

Another stanza from the same poem, however, avoids abstract nouns like *number, alphabet, theory,* and *concept,* and uses a more homely, intimate, strictly Semitic vocabulary:

> jekk taf kif kien il-bidu
> u kif se jkun it-tmiem,
> jekk taf kull fuq, kull isfel,
> kull wara, kull quddiem . . .

> [if you are aware how it all began,
> and how the end will be,
> if you know what's up, what's down,
> what's prior, what's posterior . . . ][65]

Ought the poet to emphasize the Arabic lexemes in the language? When I asked Friggieri this question, he replied that he often preferred a Semitic word, but because he had to think about the legibility of what he wrote—because he did not want to interrupt the reading experience by using a word that would send the reader to the dictionary—he would more likely than not select a word with a Romance provenance. Yet a stanza like this demonstrates the gravitational pull that Semitic lexemes hold for the literary writer.

There are indications that the percentage of Romance lexemes used in literary Maltese may be increasing. As the twentieth century progressed, an increasing emphasis on realism in literary language—a desire to forge a literary medium that cleaved to the vernacular as it is spoken—changed the nature of written Maltese. And diglossia and code-switching among native speakers resulted in the domestication of a number of Romance (and global English) lexemes. According to a recent study, only 32.41 percent of modern Maltese vocabulary is derived from Semitic sources; 60.23 percent of its words come from modern European languages, chiefly from Italian.[66] Certainly younger writers embrace the Romance cognates in the language with greater enthusiasm than their elders, if only to represent the technological and political actualities of the world they live in and their allegiance to postmodern, transnational ideals. I asked Immanuel Mifsud, one of the most dynamic and interesting young writers in Malta today, how he chose between Romance and Arabic synonyms. He answered without hesitation that he prefers Romance words. I mentioned that other Maltese had told me that to their ears the Semitic words in the language are more beautiful. Mifsud agreed that the Semitic lexical pool had greater aural variety than the Romance in general or the Italian in particular but maintained his preference for the Romance.

The Romantic belief in the purity of origins and hence the beauty of antiquity encouraged the promotion of the language's Semitic lexical resources for those who forged literary Maltese. For—as Averroes' and Hermannus's *Poetics* reminds us—invention, not nature, produces a literary language. When you study poems that move you, Averroes and Hermannus write, you will find that the poet has used linguistic artifice to transform speech into poetry: some simile or metaphor, some unexpected turn of phrase, some "enigmatic concealment."[67] Thus did Dun Karm craft a pure, semiticized Maltese for his poetry, a literary artifice that distanced his diction from the spoken tongue; he used Romance and Semitic lexemes indiscriminately in his correspondence.[68] But another sensibility guides the poets of the late twentieth and early twenty-first century; and, indeed, it may prove that the genius of the language itself is suffering a sea change. Today, Oliver Friggieri laments the loss of the Arabic inheritance of literary Maltese, saying that the language is losing vocabulary at an alarming rate: "if you look at a page of a dictionary," he told me, "the entries seem like tombstones." The outsider may feel the melancholy of this statement even while sympathizing with the writers of a younger generation, who infuse their literary language with the Italian and global English findings that wash up on Maltese shores. The writers of twenty-first-century Malta must walk a high wire strung between linguistic history (the tombstones of the dictionary), on the one hand, and on the other the contingent and transient lexemes of global English and the Italian broadcasts that Maltese televisions pick up from neighboring Sicily.

I chose to begin my account of the history of the emergence of Maltese as a national language at the historical moment when European visitors first began to talk about the language as a regional curiosity, and throughout I have emphasized outside observers' perspectives on the language. This narrative strategy has naturally had an effect on the story I have told. Like a philologist of days of yore I have performed a taxonomic analysis of the language, separating its substance into two alembics—dividing the Semitic from the Romance—in order to measure and analyze the stuff it is made of.[69] This approach owes much to the classifying genius of nineteenth-century scholars who used an analytic approach to dissect the objects of their study. But the Maltese language possesses (or is possessed by) a very different genius. It does not separate elements, like cartoon scientists with their brightly colored (and invariably combustible) liquids ranged in rows of vessels. Rather it fuses disparate substances into a whole of odd and rare beauty and animates them. Maltese, like Spanglish, is a mash-up generated in a borderland and nourished by the cohabitation of linguistically distinct populations over an extended historical period. European observers who wrote about the language between the sixteenth and twentieth centuries described it as a *rara avis* and occasionally expressed distaste for its compound nature, as the title of a 1943 book—*The Maltese Centaur, or Linguistic Monstrosities of the Island of the Knights*—demonstrates.[70] And yet it is only one of the contact languages generated during the long centuries of commerce between Arabs and Romance-speaking Europeans in the Mediterranean. It, however, unlike other lingue franche of the age, survived to become a written language and a literary medium.

The term *lingua franca* itself is a linguistic alloy produced by the encounter between speakers of Arabic and the Romance vernaculars in the medieval and early modern Mediterranean. It is Italian; hence the plural form *lingue franche*. The adjective *franco* derives from the Latin *Franci*, which referred to the Germanic tribes who lived near the Rhine, and during the Middle Ages was used to refer to the Frankish peoples who had expanded into territory that is now France. In the Italian phrase "lingua franca," however, its semantic range is different. During the late Middle Ages the Arabs used the word *al-ifranj*, from the Latin root and its medieval Romance derivatives, to refer not to the Franks in particular but Western Christians in general. And the *lingua franca* to which that term was first applied—spoken by the European residents of the Levant during the era of the crusades—was not Frankish (a Germanic tongue) or French but an Italianate Romance fused with vocabulary from the other Romance languages as well as Arabic. The term we use to refer in general to languages of convenience adopted in contact zones memorializes the Italian merchants and mercenaries of the late medieval and early modern period and the Arabs with whom they battled and traded.

Unlike the other tales I tell in this book, the story of Maltese is not in fact history. Maltese is a vital language with a young and growing literary tradition, and its short literary history poses a number of compelling questions which cannot yet be answered. My effort to describe the evolution of the language as a competition between Semitic and Romance is not, after all, a radical innovation. Most accounts of the language, whether diachronic or synchronic, use the same narrative structure, characterizing it as what happens when two radically different linguistic systems collide. And most historians and linguists perform the classic philological maneuver when discussing Maltese: they *analyze*, isolating the constituent elements of the language, measuring their prevalence, and studying their effect on each other. There are certainly other ways to tell this story. By choosing to emphasize the Semitic-Romance dialectic I have marginalized the story that is in many ways the most striking and beautiful in Maltese linguistic history: the emergence, particularly in the last fifty years, of a Semitic-Romance linguistic amalgam, a truly hybrid language that links the northern and southern shores of the Mediterranean.

But the story I have chosen to tell—the tendency to dissociate the elements of Maltese and to purify the tongue by purging or reducing one element or the other—represents an important and neglected chapter in the history of philology and of Mediterranean Europe. Therefore it is central to the themes I address in this book. The attempt to create a national tongue by emphasizing the Romance elements in Maltese—even to the point of declaring the language an Italian dialect—was a natural response to the political exigencies of the Maltese nineteenth century. Yet when a successful literary language emerged it took a form very different from what the nationalists might have wished for their national tongue, the wellspring of the national character: not an Italian dialect but rather a colloquial Arabic. In Malta scholars and writers used the philological model of linguistic investigation to isolate the genius of the national language. They compared parallel grammatical and lexical forms and constructed genealogical trees in order to demonstrate the close family ties between Maltese and Maghrebi (and to a lesser extent

Levantine) Arabic. For better or worse, philology can claim responsibility for the conclusion they reached: that Maltese was an Arabic colloquial and should look, act, and sound like one.

I close this brief on the Maltese tongue with the testimony of a minor hero in this philological drama. In 1931, during a constitutional crisis, the Royal Commission met to hear evidence (yet again) on the language question. During the course of the hearings a lawyer by the name of Giuseffe Micallef appeared before the commission. Micallef was not a scholar; he was self-educated Orientalist and did not, as far as I am aware, play a major role in the language debates of the early twentieth century. He had presented a memorandum on the language question to the colonial government and received an invitation to address the Royal Commission in person in order to respond to their questions. His level-headed testimony, his modest and dispassionate witness to the nature, present state, and potential of the language, represent a watershed in public debates on the language question.

In Micallef's statement, for the first time in the government hearings, the British colonialists heard a thorough and accurate philological account of the language. Micallef defined the language as "a dialect of vulgar Arabic with abundant accretions of Romance elements, especially medieval Sicilian, Italian, and some relics of Latin."[71] He explained to the gentlemen of the commission that although written Arabic was a unified tongue its dialects were many, and he classified Maltese as one of these. He explained, with patient clarity, that although previous scholars had attempted to cast Maltese as a form of Phoenician, Hebrew, Italian, and other languages, more recent scholarship had described its relationship to Arabic with accuracy.

Micallef, however, recognized that the language was at an impasse. The transformations of modernity imposed on all the languages of Europe the need to form new vocabulary in order to describe new scientific and bureaucratic technologies and debate new ideas. And Maltese had scant resources to meet that need: "Maltese is now the poorest dialect of the richest language." Micallef used simple vocabulary to explain to his nonspecialist audience the linguistic challenge that faced Maltese:

> In Italy, France or England the pioneers of progress are never at a loss for a word to give expression to a new thing or a new idea. Besides the immense stock at their disposal in their own languages and sister languages, they have two inexhaustible mines, Latin and Greek, whereat to make good their wants. But Maltese does not belong to the Indo-

European stock of language, and any word grafted upon Maltese is absorbed with great difficulty. Arabic might have been the feeder of Maltese as its parent language. But the Maltese, as it were, cut the bridges with the Semitic world seven centuries ago. Loan-words find their way into a language on the vehicle of trade and culture. Besides the barrier of religion there is the culpable negligence of the Maltese Government, which so far have not opened their eyes to the inestimable boon the acquisition of Arabic would mean to Malta.[72]

Micallef told the Royal Commission that the importation of vocabulary from Italian and English would not benefit the language: "that is a source of corruption." Rather he recommended the creation of a chair in Arabic at the University of Malta. This, he believed, would give the Maltese the connection to Arabic as a living language that they needed in order to revitalize the tongue.

Micallef was not a toady of the English government. He explained and defended the position of those who supported the Italian language in Malta with passion (and in impeccable English). However, he was also a writer who wrote in Maltese and who believed that in its most beautiful and most effective form Maltese must imitate its parent language, Arabic. "I must confess that I am a purist," Micallef told the Royal Commission. "I write in Maltese, but when I write in Maltese I try to discard words which are not of Semitic origin."[73] Micallef saw Maltese as an Arabic colloquial. And he saw the learned form of the Arabic language as it was written in the contemporary world as the lifeline of the Maltese language. Only by drawing on the reservoir of *fusha* Arabic would Maltese become a modern language able to communicate with the "pioneers of progress" and debate their innovations.

The language question in Malta ended in 1936, when Maltese was made the official language of the country. Three years later Dun Karm's manifesto in defense of the national tongue, "Għaliex?," appeared in a collection of his verse. In 1964 Malta finally became a sovereign and independent state within the Commonwealth. At the same time, during the 1960s, a new generation of writers prepared to rejuvenate the national tongue as a literary language by moving it closer to the spoken tongue. They did not—as earlier generations of Maltese writers had done—vet their literary Maltese by semiticizing it. The Romance words which they would use in speech appeared in their literary texts; they began to avoid Semitic words heard less frequently in contemporary Maltese and to substitute Romance synonyms.

Maltese has followed a path similar to other European vernaculars on the way to becoming a language of literature. It has negotiated between an ideal form defined by refined literary concepts—historical memory, aural and intellectual beauty—and the pragmatic goal of comprehension to a reading public. The dynamic role that the Arabic language played in the evolution of Maltese is central to the story I am telling in this book. Maltese intellectuals saw Arabic as a touchstone for a modern national language on the European model. They believed that only by using Arabic as a resource would Maltese successfully vitalize itself, acquiring both the beauty and dignity to serve as a medium for literature and the lexical range to participate in the debates at the center of modern life.

The drama of the emergence of Maltese as a literary language, however, poses another question that goes to the heart of the themes of this book, a troubling question that can only be sketched here. Philology played a vital role in defining the nature of the Maltese language. Without the positivism and the scientism of philological method, it seems unlikely that scholars—Maltese or foreigners—would have come to understand the nature of Maltese as thoroughly as they did. The genius of philology (like the genius of nineteenth-century scientific method in general) is first and foremost an *analytic* genius. It breaks apart in order to understand; it dissociates in order to create a schematic of constituent elements and their relation to each other.

Recent models of literary and linguistic history, however, have had resource to more complex narrative techniques for describing what happens to languages and literatures in contact zones. In a study of the lingua franca in the Mediterranean, historian John Wansbrough proposed the electrical circuit as a model for communications between the cultures in motion through the inland sea, "susceptible to variable conductors (resistance), voltage gaps (collapse), and inconsistent amperage (motivation). The model is one in which feedback, both positive and negative, is the norm, and fresh input always liable to adjustment, diminution or oblivion."[74] Which model will produce the most accurate picture of literary history in a landscape that predates the emergence of national languages and national literary traditions? Must we isolate in order to understand? Are our alembics a scholarly necessity? Or do we do violence to the object of our study by separating it from the linguistic tempest in which it was generated? Wansbrough's image of the electrical circuit as a historical model suggests that any analytic technique that conceals the dynamics of contact—that blocks our vision of the sparks that fly when languages meet—will distort the history we seek to describe.

The history of the Maltese language that remains to be written is one that does not use an analytic philological model to describe the encounter between Arabic and Italian in Malta, but rather sees that history as a series of electrical charges. The analytic move is intellectually useful, even at times necessary, for the historian. Yet the scholar must approach every text prepared to be surprised by what happens when cultural live wires come into contact. The Maltese language challenges the scholar to forge a vocabulary to characterize the emergence and evolution of a language characterized by Semitic-Romance linguistic symbiosis, despite the apparent incompatibility of Semitic and Romance linguistic structures and despite ongoing military tensions between Arabic and Romance-speaking peoples in the Mediterranean. The obscure origins of Maltese make it tempting to characterize the language—to carry the Frankenstein metaphor beyond all decency—as a wildfire started by a lightning strike: God's joke on the Mediterranean. As ludicrous as the image seems, it may be as useful as any I have offered in this chapter. For what philological analysis of the language can prepare us for the startling, wholly unanticipated beauty of Maltese in its maturity, and gives us a sense of what to expect from its future?

*Chapter 5*

# The Life and Times of Enrico Cerulli

THE SICILIAN ORIENTALISM of the nineteenth century was a thoroughly insular movement. Only Michele Amari left Sicily to study Arabic in the capital of nineteenth-century Orientalist scholarship, Paris; only Amari traveled to consult the great European collections of Arabic manuscripts; only Amari taught on the Italian peninsula. And he did not create a school. He trained a single student, Celestino Schiaparelli, but Schiaparelli published relatively little and left no successors.

In Italy the evolution of Orientalist studies was affected by three factors in particular. First, although the oldest school of Orientalism in Europe was located in Italy—the Istituto Universitario Orientale, now generally known as L'Orientale, in Naples—academic Orientalism had a slow start there. The program in Arabic started by Amari at the Istituto di Studi Superiori in Florence would not become an important center for Semitic studies; Rome had no school in Orientalist studies until the founding of the Istituto per l'Oriente (or IPO) in 1921. Second, before the creation of the Istituto per l'Oriente, Italian Orientalism—if it found institutional support outside the university—contributed not to the colonial programs of the state but the missionary ambitions of the church. The Istituto Universitario Orientale in Naples was founded by a missionary and provided linguistic training for missionaries. The Vatican, too, played a role in early Italian Orientalism; its library and its connections (and competitions) with Eastern Christians made it a natural patron of Orientalist studies, as evidenced by the career of Pietro Valerga (see Chapter 2). And finally, when a secular school of Orientalist studies was established in Italy during the 1920s, it was indeed linked to a colonial program. But because this happened not during the nineteenth century but during the twentieth, the birth of an Italian Orientalist school coincided with the emergence of Italian fascism. And the colonial ideology of fascism was grafted onto a neoclassicizing vision of the Mediterranean and the role that Italy had played historically and should in future play in the Mediterranean. In the inaugural essay of the first issue of the philological journal *Cultura neolatina,* published in 1941, Giulio Bertoni wrote that "the object of philology is a reality to be conquered": a succinct statement of the extent to which the philological reading might absorb the sentiments and vocabulary of the fascist manifesto during the 1930s and 1940s.[1]

The colonial program with which Italian Orientalism's fate was intertwined had had an ignominious beginning. The attempt to establish an Italian presence in the Horn of Africa (Ethiopia, Eritrea, and Somalia) culminated in the battle of Adwa (Ethiopia) in 1898, in which the Ethiopian army routed the Italians—the only time during the nineteenth century that an indigenous army defeated a European colonizing army. The defeat slowed but did not stop Italy's colonial ambitions, which matured during the opening decades of the new century. With the Italo-Turkish War of 1911–12 the Italians claimed the Ottoman provinces of Cyrenaica and Tripolitana, christening the colony with its ancient Roman name, Libya. And they persevered in the Horn of Africa. Italy had acquired two small protectorates in Somalia in 1889. Under Mussolini the Italian army recovered from the humiliating defeat at Adwa, eventually creating a colonial state in Ethiopia, Somalia, and Eritrea known during the fascist years as Italian East Africa (in Italian, Africa Orientale Italiana or simply AOI). The Istituto per l'Oriente in Rome and the Istituto Universitario Orientale in Naples produced Orientalists whom Mussolini tapped for their expertise in administering Italy's colonies.[2]

Some Orientalists, of course, refused to collaborate with the fascists, the most notable examples being Leone Caetani and Giorgio Levi Della Vida. Caetani (1869–1935) was an aristocrat and adventurer; he traveled extensively in the Maghrib, Egypt, and the Levant. He had a habit of taking on larger-than-life projects, like the *Annali dell'Islam* (1905–26), meant to be a year-by-year history of Islamic civilization from the hegira to the present; so detailed did the digest become that it only reached only the fortieth year of the Islamic era, in ten massive volumes, before Caetani's energy and budget were exhausted. He pioneered critical readings, using the analytic techniques devised by modern philologists and historians, of early Islamic sources. Today conservative Christian websites regularly post English translations of his scholarship questioning the authority of the early historical sources on the life of Muhammad. In 1927 Caetani immigrated to Canada, in part because of his antifascist sentiments and in part because of financial and romantic difficulties. He abandoned his academic pursuits and spent the rest of his life working as a gentleman farmer; he would leave the prodigious projects he had begun in Italy unfinished.[3] And Giorgio Levi Della Vida (1886–1967), a Jewish Islamist who worked on Caetani's *Annali dell'Islam* as a young man, refused to take the oath of loyalty to the fascist regime in 1931. He lost his university position and went into exile, first at the Vatican, then at the University of Pennsylvania. After the war he returned to Rome and taught Semitic studies at the Istituto per l'Oriente. He would represent the major continuity between the prewar and postwar years in the institutional history of Orientalist studies in Rome.[4]

Those Orientalists who continued to work in Italy during the fascist years, of course, took the fascist pledge of loyalty required of all public employees. And Italian Orientalists reported to the government on topics with direct relevance to colonial policy. Yet the relation between Italian Orientalists and the fascist government was complex; Orientalist scholarship most frequently acted as a corrective to abuses of power on the part of the fascist government. The Orientalists typically stated in forceful language the delicate nature of the philological investigation and insisted on the importance of nuance and, in particular, immediate experience of the object of study in order to interpret the data correctly. That is, twentieth-century Italian Orientalism, even scholarship produced in support of the fascist government's colonial interests, did not generally display the tendency to flatten the object of study in order to facilitate domination of the subject that we associate with the Orientalism of colonizing nations. Here, for instance, Michelangelo Guidi (1886–1946) explains to an audience of nonspecialists the duties that faced modern scholars reporting on the Orient:

> to give above all—and this is the most difficult and most subtle task—a sufficiently vivid consciousness, a sense of the life that seethes there, a sympathy, in brief something more than passive contemplation or a cold, though quite exact, assertion. . . . The complexity and delicacy of the material renders difficult the task of hitting on the right expression and neglecting nothing in such brief summaries; but we do well to heed the words of the Apostle, "aporiamur, sed non destituimur," *we are perplexed, but not discouraged:* we are above all animated by the desire for

an ever richer accord between science and action, between speculation and life.[5]

Guidi's statement—which appears in a pamphlet published by the Istituto Nazionale di Cultura Fascista in 1937—warns against the kind of slipshod argumentation that characterizes polemics-cum-scholarship. Such moments of clarity do little to mitigate the brutalities of fascism or, for that matter, colonialism. Yet they do signal a consciousness of the cost of distortion of the facts on the part of a scholar whose career coincided with both.[6]

Carlo Alfonso Nallino (1872–1938) contributed even more directly to the fascist colonial program. And he is the outstanding example of the paradox of early twentieth-century Italian Orientalism: his scholarship is exemplary for its precision and balance and for his consistent efforts to resist the colonial officials' tendency to brutalize the colonized or to impose Italian culture upon colonized regions. When Prince Fu'ad of Egypt (later King Fu'ad) decided to create a new Egyptian university on the European model, at which the Arabic language and Arab literary and intellectual history would be studied using the philological method imported from Europe, he invited Nallino— then teaching at al-Azhar—to serve as one of his first lecturers. Fu'ad was an Italophile; he also hired Ignazio Guidi (Michelangelo's father) and David Santillana to lecture at Cairo University. The Egyptian novelist Taha Husayn was a student at the university during its earliest days. He reports the wonder that he—an Azharite, accustomed to the rote instruction typical of that university—felt at studying with Italian professors who spoke extemporaneously rather than reading from a book and who taught history as a rational science. His first lesson with Ignazio Guidi was a revelation: "When the third day's lesson came, my ardor was keener and sharper than ever. It was to be by an Italian professor, and in Arabic—an Italian talking to Egyptians in their own language, learnedly, about a theme of which I and my Azharite contemporaries had never even heard till that very day. . . . 'The Literature of Geography and History' it ran. . . . What was this word 'literature,' 'belles lettres'? and what had it to do with geography and history?"[7] The Azharites (Husayn would recall elsewhere) doubted that a foreigner could teach them anything about Arabic literature. But Nallino's erudition banished their skepticism. "It was Nallino who taught them how Arabic literature was born, how it developed, what the relations between literature and politics, literature and the intellectual environment had been, from the earliest centuries. And at

Nallino's lectures a whole new vision of Arab civilization appeared to the young men, truly a revelation of something new."[8]

Nallino started teaching at Cairo University in 1909. With the start of the 1911–12 Italo-Turkish War (in which the Italians claimed a colony in Libya), Fu'ad's support of the Italians teaching in Cairo became impossibly awkward. Nallino was the last of the Italian professors to leave, in 1913. He lived briefly in Tripoli, Libya, where he helped to establish a translation office, and by 1914 was teaching at the University of Rome. In 1921 Nallino founded the Istituto per l'Oriente in Rome.[9] The first issue of the IPO journal, *Oriente moderno*, appeared under his editorship in the same year. The journal furnished a reference for European scholars of the Arab and Islamic world; it included a pragmatic and eminently useful digest of current events throughout the Muslim world, from Morocco to the Indian subcontinent. The opening statement from the editorial staff delineated the scientific standards that the journal's editors intended to uphold:

> While the Orient, after the World War, is opening itself to new forms of life, and while creating numerous and solid cultural and economic ties with the Orient would be of great advantage to Italy, our public for the most part knows nothing of the past and present affairs of the Oriental populations. The Italian periodical press gives nothing but scarce notices on the topic; and these are often vitiated by two disturbing elements: first, the repetition of inveterate errors concerning some of the most common and fundamental institutions of those populations (let it suffice to mention the question of the Caliphate); secondly, the fact that reports are too often second or third hand, and therefore they reflect foreign points of view interested in manipulating events and their significance.[10]

Even scholars critical of European Orientalists' engagement in their nations' colonial programs tend to admire Nallino for his professionalism and his resistance to the thoughtless brutalities of the colonial regime—his (tragically fruitless) efforts to warn the colonial office away from the "politics of oppression, which would be in profound opposition to both the principles of the liberal Italian tradition and the current understanding of humanity generated by the errors of the war."[11] When Nallino died in 1938, Giorgio Levi Della Vida—in exile because he would not pledge his loyalty to fascist principles—wrote a glowingly respectful memorial for *Oriente moderno*. Because he was persona non grata in fascist Italy, Levi Della Vida was asked to publish it under a pseudonym. He refused; finally, with the support of the new editor of *Oriente moderno*, Ettore Rossi, it appeared with his signature.[12] In his memorial essay Levi Della Vida recalls a statement now regularly cited to illustrate Nallino's rigor and professionalism: "Non voglio lasciarmi tentare a uscire dallo studio esclusivo degli Arabi; ma, degli Arabi, voglio saper *tutto*" ("I do not want to allow myself to be tempted away from the exclusive study of the Arabs; but about the Arabs, I want to know *everything*").[13]

Of course, Italian Orientalists were not entirely innocent of the negative qualities associated with European Orientalism. Though he did not descend to the blanket statements of condemnation that we find in some scholars of earlier generations—he was, after all, no Renan—Francesco Gabrieli's scholarship is bracketed by an attitude of indifference and even contempt toward the culture he studied. Gabrieli (1904–96) was born to Orientalism. As Michelangelo Guidi was son of one of the founding fathers of Italian Orientalism (Ignazio Guidi [1844–1935], who lectured at Cairo University and taught Leone Caetani in Rome), so too Francesco Gabrieli was the son of an Orientalist: Giuseppe Gabrieli (1872–1942), who studied Arabic at the institute in Florence founded by Michele Amari, wrote important studies on the Arabic language and worked as a librarian at the Accademia dei Lincei in Rome.

Francesco Gabrieli studied with Nallino at the IPO. Unlike Nallino, however, he lived through the period of institutional self-examination and recrimination that followed the collapse of Italian fascism. And he would engage in one of the first scholarly polemics over the motives and legitimacy of European Orientalism following the war. In 1963 Anouar 'Abdel-Malek published a withering critique of Orientalism, anticipating many of Edward Said's arguments against Orientalist scholarship, in the journal *Diogenes:* "Orientalism in Crisis." Gabrieli responded to the attack on his métier in a 1965 issue of *Diogenes*. In this essay Gabrieli acknowledges the charges of irrelevance that have been leveled against the profession: "The Orientalist was, and still is in some of the less up-to-date sectors of European *communis opinio*, a scholar who chooses as the object of his research one of the most remote fields of knowledge, far removed in space or time, or both, barred from access by incomprehensible languages and writings, whose religions, philosophies and literatures are quite apart from the main stream of classical and Western tradition." He recognizes the implication of Orientalism in the ignominious history of European colonialism: "Colonialism has risen, it has celebrated its misdeeds and its splendors (and not only misdeeds, friends from the East, with or without your permission). It is dead and buried as,

everything considered, it deserved to die." And he points out unapologetically the Eurocentrism of "Orientalism." Without the methods of the Western Orientalist—without *philology*—there would be no study of the Orient,
whether by Arabs or Europeans: "Our friends from the East should therefore
not come to ask us to start studying their past and present in the light of a
modern Eastern historiography, philosophy, aesthetics and economics, inasmuch as these are today nonexistent."[14]

There is much to make the scholar uncomfortable in Gabrieli's statements (although in his defense I should point out that 'Abdel-Malek pulled
no punches in the *Diogenes* article to which he responds). His apparent willingness to admit the faint import of the object of his study is lamentable;
but this is a moral failing to which many humanists, not only Orientalists,
occasionally fall victim. More worrisome is his inability to offer a positive
defense of the encounter between the Western scholar and the Orient he
studies. The philologist's suspicion that Gabrieli had scant affection for the
traditions to which he devoted his professional life seems to be confirmed by
the pages from his diary that were privately published following his death.
Here Gabrieli sings the praises of Italian literature and of the Greek and
Roman literature which—though it too was produced in a god-haunted
age—still seems to him less oppressively clerical than Islamic letters. Nowhere
do we find a hint of appreciation of the Arabic literary tradition. And following Saddam Hussein's 1991 invasion of Kuwait he writes: "I find myself
tempted to repeat for them the 'odi genus universum' ['I hate the whole race']
of Petrarch, with more reason than him. Incapable of adapting to modern
civilization."[15] The philologist's unease is not reduced by Gabrieli's ability to
quote, apparently from memory, the Latin of Petrarch's notorious condemnation of the Arabs.

Though his attitude toward the Arabs whose culture provided his living
may raise doubts (and eyebrows), however, Gabrieli unambiguously, vehemently, and consistently condemned the fascist regime that rose and fell as
he filled the pages of his diary. The man whose life and career I will discuss
in this chapter, Enrico Cerulli (1898–1988), did not critique fascism. Unlike
most Italian Orientalists of his generation—unlike *all* Orientalists whose
work was (and remains) widely read and cited—Cerulli actively supported
the actions and ideals of the fascist regime. Furthermore he contributed to
one of the most objectionable arenas of fascist activity: the brutally inept
colonial administration of Ethiopia. Cerulli's colonial career made him an
object of nearly universal contempt in Ethiopia; I know of no apologists who

have attempted to redeem his reputation as an administrator. However, Cerulli was also a widely respected Orientalist scholar. Though he was a professional diplomat, not an academic, he wrote essential volumes on the languages, literary traditions, and history of the Horn of Africa. He also wrote on the Arabic and (because he, like most Italian Orientalists of his generation, received a classical education as well as training in the languages specific to his research) the Romance and Latin traditions of the medieval Mediterranean. No historian that I am aware of has used his colonial record to challenge the probity of his indispensable scholarship.

Cerulli's scholarship on Ethiopia does not (as one might expect, given his colonial record) reduce the object of his scientific inquiry to a two-dimensional, inert abstraction. Whether he discusses historical events or texts or the contemporary world, his reportage is dynamic and alive to nuance. This paradox—suggestive though it is—will not be my first concern in this chapter, however. Rather I am interested in Cerulli's reconstruction of the medieval Mediterranean as a theater for communications between Muslims and Christians, and in particular his description of the vivid and generative connections between medieval Italy and the Muslim culture of the medieval Mediterranean. Although Cerulli liked to refer to himself as a "*zôon politikòn*," a "political creature,"[16] by all accounts his attempts at political administration in Ethiopia were an unqualified disaster. But in his historical scholarship Cerulli hinted at what he hoped the Italian colonial project would achieve in Ethiopia. And his notion of Italy's colonial program initiated in a startlingly (and somewhat poignantly) sophisticated reading of Italy as logical successor to the Arabs, whose domination of the Mediterranean he saw as the origins of a Mediterranean modernity.

Cerulli was born in Naples in 1898 and began his academic career at the oldest school of Orientalist studies in Europe: the Istituto Universitario Orientale, now known as L'Orientale, in Naples. The university—before the founding of the IPO in Rome in 1921, the most important center of Orientalist studies in Italy—got its start in 1724 when missionary Matteo Ripa returned from a voyage to China with four young Chinese Christians. In 1732 Pope Clement XII sanctioned the university to train missionaries for service in the East. Over time the school added languages to its curriculum, including in the mid-eighteenth century the languages of the Ottoman Empire. The Istituto Universitario Orientale continued to tutor missionaries until a reform following the unification of Italy, in 1888, when the institution was secularized.[17] At the Istituto Cerulli studied Semitic languages with Nallino and Levi Della Vida, and he embarked upon the study of the spoken and literary languages of Ethiopia with Francesco Gallina, Italy's foremost scholar of Ethiopian letters.[18]

Ethiopian scholarship in Italy had a long pedigree and was closely linked with the Vatican's interest in the Ethiopian church, one of the oldest Christian communities in the world. The earliest works published in Italy in and about Amharic, the chief language of Ethiopian Christians, date to the sixteenth century. They were sponsored by the Propaganda Office and were aimed at bringing the Ethiopian church into line with normative Catholic practice. Cerulli's interest in Ethiopian languages and culture, however, was more worldly. In his first publications Cerulli already demonstrated his engagement with Italy's colonial project. And he argued a liberal perspective on the administration of the colonies, consistent with his education in the cultures of the regions colonized. In 1917, at the age of nineteen, he addressed the Convegno Nazionale Coloniale on the topic of Libyan attitudes toward the caliphate. Italy had invaded Libya in 1911 but could not extend its armies beyond the coastal region. In the 1917 Arcoma agreement, Libyan Sanusi leader Idris I secured autonomy and support for an inland kingdom based in Cyrenaica. Cerulli's report explicated the relation between Idris and the other Muslim authority who worried European leaders at the time, the Ottoman caliph. And Cerulli (like Nallino, who himself wrote a brief on the caliphate published in 1917) argued passionately for liberality of rule and recognition of the cultural autonomy of the Libyans. Cerulli exhorted policy makers to "leave our subjects in the most complete religious liberty . . . The respect for the Muslim religion that Italy has practiced in her dominions from the beginning of her colonial activity is an Italian question and a question of Italian colonial politics."[19] And in a relation delivered two years later to the Convegno Nazionale Coloniale, Cerulli envisioned Italy's potential relation with Ethiopia—its other African interest, but not yet a colonial possession—as one of collaboration and mutual benefit. Italy would gift to the Ethiopians the industry and science of modern Europe. "And Ethiopia, remaining the only independent indigenous African state, can be proud of having allowed Europeans to understand better her long and glorious history, facilitating the study of those documents that with just pride she guards jealously and that are the most handsome evidence of her millennial civilization. Thus the reciprocal benefit of collaboration also in the field of culture."[20]

Cerulli completed his studies with breathtaking rapidity. At the age of twenty-one, in 1919, he was in the Horn of Africa, serving as an officer with the Italian army in Somalia. At the close of World War I Italy sought to expand its presence in East Africa, and a concession of land from British Kenya in 1924 allowed the Italians to extend their colonial reach into southern Somalia (Jubaland). Because of his linguistic skills Cerulli was touched for service in Somalia. He remained in Africa until 1932, working first for the Ministero delle Colonie and then for the Ministero degli Affari Esteri in positions (as his resume might put it) of increasing responsibility.

During these years, in addition to his bureaucratic responsibilities, Cerulli would join two Italian parties exploring the largely unknown interior of the region. In 1927–28 he traveled from Shoa (a central province of Ethiopia, where Addis Ababa is located) to the border of the Sudan. His published report on this voyage conveys the sense of urgency and the thrill of discovery that drove him toward the frontier:

> If the voyager today wishes to see, he has to *know how to see*. . . . Because walking on paths never before traversed by anyone is a noble thing; but to be able to show to others what a human community has made of its life signifies being able to make another appreciate the political actuality of that people, and thus the probability of its future evolution. . . . He will see that the famous era of the great voyages, which one generally considers to be over, will never end so long as there still remain experiences "of human vices and valor" amongst the peoples of the earth; and that very much remains still to be seen and said concerning lands considered "exhausted" by the ordinary voyager: "exhausted" only because in some region a pair of wobbling train tracks has replaced, during the dry season, the zigzag paths of the caravans.[21]

An Italian reader would recognize the citation from Dante's *Inferno*— "experiences 'of human vices and valor'" ("esperienze 'dei vizi umani e del valore'")—embedded in Cerulli's account of his adventures. Cerulli lifted these words from Ulysses' description of his final voyage (*Inferno* XXVI, 98– 99). Dante defined the border between the known world and the unknowable as moral—the limit that God imposed on human knowledge—but implicitly acknowledged the heroism of Ulysses' hubristic voyage beyond it. And Europeans had long used Dante's Ulysses to symbolize the European voyages of exploration beyond the frontiers of the world known to Dante. Thus the frontispiece of Francis Bacon's *Novum Organum* (1620) showed a ship sailing through the Strait of Gibraltar (as Ulysses' crew so fatally did) with the motto *Multi pertransibunt & augebitur scientia* ("many shall pass through and knowledge will increase"). Cerulli's prose elegantly conveys his passion for exploring terrain untraversed by Europeans before him (and after the age of exploration had been declared dead!) and, not less important, his satisfaction that his studies have prepared him to be an articulate witness to the fantastic scenes that he would be the first European to describe. Nallino praised the quality of Cerulli's reportage in his publication of the voyage, saying that his "level of preparation, in all matters that regard the indigenous world, [is] immensely superior to all the other Italian explorers in Africa."[22]

The next year, in 1928–29, Cerulli joined a party of Italian explorers who journeyed from the Wabi Shebelle river valley in Ethiopia to the border of Italian Somalia. Luigi Amedeo di Savoia (1873–1933), duke of the Abruzzi, led the expedition. Because of his linguistic expertise Cerulli was chosen to serve as the front man in negotiations with local populations. Largely (one suspects) because of the duke's involvement in the mission, the party's voyage was immortalized in a sumptuous volume complete with photographs of the Italian explorers—in white pith helmets and khaki trousers, with wide smiles—against backdrops of native flora, exotic animals, and Ethiopian porters. The pseudo-Victorian photographs and the poetic evocations of the mysterious savagery of the land they traverse grant the book a strangely melancholy feel. It seems a work of science fiction in reverse: the explorers have been thrust not into an imagined future, but into a pocket where the past—the age of Richard Burton and David Livingstone—lives on.

> Often, in the evening, we passed some time listening with the head-phones to broadcasts of distant concerts on the radio. The European music, interrupted now and then by the cries of the hyenas and jackals that were always to be found just outside the camps, made us think yet again of the power of the human genius. . . .
> We found ourselves in the presence of a natural spectacle not to be forgotten for all our lives: nature as it must have been on this earth before the coming of man, the result of an unrestricted liberty of life and of growth, wild and strong, yet still pervaded by serenity, by a quiet so great and solemn that it gave the spectator almost the sensation of profaning with his presence something pure and sacred.[23]

Cerulli began his career as a gentleman colonial, a man of profound linguistic and cultural knowledge, and an anachronistic explorer long after the heroic era of European exploration had ended—his life and career proof that "the famous era of the great voyages, which one generally considers to be over, will never end so long as there still remain experiences 'of human vices and valor' amongst the peoples of the earth."

Cerulli knocked around Ethiopia until 1932, when he returned to Italy and was named head of the political office for East Africa and then general director for political affairs at the Ministero delle Colonie. In 1935, Italy— flouting the peace-keeping efforts of the League of Nations—invaded Ethiopia. Readers of English were kept abreast of events in Ethiopia (or Abyssinia, as it was then known to the general public) by the reportage of Evelyn Waugh, who had left England in search of adventure and landed in Addis Ababa. After the Italian invasion Waugh filed a story in the London *Evening Standard* under the title "We Can Applaud Italy." In his account he defended Italian aggression:

> Now Abyssinia is a barbarous country. By this I do not mean that it is simple. It is not merely a country where the inhabitants choose to live without cinemas and patent medicines and safety razors and motor-bicycles; nor even where they prefer to retain their natural wealth unexploited. I mean that it is capriciously and violently governed and that its own governmental machinery is not sufficient to cope with its own lawless elements. It is entertaining to find a country where the noblemen feast on raw beef, but less amusing when they enslave and castrate the villagers of neighboring countries. . . . Sentimentalists in Europe like to imagine a medieval, independent race living according to their own immemorial customs, just as they like to find villages where the people still dance round maypoles in their national costume, but the reality in Africa is more formidable.

"Sentimentalists in Europe," of course, also liked to imagine that the League of Nations might resolve international disputes more effectively than wars. Nonetheless Waugh's account provides a window onto a sympathetic contemporary perception of the Italian invasion of Ethiopia. (And, in other articles, Waugh presents an Orientalizing, outsider's portrait of the country that Cerulli knew with intimate, unromantic precision: "The crowds in the streets are practically all armed with obsolete rifles; they chat and bow and kiss one another. Occasionally a woman of high rank passes on a mule under a dome-shaped straw sunshade. She is voluminously draped and her face completely bandaged up in white shawls, leaving only dark apertures for her eyes."[24]) In a book-length account of his travels in Abyssinia published in 1936, Waugh would celebrate the first achievements of the Italian colonials. He describes the sight of Italians working in the field like common laborers: "To the other imperial races it was slightly shocking. . . . The idea of conquering a country in order to work there, of treating an empire as a place to which things must be brought, to be fertilized and cultivated and embellished instead of as a place from which things could be taken, to be denuded and depopulated; to labor like a slave instead of sprawling idle like a master—was something wholly outside their range of thought. It is the principle of the Italian occupation."[25] Waugh, of course, could not imagine the critiques of colonization that would emerge following the war. He represents the uncritical attitude of his age: European colonialism would bring civilization to Africa. Contemporary European critics of Italy's invasion resented not the fact of colonization but the worrisome display of fascist Italy's military power. The colonization of Ethiopia, Waugh acknowledged, "will be the supreme trial of Mussolini's regime."[26]

In the atmosphere of international protest following Italy's invasion of Ethiopia, Cerulli served as a diplomatic liaison to the meetings held in Europe to resolve the Ethiopian question. But while Cerulli defended Italian actions before European courts, the situation in Ethiopia was rapidly unraveling. Early in 1937 the Ethiopian resistance seriously wounded Rodolfo Graziani, the viceroy of Italian East Africa, in an assassination attempt. Graziani remained in office, but there was considerable unrest in the colony; he was a cruel and unloved ruler, and the colonial office in Italy recognized the necessity to replace him.[27] Before the end of the year Mussolini appointed Amedeo di Savoia (1898–1942), duke of Aosta and nephew of the Luigi Amedeo who had led the expedition from Shoa to Somalia, as the new viceroy of Italian East Africa. Cerulli received an appointment to the office of vice governor general.

Mussolini and his colonial minister, Attilio Teruzzi, supported Cerulli's appointment and insisted that he remain in office because of his party loyalty and his expertise in local languages and customs.[28] But Cerulli's years in office were, by most official accounts, a catastrophe. Some defended him, particularly for his profound knowledge of and sensitivity to local cultures. Thus Tadesse Tamrat, in a memorial article largely critical of the Italian colonial government in general and of Cerulli in particular, made efforts to acknowledge the respect and affection he earned in certain circles: "At the

ordinary personal level . . . we still have very fond memories of Cerulli among
a number of senior people in Ethiopia for ameliorating difficult prison conditions, his declared respect towards Ethiopian culture and tradition and for
his admirable fluency in Ethiopian languages with Amharic, Oromiñña and
Wolaitiñña cited in particular."[29] But most reports on the Ethiopian colonial
administration stress Cerulli's incompetence as an administrator and in particular the disastrous effects of the ongoing tensions between Amedeo di
Savoia and Cerulli. Cerulli seems to have perceived Amedeo as little more
than a figurehead. He aimed to take the administration of the colony into
his own hands and communicated directly with the Colonial Office in Rome
rather than with Amedeo, his superior.[30] Rome's attention was distracted by
the war, which Italy would officially enter in June 1940. And Amedeo, called
away frequently to Rome on official business, found it impossible to keep
Cerulli in line. Finally, exasperated with Cerulli's interference, Amedeo removed him from office. Cerulli returned to Rome in February 1940. He had
no political appointment for the remainder of the war years; he worked in
the Vatican archives on a series of scholarly projects.[31]

   During his years in Ethiopia Cerulli had published widely in academic
journals, primarily on the modern and contemporary cultures of the Horn of
Africa. Between 1926 and 1933 he produced a fascinating occasional digest of
contemporary Ethiopian literature for the journal started by Nallino, *Oriente
moderno*. These reviews outline Cerulli's conception of the ideal, beneficent
interaction between colonial government and colonized state (as his first relations to the Convegno Nazionale Coloniale had done). And they model the
crucial role played by the colonial official who is also an intellectual with a
thorough grounding in indigenous culture (as his contributions to the reports
on his voyages of exploration had done). The range of books he selects for
review in *Oriente moderno* is eclectic, suggesting the breadth both of Ethiopian literary production and of Cerulli's intellectual interests. Many are religious works; others are nationalist hymns to a new, modern Ethiopia or to
modern agricultural practice; one aims to prepare Ethiopians who visit Europe for unanticipated surprises: the traveler will find that public restrooms
are segregated by gender, the author informs his readers, and so one must do
the proper research before entering. Cerulli attributes the emergence of this
vibrant range of new literary works in the languages of Ethiopia, and their
particular attention to the troubles and challenges of Ethiopian nationhood,
to the effects of European influence and "la civiltà moderna" that Europeans
have brought with them to Ethiopia.[32] And he celebrates the influence of

European civilization on nascent Ethiopian identity: "Typically, European culture is represented [in the works he reviews] as the best means to resist the impudence of foreigners."[33] Like Nallino in Cairo teaching "a whole new vision of Arab civilization" to the young Azharites, Cerulli used the instruments of European literary science to articulate Ethiopian culture. In his eyewitness reports on the birth of a modern Ethiopia, European civilization functions not merely as hermeneutic tool or even a modernizing force; it is the means by which an Ethiopian people can become more themselves.

In another of his notes from the cultural front lines, he reports that the development of Ethiopian literature has been so swift and dramatic that the old dictionaries won't serve any longer.[34] Here Cerulli erodes the difference between the colonial official and the Orientalist. In order to understand and administer the life of the colony, the official must live in-country, know the language intimately, and participate in contemporary intellectual life. In a 1941 article on Islam in Africa written for a volume of essays on the contemporary Islamic world, Cerulli argued again that the colonial administrator must combine the expertise of Orientalist and bureaucrat in order to bring optimum benefit to the population of the colony. After sketching the history of interactions between Muslim and Christian communities in the Horn of Africa, he concludes:

> What I have written should prove the complexity and the delicacy of these problems, and not only for historical understanding but also for the action of the Government which is securely grounded only in an effective knowledge of the populations: knowledge in which Italy—who has given great, often the greatest names to European Orientalism, can claim a solid and secure tradition. This tradition, which our young men continue and will continue, is a guarantee of the lofty work of civilization that will be taken up once again by the new Empire after the certain victory of our military.[35]

Most of Cerulli's publications before his dismissal from public office in Ethiopia dealt, like these works, with contemporary Ethiopian and Somalian literary and political culture. He published, in particular, on folk and popular culture in the Horn of Africa, on legal institutions and aspects of contemporary culture of interest to colonial administration, and on the languages of the region. All his publications, with the exception of the monographs on the voyages of exploration, were brief, article-length works. However, following his dismissal from office, working at the Vatican library, he completed a series of monographs that stand in stark relief to this earlier scholarship for their historical distance from the present, meticulous detail, authority, intellectual passion, and sheer length. During the 1940s Cerulli produced three of the most vital and synthetic Orientalist studies of the twentieth century: *Etiopi in Palestina: Storia della comunità etiopica di Gerusalemme* (*Ethiopians in Palestine: History of the Ethiopian Community of Jerusalem*); *Il libro etiopico dei miracoli di Maria e le sue fonti nelle letterature del medio evo latino* (*The Ethiopian Book of the Miracles of Mary and Its Sources in the Literatures of the Latin Middle Ages*); and *Il 'Libro della Scala' e la questione delle fonti arabospagnole della* Divina Commedia (*The 'Book of the Ladder' and the Question of the Hispano-Arabic Sources of the* Divine Comedy).

The release from public office certainly gave him more time to devote to his studies; at the same time the difficulty of working in wartime Rome created extraordinary hurdles for the scholar. Cerulli referred to the challenges that faced him in the introduction to one of the monographs of the 1940s: "I could not have completed a work of this sort, *hic et nunc*, without the friendly and kind collaboration that I have found on every side." And indeed the help he received seems to have been extraordinary. He acknowledged the general director of the libraries and academies of the National Ministry of Education, the German Historical Institute, the Swiss legation in Rome, and the director of the Staats-Bibliothek of Berlin, which— "surmounting many difficulties—has sent me photographs of a codex now placed in a shelter."[36]

Yet in these far from ideal conditions, Cerulli completed three monographs of striking breadth and historical texture. In 1943 he published the two Ethiopian volumes. And following the end of the war, in 1949, he published the work for which he is most widely remembered by medievalists today, his study on Dante and Islam. In this monumental and meticulously researched work (discussed above, in Chapter 2) Cerulli presented editions of the Latin and Old French translations of the Arabic *kitab al-mi'raj*, the story of the Prophet Muhammad's ascension to the next world. And he produced a detailed argument in support of his thesis that Islamic depictions of the Prophet's visit to the next world functioned a bit like the grain of sand that produced a magnificent pearl—the *Divine Comedy*. Today scholars celebrate it as philological research of the first water and as a decisive intervention in a thorny historical question. It also wins sentimental honors as the work of a heroic scholar who slogged away in the Vatican archives through the most difficult years of the war. The other two books are no less remarkable in their erudition and breadth. *Il libro etiopico dei miracoli di Maria* traces the progress of a collection of legendary tales about the miracles of Mary from twelfth-century France into Iceland, Hungary, Italy, and Spain, across the Mediterranean into the Arab Christian communities of Syria, Palestine, and Egypt, and finally into Ethiopia. Like the book on Dante and Islam, the work includes editions of medieval texts in a number of languages.[37] And in *Etiopi in Palestina* he writes the history of a vital premodern expatriate community whose existence previous historians had all but overlooked. The three monographs individually are dazzling works of scholarship; taken together, Cerulli's accomplishment during the 1940s is breathtaking.

Despite the variety of the scholarship of the 1940s the works have a common theme.

> The history of relations between Europe and Ethiopia during the Middle Ages can reveal itself to scholars in a new and complex light as long as it is considered not as an isolated phenomenon, but rather as part of the whole of that grand phenomenon of communications between Orient and Occident which was such a large part of the religious, political, and cultural life of the Middle Ages . . . The Ethiopian community of Jerusalem served as an intermediary for centuries (we can document it at least starting with the thirteenth century) between Europe and Ethiopia.[38]

> Beyond these literary historical considerations, we look to yet another problem: that of the relations and thus of the reciprocal cultural influences between Western Europe and the Near East during the Middle Ages. . . . This is a concrete and incontestable proof of the role played by the Latin Orient of the Crusades: it brought into contact not only Europe and the Muslim world, but also Western Christendom and the Christian East.[39]

> And this [that is, cultural exchange between Muslims and Christians] can give a new value to the verses of the Poet [Dante] concerning the "sacred poem on which heaven and earth have laid their hand"; a sacred poem, therefore a solidly Catholic synthesis of poetry, where also (it is beautiful to think) there is an echo of the history of the glorious races of the Occident and the Orient, which for centuries and centuries transmitted to one another—in their diversity and community, in consensus and

dissent—all along the Mediterranean Sea the light of art and of civilization.[40]

A year after the publication of his book on Dante he would give a talk at the
Centre d'Études de Politique Étrangère in Paris in which he would underscore the thematic thread that runs through the three monographs of the
1940s, the crucial importance of the connections between Islamic and Christian civilization. And he would connect that cultural encounter to the inception of *European* civilization: "The function of the Arabs and of Arab culture
in the Mediterranean basin, in the various domains that we have examined,
was such that one can characterize it as a factor in our own cultural history.
We carry within ourselves, inasmuch as we are Europeans, the heritage of
Arab culture."[41]

In his scholarship of the 1940s, Cerulli traces a culture of synthesis that
fused Arab-Islamic and Latin-Christian cultures into a single, indivisible
Mediterranean civilization during a watershed moment in the Middle Ages.
He describes the Arab culture of the medieval Mediterranean as a quasi-
mystical force—the leavening, the bolt of lightning that quickened the som-
nolent Christian civilization of the era. Much like the European civilization
brought to the peoples of the African continent by the colonizing nations of
his own era, the Arab civilization of the medieval Mediterranean served as
the means by which the Christian communities of that time and place might
become more themselves. At the same time, Cerulli recognizes the cultural
particularities of the lands that bordered the Mediterranean and the regional
manipulations of imported material when it crossed cultural boundaries. He
does not reduce the complexity of the medieval terrain; he does not deny the
territorial competitions between Muslims and Christians, Christians' willingness to misrepresent Islamic thought for polemical purposes, or the ideological tensions between the Eastern and Western churches. Yet he affirms the
contacts between the diverse cultures of the medieval Mediterranean as the
decisive element in the alchemical transformation of the primitive Christian
culture of the Middle Ages into the triumphant European civilization of
modernity. Thus he describes both the Spaniards' conquest of Arab Iberia
(their "defense of Christian Europe"[42]) and their reception of the cultural
achievements of the Arabs of al-Andalus as *heroic*.

In his philological tours de force on cultural exchange in the medieval
Mediterranean, Cerulli achieves a task of surpassing intellectual difficulty.
He reproduces in opulent detail the particularities of Mediterranean textual

cultures; the monographs include extensive citations from medieval texts in Latin, Arabic, and Amharic, in addition to a staggering array of medieval European vernaculars. And he traces the fusion of those isolate cultures through the exchange and manipulation of common texts and ideas. Thus these three studies—Babelian agglomerations of texts, extravagant in their accumulation of languages yet precise in their synthesis of a mountain of analytic detail—succeed in representing the paradox of the Mediterranean. Cerulli shows the enduring power that ideas possess when they are traded far outside the boundaries of the cultures that produced them, "in a manner that adapted them to the tastes of those [new] environments, while still conserving the firm inspiration of their origins."[43]

Cerulli's move to the past at a peculiarly troublesome moment may suggest a straightforward, somewhat heavy-handed interpretation. It seems evident that the events of the late 1930s compelled him to invest a distant history with a message uniquely relevant to the present. In the three monographs of the 1940s he described the Middle Ages as a time when mediation between a Europe unified by Latinity and its others was possible. Ideas pass effortlessly from the vibrant, plurilingual cities of the Mediterranean to the farthest shores of Britain and Iceland. In a new environment they take on a dynamic new significance. But they never quite shed their cultural specificity, a historical memory of their Arab origin. Certainly the cultural communications between Arabs and Europeans that we read about in the three studies seem utopian in comparison to the brutalities of the First World War and of the Italian colonial experience in East Africa, not to mention the horrors unfolding around him as he wrote in Rome during the 1940s.

But this rather pat interpretation—the medieval Mediterranean as a tonic against the discontents of modernity—does not do justice to Cerulli's complex professional investments as a scholar and as a colonial functionary. The best place to begin a more comprehensive account of the impact his intellectual formation had on his bureaucratic career is the startling assessment of Italy's colonial experiment that he wrote for a special 1959 issue of the journal *Ulisse*. The issue, entitled "Il tramonto del colonialismo" ("The Decline of Colonialism"), reconsidered the legacy of European colonialism; Cerulli contributed the introductory article to the collection. This essay ("La fine del colonialismo") is an extraordinary backward look at his career as a colonial official—as harrowing, it seems, as the one that turned Lot's wife into a pillar of salt. In it, Cerulli refuses to apologize for colonialism. Rather he describes the colonial project as an inevitable developmental stage in the *civilizational* project. "At the beginning of 'colonialism,'" he writes, "take it as a good thing or a bad thing, is Europe."[44] And he asserts that the generative force that produced European civilization itself induced that civilization to expand beyond its borders. The logic of European civilization engendered colonialism as an inevitable product of its "forza di irradiazione."[45]

In an extremely slippery passage, Cerulli suggests that the failure of European colonialism signals the failure of modernity. He argues that European civilization produced systems of "concrete economic and political power" which found their natural expression in the "domination and subjection" of other peoples. And he asserts that we should understand this statement not as an ideological concession nor as cold Realpolitik, but rather as intellectual optimism. It signifies that the colonial movement would have outgrown the necessity for domination and subjection and transformed itself into a medium for the expansion of civilization and of culture. This dream, Cerulli writes, ended when Europe sought to destroy itself twice in the course of fifty years. Now it is no longer a dominant power, and thus no longer capable of conceiving a colonial enterprise. Because Cerulli sees colonialism as nothing more or less than the fruition of the *European* experiment, he must understand the end of colonialism as the sign of a much broader failure. He glances back to 1789, suggesting that the emergence of the colonial system represented the logical transformation of the ideals of the Enlightenment into political policy. And he is too meticulous to exclude the inevitable corollary of this argument: the collapse of the colonial project reflects the downfall of Europe as the laboratory of modernity and of Europeans as the missionaries of modernity.[46]

Cerulli's memorial for colonialism anticipates the bitter tone of Gabrieli's response to 'Abdel-Malek's attack on Orientalism (see note 14 to this chapter): "Colonialism has risen, it has celebrated its misdeeds and its splendors (and not only misdeeds, friends from the East, with or without your permission). It is dead and buried as, everything considered, it deserved to die." But Cerulli tempers his disdain with a genuine lifelong passion for the contemporary culture of the Ethiopians, with personal experience of the verities of colonialism, and most importantly with an intimate understanding of the bureaucratic articulation of the colonial project. Certainly he, like many of his colleagues in the colonial office, saw the role of Italian colonization in light of Italy's historical role in the Mediterranean. In her discussion of Italian colonialism, Bruna Soravia points out that Italian colonial officers represented Italy's colonial program in the context of the history of ancient Rome and understood Italy to be the legitimate civilizing state in the Mediterranean, "the natural center of gravity of the Mediterranean world, whose civilizing action is able to encourage cultural currents and modernizing and nationalizing politics."[47] What Cerulli added to this formulation was his unique capacity to correct the distortion of Mediterranean history that occurred during the Renaissance. He did not leap the Middle Ages to insist on the affiliation between Italian modernity and the classical era; his Italy spreading her wings over the Mediterranean was not the Roman eagle. Rather, the passages from the monographs of the 1940s cited above suggest that he saw the Italian colonial program as a logical extension of the *Arab* movement through the Mediterranean during the Middle Ages, which had superseded the Roman domination of antiquity. Because the Arab Mediterranean was historically closer to the present, because the Arabs were recipients of a monotheistic revelation, because the Arabs had brought the seeds of modern scientific inquiry to the shores of Europe, the historian must recognize them as the fathers of modernity in the Mediterranean. Cerulli saw modern Europeans not as Romans reawakened, but as cousins and heirs of the Arabs.

The tension between the two components of Cerulli's career—the expansive liberalism of the Orientalist, the hauteur and brutality of the colonial functionary—exemplifies, in a magnified form, the fundamental contradictions and anxieties that haunted the careers of twentieth-century Western Orientalists. Is the Orientalist no more than a toady of the government? Does the cold logic of our grammatical paradigms and literary genealogies betray the anguish of those living through the reality of hot wars on the ground? From one perspective Cerulli's career challenges standard critiques of Orientalism, asserting the sophistication and (at the most charged emotional level) the utopianism of philological research. In retrospect his great monographs of the 1940s maintain their scholarly importance not only for their analytic sophistication but also for the synthetic spirit that infuses them, an idealism astounding for the time and place in which they were produced. Cerulli argued that Europe was beneficiary to a powerful pan-Mediterranean culture which it had inherited from the Arabs. He was sensitive to both the cultural specificity—the imprint of particular languages and religious cultures—and the commonalities of the ideas and texts that passed between cultures. He was (to borrow F. Scott Fitzgerald's definition of the first-rate intelligence, as it was borrowed by María Rosa Menocal to describe the brilliance of medieval al-Andalus[48]) able to hold two ideas in his mind at once. He saw the genius of the medieval Arabs and the genius of the medieval Italians as two distinct qualities, and he saw how they joined to form something new.

Viewed from another angle, however, Cerulli's career affirms the notion that the Orientalist is no more than the sinister doppelganger of the bright intellectual heroes—the poetic philosophers and philosophical poets—of the Enlightenment. His character had a tragic flaw, an antinomy that he could not reconcile as he did the knot of the medieval Mediterranean. He was not able to resolve the discontinuities between the logic of colonialism and the logic of his scholarship as an Orientalist philologist. To a great extent his failings as a colonial bureaucrat were the failings of colonialism; he was a brutal administrator because colonial rule is brutal. But the difficulty of his bureaucratic career may be taken as a confirmation of the validity of the attacks on Orientalist scholarship launched in the wake of World War II. Other philologists served in colonial regimes, but I know of none who advanced as far as Cerulli did in both careers. Could the philologist not redeem the colonial official? What good does our scientific understanding of foreign cultures do us if we derive no moral benefit from it?

For—despite the occasional positive assessment of his interactions with Ethiopians and Somalians—there seems no question that Cerulli made objectionable use of his intimate familiarity with the languages and cultures of Ethiopia and Somalia while in office. After the end of the war, the Ethiopian government lodged charges against a number of high-ranking officials in the colonial government. The list of ten Italian "suspects for complicity in systematic terrorism" presented by Ethiopia to the United Nations War Crimes Tribunal in 1948 included Cerulli's name. Italy's record in Ethiopia was as scandalous as any other European colonial power's; among other things the colonial administration was accused of the massacre of six thousand Ethiopian men in Addis Ababa, using mustard gas on civilian populations and livestock, and bombing Red Cross installations.[49] And the evidence suggests that Cerulli, despite his understanding of and respect for local cultural traditions, did not distance himself from fascist policies and actions. He played ethnic parties against each other in an effort to destabilize Ethiopian resistance to Italian rule.[50] A letter in his Polizia Politica file shows him trying to hire the notorious fascist thug Ermanno Menapace to silence Ethiopian dissidents banished to Rome.[51] One British adviser described him in a memo as a "poisonous character."[52] The War Crimes Tribunal dropped his name from their list of suspects on grounds that later proved false. Thus he was never officially accused of war crimes, but his name was never truly cleared either.[53]

There is, certainly, no need to dwell on his war crimes or criticisms of his character in order to understand Cerulli's contribution to twentieth-century Orientalist thought; nor is there any point in denying his culpability in a sentimental effort to protect him from the criticism his political career earned. However, one aspect of his colleagues' critique of Cerulli is relevant to his dual career as bureaucrat and scholar. Those who knew him in office described him—as Attilio Teruzzi wrote to Mussolini—as a "cultured but theoretical man": "though an expert linguist," wrote British Acting Consul Hugh Stonehewer-Bird in a memo, "he is not an administrator."[54] Cerulli's hybrid professional identity posed a challenge for his colleagues. They did, of course, list other (more valid) reasons for questioning his professional capabilities, chief among them his ongoing competition with Amedeo di Savoia; what interests me here, however, is his contemporaries' perception of the incompatibility of his intellectual and administrative careers. Cerulli, an intellectual, could not be truly a bureaucrat. At the same time, as a man of action he could not be wholly a philologist. After retiring from diplomatic service he was elected to the Accademia dei Lincei; he wrote a vast number of scholarly works during the last three decades of his life. The lengthy memorials published following his death in the academic press typically mention his diplomatic career only en passant. They do not regard it as relevant to his intellectual life.

Cerulli had the extraordinary misfortune to be born to a world that no longer recognized the logic of a career like his. From his journeys of exploration to the philological research of astonishing breadth and depth that he completed throughout his life—though in this study I have celebrated almost exclusively his pages on Dante and Islam, he is still widely cited as an authority on the languages and history of Ethiopia—Cerulli looks like a consummate hero of the nineteenth century, not the twentieth. He certainly suffers from the inevitable comparisons between him and the man whom he battled for control of Italian East Africa at the end of his colonial career. Amedeo di Savoia was born to heroism on the twentieth-century model. An aristocrat, heir to the title of duke of Aosta, he alone among the Italian high officers was loved by Ethiopians and Italians alike. A colonial colleague called him *simpaticissimo*; the Ethiopians declared him to be *in gamba*, savvy and capable.[55] Italy entered the war in 1940—after Amedeo dismissed Cerulli from office—and Amedeo was made commander of the Italian forces in East Africa. Under his command the Italians invaded British Somaliland; when Britain began a counterattack late in 1940 the Italian position eroded quickly. Amedeo surrendered to the British in May 1941 and was interned in a prison camp in Nairobi. Less than a year later, in March 1942, he died in prison, apparently of tuberculosis.

A Futurist pamphlet celebrating Amedeo's martyrdom appeared in Rome two months after his death: "Ad Amedeo Savoia Aosta omaggio di aeropoesie guerriere" ("Homage of warrior aeropoems for Amedeo Savoia Aosta"). The poems in the pamphlet honor—in the mystico-martial mock-Christian style that is the hallmark of late Futurism—Amedeo's adventurous life and valiant death, describing him as a hero who died in support of Italy's battle to regain control of the Mediterranean:

Là sul soglio marmoreo
nella selva di cannoni al sole
mitragliere
bandiere
il fragore delle onde Mediterranee
finalmente libere
la Vittoria attende
aleggiare sul capo coronato
austero
maestosa l'Aquila di Roma[56]

[There upon the marble throne
in the forest of cannons in the sun
machinegunner
flags
the din of the Mediterranean waves
finally free
Victory waits
to hover above the crowned austere
head
the majestic Eagle of Rome]

Amedeo, with his combination of aristocratic blood and martial vigor, possessed the qualities required for heroism in early twentieth-century Italy. No Futurists wrote paeans for Cerulli. But he too—although he certainly was guilty of war crimes; although he certainly seems to have been a prickly character—was a man with qualities. Cerulli's professional life was grounded in the conviction that neither erudition nor field experience were in isolation sufficient foundation for intimate knowledge of a culture not one's own. He argued in his monograph on his travels in eastern Ethiopia that his studies at the Istituto Universitario Orientale provided a necessary prerequisite for direct experience of the untraveled backcountry he explored. In the same way he advocated field experience to support the knowledge gained from study. In an article written after the death of his mentor in the colonial office in Ethiopia, Giuliano Cora, Cerulli recalled words of advice he had received from another senior official, who—interrupting Cerulli at study at the legation in Addis Ababa—said, " 'What's this? Have you nothing to do today, that you stay in the office writing postcards?' And he wanted to teach us that the 'profession' consists in having contacts with the maximum number of environments and persons and not in writing up accounts more or less brilliant and yet more or less false and falsifying, if they were the fruit of personal excogitation and not of verified realities." Cerulli recalled this encounter as an "unforgettable work lesson."[57]

Cerulli seems never to have lost his instinct for viewing his scholarly work in intimate association with existential verities. But he would not have immediate, personal contact with Ethiopia during the second half of his career; his war record made it impossible for him to return. He organized an International Conference of Ethiopian Studies, hosting one in Rome in 1959 and a second in 1972; but when the conference was held in Addis Ababa in 1966 he could not attend. When in his postwar reflection on colonialism Cerulli abjures Realpolitik as a foundation for his colonial ideology, the historian who knows the contours of his colonial career may be allowed her skepticism. Yet in the pages of the three extraordinary monographs of the 1940s we find a construction of a Mediterranean past that achieves the ideal Cerulli seems to imagine for the Mediterranean of the present. The "optimism" that he evokes in "La fine del colonialismo"—the optimism that informs his defense of European colonialism—is difficult to imagine in the context of the brutalities of the Italian occupation of Ethiopia. But at the safe distance of six centuries, as we look back at a text passed in cabotage along the Mediterranean shores, acquiring accretions of meaning each time it makes port—though this intellectual transfer was most certainly accompanied by military and economic conquest and the suffering that causes—we are more likely to think it a marvelous, beautiful, and hopeful thing.

Cerulli was, in fact, both an intellectual and a man of action; it was part of the tragedy of his life (and, more pointedly, the tragedy of those whose lives he governed) that his proper sphere of action was the Mediterranean of the distant past. In 1972, after he retired from diplomatic service, Cerulli wrote a second book on Islamic influences on Dante, one that—like the first book—collected a dizzying number of references to the miʿraj tradition, the legend of the Prophet's ascent to heaven, in medieval and early modern European letters. I quote at some length the concluding passage of that book in order to demonstrate Cerulli's capacity to knit the consummately Italian Dante into the fiber of his multilingual, multiconfessional, transhistorical Mediterranean:

> We have presented in these two volumes a wide range of data from which hypotheses might take flight; and I hope to be able to say of my efforts, in the words of the *Paradiso*:
>
> > Think, reader, if what here has begun
> > did not proceed, how you would have
> > anguished greed to know more. (*Par.* v, 109–11)
>
> Still we cannot but hope that the extensive reports of the diffusion of the Book of the Ladder in space and time render less absurd the notion that Dante, directly or indirectly, might have had knowledge of it.
>
> But what interests us more generally is the great historical phenomenon of intellectual exchanges between the Islamic world and Europe and the renewal of Western thought that resulted from that contact, leaving a profound mark on human civilization in that milieu of cultural unity among the Mediterranean nations that has been, every time that it was realized, the mother of human progress.[58]

When Cerulli speaks of the "milieu of cultural unity among the Mediterranean nations that has been, *every time that it was realized,* the mother of human progress," the historian must wonder how many periods of Mediterranean unity Cerulli is counting. Certainly Roman antiquity, undoubtedly the Arab Middle Ages; and his apology for colonialism suggests that he considered the first four decades of the twentieth century to be an era of Mediterranean cultural unity manqué.

Cerulli was, more than any other figure discussed in this book, a Saidian

Orientalist. Regardless of what he did with his knowledge of indigenous culture before and after his term as vice governor general of Italian East Africa, he used it to deleterious ends while in office. Yet—unlike the scholars whose philological studies Said critiqued in *Orientalism*—Cerulli's colonial investments did not distort his accounts of the language, culture, or history of Ethiopia or Somalia nor (as far as one can tell from this distance) of the medieval Mediterranean. It is small comfort to the dominated, certainly, but nonetheless historically accurate, to say that Cerulli strove for and largely achieved accuracy in his philological scholarship and that he represented the culture of the Ethiopians and Somalians with respect and dignity. One might still argue that Cerulli had no right to use European science to scrutinize a non-European culture. To that challenge Cerulli would undoubtedly reply—with Francesco Gabrieli—that "our friends from the East should not come to ask us to start studying their past and present in the light of a modern Eastern historiography, philosophy, aesthetics and economics, inasmuch as these are today nonexistent" (see note 14 to this chapter). The cynicism of such a statement may make us blanch; but a logic identical to Gabrieli's also informs such capable critiques of Eurocentrism as Dipesh Chakrabarty's. Chakrabarty unapologetically mobilizes the "unavoidable—and in a sense indispensable—universal and secular vision of the human" that global intellectuals have acquired from the European Enlightenment in order to read a non-European history.[59] This is not to say that Cerulli is blameless, of course, but simply that the philologist may not be convicted for the crimes of the colonialist.

Yet it would be mistaken (and somewhat dreary) to conclude that our intellectual careers have nothing to do with our political investments or the actualities of our lives. Cerulli, like Miguel Asín Palacios (whom I discussed above in Chapter 2), Michele Amari (who was discussed in Chapter 3) and Emilio García Gómez (whom I will discuss in the next chapter), completed heroic philological studies under extraordinary duress. Miguel Asín Palacios wrote his lengthy study on Dante and Islam in Spain during the 1910s. Emilio García Gómez drafted essays that read like manifestoes on medieval Arabic poetry in Spain during the 1940s. And Michele Amari is arguably the only philologist who might inspire an action figure. In March 1849 he wrote a letter from Palermo (where the fires of 1848 still burned) to the editor of his *Storia dei musulmani di Sicilia*, from whom he had received an advance against publication of the manuscript, explaining why the manuscript had not yet arrived. The letter is a monument in the history of authors' correspondence with their editors. You ask me to report on the manuscript's progress, Amari writes. "I reply to you that the rough draft already completed of the major part of the history and the unedited materials in Arabic that I have collected will guarantee the money you have advanced me, *only* in the event that I should fail to fulfill my obligations—that is, if a Neapolitan, Austrian, or Russian bullet should send me to the other world. I have told you frankly that I will do nothing to avoid this bullet." The manuscript, he tells his editor, is in Palermo. He gives instructions that will help him to find it in the event of Amari's demise—unless, of course, a fire destroys it, "not difficult in a city which one day or the next might find itself under a rain of bombs." Amari would retrieve the manuscript before his departure from Sicily in the following month. The ship that he boarded for his flight from Palermo in April 1849 had the ill luck to be shipwrecked. In July, Amari would write to his editor from Paris that he emerged from the catastrophe with the manuscript under his arm—"the only thing I bothered to save"—and that he was now at work on it once again.[60]

The biographies of heroic scholars like Amari, when we find them, may blind the historian to the weaknesses of the scholarship. Emily Apter's recent rereading of the life and work of Erich Auerbach, who undertook to rewrite the history of European literature while exiled from Nazi Germany to Istanbul, should be prescribed as an immensely useful corrective to this tendency.[61] Auerbach's *Mimesis*—the result of his Istanbul experiment—is undeniably a masterpiece of nuance and a hauntingly beautiful work of scholarship. Apter, however, reminds us not to overlook Leo Spitzer, also an exile from the Nazis and Auerbach's senior colleague in Istanbul. According to his postscript to *Mimesis*, regularly read as a hermeneutic key to understanding his project in that book, Auerbach wrote about the "great books" because he had no library. In Babylonian exile he recreated, in loving detail, the grand sweep of the European literary tradition. His isolation and solitude grant the period in Istanbul an atmosphere of melancholy splendor, a bit like Petrarch's majestic withdrawal from the world in his *Secretum*. Spitzer, however, did have a library and a community in Istanbul: he learned Turkish. In Istanbul, Spitzer—like Auerbach a Romance philologist by training—*worlded* the received narrative of European literary history that asserts the Indo-European genealogy of European letters (and denies the relevance of any other traditions to that family history). Spitzer's congeniality and openness model a philological third path, an omnivorous *love of the word* that short-circuits the agonistic narrative that generates philological heroes.

Although the philologist may feel profound respect and even the urgency of affection for Cerulli's scholarship, no one could mistake him for a hero. Contingencies shaped the options open to him and the choices he made (as in the case of any human life). Had he been born a century earlier his life would have followed a very different, possibly even more heroic, path. His turn to philology, however, has an air of inevitability. Scholars may be drawn to philology during periods of national crisis (or philologists may draw larger audiences during national crises) because philology allows the historian to describe where *we* have come from: it is the scientific methodology of choice used to account for the origins and evolution of human communities. Because of its emphasis on the constitution of meaning, it focuses on language—or perhaps I should state it the other way: because it focuses on language, it illuminates the constitution of meaning. In either case, because of its linguistic emphasis, it compels the scholar to talk about *constellations* of meaning: the communities that use language to define their identity and their difference from others; in nineteenth-century parlance, the nation. For fundamentalist philologists, the philological inquiry transcended the contingent particularities of the spoken languages and the modern nations to create communities united by the equally intimate ties of doctrine and belief.

In the hands of some philologists (Renan is, deservedly, the standard whipping boy here), philological method was used to deride difference: to denigrate *them* for their difference from *us*. This brand of philology fragmented the Mediterranean into constituencies and Orientalized the Arab Mediterranean, flouting historical and geographical accuracy in the process. Cerulli, despite his bureaucratic brutality, represents another and (somewhat paradoxically and somewhat ironically) more optimistic branch of philology. For all his failings, he was no Nazi. He did not generate racialist theories, nor use those in wide circulation at the time, and deploy them to assert the superiority of Italian civilization. Instead he used philology to represent another truth about Mediterranean history, one with a more impressive claim to historical accuracy. He affirmed the investment of the cultures of the Mediterranean in each other's fates and the significance of historical encounters across the Mediterranean to the history of human civilization. The scholar may challenge the agonistic narrative that generates heroic national epics by "turning Turk," as Spitzer did in Istanbul—adding Turkish to his bouquet of languages, although contemporary literary historical narratives insisted that the Turkish language was exterior to his discipline, Romance philology. Or he may "Turk" literary history, revealing the investedness of the Mediterranean nations in each other's histories. This was Cerulli's great achievement: to investigate and describe, in opulent philological detail, the synthesis and radical complexity at the origin of what we speak of as "European" modernity.

*Chapter 6*

# Amalgams: Emilio García Gómez (s. xx), Alvarus (s. ix), and Philology after the Nation

> **amalgam**. Forms: malgam, amalgame, (amalagma), amalgama, amalgam. . . . Usually taken as a perversion of L. *malagma* (in Pliny and the physicians) a mollifying poultice or plaster, a. Gr. μάλαγμα an emollient, f. μάλασσ-ειν (stem μάλαϰ-) to soften; or of an Arabic adaptation of μάλαγμα with prefixed *al-* (as in *al-chemy*, *al-embic*, etc.): see the form (of the vb.) *almalgamynge* in one MS. of Chaucer, and *algamala* in Du Cange. . . . Other early writers associated it with Gr. ἅμα together, and γάμος marriage. Devic (Littré *Suppl.*) suggests a direct Arabic derivation, taking an early variant *algame* as ad. Arab. *al-jam'a* (orig. *al-gam'a*) union, conjunction, f. *jama'a* to unite, and conjecturing for *amalgame 'amal al-jam'a* 'the operation of conjunction,' or *al-mojām'a* marriage union. But no instance of the use of these, as chemical terms, is cited from Arabic writers.
> —*The Oxford English Dictionary* s.v. *amalgam*

CAN THE PHILOLOGICAL reading challenge the narratives of national history generated by traditional historicism? Once a philological analysis questions the place allocated to a text within a narrative of literary history, does it thereby compromise the structure of scientism upon which philology depends, the pedigree that guarantees the historical accuracy of the philological reading? Narratives of national origin lend the awesome weight of their authority to the philological readings that (in a neat quid pro quo) contributed to the construction of those narratives, those nations, and those origins. Thus the reading of the *Chanson de Roland* as the origin of the French literary tradition, to cite an eminent example, has become self-sustaining. Though scholars have chipped away at it—by pointing out, for instance, the extent to which Joseph Bédier's readings of the text were informed by anti-German sentiment; the work's indebtedness to a Spanish epic tradition; or its radical contingency, its response to a host of immediate contemporary factors—still the position of the *Roland* as progenitor of a literature (and, by extension, the birth certificate of a language and monument to a national identity) has proved resilient.[1]

The conundrum troubles even the literary histories of France or Great Britain, for instance, cohabited during the Middle Ages by Germanic and Romance literary traditions. The intricacies of the literary history of Mediterranean Europe, however, put it (speaking metaphorically, of course) off the map. As distinct as Germanic literary history may be, it has common ground with French. The two traditions share—to speak not metaphorically but, by philological standards, *literally*—a genealogy. And because philological analysis is powered by genealogical structures, comparative studies of the French and German literary traditions look motivated—both are Indo-European languages; both were spoken during the Middle Ages by primarily Christian peoples; both would become the national languages of European nations—in a way that comparative studies of Semitic and Romance literary traditions do not. The Mediterranean demands a much more ambitious system of classification. Indeed, it is difficult to imagine what a comparative pan-Mediterranean philology would look like. It seems that no one short of God could create the taxonomy capacious enough to encompass and compare a Semitic and Islamic system on the one hand and an Indo-European and Christian system on the other.

The difficulty of using phylogenetic philological taxonomies to describe a Semitic-Romance hybridity accounts in large part for the failures of the scholarship I have described in this book, philological readings that located the emergence of a recognizable modern national identity in the Arab Middle Ages. The accounts of Sicily's Arab past and Enrico Cerulli's scholarship on Dante and Islam used scientific methods of textual analysis to reveal a truth about the past that corrected a received narrative. Modernity was not alien to Sicilian soil, it need not be imported from Paris; the Sicilians themselves had exported the modern sciences and technologies to the continent. Dante was the beneficiary of a pan-Mediterranean theological science that originated in the Islamic reading of Aristotle and saw reason and revelation in a continuum with each other.

These readings, however—startling and lovely as they are—have failed in two distinct but related ways. They have not dislodged normative narratives of the origins of national identity or of European modernity. And they do not uniformly uphold philological standards of textual analysis. The Sicilian historians and Enrico Cerulli, by and large, accept the presuppositions of the philological reconstruction of history; they use a scientific reading of the textual record to modify received narratives of national origin. At moments, though, a logical lacuna or a poetic liberty disrupts the hierarchical paradigms of philological method. When Salvatore Cusa allows the mysterious word *debbiare* to derive from both Arabic and Latin, for instance—when he cites a dual etymology for the word, without attempting to give historical precedence to one or the other—he generates not a hermeneutic narrative of cause and effect but a lexical still life that evades historicism (see Chapter 3, note 58). The debates over the nature of the Maltese language reveal more starkly some of the limitations of philological method. While the scholars used the scales and measures of modern linguistic science to define the language and attempted to shape its future, literary Maltese forged its own path, first modeling itself closely on Arabic and then veering precipitately toward a Semitic-Romance hybridity.

Of course, one could turn this moralizing account of intellectual history on its head and propose that what I have identified as scholarly failure—the unmotivated conclusion; the intuitive leap—represents rather innovation intended to compensate for the shortcomings of the instrument of scholarly analysis. Philology—of ancient pedigree, indubitably, but reconstituted under the banner of nineteenth-century scientism—possesses a fundamentally analytic genius. It separates in order to understand. No strategy of textual criticism is better suited to parse the structures of an individual text or to categorize variant versions in a given manuscript tradition. However, it may stumble when used to study texts constituted by hybridity. The genealogies of philology—the stemmata, the paradigms, the textual and linguistic hierarchies—seem at times almost sublime in their scope and analytic power. But when multiple parentage generates a hybrid text, when disparate elements are amalgamated and engender something rich and strange, can analytic paradigms plumb their mysteries?

Spanish philology in particular has proposed intriguing and at times even scandalous answers to this question. Spanish historians have, of course, used philological method to recount the history of Hispano-Arabic literature. At the same time they have gone to great imaginative lengths to circumvent categorical analysis in order to produce a portrait of a nation Arab in its youth and Spanish in its maturity. Thus the startling trope with which José Antonio Conde introduced his 1820–21 history of Islamic Spain: "The readers who happen to pick up this book should imagine that it was written by an Arab author" (see Chapter 2, note 49). Conde turned Turk in order to represent accurately the radical complexity of Spain's medieval history. He wrote a manifesto of lyric nationalism in which it is difficult to tell which is the mask and which the author's true face. Is he a Spaniard masquerading as an Arab? Yet he encourages modern Spaniards to celebrate medieval Arabs' accomplishments as their own!

Emilio García Gómez achieved an even more striking and more beautiful sleight of hand in his memoir recalling his residence in Granada between 1930 and 1935. The book—entitled *Silla del Moro* (*The Moor's Chair*), after a hillside overlooking the Alhambra—is a work of poetic synthesis, drawing together characters, elements, and episodes from García's public, professional, and personal life. Because he was the leading Spanish Orientalist of his generation, his reflections on the Arab past of Granada are particularly rich. The book looks back from the confusion of the immediate postwar years (it was published in 1948) at a period even more chaotic for Spain ("turbulent years—but which have not been, for our generation?"[2]), an era for García gilded by the passage of years and ennobled by the shadow of the Alhambra.

In *Silla del Moro*, García depicts the city of Granada as a palimpsest; he scrapes away the layers to reveal not only the Moorish ghosts that still linger in the city streets but also the traces of subsequent visitors to the city. Thus he pauses to admire a memoir of Granada written by Washington Irving (who served as U.S. ambassador to Spain in 1842–45), *Tales of the Alhambra*. García celebrates the musicality of Irving's Alhambra and his *Alhambra*—of the place when Irving knew it and of the literary texture of Irving's description of it: "Where the Arab *guzla* does not sound, someone strums an Andalusian guitar. Fandangos and boleros are heard. There is scarcely a page where we do not hear the echo of the lovely songs of Spain: the verses of bandits and smugglers, bullfighters' ditties, songs of love and war, delightful histories of Moors. . . . Wondrous Andalucía of the Romantics!"[3] García's Alhambra is an Aeolian harp responding to the emotions and the anxieties of the years leading up to the Spanish Civil War; and it echoes with the voices of poets (modern Spaniards and medieval Arabs), Romantics (not only Washington Irving but also Chateaubriand), the gypsies and the Bourbon court who inhabited the Alhambra (not, of course, at the same time). García's Alhambra is a curious construction. *Silla del Moro* is not an unphilological or antiphilological work. It is not dehistoricized but rather hyperhistoricized, saturated with precise historical reference.

In another passage García transforms this symphonic portrait into a fugue, when he uses the Alhambra to evoke the genius of medieval Islamic civilization and contrast it to the essential character of Greek antiquity. "Each word is a world," he writes. "Now I will be so bold as to invite you to follow me into the little world of the 'arabesque.'"⁴ For García the *arabesque* evokes at once a lexical world and a very physical universe exemplified (it will surprise no one) in the Alhambra: a forest of arabesques, an architectural masterpiece that could be conceived and executed only by a civilization that sees God as mathematician and the created universe as an exquisite equation. The Greeks, García writes, loved geometric forms that were closed and self-contained. The Arabs, however, loved the combinatory: forms that could be linked in endless repetition and infinite variety. How foreign the Arab genius is to the spirit of Europe! García is sure that his European friends who visit the Alhambra miss the representational art that adorns the architectural masterpieces of the continent. They must feel lost in a sea of abstract adornments; unmoored, with no sculptures or frescoes to orient their experience of the building.

Yet García finds an approbation of Islamic abstraction in a comment from poet Paul Valéry, who (in a passage from an unnamed source) admires the creative genius of the Islamic artist. Faced with the prohibition against representation, Valéry writes, the artist "could not think of *remembering* anything; on the contrary, it was incumbent on him to *denominate something* [*denominar alguna cosa;* emphases in the original]."⁵ Whereas the Greek genius of Europe represents the physical world as visual image, the Islamic spirit of the Alhambra translates the physical world into lexeme. García opposes the Islamic and Greek plastic arts to each other as if he were weighing and comparing the two voices that claim parentage of European modernity. He confesses to a feeling of inferiority: his Granada is bereft of the sculptural portraits and frescoes that confer the title of masterpiece on the great European buildings. But his demurrer is disingenuous. Surely the reader recognizes that in this brief excursus he has created the literary equivalent of the artistic arabesque he describes. He has not *remembered* the Alhambra, but rather elucidated the principles that guided its construction: "If I might be permitted an audacious and unusual comparison, I would say that the palaces [of the Alhambra] are like a school of advanced mathematics from which the teachers have been expelled, leaving the blackboards—in this case, everything: roofs, floors, baseboards, walls, galleries—filled with sublime and infinite equations."[6] García uses a philological gesture to construct his textual Alhambra. He deploys a taxonomy that separates the Greek from the Arab, the genius of European modernity from the genius loci of the Alhambra. But rub his alembics and a genie emerges: "sublime and infinite equations," like pages of abandoned calculations from God's rough draft for creation. García concedes nothing to the Greeks. His Alhambra is every bit as timeless, every bit as modern as those monuments that welcomed modernity to the capital cities of nineteenth-century Europe—the Eiffel Tower, say, or the Place de la Concorde cradling its Egyptian obelisk.

Emilio García Gómez (1905–95) was a rough contemporary of Enrico Cerulli. Like Cerulli he had a diplomatic career, serving between 1958 and 1969 as Spanish ambassador to Baghdad, Beirut, and Ankara. However, unlike Cerulli, he was at the same time a professional academic; indeed, he was the foremost Spanish Orientalist of his age. He studied with Miguel Asín Palacios—whose lessons in the Arabic language inspired him to change his major from law to Arabic—and Julián Ribera and, while he was living in Cairo, with Taha Husayn. In 1930 he was appointed to the position of professor of Arabic in Granada, and in 1932 he founded and became the first director of the Escuela de Estudios Árabes in Granada. Furthermore—as his tribute to the Alhambra suggests—García was a man of profound literary sensibilities. He was intimate with some of the great poets of his generation, and his translations of Hispano-Arabic poetry inspired writers like Federico García Lorca and Dámaso Alonso; he brought the poetry of medieval al-Andalus into the twentieth century and engaged it in a dialogue with the poets of modernity, a contrapuntal conversation similar in some respects to the environment in which it was composed.

García is best remembered by medievalists today for his decisive contributions to the difficult task of deciphering the bilingual *kharja*s, the final stanzas of the Arabic *muwashshaha* poems of medieval al-Andalus, and this is the story I will tell here. During the middle decades of the twentieth century Spanish, English, and American philologists—both Orientalists and "Romanists," or specialists in Romance languages—cracked the code of the kharja and revealed that these telegraphic and enigmatic lines of Arabic letters concealed the voice of the poet's beloved speaking (in some cases) the archaic Hispano-Romance of the eleventh or twelfth century. Thanks to the work of these scholars, voices silent for almost a millennium spoke again. And when the philologists presented their interpretations of the kharjas to a Spanish public, Spaniards learned to recognize them as the dawn of the Spanish literary tradition. As in Conde's history of Spain, an Arab bore witness to the Spanish past; but the language she spoke in this case—mirabile dictu!—was Spanish. The recognition of the kharja as the mother of a European literary tradition is the most successful of the microhistories I have traced in this book: it culminated in the integration of an Arab past into a narrative of national origin and the identification of an Arab voice as the earliest expression of a modern European identity. At the same time, by a delicious irony, the history of the interpretation of the kharjas reveals the extraordinary difficulties that emerge when a narrative of European national identity situates its terminus post quem in a text characterized by radical Semitic-Romance hybridity.

The part that Emilio García Gómez played in the drama of resuscitating the muwashshahas—illegible to an age not attuned to its oscillations between tongues—was heroic, but heroic in a melodramatic key; briefly stated, the role did not bring out the best in him. García, it seems, possessed a genius for mediating between Spanish and Arabic. Unlike Enrico Cerulli, he had a passionate and personal attachment to the culture of the Arabs; he could not describe his affection for Granada, for instance, without recalling in luxurious detail the traces of the Arab craftsmen he saw everywhere in the city and the voices of Arab singers he still heard in the streets. We do well to remember his talent as ambassador to the Arab past of his nation and to the Arab cities of the contemporary Mediterranean when we see him working clumsily to disenfranchise the non-Spanish philologists who attempted to contribute to the work of interpreting medieval Andalusian poetry. It was not the intricacies of the Mediterranean that flummoxed him but rather the thorny difficulties of contemporary Europe, fractured into distinct and competing nations.

In this chapter I will read through some of the major documents in the record of kharja studies—not the medieval manuscripts recording the kharjas, but the pages of modern academic journals in which the labor of deciphering those baffling texts (and the skirmishes to claim ownership of them) occurred. Then I will glance backward to another Andalusian episode: a brief, disturbing paroxysm of violence from the early years of Islamic rule of Iberian territory. During the 850s, fifty Christians from the administrative capital of al-Andalus, Cordoba—some born to the faith, others converts—were executed for open defiance of Islamic law. Paulus Alvarus, a central figure in the Christian community of Cordoba, wrote a treatise defending the cause of the Christians who died. Alvarus closed this polemic (though it seems likely that we possess an incomplete version of the work) with a lament on the demise of Latinity in Cordoba, complaining that the young Christians of his day did not know the language of their own scripture but aspired to eloquence in Arabic. And then, for reasons not apparent at the distance of eleven and a half centuries, Alvarus gave the reader a rather detailed synopsis of one feature in particular of the Arabic verse which Christian youths wrote so well. The passage has become—like Petrarch's dismissal of the poetry of the Arabs (see Chapter 2), but among a much wider public—a topos and a puzzle. Scholars regularly cite it to demonstrate the thorough Arabic acculturation of Iberian Christians. Yet a closer study of Alvarus's polemic suggests that behind the pitched standoff he described lay a culture of accommodation, or more precisely of agglomeration; I will argue that Alvarus's Latin shaped itself to the contours of the literary Arabic which (the texture of his prose suggests) Alvarus knew very well.

By describing the combinatory genius of Alvarus's Latin prose, this reading aims to follow through on one of the implications of the failures (or the audacious innovations) of the scholarship I have discussed in this book: Emilio García Gómez's Granada, which the Arabs have never truly left; Michele Amari's exilic reconstruction of Norman Palermo as a fulfillment of the Arab dream of what Palermo might be; and all the scholarly dream palaces in between. These scholars' investigations of medieval history showed that the Arab Mediterranean—which was always also a Spanish Mediterranean and an Italian Mediterranean—informed what Europe was and saw itself becoming. The millennial opposition between Arabic and Latin culture, or between Islamic and Christian culture, is a chimera, a mirage that recedes as our knowledge of the past advances. Make no mistake: Arabs and Latins have competed bitterly through the centuries over territory, over the accuracy of their sciences, over the legitimacy of their scripture. But by generalizing this antagonism—by presuming it as a constant in the literary record that is our witness to medieval history—philological method has, all too frequently, blinded us to the processes at work in some medieval texts. How can the process of *analysis*—and in particular an analytic strategy that draws its principal categories of examination from the modern European system of nations—serve to decipher a textual record whose logic is rather one of *agglomeration*? The medieval Mediterranean texts which these scholars read so intently, texts which led them to mount an implicit challenge to the analytic logic of literary scholarship, themselves point the way toward a new understanding of philology. They demand a reading strategy that can articulate not (or not only) the rhythms of a fragmented modernity but rather an agglomerative movement, the beat of another millennium. Arabic is not inimical to Latin in this textual universe; the learned tongues do not exclude the vernaculars, the sacred does not exclude the secular, the Semitic does not exclude the Romance. Rather, linguistic segments adhere—without necessarily cohering—into a totality from which no thread can be removed, lest the structural integrity of the whole be compromised. Each word is a world; and very little lexical history is lost or altogether forgotten, but endures to be extracted by a diligent and dedicated reader.

To be sure, the difficulty of reading these texts is considerable, and the linguistic demands they make on the scholar can be exasperating. Must the scholar learn Arabic in order to study Spanish literary history? Consider, for instance, the Spanish etymon *cid*. The word is most familiar to speakers of English as the title of the epic that occupies roughly the same position in the Spanish literary tradition as *Beowulf* in the English or the *Chanson de Roland* in the French: *El Cid*. During the Middle Ages the word was used not only by Andalusian Arabs but also by Romance-speaking Christians and Hebrew-speaking Jews, as is attested by its presence in one of the crucial documents of medieval Andalusian cultural exchange. In an Andalusian kharja from a Hebrew muwashshaha published and interpreted by Orientalist S. M. Stern, the beloved (speaking a Spanish inflected by the Hebrew alphabet through which it is mediated) sings, "*ben sydy ben.*" The word *ben* is Spanish; in modern orthography it would be spelled "ven." *Sydy* is the Arabic *sid* with an attached personal pronoun: "my master." In this refrain the beloved, made wretched by the absence of her lover, beseeches him to return: "come, my master, come."[7] Framed by stanzas written in the macrolanguages of the medieval Mediterranean, Hebrew and Arabic, the kharja itself oscillates between languages: is the beloved's plaintive cry—*ben sydy ben*—Hebrew, Arabic, Romance, or all three at once, an amalgam of languages written in letters ill-suited to record such sounds? Because of their linguistic density, during the second half of the twentieth century scholarship on the kharjas became a battleground where fierce battles were fought over the legibility of the past.

*Kharja* is an Arabic word meaning "exit" or "departure," or denoting something that protrudes or extends. Used as a prosodic term, it refers to the closing line of the muwashshaha, a sort of Arabic or Hebrew poem (or song, as the form could be either recited or sung) invented by Andalusian poets. Unlike classical Arabic poetry, the muwashshaha was strophic. Its lines were fragmented into short sections linked by internal rhyme. The name *muwashshaha* referred originally to a kind of belt made by stringing beads in horizontal rows; as the beads aligned in vertical stripes of color, so the internal rhymes in the lines of the poetic muwashshaha created repeated patterns of sound. The body of the muwashshaha was written in classical Arabic. But the closing line of the poem, the kharja, was (in the nonpanegyric muwashshahas) written in a different lexical register. The erotic muwashshaha was spoken in the voice of the lover, and in classical Arabic; the kharja gives us the voice of the beloved, who speaks in her vernacular tongue—in the earliest muwashshahas, colloquial Arabic, Romance, or a mongrel combination of the two. It is the kharjas written partly or wholly in Romance that have attracted the attention of medievalists.

The kharjas are a recent addition to the medieval canon. And their rediscovery and recovery, which coincided with a period of intensified evaluation of the Arab contribution to medieval European literary history, were received as a revelation by Arabists and Romanists alike. The muwashshaha corpus had fallen into obscurity, and the kharjas, which contained a large proportion of words that could not be read as classical Arabic, were not understood. In 1948 S. M. Stern, a British scholar (actually a Palestinian Jew with British citizenship—the fact will become important) published an article in the pages of the Spanish journal *Al-Andalus* in which he argued that the kharjas from Hebrew muwashshahas that for centuries had resisted interpretation in fact contained Romance words transliterated into the Hebrew alphabet.[8] In response to this seminal article and a codicil to it publishing a kharja with Romance elements from an *Arabic* muwashshaha,[9] Emilio García Gómez— one of the founding editors of *Al-Andalus*—published a series of articles auguring the opening of new literary horizons. "Thanks to Stern's study," he wrote in one of these, "and to his critics and commentators, the intuitions concerning the true nature of the muwashshaha have been verified in full; we have understood the part that the kharja played in it; we have been able to formulate new hypotheses concerning the origins of Arabic strophic poetry; we have arrived at the source of Spanish literature, which now originates in lyric rather than in epic; and we have changed almost all the dates in the problem of the dawn of popular European lyric." And García attributed Stern's discovery of the Romance kharjas to providence.[10]

With this rallying cry *Al-Andalus* established itself as the journal of kharja scholarship, and it regularly published new kharja research—mainly written by García himself—for the next thirty years.[11] In the course of these publications the issues that would consume kharja scholarship for the remainder of the century became clear. García argues, for instance, that the kharjas constitute the trace of a "primitive Romance lyric," against scholars who would posit that they are merely isolated fragments produced by Arab poets to embellish an essentially Arabic prosodic form.[12] He contends that the kharja's meter is a stress meter and thus the form represents a substantial departure from the quantitative meter of traditional Arabic verse.[13] And he asserts that the hybrid textuality of the kharjas calls for a unique kind of scholarly cooperation. Because the texts are positioned on an academic borderland, "un terreno fronterizo," kharja scholarship must be undertaken by Orientalists and Romanists together.[14]

Kharja scholarship as it was represented in *Al-Andalus* quickly took on a polemical tone—or, since most of the articles on kharja scholarship published in the journal were written by García himself, faux polemical. Some of García's articles responded to the work of other scholars, but those dissenting views weren't generally published in the pages of *Al-Andalus* itself. García's autopolemic culminated in one of the most extraordinary academic conflagrations of the twentieth century. On the occasion of the untimely death of S. M. Stern, who had first interpreted the Romance kharjas, and the posthumous publication of Stern's *Hispano-Arabic Strophic Poetry* (which included the text of the doctoral thesis he had written on the muwashshaha), García published an article under a pseudonym that, because of its vitriolic nature, was accompanied with a disclaimer by the journal's editorial board. The article begins as an elegy for Stern, remembering the extraordinary impetus that his discovery gave to kharja scholarship. But it degenerates rapidly into a scathing and distasteful critique of Stern's final contribution to the field. Stern—whom García is careful to identify as a "Palestinian Jew living in England" in the opening sentence of the article—was finally incapable of keeping pace with developments in kharja scholarship because of his lack of competence in Romance philology. And so, García speculates, he abandoned the field and viewed it ultimately with a rancor inspired not only by his inability to assert intellectual ownership over the texts he had discovered but also by a "racial complex and other personal circumstances."[15]

García would publish three more pseudonymous articles in subsequent issues of the journal, works that would seem to merit the attention of the psychoanalyst as much as the philologist.[16] Kharja scholarship has by now generated its own arcane idiolect; the kharja scholar has become obsessively consumed with questions that would be incomprehensible not only to the average literary historian, but even to the average medievalist without training specific to kharja studies. The final pseudonymous article, a venomous critique of a work by Jareer Abu-Haidar, appears in the same issue as a piece published under García's name in which he attacks the work of T. J. Gorton;[17] García, again writing pseudonymously, had produced an earlier attack on Gorton's scholarship:[18] in each of these cases, the assault is so acerbic that one suspects incipient paranoia. Most puzzling, at least from the psychoanalytic point of view, García writing under the pseudonym Angel Ramírez Calvente makes frequent reference to his work as García.[19] In part as a result of the degeneration of the kharja polemic the journal ceased publication soon after the appearance of the last of the pseudonymous articles. And so, by a strange circular logic, as Stern's discovery opened the debate on the kharjas it was Stern's death and the publication of his initial research on the kharjas that ultimately brought the *Andalus* kharja polemic to a close.

Following the demise of *Al-Andalus* the torch crossed the Atlantic; a series of increasingly polemical articles on the status of kharja scholarship appeared in the American journal *La Corónica*.[20] Here the disputes focused on the usual suspects. Scholars debated the nature of the metrics of the muwashshaha, for instance, and the notion that the kharja should be read as the trace of a primitive Romance lyric. But underlying the philological concerns that occupied the scholars was a consistent focus on the "ownership" of the kharjas. Already in García's interventions this had become a crucial topic. Both Arabists and Romanists must contribute to the project of interpretation, García asserted, if the texts are to be adequately understood. But it should be noted that, in García's reading, the Arabists and Romanists best qualified to work on the kharjas were also Spaniards.[21] In the New World the issue was not the national identity of the scholars who should work on the kharjas but their *institutional* identity. To whom do the kharjas properly belong: to the Arabists, or to all those who can contribute to our understanding of the texts, including both Arabists and Romanists? The Arabist camp argued that the texts must be understood in the context of Arabic literary history; in one of the first entries in the *Corónica* polemic, Arabist Alan Jones detailed the damage done to muwashshaha scholarship by the exaggerated emphasis given to the kharja in general and to the Romance kharjas in particular. Those kharjas that do contain recognizable Romance words are few—in one medieval anthology of muwashshahas, for instance, out of a total of 352 kharjas, Jones counts twenty-nine with Romance words[22]—and some have protested the disproportionate amount of attention granted the Romance kharjas. As a corrective to this scholarly imbalance Jones called for more concentrated work by Arabists, who can understand the difficulties peculiar to medieval Arabic literature and its manuscript transmission.[23]

In response a set of scholars with a more catholic approach to literary history—most notably James T. Monroe and Samuel G. Armistead—invited contributions from all whose competence gave them access to the texts. For, they pointed out, the set of skills that the field requires is so extensive that reserving it for certain specialists will impoverish research and impose limits on our progress in understanding the text. Thus Monroe: "There is no room in this difficult field for simplistic or one-sided solutions, nor for narrow appeals to professional insularity. Little can be gained from pitting Arabists against Romanists. A serious study of muwashshah poetry requires that one be an Arabist, a Hebraist, a Romanist, and much else besides (musical expertise and literary competence are essential), yet since it would be unrealistic to expect all of these areas of knowledge from a single individual, modesty and a spirit of collaboration are the least that may be expected."[24]

Rather than await the philological Hercules with competence in all the necessary fields and languages, disciplines and subdisciplines, the Monroe-Armistead camp called for a more holistic approach to kharja scholarship. These scholars' work was philologically rigorous. In response to a critique of their vocalization of an Arabic word as "albo" (a Spanish word meaning "white" or "dawn"), for instance, Armistead and Monroe produced a detailed and extensive list of Spanish and Arabic texts in which the word appears.[25] But their philological readings were also tempered with a consideration of the situation of their work in the context of a broader understanding of cultural history, both medieval and modern. In an intervention that appeared in a late stage of the polemic, María Rosa Menocal begged for recognition of the contingency of the muwashshaha and the multivalence of the cultural environment from which the poem emerged. In order to produce accurate and relevant readings of these texts, she asked "whether we all need to become Arabists and Hebraists as well as Hispanists in order to be Hispano-medievalists or is there a way of justifying using other versions of texts, of using some of the precepts of a post-deconstructive world and availing ourselves of translations as other versions of texts that would otherwise fall almost completely by the wayside?"[26] By questioning the notion of scholarly legitimacy as it was narrowly understood in the context of kharja scholarship, Menocal (like Monroe and Armistead) called upon the philologist to defend her or his work in another respect: to use the critical tools developed during the waning decades of the modern era in order to articulate the relevance of the kharjas to a world where (as in medieval al-Andalus) borders are prone to shift and identities spontaneously morph.

In a work first published in 1958, philologist Erich Auerbach wrote: "Not only the scholars and critics among us, but also a large and steadily growing section of the general public, have ceased to be frightened by the diversity of peoples and epochs."[27] Yet some kinds of diversity retain the power to disturb us, and the categories of philological analysis we use when studying the medieval past may be complicit in the perpetuation of textual difficulty (as Auerbach's own career suggests; see Chapter 5). Consider, as an example of this phenomenon, the first Arabic kharja deciphered by S. M. Stern, and published in *Al-Andalus* in 1949. In this brief article, an addendum to his groundbreaking article on Romance kharjas in Hebrew muwashshahas, Stern gives the Arabic text of the muwashshaha and suggests Romance readings of several of the words in the kharja: *meu l-habib enfermo . . . de meu* (my lover is sick . . . [when he's away] from me). The editors of *Al-Andalus* append a note to Stern's article in which they translate the body of the muwashshaha, and call on "los romanistas amigos" to help them in the task of interpreting the remainder of the kharja.[28]

The muwashshaha, by al-A'ma al-Tutili (d. 1130; the name means "the blind [poet] from Toledo"), is a particularly tender and elegantly constructed love song.[29] The opening line delicately balances two opposed elements: water (the tears that the lover sheds) and fire (the fire that burns in his heart). The phrase is common in Arabic love poetry, but not for that reason less treasured. On the contrary, where it is expressed in a delicate turn of phrase (as here) it is a particularly valued gesture. The poet mourns the absence of his beloved. He calls out to the Ka'ba to witness his pain (and his contrition); and the Ka'ba, the ultimate goal of the Meccan pilgrimage and thus a sign of spiritual presence, symbolizes in the context of the erotic poem the sort of presence that is denied to the poet, who suffers the absence of his beloved. There is a consistent emphasis throughout the poem on mediation: the heart on its journey toward the Ka'ba is caught between (*bayna*) "passion that calls and love that responds" (v. 5); the lover's tears are like swords balanced between (*bayna*) his eyelids (v. 10); the beloved sings the closing kharja "between (*bayna*) boldness and love" (v. 15). The lover's heart, in short, is fragmented by the absence of his beloved (as the muwashshaha's lines are fragmented into brief, rhyming hemistiches) and craves the unifying presence represented by the beloved or by the Ka'ba as the pilgrim's goal.

In the years since Stern published the body of al-A'ma al-Tutili's muwashshaha and indicated the presence of Romance words in its kharja, a number of scholars have had a stab at interpreting it—Emilio García Gómez, Josep M. Sola-Solé, James T. Monroe, Álvaro Galmés de Fuentes, and Otto Zwartjes, to name only those scholars who have discussed and translated the text in book-length studies of the kharjas.[30] It seems likely that the lines (spoken, like all kharjas, in the voice of the beloved) play on the themes central to the rest of the muwashshaha: love for one that is absent. But little of the kharja can be interpreted with precision. The text, as the modern scholars understand it, is—apart from the single Arabic word *habib*, here "lover"—entirely Romance. The difficulties in interpretation that produce the divergences between the scholars' readings are the result of the fact that the words are filtered through the Arabic alphabet and through a series of manuscript versions made by copyists who did not understand what they were copying. The kharja (like the body of the poem itself) must have to do with proximity and distance, with the difficulty of access to the beloved and the beneficent effects of the beloved's presence. But what *does* the woman want?

The scholar who turns to Alan Jones's book-length study of the Romance kharjas in search of elucidation will find little comfort. Jones, it will be remembered, participated enthusiastically in the *Corónica* kharja polemic, arguing the "Arabist" position. He maintained that the texts of the kharjas were difficult, at times impenetrable, and only Arabists familiar with the intricacies of the Arabic literary tradition and its manuscript transmission could hope to unravel their difficulties. In support of his position, and as an aid to Romanists who wished to work with the kharjas, Jones published a catalogue of the entire extant corpus of kharjas containing Romance words. Jones does not translate the kharjas. He gives the final stanza of the muwashshaha itself, followed by a stich-by-stich explication of the kharja, reproducing the surviving manuscript versions and transliterating these versions into the Latin alphabet letter by letter. Finally, he offers a reading of the kharja as a whole that is plausible based on the manuscript evidence—though again he does not translate but merely transliterates the Arabic text—and discusses the difficulties that remain.

And the difficulties in this case are formidable. I give here an approxima-

tion, in Latin transliteration, of Jones's transcription of the surviving manuscript versions of the text:

MW 'LḤBYB ANFRM D̲H̲Y MW AMAR
KĀN D̲H̲Ā S̲H̲NRĀ or NTNRĀ or TNNRĀ
YNQYS AM BYN KS̲H̲ĀD MW LG̲H̲ĀR

MW 'LḤBYB Da MW ṢĀR
BĀDR S̲H̲NĀR
BNFS AMNT KSĀD MW L'ĀR

MĀ W'LḤBYB D MW ṢĀR
FĀDR S̲H̲NĀR
BNFS AMNT KSĀD MW L 'ĀR[31]

Beware of Greeks bearing gifts! Jones's Arabist reading voids the text of meaning; rather than restore the beloved's voice, he renders her mute. The kharja,
with the exception of a word or two, makes little sense whether you come at
it from Arabic or from Romance. The disagreement between the manuscript
versions signals the difficulty these lines posed for those who recorded them.
Al-A'ma al-Tutili's twelfth-century muwashshaha and its kharja have been
preserved in three distinct recensions, attested by five manuscripts, all of
which appear to date to the eighteenth century and later—long after the
extinction of the last of the Arab settlements on the Iberian peninsula.[32]
And modern Orientalists, despite prodigious efforts, have not (in this case)
managed to undo the damage that time has done. Nor does it seem likely
that they will. Jones cautions that much of the kharja is "distinctly unpromis-
ing. The three surviving recensions have become corrupted in different ways,
and so badly that, even when carefully collated, they fail to provide a basis
for non-intuitive restoration."[33] Studying Jones's edition of the verses that
first showed Western Orientalists that lines of Romance poetry could hide
behind the opaque screen of the Arabic kharjas, one scarcely knows what is
more remarkable: that Arab scribes continued for so long their stewardship
of words that no longer held any meaning for them, or that Western Orientalists have continued for so long to scrutinize these epitaphs of medieval
songs in the hope of unlocking their secrets.

When does textual difficulty become a *fatal* difficulty? At what point
does a dead language become idiolect, the text itself indecipherable, the phil-

ological analysis not a reading but a post-mortem report on the site where meaning died? Thankfully, not all texts constituted by translinguistic hybridity frustrate our efforts to interpret them so successfully. In order to construe them, however, the philologist must learn to recognize and decode the logic of agglomeration that informed them: in the case of the kharjas, the layering of Arabic, Hebrew, Romance, sometimes present as distinct languages, sometimes fused to form a single, dense textual substance. The philologist might, in fact, have to learn Arabic or Hebrew in order to understand Spanish history; we might need to develop a feel for the rhythms of Arabic prose in order to read the Latin written by men steeped in the Arabic rhetorical tradition, as we sometimes need Italian to parse the Latin written by Boccaccio or Petrarch. And at times we might need to allow intuition to guide us; at such moments, we do well to remember that we are following a venerable philological tradition.

As an example of such a literary monument—a work in which Latin and Arabic prose styles fuse to create a textual amalgam—consider the document most frequently cited to demonstrate the anxieties unleashed by Andalusian cultural fluidity, Paulus Alvarus's indignant diatribe against the young Christians of his era and their obsequious emulation of Arabic eloquence. Alvarus's oft-quoted statement comes from a polemic written in response to a brief, intense era of murderous violence that pitted Muslims against Christians and divided the Christian community against itself. During the ninth century, 150 years after the Islamic conquest of the Iberian peninsula, the Muslim rulers of Cordoba put to death a number of Christians for apostasy (in the case of those born to Muslim families) or for defamation of Muhammad or proselytizing (in the case of those born to Christian families). The series of events has drawn the interest of historians in recent years for three reasons. The executions occurred during a brief period of time—fifty Christians died in the course of a decade, between 850 and 859.[34] And the episode is historically unique; nowhere else during the early years of Islamic governance in Iberia did tensions between confessional communities reach such a pitch. Historians have worked to untangle the motives for this parenthesis of murderous violence that affected one city in particular during one generation in particular. Furthermore, a number of these men and women seem to have courted martyrdom. They publicly denounced Islam and its prophet, thus incurring the wrath of the Muslim governors. And—although the extant record is extremely scanty—the documentary evidence suggests that the Christian community of Cordoba as a whole disapproved of their actions. To judge from the treatises written in defense of those who died, the Christian community argued that these men and women did not die martyrs: they did not live under systematic persecution from a nonmonotheistic government, but rather under the enlightened rule of Muslims, themselves monotheists; and they went out of their way to offend the sensibilities of the Muslim community, seeking a death which could not, for that reason, be deemed a martyrdom. Historians have sought to explain the spectacular nature of the executed Christians' crimes—their defiant public flaunting of their Christian belief, their flouting of Muslim sensibilities, their willingness to invite execution as the price of religious conviction. Finally, a number of those who died came from a background of cultural and confessional complexity: roughly a third were the children of mixed marriages or were themselves converts. And the crimes for which they were executed—professing their Christian faith in a way that offended the Muslim population—presupposes, in some cases at least, proficient command of the Arabic language. Historians have attempted to explain the unraveling of these Christians' lives in the context of the transition from a Latinate Christianity in decline to an Arabic Islamic culture undergoing swift growth and consolidation.[35]

Paulus Alvarus (d. ca. 862) and his close friend Eulogius (d. 859) produced the core of the surviving textual record describing the executions of the Cordovan Christians.[36] Eulogius wrote a "Memoriale Sanctorum" to celebrate the actions of those who died and honor their deaths. Like a shadow image of the *Thousand and One Nights*, the treatise continues as long as there are deaths to record. Eulogius ended it once, apparently in the belief that the executions had ended, and then resumed it when the deaths resumed.[37] His own execution would bring the treatise to an ineluctable end. And Alvarus left a "Vita Eulogi" and the "Indiculus Luminosus" (or "Illuminating Disclosure"), a brief arguing that Muhammad was the Antichrist, that his age was living through the end times, and that Christians must mount and sustain an obdurate resistance to Islamic civilization—its beliefs, customs, and above all its language.[38] Alvarus's argument provides convincing support for historian Jessica Coope's thesis that the real enemy in ninth-century Cordoba was assimilation. Coope sketches the historical context for the episode as an era of swift and (for the Christian community, at least) dismaying cultural transition:

The government grew stronger, the bureaucracy expanded, and the cultural life of the court became more vital. As a result, Christians were increasingly drawn to Arab Islamic culture, and the rate of conversions to Islam accelerated, leading to changes and disruptions at every level of Cordovan society, from government to the family. The voluntary martyrdoms can best be understood in this Islamic context; they represented an attempt to resist assimilation and conversion to Islam and to strengthen Christian identity by invoking the heroic image of the Roman martyrs.[39]

The anxieties provoked by assimilation certainly informed the passage from the "Indiculus Luminosus" which has become most familiar to modern historians. At the end of the treatise (although it seems probable that we possess a truncated version of it) Alvarus details the concessions that ambitious Christians make to Islamic culture and custom.[40] They undergo circumcision in order to work in the caliphal palace. And they are steeped in the language and the literary tradition of the Arabs. They do not know their own Latin language, he writes, and yet they are capable of prodigious achievements in Arabic verse. Modern scholars typically cite this passage without the final clauses, which use enigmatic vocabulary and ambiguous grammatical constructions and are perversely difficult to parse:

> Et repperitur absque numero multiplices turbas qui erudite Caldaicas verborum explicit pompas, ita ut metrice eruditjori ab ipsis gentibus carmine et sublimiori pulcritudine finales clausulas unius littere coartatjone decorent, et iuxta quod lingue ipsius requirit idioma, que omnes vocales apices commata claudit et cola, rithmice, immo ut ipsis conpetit, metrice universi alfabeti littere per varias dictjones plurimas variante uno fine constringuntur vel simili apice.[41]

> [There are found countless crowds of people who, in their erudition, create ostentatious Chaldean (i.e., Arabic) displays of words, so that in a song metrically more skillful than those of the Arabs themselves and loftier in beauty, they embellish the final clauses by binding them with a single letter. And as the idiom of that language requires, which ends the hemistiches with vowels (*or* long vowels), in rhythm—or rather, as befits them, in meter—the letters of all the alphabet are constrained, by means of a great diversity of expression, to one ending or a similar letter.]

What strikes us in Alvarus's comments is not only his tone of querulous anxiety but also his effort to explain in some detail the literary tradition that young Christian men (to their detriment) emulate. He hesitates over his selection of a word to describe the architecture of Arabic verse: *rithmicus* or *metricus*. The word *rithmicus* (or, in classical orthography, *rhythmicus*) might indicate either end rhyme or stress meter (rather than the quantitative meter of the Latin poetry of the ancients); in the final phrase, he is unambiguously describing the monorhyme typical of classical Arabic poetry. As Dwight Reynolds has pointed out in a recent comment on the passage, Alvarus here translates an Arabic term used in the analysis of poetic rhyme—*rawiyy*, or "binding letter," which designates the sound repeated at the end of each verse—with the Latin *constringo*, a verb which means "to bind together."[42]

Traditional Latin verse, of course, did not use end rhyme, and so the Latin language did not have a technical vocabulary to describe it. In this passage Alvarus pushes the Latin language to the limit of its descriptive capacity—or, perhaps, to the limit of his own capacity to use the language as descriptive tool. Using Latin to comment on the poetic conventions of the Arabs, he seeks to describe the structures of an Arabic poem using a language whose own poetic tradition was apparently as much an acquired taste for Alvarus as the Arabs'. For Alvarus tells us elsewhere that as a young man he was steeped in another kind of literary tradition: not one native to the Latins, but (again) a "rithmicus" poetry.

> Nam pueriles contemtjones pro doctrinis quibus dividebamur non odiose, sed delectabiliter epistolatim in inuicem egimus, et rithmicis uersibus nos laudibus mulcebamus; et hoc erat exercitjum nobis melle suabior, fabis jucundior. Et in ante nos quotidie extendentes multa inadibilia temtare in scribturis puerilis inmatura docibilitas egit ita ut uolumina conderemus que postea etas matura abluenda ne in posteros remaneret decreuit.[43]

> [As young men we wrote letters to each other—not hostile, but agreeable—debating the teachings upon which we disagreed, and we delighted in the merits of our rhymed verses; this exercise was sweeter to us than honey, more pleasing than the honeycomb. Before (the arrival of Eulogius), exerting ourselves daily, a boyish, youthful eagerness to learn compelled us to attempt many outrageous things in our writings, and we composed volumes of writings which afterward maturity decreed must be purged, that it not remain in later years.]

Elsewhere, Alvarus explains what made the difference in the poetic practice of the young men of Cordoba: Eulogius's acquisition, on his travels through northern Spain, of the writings of the ancient Romans, including Virgil's *Aeneid* and the *Satires* of Horace—works unknown in Cordoba at the time.[44] Eulogius, having learned the traditional technique of writing Latin verse in quantitative meter, experimented with it himself. In an epistolary poem extolling the virtues of two women, converts to Christianity executed for apostasy, Eulogius revealed to the young Christian men of Cordoba—along with the virtues of the women—the beauty of quantitative Latin verse: "Ibi metricos quos adhuc nesciebant sapientes Hispanie pedes perfectissime docuit" ("In this letter he taught us to perfection the metrical feet which the learned men of Spain did not know at the time").[45]

Alvarus himself would become a practitioner and proponent of "metricos pedes"—the weighted measures of classical Latin verse. In his extant poetry he uses the quantitative meters of the ancients. And in one poem he scorns the stress-meter, rhymed verse that he wrote as a young man and destroyed following Eulogius's revelation of the true nature of Latin poetics:

> Ergo vos, cigni lautique decore pauones,
> Cum suaui meatim philomela ducite carmen,
> Et pedibus metricis rithmi contemnite monstra,
> Que segnis Harrabs floxa[s] sic rancide sanna[s]
> Deuio mugitu pangit, ut cantica turpet
> Eclesie pleuis, que semper fulgide claret.[46]

> [And so, you swans, you peacocks glorious in beauty,
> Lead the song with the sweet nightingale in my manner
> And abjure the freakish (songs) in rhymed meters
> Which—meandering, dissolute—the listless Arab composes,
> In such loathsome manner, with a foolish bellow, that he defiles the
>    songs
> Of the ecclesiastical congregation, which always shine with a glittering
>    light.]

Both the eccentricities of Alvarus's orthography and an extremely exiguous manuscript tradition make it difficult to be certain that the reading of the verses offered here is correct. The text of this poem (like most of Alvarus's writings, including the "Indiculus Luminosus") survives in a single manuscript copy, most likely dating to the tenth century (roughly one hundred years after Alvarus's death).[47] The word represented here as *Harrabs*—Arab—appears in that manuscript as *harrans*, or in classical Latin orthography *errans*: meandering, aimless; one who wanders from the truth. Editor Juan Gil suggested the emendation reprinted here. In either case, in these lines Alvarus repudiates those who defile poetry by writing "rhythmic" verse; he calls for young Christians to write "in [his] manner"—these lines of thundering censure are composed in dactylic hexameter—and to shun rhymed trumperies, deformations of verse.

It is difficult to determine precisely what Alvarus inveighs against when he denounces the versification of his age, or what manner of versification he and his companions outgrew when Eulogius taught them the rules of Latin scansion. In the lines quoted above Alvarus tells us that in their youthful verse, he and his mates attempted "multa inadibilia," "many outrageous things." And a number of clues suggest that Alvarus himself linked rhymed Latin poetry with the deleterious cultural influence of the Arabs: the use of the same adjective—*rithmicus*—to describe (and condemn) both; the plausible association of "rhythmical" verse with the Arab poet in the lines just quoted; the vehemence of Alvarus's condemnation of rhymed poetry. Did the young Christian men who wrote such poetry in Latin develop the technique in imitation of the monorhymed *qasida*s of the Arabs? Did some of the young men in Alvarus's circle actually write their poetry in Arabic: was Alvarus closer to the Christians whose Arabic poetry he deplores than historians suspect? This last suggestion seems no less outrageous than the poems themselves, in Alvarus's characterization of them. Yet given the evidence—a flimsy record; but it is all we possess—we cannot rule out the possibility altogether.

For Alvarus tells us little indeed about the poetry of his peers. His description leaves open the possibility that the Latin poets of ninth-century Cordoba developed a rhymed stanza in imitation of the Arabs. His own familiarity with the technique of Arabic versification suggests that he knew enough about the language and the literary tradition to interpret and analyze Arabic poetry himself. And, in the "Indiculus Luminosus," Alvarus models another simulation of literary Arabic, a Latin literary device that mimics a rhetorical practice fashionable in contemporary Arabic prose. At the beginning of that final section of the treatise in which he denounces the young Christian men showing off their "Chaldean finery," Alvarus (again) inveighs

against the cultural influence of the Arabs, here condemning the Christians'
taste for both Arabic poetry and prose:

> Et dum eorum uersibus et fabellis Milesiis delectamus eisque inseruire
> uel ipsis nequissimis obsecundare etjam premio emimus et ex hoc vitam
> in seculo ducimus uel corpora saginamus ex inlicit serbitjo et exsecrando
> ministerio abundantjores opes congregantes fulgores odores uestimentor-
> umque siue opum diuersarum opulentjam in longa tempora nobis filiis-
> que nostris adque nepotibus preuidentes nomenque nefande bestie cum
> honore et precamine illis solitum uice eorum nostris manibus preno-
> tantes numquid non patule nomen bestie his affectibus in manu dextra
> portamus[48]

> [And while we delight in their verses and Milesian fables; while we even
> pay a price to serve them and to emulate their base deeds; and in accor-
> dance with this we lead our lives in this world or fatten our bodies on
> unlawful servitude and detestable work; amassing abundant riches, re-
> nown, perfumes, the opulence of clothing or of diverse riches, storing
> these things up for ourselves and our sons and our grandsons; recording
> the name of the nefarious beast with honor and reverence, in their man-
> ner and custom, with our own hands—do we not openly carry the name
> of the beast, with these affectations, in our right hand?]

The sentence is long, tangled, and difficult to interpret, beginning with Alvarus's use of the term *Milesian fables*. This expression, in reference to Latin
letters, might imply a framed tale, a licentious tale, a witty tale, or all three
at once. But what *Arabic* genre does it designate here?[49] Recall that Alvarus
wrote in the middle of the ninth century. During the previous century, and
east of the Mediterranean (in Iraq), Ibn al-Muqaffa' had written the *Kalila
wa-Dimna*—the best-known and most widely disseminated single work of
the first century of imaginative prose literature in Arabic. And al-Jahiz, the
greatest prose writer of the first three centuries of Islam, was Alvarus's contemporary (he lived in Basra and Baghdad, and died in December 868 or
January 869, less than a decade later than Alvarus). Alvarus's reference is
tantalizing in the circumstances, suggesting as it does the avid consumption
of imaginative tales in Arabic—and among a Christian audience, no less!—so
early in the history of al-Andalus, and indeed in the history of Arabic art
prose.

But the connotation of Alvarus's "Milesian fables" is not the only problem with this passage. The syntax throughout is difficult—the sentence lacks the conjunctions and relative pronouns that Latin prose typically uses to indicate syntactic coordination and subordination—and the vocabulary not easy to grasp. I have removed the punctuation that appears in the modern edition because I do not believe that it helps appreciably in parsing the sentence. It is my sense that Alvarus does give us a way to analyze and understand this sentence, along with the three other sentences (one preceding and two following it) with which it is structurally paralleled. This is the second of four sentences that begin with an extended "dum" clause and end with a question phrased in the negative; in each of these sentences, Alvarus asks, in essence: While we allow the seductive culture of the Arabs to beguile our senses and lull our conscience to sleep, do we not play into the hand of the devil? Each of the sentences ends with a verb in –are, and in the third-person plural (*portamus*; *portamus*; *peccamus*; *conlocamus*): in the first two sentences, we carry (*portamus*) the image of Muhammad within our hearts; in the final sentence, we bear him, like an idol, into our very bedchambers ("in cuuiculo nostro quasi idolo conlocamus"). And within the sentences, Alvarus uses rhyme to structure meaning. Thus the sentence just quoted breaks down into rhymed fragments which parcel out the meaning of the phrases:

> Et dum eorum uersibus et fabellis Milesiis delectamus
> > eisque inseruire uel ipsis nequissimis obsecundare etjam premio
> > > emimus
> > et ex hoc vitam in seculo ducimus
> uel corpora saginamus
> > ex inlicit serbitjo
> > et exsecrando ministerio
> > > abundantjores
> > > opes congregantes fulgores
> > > odores
> > > uestimentorumque siue opum diuersarum opulentjam in
> > > > longa tempora
> > > > > nobis filiisque nostris adque nepotibus preuidentes
> > > nomenque nefande bestie cum honore
> > > > et precamine illis solitum uice eorum nostris
> > > > > manibus prenotantes
> numquid non patule nomen bestie his affectibus in manu dextra
> > portamus

In an article that appeared in 1953, Allen Cabaniss cited a handful of passages in which, he argued, Alvarus used rhyming prose—an example, Cabaniss argued, of the "'Chaldean' style" which Alvarus, despite his denunciation of the literary pomp of the Arabs, nevertheless imitated in his prose.[50] Here, too (as in the two sentences that follow this one), Alvarus seems to employ the device, which in Arabic is called *saj'*. The sentence relies upon rhyme—rather than conjunctions or relative pronouns, as befits Latin prose—to structure meaning. This may explain some of the eccentricities of Alvarus's word choice: the odd pairing of "fulgores odores" ("flashing lights"; "odors" or "perfumes"), "*ex* inlicit servit*io*" and "*ex*secrando ministe*rio*" ("unlawful servitude" and "detestable work"), "*pre*uiden*tes*" and "*pre*notan*tes*" ("storing up" and "recording").[51]

So too in this passage does Alvarus use multiple words derived from the same etymological root in close proximity to each other: *opes; opum . . . opulentjam.* This device is found in Latin as well as in Arabic, of course, but in Arabic is developed to a rarefied degree, ranging from alliteration to puns to the situation of words from the same semantic root in balanced positions in a clause or a verse of poetry.[52] He sets two brief phrases that mean essentially the same thing next to each other: *illis solitum uice eorum* ("according to their custom; in their manner")—a repetition that appears somewhat bizarre in Latin but was prized in contemporary Arabic poetry and prose.[53] Both of these rhetorical strategies for refining the meaning and elaborating the structure of a prose sentence became popular in Arabic art prose during the Abbasid period—that is, contemporaneous with Alvarus's life. Finally, in perhaps the most striking imitation of the texture of Arabic, we do not find the verb *to be* in this final section of the treatise, except to form the passive. Rather Alvarus uses the most common Arabic circumlocution to express the existential sense of the verb: passive forms of verbs meaning "to find" appear four times in the two printed pages of the modern edition.[54]

Thus in this section of the treatise—in which he castigates Christian youth who vie in eloquence with the Arabs—Alvarus himself uses the kinds of "affectations" he denounces in the closing words of the long sentence quoted above. Why does he model the rhetorical strategies he condemns: is he, consciously or unconsciously, competing with those who practice such a hybrid style unquestioningly? Does he perhaps mean to show that Latin is capable of the same rhetorical refinement as Arabic? Has he simply so absorbed the rhetorical habits of the Arabs that they emerge unbidden in his prose, regardless of the language in which he writes?

Of course, as Richard Hitchcock reminds us in a recent study of Arabic-speaking Christians in al-Andalus, very few men in Cordoba during the mid-ninth century—Muslim or Christian—understood Arabic well enough to appreciate or compose poetry in the language. Berbers and converts to Islam from among the indigenous population constituted a large percentage of the Muslim community in the city.[55] It is important to resist the temptation to exaggerate Alvarus's understanding of the Arabic language and literary tradition. Yet, at the same time, we must take into consideration the cultural ambitions of the ruler of Cordoba during Alvarus's life, 'Abd al-Rahman II (r. 822–52), who undertook to create in Cordoba (the administrative center of al-Andalus) a court to rival the Abbasid capital, Baghdad. In 822, the year of his accession, 'Abd al-Rahman invited Ziryab (d. 852)—a Baghdad-trained musician, connoisseur of fine poetry, and *arbiter elegantiae* who would have a profound influence on Andalusian letters and especially music—to Cordoba, thus setting the tone for his cultural program.[56] Alvarus seems to have come from a well-to-do family; the quantitative meter of his Latin poetry and the sophistication of his Latin prose signal his cultural ambition; it seems probable that he viewed himself, and was viewed by others, as a cultural beacon for the Christian community.[57] Certainly the sense of cultural innovation that infused the time and place (a capital city, a century and a half following its conquest by foreign invaders, entering an era of brilliant achievement) provides the context for the activities of the young Christian men whose cultural ambitions Alvarus condemns, if not for Alvarus's own literary achievements.

Furthermore, recent historical research has unearthed another shred of evidence suggesting that Alvarus was closer than we might assume to the atmosphere of cultural miscegenation that saw Christians appropriating the (official, if not de facto) language of the Muslim rulers. During the early centuries of Muslim rule of the Iberian peninsula, an otherwise unknown Iberian Christian by the name of Hafs ibn Albar al-Quti produced a translation of the Psalms into Arabic. The translator's name tells us that he was a "Goth" (al-*Quti*) and that he was the son (or more remote descendent) of a man named Albar (or, in Latin orthography, Alvarus). The internal dating of the single manuscript which preserves Hafs's translation of the Psalms could be read to indicate that the translation was completed in the year 989 or 889. Thus, if the "Albar" from whom Hafs took his name was the author of the "Indiculus Luminosus," the translator of the Psalms may be either the son or a more distant descendent of our Alvarus.[58]

It is—depending on how one reads this trickle of evidence—either possible or probable that Alvarus was closer to Arabic literary culture than the demographics of contemporary Cordoba and the tone of his denunciations in the "Indiculus Luminosus" would suggest. Certainly, at a minimum, the historical context requires us to seek in the meager textual record he left behind reflections of the intricacies of the environment in which he lived. Scholars have assumed that Alvarus knew little about the culture he condemned, despite the curious detail of his description of the Arabic poetic tradition. Yet, again and again, the historical record demonstrates the absence of a clear line of demarcation between the Romance-speaking and Arabic-speaking populations in ninth-century Cordoba (or, for that matter, in the twelfth-century Toledo of al-A'ma al-Tutili, or Emilio García Gómez's twentieth-century Granada). The Christians who died in ninth-century Cordoba were able to communicate in Arabic. Indeed, it was their capacity to convey to the Muslim authorities a credo, a defiance of Islamic belief, a provocation that defined the movement. In some cases translators may have mediated their testimony to speakers of Arabic, or an Arabic-speaking judge may have heard and understood a statement in Romance.[59] But the number of the dead requires us to view the string of executions in ninth-century Cordoba as a phenomenon rooted in a contradiction: a culture of mutual comprehension and competition, of intimacy and distrust. Those executed died because of their capacity to scandalize a society that used Arabic—at this point in its history, with rapidly increasing sophistication—to conduct its public life.

An even narrower gap separated those who read Latin and those who read Arabic. Alvarus's description of Arabic poetry indicates a detailed understanding of it; and the Arabic poetic tradition does not yield its secrets easily. The literary scholarship of the last two centuries has emphasized those works that can be viewed as ancestors to the literatures of the modern European nations and has marginalized or ignored evidence of more hybrid strands in literary history. Indeed, mere happenstance has preserved the works discussed here to the present day: Alvarus's "Indiculus Luminosus," his letters, and most of his poetry survive in a single tenth- or eleventh-century copy (made by a man whom Alvarus's twentieth-century editor deemed a "dolt").[60] Though Hafs ibn Albar's translation of the Psalms was cited in subsequent years by the Andalusian Jewish community, the single known complete manuscript—once in the collection of the Escorial Library in Madrid—has been lost (presumably in the fire of 1671). We owe the modern edition of it to a Scottish scholar and student of Arabic who made a copy of it during the first quarter of the seventeenth century; his transcription is now in the Ambrosian Library at Milan.[61] A new sensibility in medieval scholarship—one more attuned to the contingent literary traditions that emerged from cultural and linguistic borderlands like ninth-century Cordoba—has in recent years focused historians' attention on works like this, deemed marginal for centuries.

And the interest in documentation of such "hermaphrodite" works (to borrow Francesco Vella's description of an early Maltese alphabet; see Chapter 4, note 33) has, in turn, brought more such works to light from the dusty corners of European libraries—including one fragment which I cannot resist citing, so poetic is its witness to the history under discussion and the reception of that history by subsequent scholars. In 1989, Marie-Thérèse Urvoy— editor of Hafs ibn Albar's translation of the Psalms—published a brief notice concerning a scrap that emerged from the binding of a book held in a Portuguese library: four pages from a legal document produced in an Arabic-speaking Christian community in al-Andalus. Urvoy here comments on the linguistic processes visible in the few lines of text she examined: "It is very moving to see thus assembled on the same two leaves all the stages of the de-Arabization of the Mozarabs [or Arabic-speaking Christians of the Iberian peninsula]: 1) the canons in their original presentation, not vocalized; 2) certain canons, judged worthy of preservation, which are fully vocalized; 3) these same canons—or nearly the same—translated into Latin in the margin; 4) finally the simple scraping away of the text in order to recuperate the parchment."[62] Urvoy finds evidence of the gradual erasure of Arabic, but also ignorance of Latin—the person who recorded the text reconstructed Latin words through the Spanish which he obviously knew much better than Latin—as well as words that seem to come from ecclesiastical Greek rather than the terminology of the Latin rite. Here, from a text so thoroughly excluded from the literary record that it cannot even be termed *marginal*, Urvoy excavates a sliver of the linguistic actuality of medieval Iberia: a mediation between sacred languages and profane, spoken languages and written, Indo-European languages and Semitic.

In recent scholarship, scholars have begun to exhume and study fragments of lost words, like this one and like the fragmented, miscopied, and misunderstood kharjas. And they have begun to approach the written record of these beguiling and baffling centuries of European history with a better understanding of their confessional and linguistic subtleties, and from this perspective to produce thoughtful rereadings of familiar texts. I discussed above (in Chapter 2) the famous denunciation of the "poetry of the Arabs" from the pen of another, appreciably better known, author, one who (like Alvarus) was given to writing extended passages of vitriolic vituperation—Petrarch. The differences between the two men are so substantial that any historicist reading of the two men's work will obscure more than it reveals. Alvarus wrote near the beginning of the Arabs' adventure on the northern shores of the medieval Mediterranean, Petrarch near its end; Alvarus wrote from a state ruled and largely administered by Arabs, Petrarch from cities never conquered by the Arabs; Alvarus was an obscure literary doodler, all but forgotten by literary history, and Petrarch is widely recognized as the progenitor of poetic modernity. Yet in curious ways their stance regarding Arabic poetics begs a comparatist reading. Both men insist that they know the poetry of the Arabs, though modern historians have been reluctant to take them at their word. Both seem to see the Arabs as an imperious and insidious presence both morally and in the sphere of literature: recall Petrarch's waspish interjection, "after the Arabs, no one will be allowed to write!" (see Chapter 2, note 46), and Alvarus's "listless" and "loathsome" Arab poet who has so noxious an influence on Christian poets (see note 46 to this chapter). And the recent work of philologists and philologically minded historians has made it possible, finally, to begin to tease out the implications of the provocative statements these men made, declarations and denunciations that seem to place the Arabs and their poetic traditions at the heart of what the Latin and Romance writers of Alvarus's and Petrarch's age aimed to achieve.

The Manichean reading of what is typically termed the "Cordoba martyrs movement" in historical scholarship has made it difficult to view Alvarus's writings in any other than a stark dualistic light, in the context of a transcendent enmity between confessional foes. I have avoided using the word *martyr* in this account not in order to slight the religious commitment or the suffering of those who died but rather to tell another tale: one in which the instruments of revelation, the tools that God uses to communicate with humanity—the languages of ritual—are woven together into a single indissoluble fabric in the anti-Muslim polemic of a pillar of the Christian community. In telling the story of the interpretation of the kharjas in the first half of this chapter, I chose a more traditional narrative strategy: reading against the grain, making the implicit explicit, pointing out the nationalist investments of the scholars who labored to decipher the baffling textual trail of evidence left us by copyists long dead. Jones's muscular, even mannerist (over)reading of the manuscript difficulties of the kharjas and García's petty crusades to protect the Hispanicity of the kharjas signal the profound difficulty those telegraphic, ephemeral texts posed for modern scholars. First spoken eight or nine centuries earlier by a woman taxed beyond endurance by the travails of love, framed in the macaronic diction of a romance that crossed linguistic and confessional borders, copied and recopied over the centuries by scribes with an increasing ignorance of the language in which they were written: it is no wonder these texts have fragmented over the centuries. And yet, while specialists bicker over proposed interpretations of the manuscripts letter by letter, the kharjas have established themselves in the anthologies of Spain as the origins of the Spanish literary tradition. There is a certain unintended brilliance in this development: how succulent, to locate the origins of a modern national literary tradition in these texts that are so marginal, both to the poems they embellish and to literary history in general; so linguistically and culturally contingent that they were forgotten for centuries, abandoned by all three of the cultures that generated them! "We have arrived at the source of Spanish literature, which now originates in lyric rather than in epic," García wrote (see note 10 to this chapter). And it is a lyrical nationalism indeed that looks to these verses pockmarked with aporia to mark the origins of its literary identity.

Make no mistake: scholarship on the language, prosody, and poetic function of the kharja has made great strides over the last half century. We now know much more both about the texts and about the culture that produced them than we did before Stern's article brought them to the attention of an international scholarly public. Philological research—including Emilio García Gómez's articles in *Al-Andalus* and Alan Jones's catalogue of the kharjas—has produced lucid readings of many of the romance kharjas, and indeed other scholars have deemed pronouncements like Jones's on the difficulty of the kharjas to be exaggerated.[63] But even an analysis that evacuates the text of meaning, that challenges scholarly interpretation and reduces what once seemed to be words to a cluster of random letters—like Jones's "reading" that revealed a previously translated kharja to be illegible—may prove fruitful in the end. By burning away misinterpretations, such scorched earth philology may allow an insightful scholar to see a gleam of meaning in a tangle of apparently untranslatable letters.

At the same time, the kharja polemic reveals in stark relief the vulnerability of philology. Although during the nineteenth century it learned to use the vocabulary of positivism to describe itself, philology is as prone as any of the sciences (pure or humanistic) to manipulation and appropriation. García himself was alive to this fact. In a review of a work by S. D. Goitein published in *Al-Andalus*, he pointed out that when we read books of humanistic scholarship that claim to be scientific we can allow ourselves to believe in their objectivity. However, he warns, "it is an illusion. Objectivity is rarely seen in books, either because it is not sought or because it is impossible to achieve. And there is nothing bad in this. It is sufficient to rid oneself of the positivist illusion and not to seek in books the objectivity that they can rarely give us."[64] Here García in effect defangs the accusation that kharja scholarship was mired in a hermeneutic circle: that the scholars who scrutinized those opaque texts with the presupposition that they would find Romance words in Arabic drag simply saw what they already knew they would find.

For the Spanish philologists who sought, found, and celebrated the curious tale of Spain's Arab past seemed to know what they were looking for, or at least to recognize instantly what they found. The Spanish Orientalists I have discussed in this book—José Antonio Conde, Miguel Asín Palacios, Américo Castro—modeled a new vision of Spain's past. No longer a Catholic nation, medieval Spain was now defined by its complexity. Subtract a single thread from the skein—erase the contributions of Muslims or Jews to Spanish history—and the structure of the whole collapses. Spain's past was transformed; what remained ineradicable was the vanishing point for those medieval narratives, the distant goal at which they aimed: *Spain*. The nation provided a geographical and linguistic rationale for a history that predated its creation as a geographical category and the emergence of Spanish as a vehicle for literary composition. Thus did Miguel Asín Palacios locate the medieval philosophers Ibn Tufayl and Ibn Rushd "in our Spain" (see Chapter 2, note 55); thus did Francisco Javier Simonet speak of the "national hispano-Latin language" spoken by "nuestros Mozarabes" (see Chapter 2, note 57); thus did Francisco Fernández y González call the moriscos "Spaniards without doubt" (see Chapter 2, note 48); thus the sonorous titles of books by Conde, Pascual de Gayangos and Simonet: *Historia de la dominación de los Árabes en* España, *History of the Mohammedan Dynasties in* Spain, *Historia de los mozárabes de* España. The Spanish Orientalists whose work I have celebrated in this book worked in collaboration to create a new past for an old nation. Though Simonet and Fernández y González, for instance, disagreed about the details of the history of Spain, they both maintained that the nation that looked so ineluctably, timelessly Catholic today had a history characterized by linguistic, religious, and cultural complexity, and that for all practical purposes it remained *Spain* then, despite all its medieval difference.

García's work on the kharjas was immensely valuable not only for his erudition or for the historical truths he uncovered. He was a remarkably canny witness to the hermeneutic difficulties posed by the interpretation of the kharjas. In particular, no one understood better than García the fact that kharja scholarship had engaged in a losing battle against the philologist's oldest and deadliest foe, the hermeneutic circle. During the heady days following the discovery of the kharjas he enthused about the almost mystical processes by which scholars' understanding of the texts advanced: "And this consonantal text, shifting and murky (*movedizo y pantanoso*), must be interpreted by first guessing at words in a language almost unknown, which—*by a strange circular logic*—we come to know precisely through these poems deciphered so painstakingly and only with partial certainty."[65] It is difficult when reading these lines, when watching philologists pick through the kharjas to find Romance words buried in the rubble of Arabic letters, not to recall the stern Joseph Bédier mocking the Lachmannian editors who believed that their scientific methods allowed them to second guess the manuscript witnesses to the medieval literary tradition (discussed in Chapter 2). García acknowledges the hermeneutic difficulties posed by the kharjas, but he does so in a tone of wonder. The difficulty of the kharjas, simply stated, proves their worth. The kharjas are sui generis, unique in the history of letters. For this reason only interpreting the kharjas can teach us to interpret the kharjas.

Nor was García the only philologist to identify the vulnerability of philology as opportunity rather than peril. In a remarkable methodological apologia, Leo Spitzer—like García—scorns those who see the hermeneutic circle as a threat to the legitimacy of the philological reading. We met Spitzer at the end of the last chapter as he fled Nazi Germany for Istanbul, landing there a step ahead of Erich Auerbach. He left Istanbul for a job in Romance philology at Johns Hopkins University in 1936. His essay "Linguistics and Literary History," he tells us, took shape when Américo Castro invited him to give a talk on that subject at Princeton. The lecture on methodology, accompanied by a series of philological essays, would become his "first book printed in America";[66] it appeared in English in 1948. The essay is at once autobiography and philological manifesto: a scholarly Bildungsroman written not, like the Romantic genre, by a young man but rather by a man on the threshold of middle age—Spitzer was sixty-one years old when the article appeared. In the essay Spitzer pulls no punches; he begins by informing the

reader, quite disarmingly, that philology is a "sham science."[67] Yet he goes
on to speak with respect and with great intellectual passion about the power
of philology as a strategy for interpreting textual history. Spitzer affirms that
the philologist makes use of the inductive methods of the nineteenth-century
scientist in order to understand the constitution of the literary text. Yet we
also rely on deductive leaps—on what Spitzer terms the "inner click" that
accompanies the intuitive insights that allow us to unlock the meaning of the
text.[68] Because he sees intuition as necessary to the hermeneutic process,
Spitzer conceives the hermeneutic circle as, on the whole, salubrious. *This*
circle, he writes, "is not a vicious one; on the contrary, it is the basic operation in the humanities, the *Zirkel im Verstehen* as Dilthey has termed the
discovery, made by the Romantic scholar and theologian Schleiermacher,
that cognizance in philology is reached not only by the gradual progression
from one detail to another detail, but by the anticipation or divination of the
whole . . . Our to-and-fro voyage from certain outward details to the inner
center and back again to other series of details is only an application of the
principle of the 'philological circle.'"[69] For Spitzer intuition precedes rationale, and it guarantees rather than compromises the integrity of the philological analysis. "The first step" of the philological reading, "on which all may
hinge, can never be planned: it must already have taken place. . . . We see,
indeed, that to read is to have read, to understand is equivalent to having
understood."[70]

Spitzer reveals philology to be a hybrid of inductive and deductive
method, a compound of intuition and painstaking textual analysis. The
scholar must historicize. Particularly when working with texts made difficult
by the passage of time, we must make an effort to understand how the text
reflects historical event and linguistic evolution. But this work does not ex-
haust the philologist's methodological repertoire or our responsibility. While
we're reading, an "inner click" reveals to us a truth about the text or reflected
in it. This moment of recognition allows us to navigate our way out of textual
difficulties, to unravel aporia, or to perceive an author's meaning. We then
use philological analysis to coax the text to confirm that truth which our
intuition has anticipated; we ask it to teach us something we already know.

Here Spitzer's argument—though we may feel that we know precisely
what he's getting at—becomes a bit opaque; for the vanishing point of his
philology is a firm faith in the transcendence of human knowledge and in the
capacity of human language to represent the transcendent. In the culminating
paragraphs of the essay Spitzer argues unambiguously and unapologetically

that to be a philologist is to be a believer. The philologist has faith that the fragments from which he constructs his argument—texts obscured by lacunae and by linguistic and historical difference—are shot through with the light of divine understanding. There is no peril in the hermeneutic circle if we recognize the truth and beauty of the aggregate that the scholar studies: the human mind, implicitly understood as a reflection of the divine intellect.[71]

Perhaps it is easier for a twenty-first-century audience to evaluate Spitzer's argument if we phrase it in terms more familiar to us. The Spanish Orientalists whose work I have discussed in this book began with the presupposition that in the medieval past—scandalously different though it might appear—they would find an image of Spain in its youth. They demonstrated to a global audience of philologists that the nation's past might prove at moments perversely difficult to interpret—one might need to learn a Semitic language in order to read it!—and yet be no less *ours*. The Spaniards were the first to embrace an Arab past as an essential chapter in a modern European national history. In their excavation of Spain's Arab past, they celebrated a modernity that *originates in lyric*—in the diction of a love affair between languages—*rather than epic*, the genre of agonistic battles between blood lines, between linguistic and confessional communities. They found the first spark of a modern Spanish identity in the *sydy* of the Hebrew kharja rather than the valiant warrior *El Cid* of epic fame.

Yet it's my intuition that the diction and vocabulary of nationalism is now on the wane, even in the history-haunted discipline of Romance philology; it, no less than the mysticism of Romantic scholarship, looks a bit shopworn today. Certainly we know that the nation-state—that marvelous piece of bureaucratic technology that germinated in Europe and North America at the end of the eighteenth century and was in full bloom at the end of the nineteenth—is no more a going concern. It stands to reason that nationalist philology will follow suit. Even modernity, whether you believe it was invented by northern Europeans enamored of the Greeks or in the shaded wings of García's Alhambra, is (as they say) history. For these reasons García's reconstruction of the kharja as the origin of the literature of modern Spain has come to seem much less au courant than his Alhambra. His interpretation of the kharjas, the urgent message of a beloved muted but not silenced by historical distance and linguistic difficulty, brought them alive for a new audience—the scholars and poets of modernity. But he painted them in a monochromatic palette; in his hands, they became the voice of Spain. His Alhambra, though! The pointillist portrait he creates in *Silla del Moro* speaks at multiple, aleatory moments in its history. His reading of the Alhambra sacrifices neither historical texture nor the sumptuous sensual pleasures to be derived from close reading. It is at once passionately historicist and passionately intuitive; the two urges, rather than denying legitimacy the one to the other, rather support and affirm each other. *Silla del Moro* celebrates and indeed imitates the hybridity of the city itself; and in so doing it models a philological practice that does not evade the challenge of the past but answers complexity with complexity and audacity with audacity.

So, too—in homage to García's Alhambra—in my reading, Alvarus's polemic memorializes the linguistic density of his age; and, like García's Alhambra, the "Indiculus Luminosus" described above creaks under the strain of history. It is shot through with stress fractures attesting to both the vagaries of its transmission to our age and, most urgently, the difficulties of the moment when it was recorded. Alvarus's Latin functions a bit like a camera obscura in which the attentive reader can still glimpse a shadow play occurring beyond the margin of the text: the competitions between Arabic and Latin cultures in his Cordoba. Why did his conversion to the quantitative meter of the ancients make such a difference to Alvarus: why does he return to it in the "Indiculus Luminosus," in the "Vita Eulogi," in his poems, in his letters?[72] What concatenation of anxieties is codified in his excoriating denunciation of end rhyme? If my intuition is correct, Alvarus's Latin periods amalgamate two literary discoveries: the newly venerated style of the ancient and patristic Latin works which Eulogius brought back from his travels and the newly fashionable architecture of Arabic art prose. Alvarus's style is an amalgam of his masters', and if he fulminates against those who wear their cultural allegiance on their sleeve—whose verse displays the scar of the Arab invasion at the end of every line—it is, in part, in order to abjure the depth of his own intimacy with that literary tradition.

It is a crude thesis, by philological standards, but may serve as a provocation. Like the philological studies I have discussed in this book, it is informed by the presupposition that the Arabs are not exterior to the history of the Latins, and vice versa. Like those readings, it views a distant moment of Mediterranean unity as a crucial point of reference for the present. But unlike them, it does not take medieval cultural commerce between Arabs and Latins as the genesis of a modern *national* sensibility. Of course, it stands to reason that a philologist of the postnational and postmodern twenty-first century will find a substantially different significance in the prenational and premodern Mediterranean of the Middle Ages. We will study and build on the work (and the insights) of our predecessors, of course. Their manipulations of the texts we read will become part of the texture of our own readings. We must acknowledge the importance of nationalism to their readings; but that doesn't commit us to reproducing their nationalism. Our readings must represent the past to an age that is no longer consumed with understanding and projecting identities defined along national boundaries. The fault lines between communities are drawn differently in our world; and our sentiments with regard to the written text, to linguistic and confessional difference, and indeed to literacy itself have changed. The next chapter in the history of the philological Mediterranean may well take us beyond the quaint national ideologies of the nineteenth and twentieth centuries and push us toward the *worlding* of that distant, ever more familiar history.

*Chapter 7*

# Scheherazade at Home (Baghdad, A.D. 803; London and Hollywood, 1939)

Però che a un popolo licenzioso e tumultuario gli può da uno uomo buono essere parlato, e facilmente può essere ridotto nella via buona; a un principe cattivo non è alcuno che possa parlare, né vi è altro rimedio che il ferro. Da che si può fare coniettura della importanza della malattia dell'uno e dell'altro: che se a curare la malattia del popolo bastan le parole, ed a quella del principe bisogna il ferro, non sarà mai alcuno che non giudichi che dove bisogna maggior cura siano maggiori errori.
    —Machiavelli, *Discorsi sopra la prima deca di Tito Livio* II:8[1]

[Although a good man can speak to an unruly and agitated people and they may easily be returned to the good path, there is no one who may speak to a bad prince, nor is there any remedy for him other than the sword. Thus we can make a conjecture about the gravity of the malady of the one and the other: if to cure the malady of the people words are sufficient, and to cure that of the prince requires a sword, anyone can see that where a greater cure is required, there the errors will be greater.]

IT MAY SEEM churlish to trim the accretions which the *Thousand and One Nights* has acquired through its global meanderings over the last millennium, to refuse all that the *Nights* has become—the exemplary work of world literature, written in no one time or place but massaged in many—and restore to it its particularity as a work of medieval Arabic literature, particularly when what remains after the Western manipulations are trimmed away is so exiguous. The *Nights* had a dual existence, throughout its premodern history in its native, Arabic-language milieu, as light reading for educated men and fodder for storytellers. In a word, it is a work of popular literature. And, no doubt, it has always been mercurial in nature, as popular literature tends to be. The written versions themselves, were there a more robust early manuscript history, would demonstrate a high level of variance—differences in word choice, the ordering of tales, even plot structure.[2] Given the fluidity of premodern literature in general, given the fluidity of oral literature in general, given the thematics of this work in particular—a celebration, after all, of narrative invention—it seems wrongheaded to insist on textual fidelity and resist the dazzling capacity for metamorphosis that the text has displayed in its encounter with European letters. And the Galland manuscript, the most extensively studied manuscript predating its transformation in the West, seems a paltry thing in comparison to the Rubenesque Scheherazade of the West.

Yet a case can be made for a Bédierist reading of the Galland manuscript. The Scheherazade of the West—the garrulous maid who picked up a thread dropped by the *salonnières'* fairies at the end of the seventeenth century, who boldly carried her tales of the fantastic, the exotic, and the grotesque into the gathering light of the eighteenth century—that Scheherazade we know; Shahrazad, however, we don't. I discussed in Chapter 1 the extraordinary difficulties of the manuscript history of the *Thousand and One Nights*. What the West made of the *Nights* between the beginning of the eighteenth century and the end of the nineteenth contaminated the Arabic text in the versions available to scholars. Only when Muhsin Mahdi published his edition of the Galland manuscript in 1984 did it become possible for the scholarly community to read and study the work in a form that predated Western manipulation. Scheherazade, heroine of the West, we know; but we are not so well acquainted with Shahrazad, the Arab maiden with Persian, Sanskrit, and Greek forebears, the heroine who entered the Arabic literary tradition more than a millennium ago and who left so remarkably few manuscript traces of her passing.

In this chapter I will return to Scheherazade, approaching the *Thousand and One Nights* not (as I did in the first chapter) by way of the textual monument that the West has erected to her but rather by circumambulating the comparatively humble memorial to her in Arabic letters, the Galland manuscript. I must make a confession before I begin, however: my reading of the *Nights* in this chapter is not truly philological. The reader will not find here the "staged cacophony of multilingual encounters" (as Emily Apter characterized Leo Spitzer's philological practice[3]), the contrapuntal melody—at once scandalous and sumptuous—of alien alphabets encountering each other on the page. It is my duty to urge you (to paraphrase Lemony Snicket) to close this book at once and read something else, if you prefer that sort of thing. I have chosen a different approach in part because this study is intended for a more general readership. Nothing asserts the *difference* of the philological reading more shrilly than the spectacle of swarms of Sanskrit or Greek or Arabic letters disturbing the orderly ranks of our own. In part, however, I take the stance I do with regard to textual history out of a conviction about the sort of philological practice that speaks to the present.

During the past quarter of a century, philology—like a heavy-metal band of the 1970s—has staged a number of comebacks. At regular intervals scholars have augured a return to philology. In Chapter 1 I discussed Edward Said's essay, "The Return to Philology" (2004). Paul de Man, of course, had called for a "Return to Philology" two decades earlier, in an essay by that name that appeared in the *Times Literary Supplement* in 1982 and in book form in 1986.[4] But there's philology and then there's philology; the philological practice to which scholars return changes with each iteration. Paul de Man saw philology as a precursor of critical theory: "the turn to theory," he wrote, "occurred as a return to philology." The philological project for him served to focus critical attention on "the structure of language prior to the meaning it produces."[5] In so doing it foreshadowed the *theoretical* project in which de Man was himself engaged. Philology provided a lens that allowed the scholar to scrutinize the materiality of language; critical theory used reading strategies pioneered by the philologists to materialize the ideational structures of the text.

In its twenty-first-century reincarnations, however, philology seems to be taking a historical (not to say historicist) turn. Said saw philology as a critical rhetoric that professional readers use to parse the historical uniqueness both of the text and of the present reading of the text. Said cites the committed reading practice known in Islamic traditions as *ijtihad* as a model for the secular reader: "Since in Islam the Koran is the Word of God, it is therefore impossible ever fully to grasp, though it must repeatedly be read. But the fact that it is in language already makes it incumbent on readers first of all to try to understand its literal meaning, with a profound awareness that others before them have attempted the same daunting task."[6] Said understands our duties as professional readers in continuity with our responsibilities as human beings; he situates his philology in the context of his notion of humanism. His definition of philology unapologetically celebrates reading as an end in itself, as a moral exercise. At the same time it privileges the historical uniqueness of the text (and condemns the theoretical move that would attempt to disengage the text from lived reality[7]). The community of readers of whom and to whom the philologist speaks, whose witness to the reading keeps the philologist honest, includes not only the philologist's contemporaries—the immediate audience for our readings—but also those others who have "attempted the same daunting task," those who have read before us.

*Philology* connotes a peculiarly energetic reading practice, a loving attentiveness to the engagement of the text with its own history. The text at times refuses to mean; it throws up barriers to our understanding. The philologist may work to untangle a textual knot in a number of ways. Speaking in broad terms, the philological reading may focus its interpretive efforts on the materiality of language; the philologist may use his linguistic and literary erudition to unravel the meaning of the text. Or she may see the constitution of meaning in the interaction between literary text and extraliterary history, treating the text as witness to historical events occurring just beyond the edge of the page. What the two approaches share is the steady gaze at the surface of the text as such; philological practice connotes a vigorous and affectionate scrutiny of the text in all its unique, splendid, at times maddening detail. The two approaches are not mutually exclusive, of course, and we regularly use both optics—the historical and the linguistic—in a single reading. But during certain periods over the last two centuries philologists have privileged one axis or the other, in response either to personal preferences and tastes or to current styles or concerns.

Which of the two reading strategies is in the ascendant as we enter the twenty-first century? The presupposition of my reading of the *Nights* is that—while no reading of medieval literature can afford to dispense with attentiveness to the letter of the text, and indeed few medievalists would care to do so—philological readings of the literary traditions of the medieval Mediterranean at the present time aim (sometimes unconsciously) to tease out the historical specificity of the text in order to contribute to the project of worlding European and Euro-American letters. More recent readings of medieval Mediterranean literatures resist the tendency, typical of nineteenth- and twentieth-century philology, to see literary history solely in terms of genealogies—taxonomies that emphasize familial relations between languages or texts descended from the same root, the influence of like upon like. The philological reading that speaks to a twenty-first-century audience sees in the premodern text the reflection of a vanishing point still to come in its future, as nineteenth-century philology did. We still see the past as a foreshadowing of the present. But the medieval text today looks forward not toward the emergence of the modern nation in nineteenth-century Europe but rather toward an uneasy globalization in which local or regional differences mean nothing and everything. Medieval textuality, today, echoes our brave new postnational world. And *Mediterranean* medievality in particular casts an uncanny reflection of terrain very familiar to us today—because it predates the erection of a Berlin Wall between the world of Islam and Christian Europe, an artificial division which we have now seen fall—and yet starkly different.

The scholars whose work I have read in this book made such research possible by producing historical narratives that contradict some of the most cherished notions of European modernity (though the verbing of the noun *world* would, of course, have flummoxed them). The Europe invented by these Orientalists did not discover the modern sciences when it rediscovered Greek antiquity; we learned our scientific methodology from the Arabs. European poets did not invent the poetry of romantic love, thus setting in motion a Rube Goldberg machine that would ultimately generate the vernaculars of modern Europe and Romantic individualism; they borrowed romantic love, both the concept and its poetic celebration, from the Arabs. Modernity was not invented in the capitals of northern Europe but in Granada and Palermo. The philologists whose work I have surveyed in this book defended their counterintuitive theses with detailed readings of medieval literature in a gorgeous bouquet of languages, living and dead. In so doing they (explicitly or implicitly) challenged the presumption of European exceptionalism that informed most accounts of the "rise of Europe" and the "birth of modernity." And they (explicitly or implicitly) denied the validity of the confident Western belief in the timeless and untraversable distance between the Arab Orient and the European West.

There is, of course, more to the world (and hence more to world history) than the Arab-Islamic and Euro-Christian civilizations. I do not claim that my reading of history—either of European Orientalist scholarship or of the medieval literary record—is exhaustive or inclusive. I offer the readings in this book (both of European Orientalism and of medieval literature) as geographical and chronological tesserae: pivotal chapters in the history of the last millennium or so, some of them, but still only fragments of a larger picture. I have been inspired in part by a conviction that the material I document here, some of it quite marginal to the normative narratives of European history, is simply too important to fall by the wayside. In addition my readings aim to demonstrate the vitality and indeed the necessity of philological reading practice to the study of literary history—despite the fact that the bloom is long off the rose of scientism, and despite the fact that the philological reading turns out to be not all that *scientific* after all.

My reading of the *Thousand and One Nights* in this chapter constitutes a modest contribution to the effort to document the intimacy between the Arab world and the West over the last millennium. It takes as its point of departure the presupposition that European exceptionalism—in particular, the unbreachable wall we presume to exist between Arabic letters and the literary traditions of the vernaculars of Europe—is a modern invention. Manuscript evidence of literary communications between Arabic and European vernacular letters is indeed difficult (though not, as we will see, impossible) to produce. Nonetheless the historical record requires us to assume contact between the traditions, or at the minimum a consciousness of (linguistic, literary and cultural) plurality. The twenty-first-century philologist must use a dynamic of cultural difference—not the image of a European "continent" sealed off from the voices of exteriority for the duration of its Middle Ages—as the backdrop for our readings of medieval literature.

To the attentive reader, of course, it may seem I have stacked the deck in my favor. How hard can it be to demonstrate communication between Arabic and European letters if your proof text is the *Thousand and One Nights*? But that text is sui generis, a one-of-a-kind pluri-authored literary extravaganza! If the philologist is beholden to others before her "who have attempted the same daunting task," this could be a long reading indeed. I continue my confession by acknowledging that it was her appeal to a plurality of audiences that first attracted me to Scheherazade, and the thought of how dazzling a "thick philology" of such a text might be. But what kept me with her was something else, an interpretive knot that I struggled for some time to unravel. The reading that I offer here had its origin in a stubborn notion that came to me as I read and reread the text, the history of its manuscript transmission, and the various imitations and homages to it produced in the languages of the Orient and the West. Because I could not banish it I sought instead to investigate it, to substantiate or refute it, by seeking more information about the text and the history it might reflect. It is the fruit of that process that I present to you now. Briefly stated, my approach to the *Thousand and One Nights* began with an intuition that Scheherazade and Shahrazad are two different women; and that Shahrazad, the Arab maiden, casts a dark shadow over the peculiar and ambivalent textual citadel constructed to house her.

## Baghdad, A.D. 803

Certainly those who first imagined the *Thousand and One Nights* had no notion that they were creating a literary work for the ages. We have references establishing that an Arabic version of it existed as early as the tenth century of the Christian era. However, from the first it was judged frivolous and insignificant by those whose opinion mattered. Ibn al-Nadim, a tenth-century Baghdadi bookseller who wrote an exhaustive catalogue of the literary works known to him, gave it pride of place in his account of the origins of imaginative fiction: "the first book to be written with this content," he tells us—meaning stories to be told at night for the purposes of entertainment—"was the book *Hazar Afsan*, which means 'a thousand stories.'" (Ibn al-Nadim knew it by its Persian title; it would ultimately acquire a naturalized Arabic title: *Alf layla wa-layla, The Thousand and One Nights*.[8]) We don't know what the version that Ibn al-Nadim knew looked like. But his synopsis makes it clear that the frame tale, the Scheherazade story, had already taken on the form we know today. Despite its apparent popularity Ibn al-Nadim deemed it "truly a coarse book, without warmth in the telling [literally, *graceless* and *meager*]."[9] Ibn al-Nadim's judgment of the text suggests that from the first the tale found a public not among a literary elite but among casual readers and listeners. Such manuscripts of it as existed may have been unliterary by design; a vivid imagination or a skilled storyteller could add flesh to the scrawny narrative in the telling.

The fact that it was a work of popular literature, and thus marginal to the Arabic literary tradition, helps to explain why relatively few early manuscripts of the work survive. The written versions of it would have seen heavy action. They would not be sold to men who would safeguard them in private libraries but rather rented to professional storytellers and passionate if casual readers who would absorb their details and then return them. They would be loved up over the years and would vanish, as the ephemera of popular culture do. And a popular transmission, too, could explain why fragments of it (as we will see) reached the distant shores of Europe while the architecture of the frame narrative largely did not.

The Galland manuscript seems consistent with the notion that the *Nights* functioned as a seed for oral recitation. We would expect repetition of stock phrases in the extant manuscripts, the remnants of the formulas that are the professional storyteller's stock-in-trade, and these we find—the occasional bit of rhymed prose describing the beauty of a youth or maiden or underscoring the moral of a tale. Some passages have been elaborated by the writer who recorded them, recherché details and refined prose added, while others seem no more than notes to be dressed up in performance. Some characters emerge in splendid precision; others seem simply adumbrations of stock description; others still are shady outlines to be filled in by the storyteller, if he were so inspired.

Thus, for instance, Scheherazade—or, to restore to her the arabicized Persian name by which she was known in the premodern Arabic manuscripts of the *Nights*, Shahrazad. We meet Shahrazad after the dark machinery of the frame tale has been set in motion. Shahzaman has discovered his wife's betrayal and murdered her and her lover; his brother, Shahrayar, has discovered his own wife's adultery. Convinced of the irredeemable perfidy of all women, the two brothers have wandered—in search of truth or to escape from the truth, it is not clear which—and returned. Shahrayar has devised a solution to his difficulty: he will take a virgin to the marriage bed each night and order her execution in the morning, before she has a chance to betray him. And Shahrazad's father, Shahrayar's vizier, is responsible for securing his brides. It is only when Shahrayar's city has been brought to the brink of collapse by his serial "marriages" that we meet Shahrazad. And her name immediately signals her importance to the tale, echoing as it does the sound and structure of the names of the two brothers.

Who is Shahrazad? To paraphrase Todorov, she is a verb: she is the function of storytelling; she tells the tale that does not end.[10] We learn little else about her. She became a heroine during the twentieth century despite—or, perhaps, because of—the paucity of information about her revealed in the text. She has come to symbolize stealth wisdom; the power of popular resistance to undermine the brutalities of misrule; the power of narrative itself, of the human urge to use invented people and invented event to interpret and thus transform reality. Indeed it is true that—if we consider the late medieval Syrian manuscript edited by Muhsin Mahdi—the tales Shahrazad tells, particularly at the outset of the work, seem to speak directly to her plight. They return obsessively to a short list of themes all bundled together in the story of Shahrayar's madness: trust and betrayal; rule and misrule; the governance of cities and of the human heart; the deviousness of women and the devastations of romantic love. Shahrazad resists the murderous Shahrayar by leading him through a looking-glass world where he sees his faults—nightmarishly distorted, but unmistakably him—and the damage they do.[11]

For the stories that Shahrazad tells Shahrayar do not have the sparkle, the innocent charm, that the *Arabian Nights* possesses in the Disney or nursery versions that are likely to be our first introduction to them in the West. Shahrazad spins a web of tales in which sinister events occur with brutal deliberation and in uncanny repetition. Thus in a story cycle embedded in the frame narrative, the Porter and the Three Ladies of Baghdad, we hear a series of tales in which characters go underground and there become cogs in the machine of fate: in each case they are the undoing of a person they meet (or accompany) underground, despite their affection for that person. We learn as the narrative progresses that a character's descent will be another's doom. In the last of these tales (the Third Dervish's tale) the protagonist himself knows his fate; it has been foretold. Forewarned, however, is not forearmed. He descends, and he will inadvertently kill the beautiful and noble young man he meets underground. Understanding does not grant immunity from a bleak fate but only adds a sinister nuance to a character's doom.

Of course some tales do end well in the *Thousand and One Nights*, in particular the embedded frame narratives. The Porter and the Three Ladies of Baghdad, for instance, concludes with a motif not unfamiliar in the Western storytelling tradition. The three Baghdadi ladies have (unbeknownst to them) entertained Harun al-Rashid, his minister Ja'far, and his executioner Masrur in disguise. The morning after their debauched revelry (one understands better, having studied this tale, the Victorians' opinion that the *Nights* was somewhat louche), Harun orders Ja'far to bring the ladies before him in order that they might tell their own tales. One imagines their anxiety—particularly when the caliph instructs them not to lie to him, for "you should be truthful even if the truth sends you to burning hell"[12]—yet the story ends happily. He arranges a prosperous marriage for each of them, even marrying one of them himself, and we presume that they lived happily ever after.

The dramatis personae present at this little pantomime of justice—the Abbasid caliph Harun al-Rashid and two members of his household—memorialize the era when the *Nights* entered the Arabic literary tradition.

Harun ruled the Arab world from his sumptuous capital, Baghdad, from 786 until 809. The splendor of Baghdad during his reign became an article of faith for the Western popularizers of the *Arabian Nights*. For Tennyson he was the "good Haroun Alraschid," and his city sported "shrines of fretted gold, high-walled gardens green and old."[13] For the 1924 Douglas Fairbanks film *The Thief of Bagdad*, sets were constructed "on acres of glazed floor . . . so that the magnificent structures, with their shadows growing darker as they ascend, seem to have the fantastic quality of hanging from the clouds rather than of being set firmly upon earth."[14] Baghdad was, for modern Western readers of the *Nights*, a pastel citadel that provided a fitting backdrop for tales of chivalric splendor. But of course Abbasid Baghdad had somewhat earthier implications for a medieval Arab audience; and the circle of men we meet in the story of the Porter and the Three Ladies of Baghdad in particular played key roles in a narrative with a very different ending.

Ja'far and Harun were bosom buddies until the night of January 28, A.D. 803, when Harun (for reasons that still puzzle the historians) ordered the murder of Ja'far and ultimately of every member of his extended clan, the powerful Barmaki family. And his executioner features in the stories told about the massacre: Masrur refused to carry out Harun's command to murder Ja'far until Harun threatened to send another executioner after his head as well as Ja'far's. Arab historians produced a number of plausible narratives to account for the fall of the Barmakids: the caliph's servants had exceeded their station and grown overweening; the caliph (or the Arab aristocracy in general) resented the ascendancy of a Persian clan; the caliph had simply outgrown the tutelage of Ja'far and the Barmakids and, being a brutal man, chose a brutal means to celebrate his maturity.[15] And some blamed a palace intrigue for the downfall of the Barmakids. Harun had married Ja'far to his sister, 'Abbasa, so that he might enjoy the company of both of them during long evenings of wine and song. The marriage was meant to be symbolic, but Ja'far and 'Abbasa fell in love and (unbeknownst to Harun) conceived a child. One day 'Abbasa beat one of her slave girls too viciously. In a fit of pique the girl revealed the existence of 'Abbasa's child to Harun. Or, according to other versions, she told all to Zubayda, Harun's wife; and Zubayda, jealous of Harun's affection for 'Abbasa and resentful of the Barmakids' ascendancy, told Harun. Betrayed by his beloved sister and by his trusted minister, Harun had no choice but to exact a terrible revenge.

The story may be historical poppycock; it may be true but inconsequential to the ultimate fate of the Barmakids; it is yet no less compelling for that.

And when an audience familiar with the tale meets Harun, Ja'far, and his executioner prowling the streets of Baghdad in disguise, when the action moves to Harun's court and Harun must judge the exploits of the three unruly women, the history of the misdeeds of the women of Harun's family crosses wires with the invented tale. The actions of 'Abbasa and her slave girl intrude on the narrative like the letters of the *scriptura ima* or lower writing of a palimpsest just glimpsed beneath the text that has overwritten it. And the tale that follows the Porter and the Three Ladies of Baghdad in the Galland manuscript, the Story of the Three Apples, only increases the undercurrent of dread. In it, as in a nightmare, Ja'far fails repeatedly to identify the culprit who has committed a shocking crime, and Harun threatens repeatedly to put him to death for his failure.

In the popular imagination, palace intrigues—spiteful and vicious machinations behind the harem walls—caused the downfall of the Barmakids. These events are not mentioned in the *Nights*. Yet the reader who knows that history cannot help remembering it as she turns the pages of the text, because in the *Thousand and One Nights* we do hear a feminine voice in the night that works a mysterious magic on the psyche of the ruler: the voice is Shahrazad's. She has the sultan's ear. And she uses her intimacy with the ruler of the state to manipulate his emotions and influence his governance. The stories she tells her murderous husband fall (to borrow Ramón Menéndez Pidal's description of Joseph Bédier's narrative voice[16]) somewhere between prophetic and menacing. Stories do save lives in the frame tale and the frames within the frames: not only the Porter and the Three Ladies of Baghdad, but also the Merchant and the Demon, the Fisherman and the Demon, the Hunchback. In the tales embedded within those frames, however, it's a different story. We meet a man who lies to his cousin in order to consummate his incestuous love for his sister. With the cousin's help the two inter themselves in a subterranean tomb and die in each other's arms; when their bodies are found, God's wrath has incinerated them. In another tale, a vicious queen lies to her husband about her lust for a repulsive slave. She turns her husband to stone from the waist down, but the king has his revenge on her when his ally, pretending to be her lover, murders her in their bed. Perhaps the bitterest pill to swallow, the most uncanny tale that Shahrazad tells, is the Story of King Yunan and the sage Duban, in which the king—acting on the advice of an envious vizier—sentences to death the scholar who has cured him of leprosy. Duban promises the king a glimpse into a book which will answer any question he asks, but only after his own execution. And he gives the king a magic powder that will allow Yunan to reanimate his head following his death. The king has the scholar killed, coaxes his head back to life, and obeys the commands that the undead scholar's head speaks. The book that Duban has bequeathed to Yunan is blank, but its pages have been infused with poison; so as the scholar's reanimated head instructs him to turn page after page, the king poisons himself. The answer to the question that King Yunan never asks is the narrative of Duban's vengeance and the king's death. It's true that the characters we meet in the *Nights* ransom their lives with tales; but in those tales, narrative has a striking rate of toxicity.

The *Thousand and One Nights* is a spectacularly uncanny work of literature. Within a frame tale that celebrates as a heroine a woman who whispers stories into the ear of a mad governor, it reworks horrific legends about a dynasty ruined by women's pillow talk. And Abbasid Baghdad makes a shrewd backdrop for the metaliterary drama symbolized by the position of the *Thousand and One Nights* in the Arabic literary tradition: the debate over the legitimacy of imaginative narrative in a milieu characterized by cultural plurality. In Abbasid Baghdad Arabic letters first came into contact with and absorbed external literary traditions: the Pahlavi, the Greek, the Syriac, the Sanskrit. Thanks to the bibliographical genius of the early Arab historians, who regularly detailed the sources of their information, Ibn al-Nadim—who reported to us the scorn that litterateurs felt for the *Nights*—also mentioned the extra-Arabic origins of the fantastic literature of his age. "The first people to collect stories," he wrote, "devoting books to them and safeguarding them in libraries . . . were the early Persians."[17] The hybrid Persian-Arabic names by which the three central characters of the frame tale were known in the Arabic version of the work—Shahrazad, Shahrayar, Shahzaman—as well as the Persian title by which Ibn al-Nadim knew the *Nights* indicate its origin (its proximate origin, at least) in Persian letters. The Barmakid clan itself represents another, quite different facet of the process of contact and absorption. The Barmakids, who rose to a position of extraordinary political power in Harun al-Rashid's Baghdad, were themselves Arabized Persians.

As it forged an imaginative narrative tradition of its own, Arab culture struggled to reconcile fantastic tales—with their non-Arab origins and their often salacious content—to Islamic values.[18] Islamic teaching did not prohibit the invention of fictions, particularly when they were used to explicate or reinforce the precepts of Islamic belief. But scholars discouraged the telling of frivolous tales. And the *Thousand and One Nights* made matters difficult for itself with its off-color and frequently macabre content. The *Kalila wa-*

*Dimna*, a mirror for princes translated from the Persian at roughly the same time as the *Nights*, enjoyed a vogue in Arabic letters that endured for centuries. Translated into Greek, Latin, and the vernaculars of Europe, it would become a respected work in the European literary traditions as well. The *Kalila wa-Dimna* included fantastic tales just as the *Nights* did. But they typically had a plausible moral and could be read as ethical or religious exempla. The same could not be said of the ghoulish or scandalous vignettes in the *Nights*. The paucity of early Arabic manuscripts of the *Nights* tells us all we need to know about the judgment passed on the work by its Arab audience: during the interminable winter evenings, you might ask for a tale from the *Nights* and hope God was looking the other way; but it was not a work to be studied, elaborated, and safeguarded for posterity in libraries.

Abbasid Baghdad, where the Arabic *Nights* emerged from a multiple and shadowy genealogy, is both the birthplace and the setting of the *Nights* as we know it. The text does of course recall other times and places: see, for instance, the doomed, unnamed capital of the frame tale, its streets swept clean of virgins, and the vibrant Cairo of the tales told in the Hunchback cycle. I have chosen to emphasize a single time and place in my account of its origins both because philological analysis thrives on precision and because it is my sense that Abbasid Baghdad—honorary birthplace not only of the *Nights* but also of literary fiction in Arabic—casts a long shadow over the text. For it was precisely in Abbasid Baghdad that imaginative narrative in Arabic had its Prague Spring before Islamic scholars condemned it as immoral and irreligious. William Granara has suggestively used Bakhtin's formulation of the *chronotope* to refer to modern Arab novelists' return to medieval al-Andalus as a place that is also a historical era.[19] Granara argues that in Arabic fiction al-Andalus transcends geotemporal specificity to represent the historical and potential capacity of Arabo-Islamic culture to interact fruitfully with other cultural systems. The manipulation of the historical figures Harun al-Rashid and his minister Ja'far in the *Thousand and One Nights* suggests that for the medieval Arab imagination Abbasid Baghdad functioned as another such chronotope. David Pinault has shown that the story of the Three Apples riffs on historical accounts of the personalities of Harun al-Rashid and Ja'far.[20] Muhsin Mahdi has identified the episode, plucked from histories of Abbasid Baghdad, that inspired the King's Steward's tale from the Hunchback cycle.[21] And my reading locates in the tales of Shahrazad a concatenation of anxieties associated with Baghdad. If her fantastic flights of narrative liberate the city from the plague that decimates it, at the same time the dark stories she relates convey an inescapable sense of dread. Her garrulousness represents at once the brilliance of narrative invention and its moral peril, its divagations into turpitude and its heterogeneous origins; she saves her city while she evokes the threat to civic stability posed by the women of the caliph's household in the popular narratives of the Barmakids' demise. The *Thousand and One Nights* circles round the "real" history of Abbasid Baghdad as it worries over themes of governance and passion and of narration, silence, and death. It situates its interrogation of the splendors and dangers of imaginative narrative in a time and place associated with narrative opulence, political power, and the dangers of both fantastic tales and political power ungoverned by reason.

Of course, some of the specificity of this history would have been rubbed away by the time the version of it that comes down to us was recorded. Scholars date the Galland manuscript to the late Middle Ages, at least 500 and perhaps as many as 650 years after Harun al-Rashid's massacre of the Barmakids. By this time, too, the debate over the legitimacy of imaginative narrative had become background noise. What the text loses in detail, however, it gains in emotional urgency. It returns stubbornly to the themes of narration (in particular narration under duress and as a negotiating strategy) and betrayal (in particular the betrayals of cunning women and of mad governors). It suggests a disconcerting, even uncanny message: the woman whispering stories in your ear may possess a knowledge that will set you free; or she may drive you mad. The only way to understand her intent is to listen closely to what she says.

## The Medieval Mediterranean

At this point, my narrative must sacrifice precision in order to tell a tale difficult to contain within temporal, geographic or linguistic bounds. In this book I have read philological readings of the medieval Mediterranean that emphasize communications between the Arabic-language cultures of the Islamic world and the Romance-language cultures of Christian Europe. But this represents a woeful reduction of the linguistic and cultural riches of that geo-chronological terrain. It excises—among others—the Hebrew tradition, the Persian, the Byzantine Greek, the Turkish, the Armenian and Berber and Coptic. One would need that useful conceit that Jean Baudrillard lifted from Jorge Luis Borges, the map coextensive with the terrain it charts, to do justice to the reality on the ground.

The medieval Mediterranean serves philologists today precisely as *chronotope*: as abstraction, as a metaphor for a more radical and scandalous complexity. If (in my reading) Abbasid Baghdad encoded reflections on the potential and peril of imaginative narrative against a backdrop of cultural plurality in the late medieval Arab imaginary, the medieval Mediterranean has recently become for philologists a similar kind of chronotope. As in William Granara's reading modern Arab novelists use medieval al-Andalus as a symbol of the possibility of negotiation between currently conflicting monotheisms, so do historians and literary historians use the medieval Mediterranean in general to historicize contemporary tensions between Christians and Muslims. Mediterranean history gives us a way to demonstrate the historical interdependence of Euro-Christian culture and Islamic culture. Lines of cultural transmission and trade routes crisscrossed the medieval Mediterranean as well as cultural fault lines, interconfessional tensions that exploded into violence periodically during the era we study.

Given the robust quality of communication between cultures in the medieval Mediterranean, given the transmission of other sorts of cultural information between the Arabic and Latin-Romance cultural spheres, it may seem remarkable that the *Thousand and One Nights*—gold mine of narrative material that it is—did not make the Mediterranean crossing before Antoine Galland's translation in the opening decades of the eighteenth century. Indeed, it is a little-known fact that the frame story did appear in European letters during the Middle Ages, as did one of the embedded tales from the *Nights*. The story of Shahrayar and Shahzaman (Shahrazad is conspicuous by her absence) was included among the *Novelle* of Giovanni Sercambi (1348–1424), and Ludovico Ariosto retold it in canto XXVIII of the *Orlando Furioso* (1516). And we find a portion of the tale of King Yunan and the sage Duban in Bosone da Gubbio's *Avventuroso Ciciliano* (1311).[22]

The differences between the stories as they appear in the Arabic "original" (I am still reading outward from the early manuscript edited by Mahdi) and the Italian "translations" are instructive. In Sercambi's and Ariosto's version of the frame tale, a powerful man and his companion discover their wives' faithlessness. Their despair leads them to wander in a series of episodes that seem to have been lifted from a premodern buddy movie—so far the Arabic and Italian tales follow identical paths. And the Italian heroes, like the Arab princes, will ultimately bed a woman whose faithlessness astonishes even them, cynical as they have become. But the Italians take a radically different moral from the experience. *Così fan tutte*, they say to themselves; a man's

only rational response is to give as good as he gets. Sercambi—appreciably
more misogynistic than Ariosto—returns his heroes to beat their wives and
bed as many women as they like. Ariosto's protagonists give their wives li-
cense to play, as they themselves intend to do (Ariosto, it must be said, is as
affable a writer as there is in world literature). There are no virgin brides, no
murders, and no descent to the brink of anarchy and civic collapse; no Shahrazad arrives to save the day.

So, too, the version of the story of Yunan and Duban retold by Bosone
da Gubbio is stripped of the backstory that grants it its psychological complexity in the Arabic version. In the story of King Yunan and the sage Duban,
you will remember, a vacillating king gives way to a devious minister's suggestion to put to death the learned foreign doctor who had cured him of leprosy;
the scholar takes his posthumous revenge by compelling the king to thumb
through the pages of a poisoned book. In Bosone's version only one device
from this intricate narrative remains: the book that poisons its reader as he
reads. Bosone inserts that motif into a relatively banal plot involving negotiations between two monarchs that degenerate slowly into war. There is no
tension between a king—indecisive, easily dazzled, and easily manipulated—
and his learned, foreign minister. The poisoned book simply introduces a
thrillingly sinister element into a mundane tale of diplomatic intrigue.

If we peer a bit deeper into the Yunan and Duban cycle as it appears in
the oldest manuscript of the *Thousand and One Nights*, however, it becomes
evident that a sliver of the material present in that tale did penetrate more
deeply into the literary traditions of the European languages. For there is a
crossed wire between the story of Yunan and Duban and one of the most
popular framed narratives of the European Middle Ages: the work known
most frequently as the Book of Sindbad (not to be confused with the sailor)
in the East and the Seven Sages of Rome in the West.[23] The Sindbad/Seven
Sages material seems to have worked its way gradually across the Mediterranean, appearing in Arabic in Abbasid Baghdad, in Syriac soon after, in Greek
during the eleventh century and in Latin and Persian during the twelfth.
During the thirteenth century it entered the orbit of European letters; it was
translated into the Romance vernaculars as well as Hebrew.

In Sindbad, as in the tale of Yunan and Duban, we meet a king who
hires a learned minister with an odd foreign name to perform a personal
service. In Sindbad, as in Yunan and Duban, the scholar's life will be threatened by envy and court intrigues. Characters in the tale of Yunan and Duban
themselves relate tales that feature a king named Sindbad. Furthermore iden-

tical tales are told within the Yunan-Duban frame in the *Nights* and the Sindbad/Seven Sages frame in both its Arabic and European versions. David Pinault, noting this rash of parallels, has pointed out the obvious: the various traditions (the Arabic Yunan-Duban tales, the Arabic and European Sindbad/ Seven Sages tradition) represent ramifications of a common stock of narrative material.[24] The Sindbad/Seven Sages narratives, however, differ in one central detail from the narrative of King Yunan and the sage Duban. Although in the tale of Sindbad we do meet a vacillating sultan, he is not the villain in the tale; nor is his minister. It is rather his wife who attempts to orchestrate a hostile takeover from within the palace walls by telling the monarch tales that twist the truth. And one of the victims of her machinations is the learned foreign retainer who, in the Eastern versions, gives the tale its name: Sindbad (in the Greek version Syntipas, and in the Spanish translation made directly from a lost Arabic original, Sendebar). Other men attached to the court relate narratives that set the story straight; in the end the queen's nefarious plot is revealed and she is put to death.

Thus the Sindbad narrative brought a tension central to the plot of the *Nights* to European shores: the threat that women's talk poses to the stability of the polity. And it is possible that the Sindbad tradition contributed in a tangible way to the genesis of the *Nights* in its modern, Western form. Antoine Galland stated in the dedication of the first volume of *Les mille et une nuits* that he had begun his translation of the tale of Sindbad (by which he means the sailor) when he learned that it formed part of a larger narrative called *The Thousand and One Nights*.[25] His search for that work culminated in the discovery of the manuscript that bears his name today. Galland does not reveal who told him that the Sindbad narrative belonged in the *Nights* and scholars have not concurred on the significance of the statement. It seems likely, given the strong family resemblance between the narrative of Sindbad the sage and the Yunan-Duban frame in the *Nights*, that Galland (or his unnamed informant) simply confused his Sindbads. The tale of Sindbad the *sailor* never formed part of the *Nights* before Galland put the stories of his voyages in Shahrazad's mouth; but the narrative of Sindbad the *sage* had been associated with the *Nights*, in its iteration as the tale of King Yunan and the sage Duban. It befits the convoluted textual history of the *Thousand and One Nights* that its long and prodigiously productive life in the West should have been kick-started by scholarly error.

Thus the *Thousand and One Nights*, like a rather large pebble dropped into a rather large pond, disappeared beneath the surface of the Mediterranean while the ripples created by its fall washed the shores of Europe. Miguel Asín Palacios, in his essay on Thomism and Averroism, imagined the history of medieval theology as a chain reaction traversing the medieval Mediterranean and fusing the distinct theological traditions of Muslims, Jews, and Christians (see Chapter 2, note 54). The transmission of narrative material from the *Thousand and One Nights* finesses Asín's depiction of medieval intellectual history. A network of tales drawing on the reservoir of narrative associated with the *Nights* survives to attest knowledge of it in medieval Europe. However, a comparison of the treatment of the narratives in the Arabic and Romance traditions underscores the distinct historical resonance which the tales they possessed in common had for diverse populations. A version of the Arabic Book of Sindbad did reach the shores of Europe; it was translated into Spanish in 1253. The single manuscript copy of the translation languished uncopied on a library shelf, generating no new manuscript copies, no retranslations, and no imitations.[26] Like the translation of Aristotle's *Poetics* made directly from the Greek by William of Moerbeke (see Chapter 2, note 65), the translation of the Book of Sindbad that remained faithful to its Arabic exemplar simply did not speak to a thirteenth-century Romance-speaking audience. The tales that take inspiration from the Arabic Sindbad and did find success in European letters represent a radical departure from the Arabic original. They play up different aspects of the narrative, making it in some versions a simple repository for misogynistic material, in others a bureaucratic procedural and royal tell-all that peeks behind the curtains to show us how monarchs and their philosophical hired hands *really* live. In the same way, none of the Italian versions of tales from the *Nights*—Sercambi's, Ariosto's, or Bosone's—reproduces the unique cocktail of themes that made the Arabic incarnations of the story so riveting. The tales are stripped of the plot elements that link narration and intellectual expertise to danger. They do not question the probity of the protagonist as the Arabic tales implicitly challenge the judgment and the moral formation of the kings central to the narratives.

And neither the Italian tales derived from the *Nights* nor the European reconfigurations of the Arabic Sindbad showed the slightest interest in the figure of Shahrazad. Her absence in all the European reworkings of narrative material from the *Thousand and One Nights*—the versions of the frame narrative in Sercambi and Ariosto; Bosone's retelling of the story of Yunan and Duban; and the countless recastings of the Sindbad tale, itself a cousin to Yunan and Duban—Shahrazad's invisibility in all this narrative matter suggests that, to European ears, she was immaterial. In subsequent Arabic redactions of the work she remained marginal, almost invisible, but always present. The ninth-century fragment of the text discovered by Nabia Abbott names her (see Chapter 1, note 48); Ibn al-Nadim's testimony demonstrates that the dynamics of the frame tale scarcely changed between the tenth century and the era when the Galland manuscript was written, half a millennium later. In Europe, however, she simply didn't signify.

It is possible that Shahrazad did not make the Mediterranean crossing because the Europeans, unlike the Arabs, could not read backward from the uncanny tales of narration and death that she tells to the complex and sinister popular associations with the Baghdad of the Abbasids. Perhaps her evocation of the stakes of narration held scant meaning for a European audience not attuned (as her Arab audience would be) to debates over the legitimacy of profane narrative. In this light, the thematic diffuseness of the European Seven Sages narrative tradition is suggestive. In its Arabic version, the tale featured personnel closely related to the dramatis personae of tales of the Barmakids' demise: a malleable sultan, a learned foreign minister, a conniving woman. Lacking the historical details of this narrative, however—lacking Abbasid Baghdad as chronotope—Europeans used other themes to give sinew and muscle to the bones of the tale. It's difficult to say, without more study, why medieval European writers used what they did (and, perhaps more importantly, refused what they did).[27] However, it seems quite evident that before Galland's translation at the beginning of the eighteenth century Europeans lacked an interpretive lens that might make the *Nights*, in all its fulsome splendor, compelling to a hometown audience. And it was left to the passionate readers of the nineteenth and especially the twentieth century to shape Shahrazad into the heroine she has become—the transnational symbol of the persistent human will to turn life into tale and to use tale to transform life— and to find a use for the thematic surplus trimmed from her character: her evocation of the darker implications of narrative invention.

## London and Hollywood, 1939

The *Thousand and One Nights* made a fleeting appearance—virtually imperceptible to one not watching for it—in one of the literary monuments of high modernity. In Luigi Pirandello's *Sei personaggi in cerca d'autore* (first performed in Rome in 1921), soon after the Characters appear, the Father begins to explain the Characters' plight to the Actors; and the Stepdaughter—whose perspective on the melodrama unfolding is, of course, starkly different from the Father's—threatens to take the bit between her teeth and carry the narrative away. Pirandello's stage directions call for the Stepdaughter to "give a naughty rendition of a few bars from 'Prends garde à Tchou-Tchin-Tchou' by Dave Stamper, rewritten as a Fox-trot or slow One-step by Francis Salabert":

Les chinois sont un peuple malin,
De Shangaï à Pekin,
Ils ont mis des écritaux partout:
Prenez garde à Tchou-Thin-Tchou![28]

[The Chinese are a clever people,
From Shanghai to Peking;
They have put up signs everywhere:
Beware of Chu-Chin-Chow!]

The song comes from the wildly popular British stage play *Chu-Chin-Chow*, an adaptation of the tale of Ali Baba; Pirandello has the Stepdaughter sing the French version of the first stanza of the song that introduces us to the British play's eponymous villain.[29] Pirandello's Stepdaughter is a very distant cousin to Shahrazad indeed. The story of Ali Baba which provided the inspiration for *Chu-Chin-Chow* is one of the "orphan" tales associated with the *Thousand and One Nights*: stories which have no known Arabic cognate predating the Galland manuscript. Yet her saucy performance captures a truth central also to Shahrazad's tales: like Shahrazad, the Stepdaughter obeys a dictate to narrate; and, like Shahrazad's, the Stepdaughter's flirtatious opening bid for her audience's attention frames a mise en abyme of narrative, overlapping tales whose gradual, inexorable revelation will unsettle her (fictional and actual) audience.

During the twentieth century, scholars would begin the laborious task of sorting out what Galland had wrought in his translation of the *Nights*: what he translated and what he transformed (or invented wholecloth).[30] So too, during the nineteenth century, the English translations of the *Nights*, with their extensive historical commentaries, unleashed the dark matter beneath the nursery-bright confections of the early European translations and imitations. In particular, they introduced modern readers to the seamy side of Abbasid Baghdad, refining the story of Ja'far and Harun al-Rashid until it acquired the histrionic dimensions of a classical tragedy. European readers came to view the *Nights* as a window onto Abbasid Baghdad; and among the vignettes that window framed we can watch Harun's massacre of the Barmakid clan in flickering black and white, like an old newsreel. Edward William Lane—whose translation appeared in 1838–40—refused to comment in his usually exhaustive notes on the dismal chapter in Arab history. He demurs: "The stories in which this celebrated man is mentioned will, I think, be more agreeable to those readers who are unacquainted with his history, of which, therefore, I shall say nothing."[31] John Payne, who published his translation in 1879, was not so squeamish. Ja'far, he tells us, was the brilliant scion of the Barmakid clan—the architects of the Persianized culture of the Abbasid court that represented, in the Arab imagination, the golden age of Arab refinement. However, Payne had the lowest opinion of Harun, whom he termed a "morose and fantastic despot." He repeated in lurid detail the historical legends about Harun's massacre of the Barmakids—the tale of Harun and Ja'far, 'Abbasa and her maid, Zubayda's vindictiveness, and the terrible revenge Harun exacted for Ja'far's transgression—as evidence of Harun's brutality.[32] Richard Burton took a starkly different view of Harun's character. Burton's Harun was a bit of a Shahrazad himself: "fair and handsome, of noble and majestic presence . . . well read in science and letters, especially history and tradition." Thus it was necessary for him to represent Harun's massacre of the Barmakids as an unaccountable lapse: "a single great crime, a tragedy whose details are almost incredibly horrible."[33] In his account, after the death of Ja'far Harun repents his actions bitterly (and, of course, fruitlessly).

To one familiar with the history as it was represented in the Arab historiographic tradition and in the nineteenth-century English commentaries on the *Nights*, the connotations that the figure of Ja'far in particular has acquired in modern movies based on the *Nights* comes as a shock. If Scheherazade (she is no longer the enigmatic Arab maiden Shahrazad) is the darling of the twentieth-century transnational *Nights*, Jaffar (he is no longer the Arabized Persian bon vivant Ja'far) serves as our all-purpose villain. Western readers know Scheherazade as a symbol of resistance to despots, and in particular as an icon of the resistance that the imagination can mount against the tyranny of various forms of oppression, from political brutality to simple monotony. In movies based on the *Nights*, however, Scheherazade casts a shadow, which takes the dark, manipulative, conniving form of Jaffar.

The movies have codified Jaffar as the embodiment of a particularly unctuous, politically inflected evil. Contemporary readers will be most likely to remember the cinematic Jaffar from the 1992 Disney movie *Aladdin*. Literate moviegoers may be aware of the apparent source of the Disney Jaffar: the 1940 *Thief of Bagdad*, produced by Alexander Korda and starring the sinister Conrad Veidt as Jaffar. Those whose interest has been piqued by the transformation of Ja'far into Jaffar and who have dug more deeply into the cinematic record may have unearthed the 1959 Mr. Magoo vehicle *1001 Arabian Nights*, in which the character is known only as "the wicked wazir" but retains all the character elements of the Jaffar from the 1940 *Thief of Bagdad*.[34] In these movies Jaffar retains his historical professional identity. He is a vizier, a minister with a privileged access to the governor of the state—not Harun, but an unnamed inept sultan.[35] He aims to usurp his retainer's power. To that end he has designs on the sultan's daughter. Once he possesses her—sexually and legally—he will possess the power of the sultan. In addition, he is a sorcerer. He has magical powers that he uses strictly for dark and sinister purposes.

Those who know a bit about the history of the *Nights*—the structure of the Galland manuscript, the historical legends about Abbasid Baghdad that it echoes—may recognize a bit of Shahrazad in the figure of Jaffar (or, conversely and somewhat perversely, may see the medieval Shahrazad as the shadow cast by the modern Jaffar). The Jaffar of the movies is a condensation of the themes that shadow the characters we meet in the *Thousand and One Nights* and that find explicit expression in the popular historical tales of the death of the Barmakid clan at the hands of Harun al-Rashid. A combination of attributes makes Jaffar uniquely sinister in the twentieth-century films: his easy intimacy with the monarch; his desire to insinuate himself into the inner circles of power, and ultimately to usurp power for himself, by befuddling the sultan and marrying his daughter; his use of sorcery to achieve this end. This malevolent list, while it has little to do with the historical Ja'far, has an uncanny ring to one familiar with popular versions of the dynastic history of the Abbasids. In Harun al-Rashid's Baghdad, too, murky historical agents used unseen forces to overthrow a ruler. In popular histories, however, the agents were the women of the caliph's house. Whereas the Jaffar of the movies preys on the caliph's daughter, in the historical tales it was the daughters themselves who were doing the hunting, and their hapless mates were their prey. The deeds of the faithless women of Harun al-Rashid's palace reverberated beyond the palace walls; but the women themselves, of course, remained invisible. Unseen by the Baghdadis of the age, the methods of their menace would seem as terrifying as Jaffar's magic spells to a twentieth-century audience. It was gossip and mercenary sex that poisoned Harun al-Rashid's mind in the popular histories. The Jaffar of twentieth-century films displaces the fearsome feminine conniving that filled the perfumed night air behind the closed doors of the royal harem into the figure of the man who, the histories relate, those chattering women undid.

So, too, bumbling sultan central to the plots of *The Thief of Bagdad*, *Aladdin*, and *The 1001 Arabian Nights* seems to have a historical precedent in the narrative traditions associated with the *Nights*. The king Yunan, like the unnamed sultan of the movies, is a vacillating governor whose indecisiveness makes him prey to his conniving vizier's machinations. This character, of course, fathered a son and heir in the Arabic and Western offspring of the Yunan-Duban cycle. The monarch in the Arabic Book of Sindbad and the European Seven Sages of Rome, like Yunan, hedged and dithered; his evil wife recognized his weakness, and played him like a cheap violin. The Western movies that follow the machinations of the scheming retainer Jaffar and his ineffectual patron reproduce (whether intentionally or not) dynamics that have been part of the *Nights* tradition from its inception, or at least as far back as the literary record allows us to trace it. They extract the queasy sexual anxieties from the Sindbad/Seven Sages cycles and from the tale of Ja'far, his patron Harun al-Rashid, and the women of their house. And they use that narrative material as macabre undercurrent to an essentially comic depiction of a hopelessly spineless sultan.[36] In the movies, the figure of Jaffar transforms the pastel nursery Orient into a chiaroscuro kingdom in which menace lurks behind brocade curtains (but good, of course, triumphs in the end).

The movie that introduced the evil Jaffar, in all his malevolent perfection, to international movie audiences was the brainchild of producer Alexander Korda.[37] The 1940 *Thief of Bagdad* borrowed the title of the 1924 *Thief of Bagdad*, the film whose vision of Baghdad was so ethereal that its buildings were required to float. In its airiness the 1924 *Thief* was heir to the mischievous but defanged djinns of Galland's *Nuits*, produced for an audience of *salonnières* weaned on faeries, and to Tennyson's Baghdad of filigreed golden domes. But only in his fascination with "Bagdad" as mental horizon, as aestheticized space, did Korda draw inspiration from the previous *Thief*.[38] The role of Abu (played by Indian boy actor Sabu) owes little to Douglas Fairbanks's thief, and Conrad Veidt's Jaffar is Korda's (and his scriptwriters') invention. Veidt lurks and oozes through Korda's sets with palpable relish, while Sabu plays Ariel to his Caliban. The plot borrows a motif here and there from the *Nights* but is largely (in the grand Western tradition built on that humble medieval foundation) a series of free associations on Oriental themes. The movie did well with wartime audiences starved for distraction but has not been universally celebrated for its cinematic merits.

What inspired the transfiguration of Jaffar's character from hapless victim into sinister villain? The filming of *The Thief of Bagdad* took place against the backdrop of the beginning of World War II. Filming started in England, Korda's home at the time, in the late spring of 1939. While Korda and crew created a fantasy Bagdad on the British lots, Europe advanced toward outright war. The studio rushed through as much of the shooting schedule as they could, recognizing that the outbreak of hostilities would bring an end to filming. Britain entered the war on September 3, 1939, two days after Germany invaded Poland, and overnight cast members and crew found themselves working not in a Bagdad of the mind but in a propaganda film conceived and produced by Korda, *The Lion Has Wings*.[39] In order to finish *The Thief of Bagdad* Korda would move the principal actors and crew to the United States after *The Lion Has Wings* wrapped.[40] The desert scenes he had intended to shoot in Egypt and Saudi Arabia were filmed in the Grand Canyon; pickup scenes were shot in Hollywood studios. The horror of the war, Korda's perception of the public's need for escapist entertainment, and his activities as a propaganda director may account for his sense that the project needed both a lavish, fantastic setting and a standout villain.

*The Thief of Bagdad* does not have the feel of a propaganda film; yet the villain that was its chief contribution to the *Nights* in the West would prove to have, whether Korda intended it or not, a peculiar contemporary resonance. The film begins with a critique of isolationist politics—a topic of moment during the early days of the war—but soon loses itself in the hazy pastels and the sententious epigrams with oddly inverted syntax that are the hallmarks of the Oriental fantasy film.[41] And its villain is not a marauding European dictator but a lurking Arab minister-cum-necromancer. The skulking, oily scoundrel with a foreign accent was by 1939 a familiar figure in English language films. And other Oriental fantasies (most notably *Chu-Chin-Chow*) had generated a stock Oriental bad guy sharing some of Jaffar's fundamental characteristics.[42] So Korda's sinister Jaffar had precedent in earlier cinematic riffs on the *Nights*. However, the importance of the North African theater in the early stages of the war would grant a particular urgency to Conrad Veidt's menacing, vaguely Arab Jaffar. The British would retaliate for Mussolini's ill-considered invasion of Egypt by capturing Sidi Barani from the Italian forces (led by Rodolfo Graziani, the loathsome viceroy of

Italian East Africa) on December 11, 1940. They defeated the Italians at Sol-
lum, Egypt, on December 17. And *The Thief of Bagdad* opened in London
on December 19.

Korda could not, of course, predict the fortuitous timing of the film's
release. But his studio was engaged in negotiations to shoot on location in
Egypt before filming began, and Korda may have learned of the activities of
the Desert Rats, the armored division stationed to Egypt in 1938 to strengthen
the British position there. Certainly he, like all Britons, was aware of the 1936
treaty requiring Britain to remove from Egypt all but those troops required
to protect the Suez Canal. And one of his biographers, Karol Kulik, produced
a tantalizing suggestion that Korda made a significant contribution to the
war effort on the North African front. Korda was granted a knighthood in
1942, ostensibly for his activities as filmmaker, although it seems quite evident
that his service to Britain went beyond moviemaking. Those who knew
Korda (and Winston Churchill, with whom Korda was intimate) have made
it clear that he contributed in a significant way to the war effort but did not
reveal details about the nature of his activities. Kulik reported an account
that Korda, on the premise of shooting a fictitious movie, filmed the coastline
where the invasion of North Africa would occur; this footage he turned over
to the British forces before the invasion began. The knighthood, Kulik speculated, was granted him in recognition of this service in addition to his activities as a propaganda filmmaker. Kulik was not able to confirm the rumor.
Those who would know the truth kept discreet silence about Korda's activities and since have died.[43] The tale suggests a possible motive for Korda's
interest in the North African theater before the start of the war and before
the filming of *The Thief of Bagdad*. But no evidence exists to corroborate it.
All we can conclude with conviction is that his awareness of the precarious-
ness of the British position in a former colony, Egypt, may have suggested to
Korda that British audiences would be happy to hiss an Arab villain.

The literary sources for *The Thief of Bagdad*, if such exist, are even harder
to pin down. The character of the irascible Djinn in *The Thief of Bagdad*
seems to have been suggested by the demon in the story of the Fisherman
and the Demon; the Djinn's opening comments are modeled on the demon's
remarks to the fisherman in the *Nights*. So, too, the movie's plot is set in
motion by a recognizable motif lifted from the pages of the *Nights* and modified to meet the filmmakers' purposes. Jaffar convinces his patron—the monarch Ahmad, the grandson of Harun al-Rashid (played by John Justin)—to
take a turn through his city in disguise, as his grandfather used to do, in

order to become better acquainted with his people. But Jaffar then sends his henchmen out to arrest Ahmad; in Jaffar's nefarious plot, Ahmad will waste away in a prison, his protestations that he is the sultan ignored as the ravings of a madman, and Jaffar will proclaim himself sultan. The literate viewer will find the occasional motif lifted from the *Nights* and reshaped to fit the film's designs, as the character of the Djinn and tales of Harun al-Rashid's and Ja'far's nighttime revels in disguise have been here. Korda and his scenarist certainly knew the *Nights*, in one form or another. And it's possible that their knowledge of the narrative material went beyond the published versions of the *Thousand and One Nights* available to Western readers.

Although film historians recognize *The Thief of Bagdad* to be largely Korda's creation, he neither wrote nor (officially) directed the film. Lajos Biró, like Korda a Hungarian who fled the country following World War I, wrote the scenario (and Miles Malleson, an experienced writer who also played the addled sultan in the film, wrote the screenplay). A nineteenth-century philologist, Pio Rajna, unearthed a contemporary popular Hungarian version of the frame tale of the *Thousand and One Nights* when searching for the sources for Ariosto's retelling of the frame tale from the *Nights*.[44] Rajna's discovery suggests that the narrative material of the *Nights* generated a more vibrant—or at least more durable—popular tradition in Hungary than in Western Europe, where the frame tale was largely unknown before Galland's translation appeared. Korda and Biró clearly used the narrative extravaganza that the *Nights* had become in the published Western translations as raw material for the film. But it is also possible that the Hungarians drew on their common knowledge of popular tales descended from the *Nights* and its medieval European offspring, like the Seven Sages of Rome, when shaping the characters and the narrative for the film.

Despite the web of plausible links between Korda and his film, archaic versions of the *Nights*, and the contemporary Arab world, it is difficult if not impossible to determine the source and motives for the transformation of the character of Jaffar in *The Thief of Bagdad*. One of Korda's biographers thought he had found the inspiration for Jaffar when he caught sight of a painting in the National Gallery in Budapest commemorating a famous Hungarian victory over the Turks; one of the Turkish warriors, he thought, was a dead ringer for Veidt's Jaffar.[45] And, indeed, why not? The painting—a turbulent Romantic composition by Sándor Wagner entitled *Titusz Dugovics Sacrifices Himself* (1859)—depicts the titular sacrificial hero in a battlement. Behind him the Europeans defend their bastion while the Turks seethe up the stone wall, daggers drawn. One Turk has taken hold of Dugovics; we see his face in profile, swathed in a brilliant red turban; he wears flowing red trousers.

Korda's biographer thought of Jaffar when he saw this painting, undoubtedly, because of the movie's opening sequence. *The Thief of Bagdad* opens with a shot of a ship flying brilliant red sails. The second shot zooms in on the eye of Horus on the side of the ship. And the third is a zoom shot of Jaffar awaiting the ship on the dock, his head and face swaddled in a red turban, only his glowering eyes visible. The sequence prefigures a crucial scene later in the movie when Abu, the eponymous thief of Bagdad, will steal the glowing red All-Seeing Eye from the temple of anonymous, vaguely Central Asian pagans. In recognition of the film's achievements in color photography (like the striking opening sequence) and special effects (see Abu's battle with a giant spider in order to abstract the All-Seeing Eye), the Academy of Motion Picture Arts and Sciences awarded *The Thief of Bagdad* three Academy Awards in 1940, for Art Direction, Color Cinematography, and Special Effects. These were, of course, the heady early days of color filmmaking; and *Thief* was the first feature film to be made using the Technicolor three-strip blue screen process to achieve its special effects.[46] And Korda chose in the opening sequence to use the formidable technical capabilities at his disposal to emphasize formal elements that recall Sándor Wagner's painting. In the tableau that Wagner depicts, the Turk's eye (viewed in profile and framed by his red turban), Dugovics's eyes, and the flag that Dugovics's comrades struggle to hoist form the central axis of the composition, a rising horizontal line echoed by the progress of the invading Turks scaling the rampart below and the clouds in the sky above. So—in sequence rather than in composition— did the opening shots of *The Thief of Bagdad* use the color red and close-ups of eyes to emphasize content central to the narrative: the malevolent power of Jaffar's eyes and the redeeming power of the All-Seeing Eye.

What inspired the transfiguration of Jaffar's character from hapless victim into sinister villain? Korda may have taken inspiration or motivation from his intelligence work in North Africa, from versions of the *Nights* he heard or read as a boy, even from the fervent Romantic nationalist sentiment of Sándor Wagner's painting. The sense of violent action suspended at a crucial moment, the color red suggesting the blood that must be spilled in a moment yet to come (in Wagner's painting) or just offscreen (in Korda's film): did his Jaffar link, perhaps unconsciously, a visual memory of Wagner's painting to his sense of the crucial importance of the North African front to events about to unfold as the movie was shot? Or did Korda's Jaffar condense current events and Hungarian historical memory of the Ottoman threat, lifting the critique of the political and sexual dynamics of the Abbasid dynasty from introductions to translations of the *Nights* to animate his characters and give his plot teeth? My reconstruction of the progress of the *Nights* through the centuries suggests that Shahrazad and the tales she told reflected a knot of anxieties associated in the Arab imagination with Abbasid Baghdad: the perils of imaginative narrative and the massacre of the Barmakids. Medieval Europe knew nothing of that history. Thus in the medieval European retellings Shahrazad's tales lost the thematic specificity and the urgency—the sense of a headlong rush from betrayal into ruin—that they had in their Arabic cognates. But during the nineteenth century Orientalists made the narratives of the undoing of the Barmakids available once again to a European readership. Korda and his scriptwriters may well have pored over Payne's and Burton's retelling of the matter of Baghdad as they did the translations of Scheherazade's tales. Did they recognize the relevance of that history to the tales Scheherazade tells, and perceive some connection between the unraveling of the Barmakids and events unfolding around them as they wrote their script? Did they select the name *Jaffar* for their villain simply because it was an Arab name that Westerners could pronounce or in homage to the character who symbolized at once the cultural plurality and brilliance of Abbasid Baghdad and the precipitate collapse of all that Abbasid Baghdad had accomplished and become?

Alas, it is impossible to say with certainty. We do not know that Korda gathered intelligence for the British Armed Forces in North Africa; we do not know that he saw Wagner's painting in the Hungarian National Gallery. Nor do we know whether he was exposed to popular Hungarian versions of the *Nights* as a boy. Although I have spread a sumptuous banquet of possibilities, plausibilities, and probabilities, my evidence constitutes, I am sorry to say, a barmecide feast. I cannot produce a deductive argument to prove the link between putative cause and effect. Most tenuous of all is the connection I have sketched between the character Jaffar in a film made in England and Hollywood in 1939 and a deep history of sinister associations with the women of the house of Harun al-Rashid or with the nighttime tales of women.

Where, come to that, is the boundary line between Abbasid Baghdad—in all its historical precision, the birthplace of imaginative narrative in Arabic and the place where the Barmakids died—and the "Bagdad" of the movies? It is difficult to pinpoint with precision when and where the Western commentators and narrators decisively laid claim to Baghdad and began to use its simmering antinomies as an inverted representation, at once utopian and dystopian, of home. Both the Galland manuscript and the narrative material that would be gathered in the extended-play version of the *Nights* during the modern era include a preponderance of tales set in Abbasid Baghdad.[47] But *Baghdad* here is simply a name, an onomastic backdrop to the action. Like Shahrayar's unnamed capital in the frame tale, Harun's Baghdad provides the barest of stage settings, a suggestion of the archaic haunts of power. The Cairo that we glimpse in two of the tales told in the Hunchback cycle, in contrast—in particular the merchants' Cairo—lives on the page.[48] Streets in the old suq, caravansaries, and city gates are named. In one tale, a voice—the narrator's, the scribe's, the author's; perhaps the voice of Shahrazad herself—interrupts the action to report, when one character wishes another God's blessings: "And the gates of Heaven opened and received Cairo's prayers."[49] Surely this is not the comment of a disinterested outsider; this must be the voice of a Cairene. But the Baghdad cycles—the frames within the frame set in Baghdad: the Story of the Porter and the Three Ladies of Baghdad and the Three Apples—relate few tangible details about the city. In the movies of the twentieth century, Baghdad became a city of cotton candy–colored minarets built on mirrored floors, with a villainous Jaffar lurking in its inverted shadows. But already in the Galland manuscript Baghdad is a notional metropolis. It does not have the texture of a real city (as the Cairo of the *Nights* does) but of the memory of a city. It is a monument to a time and a place—precisely a chronotope; street names and topographical specifics would only shatter this effect.

I leave these fragments of a potential archaeology of the villainous Jaffar strewn about, a Cubist portrait bringing to an appropriately sinister close my notes on the astonishing transformations of the *Nights* in the West over the past nine centuries or so. The text, or portions of it, reached a European audience during the Middle Ages. These were naturalized as European tales which, though they share narrative material with the Arabic *Nights*, are thematically quite distinct from their exemplar: Sercambi's, Ariosto's, and Bosone's retellings of stories from the *Nights*; the Seven Sages of Rome in its various incarnations. Antoine Galland insinuated the work in its entirety (and then some) into the faery-saturated atmosphere of the eighteenth-century salons. It outgrew that home away from home in the West to become proof text for the Orientalists, who cut their teeth on its substantial lexical, manuscript, and hermeneutic difficulties. During the twentieth century it transmogrified once again. In this chapter I have traced what seems to me, from a historical perspective, the most remarkable of its modern metamorphoses. The textual evidence suggests that the matter of Baghdad has become relevant to Western audiences in a new way over the course of the last 150 years. Changing political environments, changes in the way a popular audience consumes narratives, changes in our perceptions of gender—all these factors and more seem to have contributed to a rekindling of interest in the thematic strands bundled together in the late medieval Arabic *Nights*. The sense of menace and the promise of salvation condensed in the Galland manuscript into the tales told by a single, enigmatic figure—the Arab maiden with a Persian name, Shahrazad—is once again present in late modern Western appropriations of narrative material from the Nights. But this thematic strand has bifurcated into two distinct characters: Scheherazade, symbol of narrative creativity; and Jaffar, emblem of political conniving.

It is difficult to know where to stop telling the story of the *Nights*. Should the philologist aim for a latter-day New Criticism, and limit her reading to the linguistic, rhetorical, and literary structures of the text itself? Sumptuous as those are in the case of the *Nights*, by contemporary critical standards a reading that resists historicism altogether risks being condemned (with justice) as irresponsible. We must situate textual history within a broader historical context. The medieval literary historian knows that the point where a text ends and begins cannot always be precisely determined, however. The *Nights*, which bleeds into the Seven Sages tradition which itself has cognates in Syriac, Greek, Hebrew, Latin, and all the European vernaculars, is an extreme example of a literary-historical dilemma that we face each time we frame a reading of a text. But all medieval texts are situated within an intertextual web, and the historian must reconstruct its affiliations, both avowed and not. This understanding of the philologist's task—a labor of tracing story to story in a network of lines of transmission that crisscross the Mediterranean like a cobweb—makes the philologist herself into a bit of a Scheherazade, telling a tale that does not end because it obeys a moral imperative to continue.

But in the real world, the tales the scholar tells follow the fundamental rules of narrative: they have a beginning, a middle, and (sorry, Scheherazade) an end. The imposition of order on the untidy business of medieval literary history has been imaged in the past as an act of violence; most philologists remember Bernard Cerquiglini's denunciation of the philologist as Procrustes, the bandit of the Attic hills who trimmed his victims' bodies to fit his loathsome bed. In honor of the mother of all narratives, in honor of the text that memorializes both the narrative imperative and the anxiety that accompanies narration, we might propose an alternate, (slightly) less brutal image of the philologist as overeager editor: the sage Duban. In the tale as it appears in the *Thousand and One Nights*, when Duban accepts his death as inevitable he presents a gift to the king: a book. He gives the king a mysterious powder and instructs him to press the severed head into the powder following his execution. When the king does so, Duban's reanimated head interprets the text as the king leafs through its (blank) pages. The circumstances of Duban's death may gall a modern reader. We do not want Duban to go gentle into that cruel night; we want a deus ex machina to pluck him from danger. By the unforgiving logic of the fairy tale, however, Duban accepts his demise and orchestrates his revenge from a murky and impossible moment between life and death.

The philologist must not die in order to narrate, of course; narration is not always and only vengeance: the facts do not really fit (and thank God for that). Yet the philological reading, a bit like Duban's narration of the book without text, begins with a brutal schism (in the case of philology, the chronological and linguistic separation of the text from the historical and textual network that generated it) and an arcane scientific transformation (the technologies of reading—from stemmata to chemical baths—that assist the philologist). Like Duban, the philologist narrates from an ambiguous and historically uncanny moment. Though we work assiduously to correct for the distance between ourselves and the text—to project ourselves into the past by emptying our critical narratives of anachronisms and inaccuracies—the disconnect between us and the text of necessity colors our readings. And any number of contingencies, above all the historical narratives we use to interpret the text, distort the stories we make it tell.

This is the vulnerability of the philological method; this is what opens it up to appropriations like the *philologies engagées* that I discussed in the first chapter of this book. It makes the philological reading susceptible to *innovations* (and I mean that word both in the negative sense that it acquires in Lachmannian textual criticism and in the Bédierist recuperation of it as a synonym for the luxuriant variance of the medieval text). The fundamentalist philologists I discussed in Chapter 1, with their nineteenth-century diction and their quest to uncover the voice of the Holy Ghost in scripture, may seem quaint to us today. But when fundamentalist readers use radical readings of foundational texts to mobilize a mass audience, the dangers of philology are impossible to ignore.

When philology co-opts the vocabulary of scientism its claims can be perversely seductive. Yet the philological reading does not proceed by means of deduction alone. It uses the inductive leap, the intuitive insight, to infuse Promethean life into the dull clay of the incremental deductive argument. In particular, philological method does not protect us from the perils of the hermeneutic circle. Some of the finest philological work of the last two centuries has deployed circular argument—by begging the question, using a conclusion to predict a beginning. I think I give away no professional trade secrets by confessing that the reading of the *Thousand and One Nights* that I have sketched here (and which my audience may or may not judge to be *fine*) did not derive solely from study of the Galland manuscript. Shahrazad has very little substance in that early redaction of the *Nights*; she is sketched in a few vivid strokes, and then she all but vanishes behind the screen of her stories. Only by reading backward from the Scheherazade invented by modern Western consumers and imitators of the modern Western *Nights* is one likely to attribute any agency to Shahrazad at all.

I framed the reading of the *Nights* that I offer here when the search for the source of the anxiety that haunts the stories that Shahrazad tells led me (through a combination of deductive steps and inductive leaps) to the realization that something was rotten in the city of Baghdad. And it is my intuition that Philologia herself—whether we represent her as Procrustes, the scholar Duban, or the garrulous and sinister Shahrazad—beckons contemporary scholars toward a recognition that, while it may not prove dystopian in the end, does have its chiaroscuro shadows. Philology, as we know it and were taught to practice it today, was constituted during the nineteenth century under the sign of the nation. Under the influence of national ideologies it learned to represent the nation as a natural phenomenon. And it learned to depict the emergence of the European nations and the articulation of a pan-European civilization as the culmination of history. It is the dark fate of philology today to narrate the extinction of the notions that called it into being, in its current form, during the nineteenth century: not only scientism, but also European exceptionalism. Nineteenth-century philology took up the call to uncover the origins of the nation, to reveal the first expressions of the national genius in its earliest literary monuments. Today it brings us to the recognition of a different set of truths: Europe, to paraphrase Prince Metternich, is a geographical expression. Civilization neither began nor culminated there. The medieval history of the Christian West is characterized by radical and ineluctable complexity. The taxonomies and genealogies of philology have obscured the literary history of the West by occluding its communications with non-Indo-European literatures. Historical narratives of the emergence of modernity have imposed a breach between the early modern and the medieval and between the Arab and the Western that the historical record disavows.

It remains to be seen whether philology will prove capable of meeting the challenges that face it today. Contemporary philological method, of course, works well as a means to analyze intralingual phenomena: the manuscript history of a premodern text, for instance, or phonetic shifts within a given language. And it has been used with great success to resolve interlingual literary and linguistic problems involving cognate languages—say, identifying Italian borrowings from the Latin or the Occitan. But it stumbles frequently when confronted with phenomena that transgress those boundaries between language "families" that it represents as natural (rather than cultural) divisions; thus the difficulties that proponents of the "Arabic thesis" have had in devising an effective defense for their claims that the Occitan poets borrowed from the Arabs or that Dante sought inspiration in Muslim descriptions of the afterlife. The extraordinary difficulties generated by the kharjas—texts that straddle the border between Arabic and Romance poetics—signal such a failure. Disciplinary rigor may provide the tools necessary to decipher texts made difficult by distance and time. The manuscript remains of the Romance beloved's reply to her Arab lover have grown opaque with time and repeated copying by scribes who did not themselves understand the words they wrote. And the careful scrutiny of such a text by a trained Arabist may dissolve a Gordian knot and clear the way for a Romance scholar's interpretive advance. But when a philological reading does not clarify but voids a text of meaning, or when disciplinary niceties are used to bar access to texts, what conceivable service does disciplinary rigor provide? Philological analysis of the kharjas has advanced slowly because of the extraordinary and sui generis difficulties of the texts. But at times it is not linguistic or literary complexity but disciplinary border wars that prevent the philological avant garde from claiming new territory.

So, too, have skirmishes over the legitimacy of scholarship on Islamic influence on Dante thwarted our understanding of the question. In those border wars, however, scholars have less frequently engaged each other in direct combat. Miguel Asín Palacios, in the second edition of *La escatología musulmana en la* Divina Comedia, included a lengthy bibliographical résumé of the debate engendered by the initial publication of the work (see Chapter

2). And on occasion scholarly communication across disciplinary boundaries has produced fruitful insights and discoveries: see, for instance, Enrico Cerulli's publication of the Latin and Old French translations of the popular tales of Muhammad's travels in the afterworld. With unfortunate frequency, however, scholarly discussion of relevant questions does not occur. Scholars fail to find common ground where they might meet for such debate. Few journals of Romance studies have sought articles by Arabists; few Arabists have moved out of their professional comfort zone to work on a question involving Italian literary history; few Italianists are willing to take the time and effort to learn a language or an intellectual history which their discipline considers irrelevant to the field. And often those contributions made by Orientalists are simply ignored by scholars in the mainstream of Dante studies: the Italian translation of Asín's study on Dante and Islam appeared did not appear until Asín's book was seventy-five years old. A philological analysis that embraces Arabic and Romance poetics may appear from the disciplinary perspective to be unmotivated and even perverse. The philological lens was devised to analyze linguistic and literary systems that have been demonstrated to have a familial relation to each other. Therefore it deems the scholarly investigation that moves between the Arabic and Romance traditions to be less *philological* than *comparatist*.

The disciplinary tensions between reading practices that define themselves as philological (historicizing readings powered by taxonomic analysis) and those that define themselves as comparatist (motivated by a theoretical or aesthetic insight) have been present but largely implicit throughout this study. Of the two, philology is generally perceived to be fustier, less robust, and less relevant to contemporary academia. Yet it is one of the presuppositions of this book that the philological reading can make a precious contribution to literary studies in a postnational era. The philological lens can train the scholar's eye on the unique historical and linguistic qualities of the text— qualities that a tradition of Eurocentric readings may have obscured. And it gives us the critical strategies we need to excavate the scandalous peculiarities even of texts at the center of the European tradition: to reveal, for instance, Dante's engagement with the Islamic sciences, Petrarch's ambivalent reading of the Arab poets, or the arabicizing rhythms of Alvarus's Latin prose.

But as the philological reading generally combines linguistic and historical optics, so too do we regularly use "comparatist" methodologies in our rigorously "philological" textual analyses. My reading of Jaffar as descendent of a distant ancestor—Jaffar as the refiguration of the darker connotations of

Shahrazad—cannot be defended historically. The suggestion is, by philological standards, unmotivated. It emerges from an intuition: a perception about his character, a perception about hers, and a speculative link between the two. And in this case, even application of philological method—historical investigation and critical evaluation of the "language" of a cinematic text—failed to produce decisive evidence of a causal link between the two. Yet the history of philology teaches us that one scholar's intuition may inspire another scholar's research and substantive defense (or rebuttal) of a hypothesis. Certainly a historian of film or Hungarian letters would produce a more textured and vivid reading of the material than I have been able to present here.

More crucial to our activities as historians of literature, even if we have not established "proof" of "influence"—I use the quotation marks of infamy here to indicate literary-historical terms whose authority my discussion in this book has challenged—has the reading produced nothing? A comparatist analysis powered by intuitive insight, wedded to the analytic strategies and historicizing genius of philology, can bring works we do not know to life and revitalize works that we think we know very well. In particular it can restore a cultural autonomy to the text. It can help us to see the literary work not as a reflection of a European literary tradition viewed always as primary and final, alpha and omega of literary history, but rather as a text with its own tradition and its own networked intralingual and interlingual affiliations to other traditions and other works. Used to sinister ends, the philological reading may be as dark an instrument as Jaffar's hypnotic eyes. Used productively it may help us to restore (linguistic, literary and cultural) texture to the text, and thus contribute to the project—crucial at the present moment—of situating European letters in a global perspective. And it represents one of the most significant contributions that literary historians can make to our understanding of history *tout court:* a sensitive witness to the historical meaning of texts that at the same time articulates their significance to the present.

If we take seriously the challenge to European exceptionalism, the necessity of honoring both the linguistic and historical specificity of the non-European text and its relevance to "our" history follows as a matter of course. And, happily, in philological method we possess a disciplinary practice that teaches us to read for difference, to do justice to the linguistic and historical texture of the text. Of course, philologists may have to be reminded that to read philologically is always, on some level, to read comparatively. Because the taxonomies that philologists use to analyze linguistic and literary form were generated by means of linguistic and literary comparatism—they were used to describe not the hapax legomenon but recurring phenomena—philological practice implies linguistic plurality, the zero degree of the comparative reading. The philological reading infers and always has inferred difference: once philologists recall this fact of our disciplinary history to mind, as the Orientalists of Mediterranean Europe recalled to Europeans the crucial role that the Arabs played in their history, we will once again be able to demonstrate the relevance of our past to the present.

# NOTES

## CHAPTER I

1. Edward Said, *Humanisim and Democratic Criticism* 61.
2. Anthony Grafton, *Defenders of the Text* 26–27.
3. Ibid. 44, 31, and 37.
4. My discussion of philology elides virtually all of the vital and immensely interesting history of the practice between antiquity and the early modern period for purely practical reasons: it requires a book to itself. I refer the reader to Karl Uitti's essay "Philology" in the *Johns Hopkins Guide to Literary Theory and Criticism* and James Turner's work in progress on the history of philology and the origin of the modern humanities.
5. Giacomo Leopardi, *Opere* 15.
6. See Helmut Müller-Sievers, "Reading Evidence" and Sebastiano Timpanaro, "Angelo Mai."
7. See Sebastiano Timpanaro, *The Genesis of Lachmann's Method*, for an authoritative discussion of the "Lachmannian method" and its reliance on models that had evolved between the humanist era and the eighteenth century.
8. Ernest Renan, *Œuvres complètes* 3:839.
9. It seems worth noting, however, that this perception—that the emphasis of aggressively engaged philological readings was split between nationalizing and religious investments—may reflect the scope of subsequent research rather than the actual interests of the nineteenth-century philologists. Some of the most intriguing "meta-philological" scholarship of the late twentieth and early twenty-first century investigates the contributions that philologists made to the construction of national identity (see below, note 13). And I will have more to say herein on the relation between religious fundamentalism and academic philology. Did the philologists also use the new strategies of reading to produce vivid readings, for instance, of love poetry or nature descriptions? This question has not heretofore engaged modern scholars.
10. Gaston Paris, "La Chanson de Roland et la nationalité française" 91–93.
11. Ibid. 100. See also David Hult's sensitive discussion of Paris's 1870 performance at the Collège de France: "Gaston Paris and the Invention of Courtly Love" 196–97.
12. Cited in Michael Caesar, *Dante: The Critical Heritage* 554 and 558.

13. See, for instance, on the troubadours: John M. Graham, "National Identity and the Politics of Publishing the Troubadours"; on the German context: Jeffrey M. Peck, "'In the Beginning was the Word'"; on the Hispanic context: Catherine Brown, "The Relics of Menéndez Pidal" and Hans Ulrich Gumbrecht, "A Philological Invention of Modernism"; on Dante and the Italian context: Andrea Ciccarelli, "Dante and Italian Culture from the Risorgimento to World War I"; on Romance philology in general: Simon Gaunt and Julian Weiss, "Cultural Traffic in the Medieval Romance World"; on Anglo-Saxon and English letters: Clare A. Simmons, "'Iron-Worded Proof'" and Allen J. Frantzen, *Desire for Origins*; as well as the essays on Gaston Paris cited in note 11 above and on Joseph Bédier in note 19 below.

14. Historians also point out that the grumbling about the German hermeneutists' methods and aims began much earlier. Already in 1812 Alexander Archibald, the Princeton Theological Seminary's first professor, had stated on the occasion of his investiture: "In the former part of the last century this [i.e., the corruption of scripture] was a subject of warm altercation in the church. For whilst some maintained that the sacred text had not received the slightest injury from the ravages of time, others boldly asserted that it was greatly corrupted. . . . Learned men, with unparalleled diligence, employed their whole lives in the collation of manuscripts, and in noting every, even the smallest variation, in their *readings*. Their indefatigable labor and invincible perseverance in prosecuting this work are truly astonishing. It has indeed, much the appearance of laborious trifling; but upon the whole, though not always so designed, has proved serviceable to the cause of truth. For though the serious mind is at first astonished and confounded, upon being informed of the multitude of various readings, . . . yet it is relieved, when on careful examination it appears that not more than one of a hundred of these, makes the slightest variation in the sense, and that the whole of them do not materially affect one important fact or doctrine. It is true, a few important texts, in our received copies, have by this critical process, been rendered suspicious; but this has been more than compensated by the certainty which has been stamped on the great body of Scripture, by having been subjected to this severe scrutiny. For the *text* of our Bibles having passed this ordeal, may henceforth bid defiance to suspicion of its *integrity*" (*The Princeton Theology* 76–77). The A. A. Hodge who co-authored "Inspiration" was named for Alexander Archibald (his father, Charles Hodge, had seen Archibald's investiture ceremony at the age of fourteen and had been deeply moved by it; see *The Princeton Theology* 72 and David B. Calhoun, *Princeton Seminary* 1:33).

15. A. A. Hodge, *Outlines of Theology* 75. In "Inspiration" Hodge and Warfield argue that "critical examination" of the text can produce useful historical conclusions. But they say that the current paper isn't the appropriate place to answer the critical challenges to scripture (244). Rather in "Inspiration" they aim to demonstrate that scripture itself has an ontological nature modeled on that of Jesus: they state in the closing words of the article that "we rest in the joyful and unshaken certainty that we possess a Bible written by the hands of man indeed, but also graven with the finger of God" (260).

16. J. J. Reeve, "My Personal Experience with the Higher Criticism" 102–3 and 112.

Reeve mentions the Old Testament in particular because he is chiefly concerned with recent scholarship on the vast and distant history that the Old Testament witnesses. For other investigations of philological method in early issues of *The Fundamentals*, see Dyson Hague, "History of the Higher Criticism" (1:87–122) and Franklin Johnson, "Fallacies of the Higher Criticism" (2:48–68).

17. Charles Hodge, "The Scriptures Are the Word of God," in *The Princeton Theology* 113. His son, A. A. Hodge, would cite 1 Cor. 2:13 ("Now we have received, not the spirit of the world, but the spirit which is of God; that we might know the things that are freely given to us of God. Which things also we speak, not in the words which man's wisdom teacheth, but which the Holy Ghost teacheth; comparing spiritual things with spiritual" [verses 12–13, cited in the King James translation]) and 1 Thess. 2:13 ("For this cause also thank we God without ceasing, because, when ye received the word of God which ye heard of us, ye received it not as the word of men, but as it is in truth, the word of God, which effectually worketh also in you that believe") to prove the inspiration of scripture (*Outlines of Theology* 67). Neither of these proof texts is likely to convince a disinterested outsider.

18. Leo Spitzer, *Linguistics and Literary History* 6–7. This passage is cited and discussed below; see Chapter 6.

19. On Bédier's life and works, see Michelle Warren, "'Au commencement était l'île'"; Alain Corbellari, "Joseph Bédier, Philologist and Writer"; Per Nykrog, "A Warrior Scholar at the Collège de France"; Hans Aarsleff, "Scholarship and Ideology"; and Mark Burde, "Francisque Michel, Joseph Bédier, and the Epic Discovery of the First Edition of the Song of Roland (1837)." David Hult, "Reading It Right," and Rupert T. Pickens, "The Future of Old French Studies in America," discuss Gaston Paris's and Bédier's contributions to debates over Lachmannian textual criticism.

20. In translation, of course, the sentence loses its elegance and some of its supple beauty of thought: "The art of editing premodern texts shares something with all the other arts: it has evolved alongside fashions that die and are reborn"; Bédier, *La Tradition manuscrite du* Lai de l'ombre: *Réflexions sur l'art d'éditer les anciens textes* 1.

21. Ibid. 22–23.

22. Ibid. 71.

23. See Corbellari, "Joseph Bédier, Philologist and Writer"; Nykrog, "A Warrior Scholar at the Collège de France"; and Warren, "'Au commencement était l'île.'"

24. See, for instance, the essays in *The Future of the Middle Ages* and Stephen G. Nichols's and R. Howard Bloch's contributions to the "New Philology" issue of *Speculum*. Sarah Kay gives an overview of treatments of Bédierist and Lachmannian theories in her review article on the "New Philology," 302–5.

25. And, of course, other scholars have attacked the Bédierist model of text editing (and defended Lachmannian method) on technical grounds. See, for two particularly interesting interventions, Ramón Menéndez Pidal, *La Chanson de Roland* 12–15 and Timpanaro, "Bipartite Stemmas and Disturbances of the Manuscript Tradition" (*The Genesis of Lachmann's Method* 157–87).

26. See, for instance, pages 11, 22, 40, and 68. In an earlier publication, however, Bédier used the word *philologie* in a positive sense, in his marvelous definition of the philologist: "la philologie n'est pas le tout, ni la fin, ni le principal de la critique; elle n'en est pas non plus l'accessoire; elle en est—simplement—la condition. En effet, elle suppose moins l'apprentissage de certaines recettes et de certains procédés de recherche, qu'une discipline générale de travail, une habitude intellectuelle, un *esprit:* et c'est essentiellement la volonté d'observer avant d'imaginer, d'observer avant de raisonner, d'observer avant de construire; c'est le parti pris de vérifier tout le vérifiable, de chercher toujours plus de vérité, en se rappelant comme le dit l'un ne nos maîtres, 'qu'il n'y a pas de moindres vérités, de vérités indifférentes, ou de vérités négligeables'; c'est le ressouvenir sans cesse présent de ce vieux proverbe, où quelque chose est enclos du génie concret et réaliste de la France, et qui assure qu'un muids remplis d'imaginations et d'hypothèses ne contient pas une poignée de savoir utile" ("Philology is not the whole, nor the end, nor the principle of criticism; nor is it the accessory; it is—simply—the condition. In effect, it supposes less an apprenticeship in certain formulas and certain procedures of research, than a general work discipline, an intellectual habit, a *spirit:* and that is essentially the will to observe before imagining, to observe before analyzing, to observe before constructing; it is the commitment to verify all that is verifiable, to seek ever more truth, recalling what one of our masters said: 'there are no piddling truths, no indifferent truths, no negligible truths'; it is to recollect constantly that old proverb [which embodies something of the concrete, realist French genius] and which assures us that a hogshead of fantasies and hypotheses does not contain a fistful of useful knowledge"; *Études critiques* [1903] ix). Of course, in the current context the insistence on the "concrete, realist" genius of the French is exquisitely revealing.

27. Here, for instance, Zachary Lockman, in his exemplary history of modern Orientalism, explains the problem with philology: for the nineteenth-century Orientalist, "the key to scholarly understanding of the Orient (as of other civilizations) was philology, the historical analysis and comparison of languages, pursued largely through the study of written texts which, it was believed, could yield unique insights into the timeless essence of a civilization. . . . [P]hilological training was often deemed all that was necessary to achieve a profound understanding of what this subset of Orientalists regarded as their object of study: Islamic civilization. As a result, the methods and approaches forged by emerging new disciplines from the mid-nineteenth century onward, including anthropology, sociology, economics and 'scientific' history, were often deemed irrelevant, even misleading, when applied to this segment of humanity" (68). Of course this is not entirely accurate; during the nineteenth century philology was believed to be the royal road to the humanist disciplines, rather than a replacement for them. But it is equally evident that all scholars did not treat it that way, and thus a corrective backlash against it became necessary: "There was a growing sense [in the 1970s] that Orientalism as a discipline, in addition to being intellectually isolated, unself-critical and lacking any methodological tools other than an antiquated philology, did not possess the kind of real intellectual foundation that underpinned the humanities and social science disciplines. It was essentially a vestige

of an early modern or even medieval way of dividing up the world, and by taking 'the Orient' or 'Islam' (understood as a distinct and unitary civilization) as its object of study Orientalism actually made it more difficult to attain a proper understanding of the histories, societies, cultures and politics of predominately Muslim peoples and lands" (*Contending Visions of the Middle East* 165).

See also Manuela Marín's synopsis of twentieth-century critiques of Orientalism: "The debate over the meaning of 'Oriental' studies takes as its point of departure a severe critique of philology as the sole instrument of analysis: the Orientalist is accused of constructing, thanks to the philological study of texts, a mythical Orient, unchanging and essentialized; but the knowledge—complete though it might be—of the language does not suffice to understand the evolution and the keys of a society." At the same time, she points out that any Western model used to analyze Islamic civilizations is likely to distort the object of its analysis. And she suggests en passant a tantalizing defense of Orientalist philology: "We should not forget that Islamic culture is intrinsically a culture of the written text" ("Arabistas en España" 380–81).

28. Particularly important book-length disciplinary reconsiderations of the last twenty-five years include Lockman's masterful *Contending Visions of the Middle East;* Robert Irwin's cabinet of curiosities, *For Lust of Knowing;* and the thoughtful essays in Albert Hourani's *Islam in European Thought.* Spanish and Italian Orientalist traditions have been largely overlooked in these surveys.

29. See Todd Kontje, *German Orientalisms;* Billie Melman, *Women's Orients;* and Lisa Lowe, *Critical Terrains.*

30. Renan, *De la part des peuples sémitiques dans l'histoire de la civilisation* 28.

31. The crucial bibliography in the field includes the seminal studies by Henri Pirenne, Fernand Braudel, and Horden and Purcell (which focus on "Mediterraneity" rather than the question of Muslim-Christian relations) and works by María Rosa Menocal, S. D. Goitein, and Molly Greene (studies that consider interconfessional relations with a secondary regional focus on the Mediterranean). Recent years have seen a number of essay collections on related topics, indicating the keen contemporary relevance of the field. See, for instance, *Rethinking the Mediterranean, A Faithful Sea,* and the collection of translated essays by Vincenzo Consolo, *Reading and Writing the Mediterranean.*

32. I follow Suzanne Akbari in borrowing the terms "intensification and abatement" from Horden and Purcell, who use it to describe patterns of agricultural activity in the Mediterranean in particular (see Akbari, "Between Diaspora and Conquest," and Peregrine Horden and Nicholas Purcell, *The Corrupting Sea* 263–70).

33. Edgar Allan Poe, "The Philosophy of Composition," in *The Complete Works* 14:204. Poe is talking here not about frames per se but rather about the setting for the action described in the literary work; the sentiment he expresses is none the less appropriate.

34. The authoritative work on the manuscript history of the *Nights* is Muhsin Mahdi, *The Thousand and One Nights.* See in addition Dwight Reynolds, "*A Thousand and One Nights*"; Heinz Grotzfeld, "The Manuscript Tradition of the Arabian Nights";

Mahdi, "The Sources of Galland's *Nuits*"; and Robert Irwin, *The Arabian Nights: A Companion.*

35. On the dating of the manuscript see Mahdi's edition of the Arabic text (*The Thousand and One Nights* [1984]) 25–36 and Grotzfeld, "The Age of the Galland Manuscript of the *Nights.*"

36. Reynolds, "*A Thousand and One Nights*" 279–80; Robert Irwin, *The Arabian Nights: A Companion* 99–101.

37. Muhsin Jassim Ali, *Scheherazade in England* 10–11; Reynolds, "*A Thousand and One Nights*" 280.

38. One of these "transcriptions" was the work of Dom Denis Chavis (Dionysius Shâwîsh) and Jacques Cazotte; Mikha'il Sabbagh produced the second. Together Chavis and Cazotte would produce the *Continuations des Mille et une nuits*, which claimed to be a translation of the *complete* manuscript of the *Nights* that had eluded Antoine Galland. Examination of this work with the aim of determining its legitimacy would be a focus of the debate on the *Nights* in the *Gentleman's Magazine*; it would be denounced as a modern invention in the early nineteenth century. Sabbagh's counterfeit transcription, on the other hand, would be unmasked only by Muhsin Mahdi during the late twentieth century. Mahdi's account of the two counterfeit texts is the most complete: see *The Thousand and One Nights* (1995) 51–72.

39. *Gentleman's Magazine* 79 (February 1799): 92. For other contributions to the *Gentleman's Magazine* debate see 64 (June 1794): 527; 64 (September 1794): 783–84—particularly interesting for the discussion of the moral content of the tales; 67 (October 1797): 815–16; 67 (December 1797): 1019–20; 67 (Supplement): 1083; 68 (April 1798): 304–5; 68 (September 1798): 757–58; 69 (January 1799): 55.

40. Beattie, *Dissertations moral and critical* 509–10. Beattie's discussion contributes to the effort to situate the *Nights* in the context of the debate between Augustan neoclassicism and emerging Romantic notions of poetic invention; see Ali, *Scheherazade in England.*

41. Nathan Drake, *Literary Hours* 1:229.

42. John Barth, *The Friday Book* 87.

43. On the nineteenth-century editions of the *Nights*—Calcutta I (1814–18); Habicht, or Breslau (1824–38); Bulaq (1835); and Calcutta II, or Macnaghten (1839–42)—see Muhsin Mahdi, *The Thousand and One Nights* 87–126; Reynolds, "*A Thousand and One Nights*" 282–84; and Irwin, *The Arabian Nights: A Companion* 42–62.

44. *Aladin ou la lampe merveilleuse* (1906), dir. Albert Capellani, Pathé Frères; *Ali Baba* (1908), dir. Georges Denola, Pathé Frères; *The Seventh Voyage of Sinbad* (1958), dir. Nathan Juran and Richard Schickel, Morningside Movies; *The Golden Voyage of Sinbad* (1974), dir. Gordon Hessler, Ameran Films, and *Sinbad and the Eye of the Tiger* (1998), dir. Sam Wanamaker, Andor Films, each produced by Ray Harryhausen; *Ali Baba aur 40 Chor* (1979), dir. Umesh Mehra and L. Faiziev, Eagle Films; *Ali Baba and the Forty Thieves* (1944), dir. Arthur Lubin, Universal Pictures; *Sinbad: Legend of the Seven Seas* (2003), dir. Patrick Gilmore and Tim Johnson, DreamWorks Animation. On the *Arabian Nights* in

Western movies, see Robert Irwin, "The Arabian Nights in Film Adaptations" and "*A Thousand and One Nights* at the Movies"; Wen-Chin Ouyang, "Whose Story Is It? Sinbad the Sailor in Literature and Film"; and Michael Cooperson, "The Monstrous Births of 'Aladdin.'" I will discuss a chapter in the fascinating history of the *Thousand and One Nights* in the Western cinematic tradition below (see Chapter 7).

45. G. K. Chesterton, "The Everlasting Nights," in *The Spice of Life and Other Essays* 58.

46. See Wiebke Walther, "Modern Arabic Literature and the Arabian Nights"; and for two interesting readings of individual authors, Fedwa Malti-Douglas, "Shahrazad Feminist" and Anna Zambelli Sessona, "The Rewriting of *The Arabian Nights* by Imil Habibi."

47. New manuscripts of the *Nights* predating Galland's translation have recently been discovered, one in a French library and the other currently in England; scholarship on these manuscripts is likely to transform our understanding of the text as a work of Arabic literature.

48. On the discovery of the ninth-century fragment and a meticulous scrutiny of it—one of the most satisfying pieces of philological detective work of the first half of the twentieth century—see Nabia Abbott, "A Ninth-Century Fragment of the 'Thousand Nights.'" On references to the *Nights* in two tenth-century bibliographical works by al-Mas'udi and Ibn al-Nadim, see Dwight Reynolds, "Popular Prose in the Post-Classical Period" 249–52; on Ibn al-Nadim in particular, see Reynolds, "*A Thousand and One Nights*" 270–72 and Irwin, *The Arabian Nights* 48–50 and below, Chapter 7.

49. Georgina Pell Curtis, *The Interdependence of Literature* 85.

50. The preoccupation is evident not only in the stories that feature Harun al-Rashid, Ja'far, and Masrur, but also in the King's Steward's tale (from the Hunchback cycle), shown by Muhsin Mahdi to be plucked from a historical account of Abbasid Baghdad. See Mahdi, "From History to Fiction: The Tale Told by the King's Steward in *The Thousand and One Nights*."

51. Azar Nafisi, *Reading Lolita in Tehran* 19; Hisham Matar, *In the Country of Men* 15.

52. A. S. Byatt, "Narrate or Die" 106.

CHAPTER 2

1. Ugo Foscolo, review of *Osservazioni intorno alla questione sopra l'originalità del Poema di Dante*, by F. Cancellieri 338.

2. Joseph von Hammer-Purgstall had also translated the *Thousand and One Nights* into French. Both this translation and the manuscript from which he translated were lost; but his French version was translated into German by Zinserling (1823) and thence back into French by Trébutien (1828) and into English by Lamb (1826). See Reynolds, "*A Thousand and One Nights*" 285 and Grotzfeld, "The Manuscript Tradition of the Arabian Nights" 20.

3. Pietro Valerga, *Il divano di 'Omar Ben-al Fàre'd* 5–6. Here and throughout I

have taken considerable liberties with Valerga's truly extraordinary Italian, making it less stumbling and inscrutably contorted in English than it is in the original. In Michele Amari's copy of this work, now in the library of the Accademia dei Lincei in Rome, the reader will find an exasperated note in Amari's hand on the flyleaf: "Il frate non sa l'italiano" ("The brother does not know Italian"); Francesco Gabrieli called Valerga's Italian "barbarico" ("Il Petrarca e gli arabi" 487, footnote 1). Valerga's rather muddle-headed grasp of his material is already evident in the confused chronology that would seem to have Francesco Petrarch born not in 1304 but ("three centuries ago" ["or sono tre secoli"]) in 1574.

4. Pietro Valerga, *Il divano di 'Omar Ben-al Fàre'd* 14–15.

5. Ibid. 19–20.

6. Saladin, for instance, appears twice in the *Decameron*, once on the first day of storytelling and once on the tenth and last. In i, iii a wealthy Jewish citizen recounts to Saladin a tale of three identical rings symbolizing the equal validity of the three revealed religions; x, ix celebrates Saladin's legendary generosity.

For Arab settings, see i, ix, which involves a character returning from pilgrimage to the Holy Land; ii, ix, in which a character runs off to work for the "Soldan"; iii, x, which is set in Capsa, Barbary; iv, iv, which features a maritime battle scene involving a ship belonging to the king of Tunis; and v, ii, in which a character travels to Tunis.

7. In addition to ii, vii (the story of Alatiel), Lee lists analogues in the Arabian Nights for i, v; ii, vi; vii, ix; viii, x; and x, viii; and he cites analogues in other Islamic sources (Turkish or Arabic) for i, v and x, viii. Lee overlooks one particularly pungent parallel: the scruffy houseguest who aspires to bed a woman above his station and is plunged into a cesspool for his hubris (*Decameron* ii:v and the Story of the Two Viziers, *Alf layla wa-layla* 248–49; *Arabian Nights*, trans. Haddawy, 177). In the *Nights* this tale is embedded in the Story of the Three Apples, listed by Lee as an analogue to *Decameron* x, viii: two men confess to the same crime, each swearing that he is the only culprit; they are brought before the governor to whom they relate their tales. So great is the governor's wonder upon hearing their story that he grants amnesty not only to the two virtuous characters but also to the true criminal, who in the meantime has confessed his own culpability.

8. Notable exceptions to this rule include Victoria Kirkham's and María Rosa Menocal's article "Reflections on the 'Arabic' World: Boccaccio's Ninth Stories," in which the two scholars argue that not only in the *Decameron* but throughout his work Boccaccio uses the number nine to signify the Arab world and in particular to convey the negative connotations that Boccaccio associates with the Arab world. Kirkham and Menocal argue that Boccaccio had a more reductive attitude toward Arab learning and was less enthralled by it than Dante. A more recent article by Alison Cornish ("'Not Like an Arab'") explores the meaning of a phrase from the *Filocolo*, in which one of the characters declares his fascination with the night sky and his intention to study astronomy "non come arabo." She concludes that the phrase suggests the character's intent to study not directly, from the (Arab) primary sources, but rather through the mediation of a "modern expert, a

learned intermediary who knows the source and also talks to us. . . . The peculiar phrase 'non come arabo,' applied to study, is an acknowledgement of cultural difference between ourselves and the object of our knowledge, particularly when remote in time or space, and an insistence on the need for cultural appropriation, vernacularization, or making the foreign one's own" (64–65).

9. Miguel Asín Palacios, *La escatología musulmana* (1919) 352; (1943) 420. The English translation of Asín's book leaves the most interesting touch out of this sentence: "The share due to Ibn Arabi—a Spaniard, although a Moslem—in the literary glory achieved by Dante Alighieri in his immortal poem can no longer be ignored" (277). Asín's Spanish, however, makes Ibn 'Arabi finally neither a Spaniard nor a Muslim but a *Murcian* (i.e., from the region of Murcia in southeastern Spain): "La parte de gloria que a este pensador hispano, aunque musulmán, es decir, al murciano Ibn 'Arabi debe corresponder en la genial empresa literaria que Dante Alighieri llevó a glorioso término con su poema inmortal, ya no es lícito tampoco desconocerla." Regionalism trumps national identity; Ibn 'Arabi transcends the divide between Muslim and Christian and transcends Spanish nationalism through the particularism of a regional definition of identity.

10. Scholars generally identify Antoine Isaac Silvestre de Sacy (1758–1838)—who became professor of Arabic at the École speciale des langues orientales vivantes in Paris in 1795 and produced an Arabic grammar as well as two anthologies for the use of students—as the father of the Parisian school of academic Orientalism. The Spanish scholar Pascual de Gayangos y Arce (1809–97) studied with Silvestre de Sacy. Gayangos would train Francisco Codera y Zaidín (1836–1917), who would train Julián Ribera y Tarrago (1858–1934), who would train Miguel Asín Palacios. Michele Amari also studied with a student of Silvestre de Sacy; see below, Chapter 3.

11. Francisco Codera y Zaidín, however, had traveled to Arab countries to acquire manuscripts.

12. James Monroe, *Islam and the Arabs in Spanish Scholarship* 83. On Asín, see also María Rosa Menocal's thoughtful review of two recent publications, a biography of Asín and a reissue of his works ("An Andalusianist's Last Sigh").

13. Foscolo, review of *Osservazioni intorno alla questione sopra l'originalità del Poema di Dante*, by F. Cancellieri 321.

14. "Dante, if compared not only to Virgil, the most sober of poets, but even to Tacitus, will be found never to employ more than a stroke or two of his pencil, which he aims at imprinting almost insensibly on the hearts of his readers. Virgil has related the story of Eurydice in two hundred verses; Dante, in sixty verses, has finished his masterpiece—the Tale of Francesca de Rimini" (review of *Dante; with a new Italian Commentary* 459). The occasion of Foscolo's review articles in the *Edinburgh Review* is indicative of the new interest in Dante: he surveys a recent English translation of Dante and a new Italian commentary in the first. And in the second he reviews a publication that considers a question relevant to the current discussion: to what extent was Dante's invention *his* invention? Did he simply assemble found elements into a new form?

15. Asín mentions this comment at the beginning of his notations for the year 1919

(*La escatología musulmana* [1943] 484) and repeats it later in a summary of the polemic (508).

16. Already in 1744 a bibliographer noted the presence in the Bibliothèque du Roi of a Latin translation of the miʿraj narrative. (This library—which will have another cameo appearance in Chapter 3—also held Galland's papers after his death, including the original Syrian manuscript of the *Thousand and One Nights*; and it is the same library in which two Arab scholars would produce documents purporting to be transcriptions of "full manuscripts" of the *Nights* between 1780 and 1810.) And in the mid-nineteenth century another bibliographer listed a translation of the miʿraj narrative into French among the holdings of the Bodleian collection in Oxford (see Giorgio Levi della Vida, "Nuova luce sulle fonti islamiche della *Divina Commedia*" 378).

In 1907 Angelo de Fabrizio published an elegant article about the miʿraj legend and Dante in which he identified references to the miʿraj tradition in two works written by medieval Italians. One of these works—*Lo specchio della Fede* (*The Mirror of the Faith*), written by Roberto da Lecce (1425–95), a noted Franciscan preacher—appeared only after Dante's death. But the other was written by Dante's contemporary, Ricoldo da Monte Croce. Ricoldo's *Contra legem Sarracenorum* (*Against the Law of the Saracens*) gives only a brief reference to the tradition; but de Fabrizio is able to point out that in his *Dittamondo*, written in the mid-fourteenth century, Fazio degli Uberti mentions the "Book of the Ladder" while describing Ricoldo's travels in the East, suggesting that the tale of Muhammad's journey to the afterworld was familiar in fourteenth-century Italy. See Angelo de Fabrizio, "Il 'Mirag' di Maometto esposto da un frate del secolo XV"; and for a brief but useful summary of nineteenth-century scholarship on Dante and the miʿraj tradition and an interesting discussion of more recent contributions to the debate, Maxime Rodinson, "Dante et l'Islam d'après des travaux récents" 203–4.

Finally, in 1944 Italian philologist Ugo Monneret de Villard signaled the existence of the Oxford and Paris manuscripts containing the translations of the miʿraj narrative, although he could not consult them because of the war: "comparison and accurate study of the writings is, unfortunately, impossible for me in the current circumstances" (Ugo Monneret de Villard, *Lo studio dell'Islam in Europa nel XII e nel XIII secolo* 54).

17. José Muñoz Sendino, *La Escala de Mahoma* xiii.

18. Two decades later—in 1972—Cerulli would publish a second book on Dante and Islam, which assembled even more material demonstrating the vibrant Christian interest in Muslim eschatology in general and the miʿraj legend in particular: *Nuove ricerche sul Libro della Scala e la conoscenza dell'Islam in Occidente*.

19. On the "Book of the Ladder," see Maria Corti, "La 'Commedia' di Dante e l'oltretomba islamico"; on Averroism, see Corti, *Dante a un nuovo crocevia* and *La felicità mentale* and Bruno Nardi, *Dante e la cultura medievale, Saggi di filosofia dantesca,* and *Dal 'Convivio' alla 'Commedia'*; on Dante's depiction of Muhammad see my "Muhammad in Hell"; and for a truly original reading of Dante's intellectual environment, see Gregory B. Stone, *Dante's Pluralism and the Islamic Philosophy of Religion*.

20. See Giuseppe Mazzotta, "Antiquity and the New Arts in Petrarch" (*The Worlds*

*of Petrarch* 14–32), especially 18–21. Mazzotta's reading of Petrarch ends with an affirmation of the power of the medieval, which emerges in Petrarch's thought as an instrument of intellectual intervention: "This in-between time, which historically we call *medium aevum*, is the unavoidable, forever recurring time of audacious thought, which is what poetry is. In this in-between time, the poet retrieves images of the past and discovers that the achievements of modernity are always inscribed in the past; that the figures of the past have the power to unsettle the complacencies of the present" (32).

21. "Unum antequam desinam te obsecro, ut ab omni consilio mearum rerum, tui isti Arabes arceantur, atque exulent, odi genus universum. . . . Arabes vero quales medici tu scis. Quales autem poetae scio ego, nihil blandius, nihil mollius, nihil enervatius, nihil denique turpius" (Petrarch, *Sen.* XII, 2; *Le "Senili"* 241; *Letters of Old Age* 2:471–72).

22. Valerga, *Il divano di 'Omar Ben-al Fàre'd* 10.

23. Julián Ribera, "El arabista español," in *Disertaciones y opúsculos* 1:465.

24. Indeed Petrarch voiced an outspoken hostility toward contemporary Greeks whom (he believed), as much as the Arabs, should be made the object of crusade. See Nancy Bisaha, "Petrarch's Vision of the Muslim and Byzantine East" 308–13.

Juan Andrés noted the sleight of hand by which Renaissance scholarship replaced the learning of the medieval Arabs with the learning of the ancient Greeks as the culture of prestige: "If the Arabs had the ill fortune to be wrongly accused as corrupters of good taste and fatal destroyers of wholesome literature, the more fortunate Greeks have enjoyed the auspicious fate of being extolled—without sufficient grounds—as the felicitous restorers of worthy studies. Certain erudite but superficial men began to demonstrate contempt for all that was Arabic and to advance an opposing idea that we owe modern culture to the Greeks who fled Constantinople; and this was enough to make all the others embrace such an opinion without taking the trouble to examine it" (1:331).

25. Ernest Renan, *Averroès et l'Averroïsme*, in *Œuvres complètes* 3:252, 253 and 253, footnote 4.

26. H. A. R. Gibb, "Literature," in *The Legacy of Islam* 192.

27. Enrico Cerulli, "Petrarca e gli arabi." In an article that appeared in the same volume ("Il Petrarca e gli arabi") Francesco Gabrieli argued that it was possible that a friend had introduced him to the poetry of the Arabs.

28. See C. H. L. Bodenham, "Petrarch and the Poetry of the Arabs." Hermannus's translation uses the word *turpis* regularly to refer to the base moral qualities that satirical poetry must condemn.

In an article published in 1997 ("Petrarch and Averroes: An Episode in the History of Poetics") Charles Burnett agrees with Bodenham's identification of Hermannus's *Poetria* as the source for Petrarch's condemnation of the poetry of the Arabs; and he reads the Arabic of the Ibn Rushd translation of Aristotle's *Poetics* in order to see how Hermannus's translation has mangled Ibn Rushd's condemnation of erotic poetry.

29. In a particularly interesting contribution to the question ("Petrarch's Vision of the Muslim and Byzantine East"), Nancy Bisaha broadens our understanding of the "Petrarch and the Arabs" question considerably. She pulls together a range of references to

the Arabs from Petrarch's poetry and letters, and situates these references in the context of Petrarch's response to the crusades and the necessity to subjugate the Arabs in order to take back the Holy Land (and to seize the northern shore of the African continent). She acknowledges the classical topoi in Petrarch's references to the Arabs but also identifies what is strikingly original in his vituperation. She herself is a historian whose work models philological technique: she uses the historical background as a crucial gloss without which we can't accurately read the textual records of historical event.

30. A translation of the *Poetics* would be made directly from the Greek text by William of Moerbeke in 1278, but this translation remained unknown to the Middle Ages and early modernity. Hermannus's translation from Averroes' text was studied instead. See William F. Boggess, "Aristotle's *Poetics* in the Fourteenth Century" 278.

31. On these translations, see William F. Boggess, "Hermannus Alemannus's Rhetorical Translations."

32. See Boggess, "Aristotle's *Poetics* in the Fourteenth Century," and Bodenham, "Petrarch and the Poetry of the Arabs" 171–72.

33. For an interesting discussion of the understanding of the Aristotelian Organon during the Middle Ages, see al-Farabi's (ca. 870–950/51) treatise on the division of the sciences (Arabic text in al-Farabi, *Catálogo de las ciencias*, Arabic pages 14–32; Spanish translation 13–39), translated into Latin by Gerard of Cremona (ca. 1114–87; al-Farabi, *Catálogo* 128–44).

34. See Boggess, "Aristotle's *Poetics* in the Fourteenth Century" 281 and 283–84.

35. "Species vero poetrie quam elegiam nominant non est nisi incitatio ad actus coituales, quos amoris nomine obtegunt et decorant" (Hermannus, *De arte poetica* 44; Boggess, "Aristotle's *Poetics* in the Fourteenth Century" 287 [excerpt number 9]).

36. Hermannus, *De arte poetica* 41.

37. On translation of Arabic verse during the Middle Ages, see Charles Burnett's "Learned Knowledge of Arabic Poetry," which looks at translations of poetry and rhymed prose from Petrus Alfonsi in the twelfth century to Leo Africanus in the sixteenth and includes a brief but thoughtful discussion of Hermannus Alemannus's translations.

38. Hermannus, *De arte poetica* 61. The poem also appears in its entirety in the florilegium used at the University of Paris (like the condemnation of poetry that incites lust; see above, note 35), and is excerpted in most of the florilegia that quote Hermannus's translation of Averroes' commentary on the *Poetics*, including Jean de Fayt's. See Boggess, "Aristotle's *Poetics* in the Fourteenth Century," 285–94 (examples B19 and B20, C25, D45, F22 and, on page 293, example 24).

The simple tale of al-Majnun—like many of the *vidas* of the troubadours—was undoubtedly a back invention suggested by the content of the poems. But medieval anthologists tended to attribute odd love poems to the legendary al-Majnun when they didn't know the author, and verses and *akhbar* (narratives or anecdotes) purported to be his proliferated. See María Rosa Menocal's unforgettable retelling of the tale of al-Majnun and Layla in *Shards of Love* (144–48).

39. On Hermannus's substitutions and deletions of Averroes' poetic examples, see William F. Boggess, "Hermannus Alemannus' Latin Anthology of Arabic Poetry" 657–60.

40. Hermannus frequently doubled the number of lines of the Arabic poetic selections by producing one line of Latin text for each hemistich of the Arabic original. At other times, however, he *reduced* the number of lines, so that his translation had fewer lines than the Arabic original. Boggess's essay "Hermannus Alemannus' Latin Anthology of Arabic Poetry," which gives the text of each of Hermannus's Latin translations as well as a transliteration of the Arabic verses he is translating, is the best resource for taking stock of Hermannus's manipulation of his source.

41. This selection from al-Majnun is the longest selection of poetry in Hermannus's treatise, and he seems to have taken care to polish it (although another selection, from Imru'u 'l-Qays, also gets special attention: Hermannus rhymes the hemistiches as well as the line endings in the Latin translation). The effectiveness of his translation is demonstrated by the frequency with which the opening verses appear in the florilegia excerpting Hermannus's *Poetria* (see above, note 38). The original reads (in literal translation, one line of translated text for each hemistich of verse):

> I burst into tears for Taubadhi
> and it cried out "Allahu akbar!" to the merciful God when it saw me
> I said to it: Where are those whom you knew,
> [those who were] around you in the safe and easy age?
> It replied: They have gone, they have entrusted their land to me;
> but who is master over the adversity of time?

The abandoned dwelling place in Arabic is a masculine rather than a feminine noun; the use of feminine pronouns and adjectives, of course, becomes a source of pathos in Hermannus's translation. Indeed the original, in the prosaic simplicity of its vocabulary and syntax, reads like a template for poetic invention. For the Arabic text, see Averroes, *Talkhis kitab Aristutalis fi al-shi'r* 122; Boggess gives a transliteration of the Arabic text along with Francesco Gabrieli's Italian translation of the Arabic ("Hermannus Alemannus's Latin Anthology of Arabic Poetry" 666).

Medieval Western readers seem to have found the passage particularly suggestive. Bodenham points out its influence on subsequent writers (the English friar Robert Holcot, who visited Avignon at the time that Petrarch was there; poet Georges Chastellain, d. 1475), and asks cautiously whether Petrarch might have drawn on a memory of these lines, "quite unconsciously," in a sonnet (#269, "Rotta è l'alta colonna e 'l verde lauro," cited below, note 44; see "Petrarch and the Poetry of the Arabs" 176–77).

42. See Charlton T. Lewis and Charles Short, *A Latin Dictionary* s.v. *fluo*. One of the words which Petrarch used to condemn the poetry of the Arabs—*mollis*, soft—is used five times alongside *fluxus* in the passages cited in Lewis and Short to illustrate usage.

43. Petrarch, *Canzoniere* 51. In this context, it is of interest that—four verses after the end of the selection cited—Petrarch writes:

> . . . a pena spunta in oriente un raggio
> di sol, ch'a l'altro monte

de l'adverso orizonte
giunto il vedrai per vie lunghe et distorte . . .
(Canzone 37, "Sí è debile il filo a cui s'attene," vv. 21–24; *Canzoniere* 51)

[ . . . no sooner shines in the east a ray
of sun, than upon the other height
of the opposite horizon
you see it arrive, by long and twisted paths.]

In his crusading poem (Canzone 28, "O aspectata in ciel beata et bella") Petrarch clearly associates "l'oriënte" with the enemy army, "l'occidental" with the Christians (see *Canzoniere* 36, vv. 10 and 15; and 39, v. 98), suggesting that his evocation of an "eastern" ray of sunlight here may carry cultural connotations along with other, more obvious implications. If he did take inspiration for this poem from Hermannus Alemannus's translation of Averroes' commentary on Aristotle's *Poetics*, the ray of poetic light did indeed trace a "long and twisted path" to reach him.

44. The lines come from the sonnet which Bodenham suggested may have been loosely modeled on Hermannus's translation of al-Majnun (#269, "Rotta è l'alta colonna e 'l verde lauro" [Petrarch, *Canzoniere* 340]; see above, note 41):

Tolto m'ài, Morte, il mio doppio thesauro,
che mi fea viver lieto et gire altero,
et ristorar nol pò terra né impero,
né gemma oriëntal, né forza d'auro.

[Death, you have taken my double treasure from me,
which made my life happy and my steps proud,
which neither earth nor empire,
neither Oriental gem nor the power of gold can restore.]

The sonnet begins (suggestively in the current context) with an image that evokes a ruined dwelling place:

Rotta è l'alta colonna e 'l verde lauro
che facean ombra al mio stanco pensero . . .

[Broken is the tall column and the green laurel
that shaded my weary thoughts . . . ]

45. Petrarch, Fam. XXI, 15; 2:204–5.
46. "Siquis Latinorum Hippocrati etiam par existeret, loqui quidem posse, nisi Graecus tamen aut Arabs scribere non auderet, et si scriberet sperneretur. . . . Post solos

Arabes scribere non licebit" (Petrarch, Sen. XII, 2; *Le "Senili"* 241; *Letters of Old Age* 2:472).

47. As the ethno-religious terminology used in this sentence makes clear, the adjectives we use to refer to the Arabo-Islamic history of the European nations begs a number of questions and blurs a number of distinctions. The "Arabs" who invaded and settled the Iberian peninsula during the eighth century included a sizeable number of Berbers; the Almoravids and the Almohads, who dominated Andalusian history following the collapse of the Umayyad dynasty during the eleventh century, were Berbers. Both Arabs and Berbers were, of course, Muslim; and an indeterminate but considerable proportion of the population resident in the territory, neither Arab nor Berber, converted to the religion of the conquerors. Speakers of Arabic could also be Christians, either by birth or by conversion; and we know that there were Arabic-speaking Christians in medieval al-Andalus. And Jews were often fluent in Arabic and acted at as cultural (as well as political and economic) intermediaries. What adjectival marker of ethnic, cultural, or linguistic identity should the modern scholar use to demonimate the population of medieval al-Andalus? I lean toward the term *Arab* because I am most interested in the Arabic-language culture of medieval Iberia; I generally use the term *Islamic* or *Muslim* when I am closely following the argument of a scholar who himself uses that term, or when referring to philosophical or theological formations.

In light of this fine yet imprecise distinction, I should point out that scholarship on Dante's contacts with Islamic culture is regularly referred to in the secondary literature as the question of "Dante and *Islam*," while work on Petrarch and poetry in Arabic denotes that literary-historical problem as "Petrarch and *the Arabs*." This habit has developed largely because the scholarship addresses precisely Dante's knowledge of Islamic philosophy (which he knew in Latin translation), on the one hand, and on the other Petrarch's knowledge of Arabic-language poetry (which he referred to as the poetry *of the Arabs*).

48. Francisco Fernández y González, *Estado social y político de los Mudéjares de Castilla* 1. *Morisco* is the Spanish term for the Muslims of medieval Iberia who remained on land conquered and occupied by Christians and who were forcibly converted to Christianity; Fernández here defends their Hispanicity. Later in the same work he refers to the *mudejars* (or Muslims living under the rule of a Christian king) as "the sons of this soil . . . the conquered conquerors of Spain" (7).

49. José Antonio Conde, *Historia de la dominación de los Árabes en España* xxiv.

50. Ibid. xiv and xxv.

51. Pascual de Gayangos, *The History of the Mohammedan Dynasties in Spain* x–xii. Gayangos's relatively gentle treatment of Conde—in particular his insistence on seeing Conde's life and work in the context of the times in which he lived—are the more striking if compared to Francisco Codera's unsentimental dismissal of Conde's work. Gayangos was close enough to Conde to feel the importance of his work (and its popularity among "a certain class of readers" [x]). Codera used different philological standards to judge Conde's work. Not *everything* in the book is wrong, he wrote. "However there are many errors in his work, and non-Arabists are in no condition to distinguish the good from the

bad: therefore *they should not use this work* (emphasis in the original; *Decadencia y desapari-ción de los Almorávides en España* [1899] xi).

52. Gayangos, *The History of the Mohammedan Dynasties in Spain* vii and viii.

53. Ribera, "El arabista español," in *Disertaciones y opúsculos* 1:468. It is, of course, also true that Ribera believed the Muslims of medieval Spain to have been thoroughly hispanized and wrote that they were not racially Semitic (for this attitude, see in particular his discussion of Ibn Quzman, "El cancionero de Abencuzmán," in *Disertaciones y opús-culos* 1:12–26). Such attitudes are wholly typical of the racial ideas of the age and are, I believe, compensated for by the graciousness of lines like the one quoted above.

54. Miguel Asín Palacios, "El Averroísmo teológico de Santo Tomás de Aquino" 272.

55. Ibid. 324; emphasis added. James Monroe notes that A. J. Arberry criticized Asín's notion that Islamic theology took its origins from Eastern Christianity as typical of certain non-Muslim scholars: "all that in their view is good in Islam is of foreign origin." He termed such presumptions "not so much honest scholarship as the worst form of sectarian bigotry." Quoted in Monroe, *Islam and the Arabs in Spanish Scholarship* 192.

56. Francisco Javier Simonet, *Glosario de voces ibéricas y Latinas usadas entre los mozár-abes* xli. The verses from Horace also show up as the epigraph to the book. On Spanish reaction to the "Arabic thesis," and to versions of Spanish history that stressed the com-munications between Christians and Muslims in medieval al-Andalus in general, see Mon-roe, *Islam and the Arabs in Spanish Scholarship* 81 and Manuela Marín, "Arabistas en España" 388.

57. For the reference to medieval Iberian Arabo-Romance as "lenguaje nacional his-pano-latino," see Simonet, *Glosario de voces ibéricas y Latinas usadas entre los mozárabes* cxviii. For references to medieval Mozarabs as "nuestros Mozarabes," see, e.g., xv, xix, xxxiii, lii, c, cxciv, cxcv, cxcvii.

58. Ibid. cxxxiv–cxxxv.

59. See Monroe, *Islam and the Arabs in Spanish Scholarship* 87. Of course the Real Academia de la Historia had awarded an earlier version of Simonet's *Historia de los mozár-abes de España* their annual prize in 1867, and the work enjoys renown to the present day (it was reissued during the 1980s): evidence of the ongoing Spanish conflicts over the Spanish past.

60. Ribera, "El arabista español," in *Disertaciones y opúsculos* 1:466–67.

61. Similarly, Miguel Asín Palacios anticipated the difficulties that would arise in response to his study on the influence of Averroism on the theology of Thomas Aquinas (which appeared fifteen years before the book on Dante and Islam, in 1904). He responded by using the vocabulary of the hard sciences to defend his thesis: "By exclusion, then, we find ourselves reduced to accepting direct Muslim influence, if we have to give a scientific explanation for the phenomenon of analogy that is presented to us" ("El Averroísmo teológico de Santo Tomás de Aquino" 310). And he includes a relatively lengthy discussion of the potential means of transmission of Islamic philosophy to Thomas (317–24), deplor-ing with verve the medieval philosophers' reluctance to footnote their sources as modern scholars do (317).

In his monograph on Dante and Islam, Asín cited his teacher Julián Ribera's criteria to determine whether influence had occurred (*La escatología musulmana* [1919], 297; [1943], 357; cf. Eng. trans. 237). But he added a crucial escape clause. Likeness alone is sufficient to demonstrate influence when the similarities between the two texts "are so typical, so concrete and precise and, what is more, so many in number, that one could not in good conscience impute them to chance" (*La escatología musulmana* [1919] 298; [1943] 358; cf. Eng. trans. 237). Having dispensed with the necessity to demonstrate the means of transmission by assuming an environment that provided abundant opportunities for exposure to Arab culture—that is, by *hispanizing* the intellectual environment of medieval Italy—Asín considered the case closed in favor of influence and left the burden of proof in the hands of those Dante scholars who denied the obvious (*La escatología musulmana* [1919] 299; [1943] 359; Eng. trans. 238).

62. Américo Castro, *La realidad histórica de España* xx–xxi. For a more recent collection that uses Andalusian history to challenge standard literary historical definitions of influence, see Cynthia Robinson and Leyla Rouhi, *Under the Influence*.

63. David Wacks, *Framing Iberia* 5.

64. My summary of the translation, edition, and publication history of Aristotle's *Poetics*—encompassing the rediscovery of the Greek original, the reprints of Hermannus Alemannus's translation of Averroes' commentary, and the Cinquecento translations into Latin and Italian made from Todros Todrosi's Hebrew translation of Averroes and from the Greek text—relies on Boggess, "Hermannus Alemannus' Latin Anthology of Arabic Poetry" 657; Bernard Weinberg, *A History of Literary Criticism in the Italian Renaissance* 1:366–73, 404, and 421–22; and O. B. Hardison, "The Place of Averroes' Commentary on the *Poetics* in the History of Medieval Criticism" 73.

65. See William de Moerbeke, *De arte poetica*; and on the medieval transmission of Aristotle's *Poetics* and Hermannus's translation in particular, see my "Beyond Mimesis."

66. Renan, *Averroès et l'Averroïsme* 79.

## CHAPTER 3

1. Vella did not publish the Arabic "original" of these letters; his career was interrupted by his denunciation and trial in 1795.

2. A word on my use of the adjectives *Arab*, *Arabic*, and *Muslim* in this chapter: Twenty-first-century English-speaking scholars insist on the distinct lexical range of these three words. *Arab* generally refers to those who speak Arabic and their culture in a broad sense; *Arabic* is taken to refer specifically to the language and literary culture of the Arabs; and *Muslim* signifies the followers of Islam regardless of their native tongue. (Believing that discretion is the better part of philological acumen, I do not broach the vast lexical range of the homely but problematic English word *Arabian*.) The Italian language does not distinguish between *Arab* and *Arabic* (*arabo* signifies the language, the people, and the culture; the Italian *arabico* is now obsolete). And nineteenth-century European Orientalists regularly used the terms *Arab* and *Muslim* as synonyms. Furthermore Sicilian his-

tory problematizes the distinction between *Arab* and *Muslim* (as does Andalusian history); today historians tend to refer to the history of *Muslim Sicily* rather than *Arab Sicily* because the Muslim settlers in Sicily were both Berbers and Arabs. The language of the documents that are our witnesses to that history, however, is Arabic (and in this chapter I will talk about how Arabic literacy transformed understandings of Sicilian history). But the Arabic language was used too by the Normans, whose history certainly cannot be termed *Muslim*. In deference to the nineteenth-century philological works I am discussing and the complexities of the history they describe, I will occasionally use the adjective *Arab* to describe those periods of the Sicilian past that are documented by Arabic-language records—regardless of the confessional or ethnic pedigree of the Sicilian majority at the time.

3. *L'arabica impostura* reprints Domenico Scinà's nineteenth-century account of Vella's fraud (until the 1978 publication of this work, the sole source of information on the events) along with a well-researched essay by Adelaide Baviera Albanese on the forces—both within the Sicilian aristocracy and the Bourbon regime—that conspired to use Vella's discovery to their own purposes. Vella's intervention remains the point of departure for accounts of the Sicilian rediscovery of Arabic; among the nineteenth-century Sicilian historians, Michele Amari (*Storia dei musulmani di Sicilia* 1:6–11) and Vincenzo Mortillaro (*La storia, gli scrittori e le monete dell'epoca arabo-sicula* 296) recount the tale as the episode that gave impetus to a truly scientific Arabic philology in Sicily. William Spaggiari discusses a series of letters sympathetic to Vella written by Antonio Panizzi in "La 'minzogna saracina.'" Paolo Preto discusses the episode, along with a number of other Sicilian historical counterfeits from the Middle Ages to the early modern period, in "Una lunga storia di falsi e falsari" (24–30). Giuseppe Giarrizzo, in a biographical essay on Rosario Gregorio, includes a brief but provocative discussion of the Vella episode (*Cultura e economia nella Sicilia del '700* 220–21). And Leonardo Sciascia's novel based on the event (*Il consiglio d'Egitto*, translated into English as *The Council of Egypt*) has garnered praise for its historical accuracy and was made into a movie, *Il consiglio d'Egitto* (2002, dir. Emidio Greco).

4. Domenico Scinà, from the introduction to Gregorio's *Discorsi intorno alla Sicilia* 1:14.

5. Intriguingly, Thomas F. Glick points out that nineteenth-century Spaniards debating the "origins" of the Spanish irrigation system reproduced a similar dynamic: they "chose Rome as the most likely ancestor if they represented a centralist position and supported a series of water laws inspired in the French civil code. Advocates of the traditional, autonomous local irrigation communities opted for Arab origins" (*From Muslim Fortress to Christian Castle* 66).

6. Salvatore Cusa, *I diplomi greci ed arabi di Sicilia* 1:x.

7. Domenico Scinà, *L'arabica impostura* 22.

8. In order to produce the original manuscript for the first batch of letters, those between the emirs of Muslim Sicily and the caliphs of North Africa, Vella doctored a medieval life of Muhammad. The second manuscript, the letters between the Normans and the caliphs, was Vella's original creation. This manuscript is now at Columbia University.

9. Richard Gottheil, "Two Forged Antiques" 309.

10. Cusa, *I diplomi greci ed arabi di Sicilia* 1:xix.

11. Indeed, as Giarrizzo points out—despite the heroic role that Rosario Gregorio plays in most accounts of Sicilians' reconstruction of the island's Arab history—the Vella affair and Sicily's Arab history in general apparently held little importance for Gregorio. See *Cultura e economia nella Sicilia del '700* 222.

12. More precisely, the letter stated its place of publication as Malta; in fact it seems to have been published in Naples. See Spaggiari, "La 'minzogna saracina'" 293, note 33.

13. Giarrizzo, *Cultura e economia nella Sicilia del '700* 221.

14. Rosario Gregorio, *Rerum arabicarum quae ad historiam Siculam spectant ampla collectio* xiii.

15. "New, pure and copious light" are the words that Scinà used to describe Gregorio's intervention, the publication of Siculo-Arabic documents in order to expose Vella's fraud (*L'arabica impostura* 44). The phrase "our Saracen history" comes from Mortillaro (*La storia, gli scrittori e le monete dell'epoca arabo-sicula* 303); "our Arabic memories" are the words of Cusa (*I diplomi greci ed arabi di Sicilia* 1:xv); "our ancestors" is the term that Pietro Lanza uses to refer to the Arabs (*Degli Arabi e del loro soggiorno in Sicilia* 52). For the phrase "i nostri Saracini" in particular, see Mortillaro, *La storia, gli scrittori e le monete dell'epoca arabo-sicula* 300 and 303 and Carmelo Martorana, *Notizie storiche dei Saraceni siciliani* 1:6.

The metaphor of shining the light into the shadows of the Arab past appears in nineteenth-century Spanish historiography as well. Thus Conde, in *Historia de la dominación de los Árabes en España* (1820–21), described his motivation for using Arab sources to write Spanish history: "The events could not be corrected, nor things as they were clarified, except by the light of Arabic memories" (xiv). Fernández y González, in his *Estado social y político de los Mudéjares de Castilla* (1866), announced his intention to "cast some light on a subject so little known as the history of the *mudejares* [Muslims living under Christian rule] of Castile, the last of a vast and formidable power, and who (just like our ancient Mozarabs and the Zoroastrians of Persia) preserved the memory of the most illuminated traditions, worthy of exaltation and of the highest praise" (11).

Simonet demonstrated that the metaphor could swing both ways. In *Glosario de voces ibéricas y Latinas usadas entre los mozárabes* (1888) he wrote that following the revelation of Islam the Arabs advanced East and West, "obscuring with the shadows of a new paganism peoples already illuminated with the light of the Gospel, retarding the rebirth and the progress of Christian Europe" (xlii).

As far as I am aware, the Spaniards did not (as the Sicilians did) tend to refer to the Arabs of Spanish history as "*our* Arabs" or "*our* Saracens." As a telling exception to this rule, see Simonet's repeated references to "nuestros Mozarabes" (cited above in Chapter 2, note 57).

16. Sicilian Arab scholarship, to an even greater extent than other European philological traditions, is alive to its own disciplinary history. Nineteenth-century Sicilians regularly traced the genealogy of scholarship in the field as a preamble (or postscript) to

their own contribution. Amari's summary of studies in Siculo-Arabic history is (as one would expect, given Amari's irrepressible personality and athletic style—Gibbon was an important model) particularly lively. A propos of the tardy development of Orientalist studies in Sicily, Amari comments on the remarkable fact that during the seventeenth and eighteenth centuries, while Rome was the center of Orientalist studies in Europe—largely because of the need to train missionaries—and Tuscany did not lag far behind, "such studies did little good in Sicily, because the progresses of the intellect were difficult to communicate from one scrap of Italy to another, and with even greater difficulty crossed the sea" (*Storia dei musulmani di Sicilia* 1:5).

17. Saverio Scrofani, *Della dominazione degli stranieri in Sicilia*, preface (unnumbered page).

18. Quoted from an unnamed English source in Robert Zapperi, "La 'fortuna' di un avventuriero" 455. I have not been able to find the source of this citation, which I have translated back into English.

19. In his obituary for Scrofani, Pompeo Inzenga wrote, "Habituated to opium, perhaps on his voyages to the Levant, he could not, having returned to Europe, wean himself from it; and he had no reason to lament, since he received comfort from that force that consumed him over the years" (Zapperi, "La 'fortuna' di un avventuriero" note 4, page 461). Zapperi points out that "it seems that [Inzenga's] personal relations with Scrofani must have been abysmal" (note 6, page 461). In the essay here cited, Zapperi demonstrated the extent to which Scrofani manipulated his public image by massaging the biographical essays he wrote for the numerous biographical dictionaries of the early nineteenth century.

20. Scrofani, *Della dominazione degli stranieri in Sicilia* 115.

21. "Come in terra di niun signore"; ibid. 107–8.

22. Ibid. 116.

23. Ibid. 108.

24. Amari, *Storia dei musulmani di Sicilia* 1:12; Mortillaro, *La storia, gli scrittori e le monete dell'epoca arabo-sicula* 300. On Scrofani, see also Giarrizzo, *Cultura e economia nella Sicilia del '700*.

25. Martorana, *Notizie storiche dei Saraceni siciliani* 1:6–7. Martorana—like other Sicilian writers of the age—fluctuates between the two spellings of the word *Saracen*, the standard Italian *Saraceni* and the Sicilian *Saracini*. *Saraceni* appears in the title and *Saracini* in this sentence; indeed, he sometimes uses two different spelling in the same sentence. On Martorana, see Amari, *Storia dei musulmani di Sicilia* 1:12; Mortillaro, *La storia, gli scrittori e le monete dell'epoca arabo-sicula* 303; Mira, *Bibliografia siciliana* 2:45; and Atto Vannucci, "Dei recenti studj sulla antica civiltà arabica" 140.

26. Martorana, *Notizie storiche dei Saraceni siciliani* 1:5–6.

27. Ibid. 2:162. The Hieros were Greek rulers of ancient Sicily; under Hiero II (r. 270–215 B.C.E.) Syracuse became one of the most powerful cities in the Mediterranean.

28. Ibid. 2:74.

29. Pietro Varvaro, "Giuseppe Vella e i suoi falsi codici arabi con un documento

inedito" 328. Jeremy Johns uses this magnificent quote as the epigraph for his masterful 2002 study, *Arabic Administration in Norman Sicily*.

30. On Lanza's biography, see Mortillaro, *La storia, gli scrittori e le monete dell'epoca arabo-sicula* 304; *Dizionario dei siciliani illustri* 287; and Amari, *Storia dei musulmani di Sicilia* 1:12. Amari's collected letters include a handful of letters exchanged with Lanza during the events of 1848–49, the last of which (dated April 9, 1849 and written from Palermo) is heartbreaking. Amari had written to him on March 28 counseling resistance, "and we all want to resist," Lanza replied; "but can Palermo resist alone? And even resisting, will it be able to recover what has been so unfortunately lost, without fundamental materials, and deprived of that moral support that awakens enthusiasm when it has been excited by success? . . . You will understand me well: if our fortune continues to be adverse (which I ardently hope will not be the case) I will stay at my post until the last, and then if I still live I will go an exile to a foreign land. Ah, dear Michele, how oppressed I feel in spirit!" (*Carteggio* 1:566–67)

31. On Amari's biography, see my "Orientalism and the Nineteenth Century Nationalist" and *The Kingdom of Sicily, 1100–1250* 17–46, with notes; and Roberto M. Dainotto, *Europe (in Theory)* 172–238.

32. On Mortillaro's biography, see Giuseppe M. Mira, *Bibliografia siciliana* 2:106–8; Angelo De Gubernatis, *Matériaux pour servir à l'histoire des études orientales en Italie* 236–37; *Dizionario dei siciliani illustri* 334–35; and, of course, his own *Reminiscenze*.

Amari and Lanza were elected to high level positions in the revolutionary government—Amari as minister of finance, Lanza as minister of foreign affairs. Mortillaro was elected to Parliament as a peer (the peerage having been significantly expanded by the revolutionary government in order to broaden the power base). And he served as a high-ranking official in the national guard, an arm of the coalition government conceived and operated by the conservatives as a means of suppressing the *squadre* in the countryside. The liberals had recruited the *squadre* to resist the Bourbon army; they spent the majority of their working hours, however, promoting lawlessness to their own purposes. Speaking of the ambitions and the failures of the *squadre* in particular and the revolutionists in general, Raffaele de Cesare—a historian sympathetic to the revolutionary cause—wrote: "if that period did not have political consistency, it was morally glorious" (*La fine di un regno* 1:4). The split between the *squadre* and the national guard was one of the more visible manifestations of the deep divisions between Sicilian liberals, the core of the revolutionary movement, and the conservatives, who were loyal to the Bourbons or in favor of institutional changes rather than outright revolution.

33. Mortillaro, *La storia, gli scrittori e le monete dell'epoca arabo-sicula* 304 and 310.

34. Mira, *Bibliografia siciliana* 2:106.

35. The comments are from private letters collected in the interminable volumes of *Works* that Mortillaro himself edited and published; *Opere* 8:184 and 165.

36. Mortillaro, *Reminiscenze* 63–64. Mortillaro blamed Amari for the demise of his own literary journal, *Giornale di scienze lettere e arti per la Sicilia*, which fell victim to the Bourbons' suppression of the press following the publication of Amari's work on the

Vespers. Mortillaro would resume publication of the journal in February 1848, after the Sicilian revolution annulled censorship of the press (*Reminiscenze* 76).

37. Amari, *Storia dei musulmani di Sicilia* 1:13–14 and footnote 3, 13–14.

38. Mortillaro, *La storia, gli scrittori e le monete dell'epoca arabo-sicula* 297; Lanza, *Degli Arabi e del loro soggiorno in Sicilia* 19; Amari, *Storia dei musulmani de Sicilia* 3:921–22.

39. Lanza, *Degli Arabi e del loro soggiorno in Sicilia* 50–51.

40. Amari, *Description de Palerme au milieu du X^e siècle de l'ère vulgaire, par Ebn-Haucal* 4.

41. Mortillaro tells a slightly different version of Sicily's pre-Muslim history. He doesn't mention the classical (Greek *or* Latin) heritage. He depicts Byzantine Sicily at the time of the arrival of the Arabs as hopelessly decadent—already a familiar trope in nineteenth-century Sicilian historiography—and describes the residence of the Arabs in Sicily as one of gradual cultural and technological innovation *ex vuoto*.

42. Lanza, *Degli Arabi e del loro soggiorno in Sicilia* 19–20.

43. Mortillaro, *La storia, gli scrittori e le monete dell'epoca arabo-sicula* 273.

44. Amari, *Storia dei musulmani di Sicilia* 1:107. Note Amari's use of the first-person plural pronoun in this passage. Sicilian historians of the nineteenth century consistently referred to the history of Arab Sicily as "our" history and to the Muslims of Sicily as "our Saracens." Amari, however, never uses first-person plural pronouns when referring to the Muslims. He uses the word *our* repeatedly and insistently. However, he regularly uses it in reference to Christian or modern history, and in particular when writing about modern, Christian, Sicilian history. In this passage, however, "our common fatherland" means *Italy,* a concept that did not exist when Lanza and Mortillaro published their works in 1832 and 1846 respectively—and that remained vague and somewhat suspect in Sicily in 1854, when this volume of Amari's history appeared.

45. The first two volumes of the *Storia dei musulmani di Sicilia* (in the twentieth-century edition, 1,097 pages) deal with the years of Muslim rule; the three-part third volume (922 pages) addresses the Normans. If one were to subtract from the Arabs' tally the portion of the first volume that recounts Sicilian history *prior to* the arrival of the Arabs, the relative number of pages devoted to the Normans would be even more striking.

46. Mortillaro, *Lettera del Marchese Vincenzo Mortillaro* 4–5. Mortillaro refers in particular to chapter 8 of volume 3, part 1 (which appeared in 1868).

47. Amari, *Storia dei musulmani di Sicilia* 3:227 (where the phrase *Italia di sopra* appears twice) and 233.

48. Italian Orientalist Angelo Mai, of course, has appeared already in these pages; see Chapter 1. And Joseph von Hammer-Purgstall, mentioned in Mortillaro's letter, also made an appearance above (see Chapter 2) and will have a cameo role later in this chapter.

In a similar way Francisco Javier Simonet claimed that not the secret *Arab* history but rather the lost *Romance-Christian* past of Spain was immanent in the written traces of Spanish history, the inscriptions on Spanish monuments, and names given to the contours of the Spanish countryside: "Although, unfortunately, we cannot benefit from any complete document written in the vulgar Mozarabic dialect, in the works of the Latin and even Arab authors of that people, in inscriptions, in the geographical nomenclature of the country dominated by the Moors, in the names of people, animals, plants and medicines, and in many other words which the Arabs have noted as pertinent to the *Aljamía* or the common language of the conquered Spaniards, we have found copious remnants and traces of that dialect" (*Glosario de voces ibéricas y Latinas usadas entre los mozárabes* cxxxiv–cxxxv).

49. Mortillaro, *Opere* 3:189

50. On the growing tension between the exiles of 1848 and those who remained, particularly in the years leading up to the Risorgimento, see Marta Petrusewicz's discussion in *Come il Meridione divenne una questione*, especially 152–56.

51. On Cusa's biography, see Mira, *Bibliografia siciliana* 1:287–88; De Gubernatis, *Matériaux pour servir à l'histoire des études orientales en Italie* 235–36; and *Dizionario dei siciliani illustri* 148–49.

52. My account of Amari's exasperation with Cusa, expressed in a series of unedited letters written to historian Isidoro La Lumia, follows the story as told by Arabist and historian Adalgisa De Simone, who published a lively summary of Amari and La Lumia's correspondence; see "Salvatore Cusa arabista siciliano del XIX secolo."

53. De Simone, "Salvatore Cusa arabista siciliano del XIX secolo" 608.

54. "Retrodatato 'con malizietta molto trasparente' al 1868"; cited in De Simone, "Salvatore Cusa arabista siciliano del XIX secolo" 610.

55. *Dizionario dei Siciliani illustri* 149.

56. Cusa, *I diplomi greci ed arabi di Sicilia* 1:vii.

57. Ibid. 1:viii–ix.

58. Cusa, *La Palma nella poesia, nella scienza e nella storia siciliana* 79.

59. On Morso's biography, see Amari, *Storia dei musulmani di Sicilia* 1:11–12; Mira, *Bibliografia siciliana* 2:103–4; and *Dizionario dei siciliani illustri* 334.

60. Scinà, *La arabica impostura* 75.

61. Mortillaro, *Opere* 2:110–11.

62. Amari, *Storia dei musulmani di Sicilia* 1:11–12.

63. Salvatore Morso, *Descrizione di Palermo antico* 190 and 194.

64. Ibid. 203–4.

65. Ibid. 178–82 and 186.

66. My translation of Amari's Arabic transcription: Amari, *Le epigrafi arabiche* 81.

67. Ibid. 78.

68. Atto Vannucci, "Dei recenti studj sulla antica civiltà arabica e della storia dei musulmani in Sicilia di Michele Amari" 145; emphasis added.

69. On the inscriptions at the Cuba, see Amari, *Le epigrafi arabiche* 83 and *Diari* 178.

70. C. A. Nallino—who taught the Arabic language and literature at al-Azhar University in Cairo, was one of the first professors of Arabic at Cairo University, and served in the Italian colonial administration in Libya—will be discussed in Chapter 5. He also taught in Palermo from 1905 until 1913.

71. Vannucci, "Dei recenti studj sulla antica civiltà arabica e della storia dei musulmani in Sicilia di Michele Amari" 169–70.

72. Amari, *Storia dei musulmani di Sicilia* 3:915–16.

CHAPTER 4

1. From a letter to Achim von Arnim; *Achim von Arnim und die ihm nahe Standen* 3:139

2. Fernand Braudel saw piracy as the reconfiguration of state-funded warfare in the Mediterranean following the battle of Lepanto (1571) and the Ottoman conquest of Hafsid Tunis (1574): "On the water, the end of conflict between the great states brought to the forefront of the sea's history that secondary form of war, piracy. Already a force to be reckoned with between 1550 and 1574, it expanded to fill any gaps left by the slackening of official war. From 1574–1580, it increased its activities even further, soon coming to dominate the now less spectacular history of the Mediterranean. The new capitals of warfare were not Constantinople, Madrid and Messina, but Algiers, Malta, Leghorn and Pisa. Upstarts had replaced the tired giants and international conflicts degenerated into a free-for-all" (*The Mediterranean and the Mediterranean World in the Age of Philip II* 865).

3. For general histories of the corsairs of Malta and Barbary, see Stanley Lane-Poole, *The Story of the Barbary Corsairs*, and Peter Earle, *The Corsairs of Malta and Barbary*.

4. On the participation of northern European aristocrats in the Maltese caravan, see Thomas Freller, "'Adversus Infideles.'"

5. On Maltese linguistic history during the rule of the Order of Saint John, see Joseph Brincat, *Malta: Una storia linguistica* 222–24.

6. Mark Abley reports that the Boro language, spoken in the eastern Himalayas, has a verb, *gobray*, which means "to fall into a well unknowingly" (*Spoken Here* 125). On the purported number of "Eskimo" words for snow—the anthropological version of an urban myth—see Laura Martin, "'Eskimo Words for Snow.'"

7. For a discussion of the Arab geographers who refer to Malta, with bibliographical references, see Godfrey Wettinger, *The Arabs in Malta* 88.

8. Jean Quintin d'Autun, *The Earliest Description of Malta* 16–18.

9. Albert Friggieri and Thomas Freller, *Malta: The Bulwark of Europe* 134.

10. On early grammars and dictionaries, see Joseph Aquilina, "Systems of Maltese Orthography" 84; Dionisios A. Agius, Review of *A Contribution to Arabic Lexical Dialectology* 172–73; G. Wettinger and M. Fsadni, *Peter Caxaro's Cantilena* 10; and Brincat, *Malta: Una storia linguistica* 226–28 and 232–38. More recent research is bringing to light word lists and even grammars dating to the seventeenth and eighteenth centuries; see Joseph Brincat, "La caccia alla fenice" and Arnold Cassola, *Il Mezzo Vocabolario maltese-italiano del '700* 7–13.

11. *Encyclopédie ou Dictionnaire raisonné des sciences, des arts et de métiers*, s.v. "Caractères et alphabets de langues mortes et vivantes"; "Malthe"; and "Punique."

12. On Peter Caxaro's "cantilena," see Wettinger and Fsadni, *Peter Caxaro's Canti-*

*lena* and Brincat, *Malta: Una storia linguistica* 167–74. On G. F. Bonamico's poem for the grand master, see Wettinger and Fsadni, and Aquilina, "Systems of Maltese Orthography" 83–84.

13. On the life of Mikiel Anton Vassalli, see Brincat, *Malta: Una storica linguistica* 238–43; C. L. Dessoulavy, review of A. Cremona, *Mikiel Anton Vassalli U Žminijietu*; and a special issue of the *Journal of Maltese Studies* on Vassalli, vols. 23–24 (1993).

14. Mikiel Anton Vassalli, *Lexicon* iii.

15. See especially ibid. vii.

16. On Vassalli's publications see Carmel G. Bonavia, "Mikiel Anton Vassalli: A Bibliography."

17. For a survey of the various alphabets—both Latin and Arabic—proposed for Maltese between 1750 and 1883 see Aquilina, "Systems of Maltese Orthography," and Cassola, *Il Mezzo Vocabolario maltese-italiano del '700* 10–13 for a discussion of orthographic innovations from older, more recently discovered manuscripts.

18. Vassalli, *Lexicon* viii and xiii.

19. Ibid. vii.

20. Ibid. xi–xiii and xv. It is also, of course, true that by tracing the language to the Phoenicians Vassalli increased its antiquity; and the antiquity of a tongue, for the Romantics, was a measure of its dignity and beauty.

21. Ibid. xiii.

22. Ibid. xix.

23. Vassalli, *Grammatica della Lingua Maltese* vii.

24. On this chapter in Vassalli's life, see Guze Cassar Pullicino, "M. A. Vassalli in 1798–1799."

25. Sir Walter Scott, *The Life of Napoleon Bonaparte* 4:60–61.

26. For a summary of Maltese resistance to Napoleon's troops, see Henry Frendo, "National Identity" 10–14.

27. Samuel Taylor Coleridge, *Collected Letters*: the first citation ("the dreariest of all dreary islands") is from a letter written to his wife on June 5, 1804; the second ("the Maltese talk Arabic mixed with Italian") from a letter to Daniel Stuart, July 6, 1804.

28. Byron, "Parody on Sir William Jones's Translation from Hafiz" (*The Complete Poetical Works* 1:340). See also "To Florence," a poem that he wrote for Constance Spencer Smith, the lover he wooed (and abandoned) on Malta, in which he described Malta as a "barren isle / Where panting Nature droops the head . . . " (*The Complete Poetical Works* 1:273).

29. Quoted in Geoffrey Hull, *The Malta Language Question* 5 and Henry Frendo, *Party Politics in a Fortress Colony* 5. See also Thackeray's description of Gibraltar and Malta (he visited Malta in 1844): "Before sunset we skirted along the dark savage mountains of the African coast and came to the Rock, just before gun-fire. It is the very image of an enormous lion, crouched between the Atlantic and the Mediterranean and set there to guard the passage for its British mistress. The next British lion is Malta, four days further on in the Midland Sea, and ready to spring upon Egypt or pounce upon Syria, or roar so

as to be heard at Marseilles in case of need" (*Irish Sketch Book and Notes of a Journey from Cornhill to Grand Cairo* 365–66).

30. Gerard Manley Hopkins, *The Journals and Papers of Gerard Manley Hopkins* 259. Hopkins wrote this entry in 1874.

31. On Giovanni Giuseppe Bellanti's Arabo-Persian alphabet, see Aquilina, "Systems of Maltese Orthography" 85 and 99.

32. The hybrid alphabet indeed looks surpassingly strange. In general the sounds that do not exist in European languages or that would require a combination of letters to represent in the Latin alphabet are written using Arabic letters: the strong *hâ', 'ayn*, and *qâf* by the Arabic forms of the letter, the English *sh* by the Arabic *shîn*, etc. See the example reproduced in Aquilina, "Systems of Maltese Orthography" 100.

33. Quoted in Arnold Cassola, *Francesco Vella* 37.

34. Quoted in Aquilina, "Systems of Maltese Orthography" 100–101; I have adjusted Aquilina's translation slightly. Here as elsewhere, where the spelling of the original differs from modern Maltese orthography, I have retained the original spelling.

The final words in the first and third lines—"xikkel," to impede or shackle, and "imfixkel," confused—come from an identical Arabic root. Thus, though the words do not rhyme perfectly, they produce a pleasing rhetorical effect which emphasizes the poet-polemicist's theme. Still Vella's polemic should not be mistaken for good poetry. Aquilina's comment (in the essay here cited) may be taken as authoritative: "Bad poetry and good sense!"

35. Reports of the Commissioners appointed to inquire into the Affairs of the State of Malta 42.

36. Patrick Joseph Keenan, *Report upon the educational system of Malta* 1–2.

37. To summarize Keenan's data, between 1842 and 1871 the number of Maltese who could speak English nearly doubled—from 5,245 to 9,690. Regarding the increase in Italian fluency during the same period he reported: "Enshrined in an antiquity of five centuries, the legacy of the Sicilians and the Knights, the language of the law, the language of polite literature, the language, to a great extent, of official life, the language of the Lyceums and of the University, and the language most specially favored in the Primary schools—this language, as I have shown, on the evidence afforded by the earliest numerical record at my command, viz., the Census of 1842, could then boast of having only 12,839 persons able to speak it. In 1871 this number had risen only to 15,591" (ibid. 87–88).

It is true that the increase in the number of English speakers relative to the increase in the number of Italian speakers is impressive. It can be argued, however, that the number of Italian speakers could be presumed to have reached a certain saturation point, and that English still was playing catch-up. But Keenan is eager to point out—with a certain justice—that the gains in English literacy are the more striking given the widespread prejudice against it, in particular on the part of the Maltese elite: "the actual position which, *under enormous difficulties,* the English language has attained in the Island is not, I think fully appreciated" (89).

38. Ibid. 98. The British administrators consistently emphasized the compassion of

their linguistic policy, in particular their recommendation of early education in Maltese. Thus Keenan spoke of the burden born by Maltese children who are obliged to be educated solely in languages that are unknown to them (91), and he quoted the views of the Maltese Chief Justice Sir Adrian Dingli: "in his native Arabic dialect, he [i.e., "the Maltese workman's child"] will very seldom, if ever, find anything to read which it is not better for himself and his fellow-men that he should not read" (90). In contrast the Maltese who argue against early education in Maltese may appear to be lacking in the milk of human kindness. However, it should be remembered that the British administrators consistently recommended that education prepare "the Maltese workman's child" for immigration or for low-level service jobs in the British colonies. Thus the 1838 report on language recommended that the ties between Maltese and Arabic be strengthened in order to make immigration to Arabic-speaking countries—in particular, those in which Britain had colonial interests—easier for the working classes (Reports of the Commissioners appointed to inquire into the Affairs of the State of Malta 43). Keenan was also eager to make it possible for Maltese workers to emigrate to Britain's other Mediterranean possession, Cyprus; for this reason he recommended expansion of the Greek programs in secondary schools and at the University of Malta (Keenan, *Report upon the educational system of Malta* 53–54).

39. Ibid. 92.

40. On the language of midwifery classes, see the Keenan Report 58 and 90. On Maltese in religious instruction, see Hull, *The Malta Language Question* 29.

41. Keenan, *Report upon the educational system of Malta* 115.

42. Ibid. 126; emphasis added.

43. Ibid. 121; emphasis in the original.

44. Thackeray, *Irish Sketch Book and Notes of a Journey from Cornhill to Grand Cairo* 382.

45. See Frendo, *Party Politics in a Fortress Colony* 46. It must be said that although Maltese historians admire Fortunato Mizzi as a courageous opponent to British colonial rule, it is difficult for an outsider to share their appreciation of his character. His attitudes toward the Maltese language were nothing short of infamous (as will become clear). Nor do his "ridiculous elections" recommend him to the twenty-first-century American sensibility. In 1883 Mizzi brought down the government by arranging the election of commoners. When his candidate, a poor man with a nerve disease, was elected, Mizzi "resigned his own seat, on the ground of decorum" (Frendo, *Party Politics* 39); the other cabinet members followed his lead. The subsequent "infamous elections" in 1886 were not as successful. The government stood, and hence cabinet ministers were treated to the spectacle of hearing Maltese spoken in chambers. Desperate times do, of course, call for desperate measures, and Maltese historians are more likely than outsiders to appreciate both the necessity and the efficacy of Mizzi's actions.

46. Debates of the Council of Government of Malta in the session 1880–81. March 30, 1881, cols. 348 and 357–58.

47. Ibid., col. 356

48. "Il diritto di Malta" (1880), quoted in Frendo, *Party Politics in a Fortress Colony* 21.

49. Debates of the Council of Government of Malta in the session 1883-84-85, May 13, 1885, cols. 958–59; emphasis added.

50. On Spanish accounts of the nation's Arab past as explanation for tardy development in Spain, see Chapter 2.

51. Debates of the Council of Government of Malta in the session 1883-84-85. May 13, 1885, col. 963.

52. The Maltese "dialect," according to this 1918 opinion piece, is "the *asphyxiating gas,* to our mind, in our progress to civilization!. . . . . I have always held Maltese to be the official dialect of idiots and rogues (among whom, doubtless, I do not include our romantic philologists and the amateur poets of all classes whose liberty of conscience and anarchy of expression I fully admit). What do we care for the little Arabian creature discovered by I do not know which improvised archeologist and expert in mental diseases in the immense darkness of our pre-oceanic history!" From an article, "Our Ideal Boundaries," written by L. A. Randon and published in "Malta," a daily Italian-language newspaper rumored to be subsidized for propaganda purposes by the Italian government. Cited (in English translation) in Paul Pace, *The Language Question 1920–1934* 1:2.

53. On Italian exiles in Malta, see Bonello et al., *Echi del Risorgimento a Malta.* Francesco Crispi, who was deported from Turin in 1853, wrote upon his arrival in Malta, "All the most ambitious and sordid characters that 1848 could spew up are here" (quoted in Salvatore Candido, "Francesco Crispi scrittore" 193 and Christopher Duggan, *Francesco Crispi* 110).

54. Gabriele Rossetti, *La vita mia* 83 and 91. On Rossetti's time in Malta, see his son William Michael's biographical essay in the same volume, 168–69.

55. Brincat, *Malta: Una storia linguistica* 264–65.

56. On the theme of the wife stolen by corsairs, see Oliver Friggieri, *Storia della letteratura maltese* 107–8 and Brincat, *Malta: Una storia linguistica* 264–65 and 276–77.

57. Keenan, *Report upon the educational system of Malta* 89. In the same place Keenan reported frankly that the supporters of Maltese tended also to favor English instruction and second language study, while the opponents of the language were advocates of Italian culture in Malta.

58. Richard Taylor's translation (*Il-Konti Ugolino mid-Divina Commedia Cant. XX-XIII ta' l-Infern ta' Dante Alighieri*) was published in 1864 and Ganni Sapiano Lanzon's (*Kant 33 ta'l-Inferno: Il-Konti Ugolino*) in 1899. On Taylor, see Brincat, *Malta: Una storia linguistica* 274–75; on Ugolino as resistance hero for nineteenth-century nationalists, see my "Dante as Poet of Exile and Resistance."

My thumbnail history of the prehistory of literary Maltese is admittedly fragmentary and biased. For a more balanced overview of the material, see P. Grech's introduction to *Dun Karm: Poet of Malta* 1–26 and Oliver Friggieri, *Storia della letteratura maltese.*

59. Quoted in Hull, *The Malta Language Question,* 164 and 176, note 48.

The notion that the Maltese nurtured the flame of a Romance tongue—masked by a Semitic veneer, but recognizably Romance nonetheless—through the long centuries of Arab-Islamic occupation was implicitly seconded by Simonet, when he speculated that in medieval Iberia both Mozarab Christians and converts to Islam "spoke a Hispano-Arabic jargon very similar to the Maltese dialect" (*Glosario de voces ibéricas y Latinas usadas entre los mozárabes* cxxix).

60. Those words are *avvanza, lingua, intelligenti, energica, Cattolica, Europa, ignoranta, pagana*, and *Asia*.

61. Note, too, the initial capital of gravitas: *Lsien*. The poem, "Ghaliex?" ("Why?"), was published in book form in 1939. See Dun Karm, *Dun Karm: Poet of Malta* 54 for the Maltese text; I have adjusted A. J. Arberry's admirable, fluent translation in order to make it more literal.

62. On Dun Karm see Oliver Friggieri, "Dun Karm, the National Poet of Malta," and Grech, "A Portrait of Dun Karm."

63. On the proportion of Romance and Semitic words used in literary Maltese, see Brincat, *Malta: Una storia linguistica* 293–301 and "Languages and Varieties in Use in Malta Today," and Alexander Borg, "Language" 29.

64. In the line "Min ibidill il miken ibidil i vintura"—"Who changes place changes his fortune"—the word *vintura* (fortune) is Romance. Brincat has speculated that here Caxaro cited a Sicilian proverb with the same meaning ("cui muta locu muta vintura"), or may use a Sicilian *senhal*, or amorous code name, to refer to a lover (*Malta: Una storia linguistica* 173–74).

Recently Arnold Cassola has proposed that a mysterious word used in the poem, *gueri*, is related to the Italian *guari*, itself kin to the French *guère*. See "On the Meaning of Gueri in Petrus Caxaro's Cantilena."

65. The poet urges the reader not to answer every question that life poses: *if* you know all, he suggests in the closing stanza, life loses its mystery and its beauty. For the Maltese text of the poem see *Il-Poeziji Migbura* 81–83; the English version is a free translation by Oliver Friggieri (personal correspondence, April 2008).

66. Joseph Brincat, *Malta: Una storia linguistica* 360. It is, of course, true that the Semitic lexemes represent the linguistic core of the language: modals, prepositions, conjunctions, and the most fundamental nouns and verbs. Thus though the corpus of Semitic words is statistically less significant the words tend to recur more frequently in average use.

67. I paraphrase Averroes' and Hermannus's statements on the artificiality of poetic language, which are essentially equivalent (Averroes, *Talkhis kitab Aristutalis fi al-shi'r* 122 [English translation, *Averroes' Middle Commentary on Aristotle's* Poetics 130]; Hermannus, *De arte poetica* 70). The phrase "enigmatic concealment" translates Hermannus's "enigmaticas latitationes," one of the elements of the moving poem, according to him. These words don't seem to correspond precisely to anything in Averroes' Arabic text he translates.

68. I owe this insight to Joseph Brincat, who generously shared with me his thoughts on Dun Karm and on the semiticization of literary Maltese.

69. In truth, native speakers themselves—or at least native speakers who are also linguists—take a similar interest in their language. The studies I have cited on the occurrence of Arabic and Romance lexemes were all authored by Maltese scholars.

70. The original Italian title of the 1943 work, by Pietro Silvio Rivetta, was *Il Centauro Maltese ovvero Mostruosità Linguistiche nell'Isola dei Cavalieri.* The author begins this rather distasteful fascist-era study by asking: "Can one, like Solomon, cut in two a single living being, which is not a man and is not an animal?" (9).

71. The Malta Royal Commission, Minutes of Evidence (1931), par. 2161 (page 363).

72. Ibid., par. 2168 (page 365).

73. Ibid., par. 2184 (pages 366–67). On language debates and language politics in general in Malta during the 1930s, see Claudia Baldoli's "The 'Northern Dominator' and the Mare Nostrum." Baldoli does not address the emergence of Maltese as a literary language, but considers the language policies of the British colonizers and the Italian fascists' attempts to use the Italian language in order to gain a foothold in Malta.

74. John Wansbrough, *Lingua Franca in the Mediterranean* 6.

### CHAPTER 5

1. Giulio Bertoni, "L' 'Istituto di Filologia Romanza di Roma'" 13. For general histories of Italian Orientalism, in addition to the works cited below, see *Gli studi sul vicino oriente* and Francesco Gabrieli's collection of memorials of the great figures in the field, *Orientalisti del Novecento.*

2. For the institutional history of the Istituto per l'Oriente, see Giacomo E. Carretto, "'Sapere' e 'potere': L'Istituto per l'Oriente (1921–1943)"; *Gli studi sul vicino oriente in Italia dal 1921 al 1970*; and Bruna Soravia, "Ascesa e declino dell'orientalismo scientifico in Italia."

3. Caetani wrote a famous letter to Giorgio Levi Della Vida reflecting on the difficulties of his life in exile ("Lettera di L. Caetani a Giorgio Levi Della Vida"). The genuine pathos of the letter, its touching reflection on the sacrifices he has made, is somewhat vitiated by its tone of unthinking misogyny.

4. Levi Della Vida wrote an autobiographical account of his professional association with Caetani and his experiences in fascist Italy: *Fantasmi ritrovati.*

5. Michelangelo Guidi, *Aspetti e problemi del mondo islamico* 5 and 32.

6. For a thoughtful reading of the limitations of Guidi's (and Caetani's and Nallino's) understanding of Islamic culture, see Enrico Galoppini, "L'oggetto misterioso."

7. Taha Husayn, *The Days* 249–50. Guidi's name—arabicized and then translated into English—becomes "Tuwaidi" in Husayn's description. On Husayn at Cairo University, see also Donald Malcolm Reid, "Cairo University and the Orientalists" 53. The indispensable work on Italian Orientalists at Cairo University is Anna Baldinetti's *Orientalismo e colonialismo*, especially 71–124.

8. "Una conferenza di Taha Husein" 105–6.

9. Because of its close ties to the government and in particular its links to the colonial program, the IPO fell under particular scrutiny following World War II; it lost the support of the government and its position of authority in Italian academic circles, and with the deaths of Nallino and Ignazio Guidi there was little continuity between the

prewar and postwar periods. Francesco Gabrieli—like Giorgio Levi Della Vida when he returned from exile in 1945—would teach at the University of Rome and kept his affiliation with the IPO. The IPO still publishes *Oriente moderno* and maintains a valuable research library but no longer trains students of the Orient. On the institutional history of the IPO during the postwar period, see Soravia, "Ascesa e declino dell'orientalismo scientifico in Italia," especially 284–86.

10. "Il nostro programma" 1.

11. Quoted in Vincenzo Strika, "C. A. Nallino e l'impresa libica" 12.

12. See Soravia, "Ascesa e declino dell'orientalismo scientifico in Italia" 282.

13. Giorgio Levi Della Vida, "Carlo Alfonso Nallino" 418. On Nallino, who edited the second edition of Michele Amari's *Storia dei musulmani di Sicilia*, see Baldinetti, *Orientalismo e colonialismo*; Strika, "C. A. Nallino e l'impresa libica"; and Reid, "Cairo University and the Orientalists."

14. Francesco Gabrieli, "Apology for Orientalism" 128, 132 and 135.

15. Francesco Gabrieli, *Pagine di diario* 104. For a discussion of Petrarch's condemnation of the Arabs, see Chapter 2.

16. Lanfranco Ricci, "Enrico Cerulli" 112. In the biographical sketch that follows I have relied on Ricci's memorial of Cerulli, as well as Tadesse Tamrat's "Enrico Cerulli" and Osvaldo Raineri's introduction to *Enrico Cerulli: Inventario dei manoscritti Cerulli etiopici*. Other sources will be cited in the course of the discussion.

17. For the institutional history of L'Orientale from its founding through the late nineteenth century, see Karl Josef Rivinius, *Das Collegium Sinicum zu Neapel*.

18. On Ethiopian studies in Italy, see Angelo De Gubernatis, *Matériaux pour servir à l'histoire des études orientales en Italie* 174–76.

19. Enrico Cerulli, "La questione del Califfato in rapporto alle nostre Colonie di diretto dominio" 11.

20. Cerulli, "I rapporti italo-abissini nel dopo-guerra" 8.

21. Cerulli, *Etiopia Occidentale (Dalla Scioa alla frontiera del Sudan)* 1:8.

22. Carlo Alfonso Nallino, "I principali risultati del viaggio di Enrico Cerulli nell'Etiopia Occidentale nel 1927–1928" 430.

23. Luigi Amedeo di Savoia, *La esplorazione dello Uabi-Uebi Scebeli dalle sue sorgenti nella Etiopia* 41 and 91–92.

24. Evelyn Waugh, *The Essays, Articles and Reviews of Evelyn Waugh* 163 and 116. There is, of course, a striking irony in the contradiction between Waugh's refusal to sentimentalize his description of Ethiopia in the first article cited and the somewhat mercenary sentimentalism of the second.

25. Evelyn Waugh, *Waugh in Abyssinia* 248–49.

26. Waugh, *The Essays, Articles and Reviews of Evelyn Waugh* 164.

27. Waugh strains his credibility somewhat by writing of his encounter with Graziani—who was, by all accounts, a loathsome administrator—"I left with the impression of one of the most amiable and sensible men I had met for a long time" (*Waugh in Abyssinia* 230).

28. On Teruzzi's support of Cerulli and Cerulli's time in office in Ethiopia in general, see Alberto Sbacchi, *Ethiopia Under Mussolini* 58–64.

29. Tamrat, "Enrico Cerulli" 97. See also Alberto Sbacchi, "Italy and the Treatment of the Ethiopian Aristocracy," for an account of Cerulli's efforts to expose and correct injustices against Ethiopians.

30. On relations between Cerulli and Amedeo di Savoia, see Richard Pankhurst, "The Secret History of the Italian Fascist Occupation of Ethiopia" 71–74 and Angelo Del Boca, *Gli italiani in Africa orientale* 3:309–10.

31. Cerulli's diplomatic career did not end with his dismissal from Ethiopia. At the end of the war he was called upon to defend Italy's administration of her colonies and support her attempt to extend her colonial rule in East Africa. He represented Italy at the Peace Conferences in Paris and London in 1945 and 1946 and at the General Assembly of the United Nations. Following the postwar period, in 1950, he was appointed ambassador to Iran and would serve there until 1954. While in Iran he amassed an extensive collection of manuscripts of popular Persian drama. On his return to Italy he granted his personal collection of 325 Ethiopian manuscripts and 843 manuscripts of Persian drama to the Biblioteca Apostolica Vaticana.

32. Cerulli, "Nuove idee nell'Etiopia e nuova letteratura amarica" 173.

33. Cerulli, "Recenti pubblicazioni abissine in amarico" 556.

34. Cerulli, "Rassegna periodica di pubblicazioni in lingue etiopiche fatte in Etiopia" 58.

35. Cerulli, "L'Islam nell'Africa Orientale" 93.

36. Cerulli, *Etiopi in Palestina: Storia della comunità etiopica di Gerusalemme* xiv and xv.

37. Gianfranco Fiaccadori pointed out to me the intriguing fact that beneath the surface of Cerulli's discussion of the progress of the legends of the miracles of Mary lies the question of the transmission of the *Thousand and One Nights*, the proof text for conversations about comparatism in Italian Orientalist circles during the first half of the century.

38. Cerulli, *Etiopi in Palestina: Storia della comunità etiopica di Gerusalemme* ix–x

39. Cerulli, *Il libro etiopico dei miracoli di Maria e le sue fonti nelle letterature del medio evo latino* 4.

40. Cerulli, *Il «Libro della scala» e la questione delle fonti arabo-spagnole della* Divina Commedia 550.

41. Cerulli, "Les arabes et l'unité méditerranéenne" 14.

42. Cerulli, *Il «Libro della scala» e la questione delle fonti arabo-spagnole della* Divina Commedia 550.

43. Cerulli, *Il libro etiopico dei miracoli di Maria e le sue fonti nelle letterature del medio evo latino* 5.

44. "All'inizio del 'colonialismo' . . . lo si apprezzi in bene o in male, c'è l'Europa." Cerulli, "La fine del colonialismo" 1551.

45. Ibid. 1552.

46. Ibid. 1552–54. For a briefer and much less acerbic rehearsal of the themes of the *Ulisse* article, see Cerulli's introduction to Teobaldo Filese's *Trasformazione e fine del colonialismo*: "The vast political movement which is usually termed 'colonization' had its apogee during the nineteenth century; and it seemed to have assured the political, economic, and (as we say) cultural domination of Europe over the other continents, in particular Asia and Africa. When Europe was reduced to quite different conditions following the two World Wars of 1914–1918 and 1939–1945, not only did the possibilities of expansion absolutely disappear; but throughout Asia and in a large part of Africa the ideas of liberty and of independence, diffused and affirmed in those same contacts with the Occident, caused the formation or the reconstitution of Asian and African states, which each day give further proof of their vivacious vitality, the largest of them acquiring also great prestige in an international arena. It is said for this reason—and with good cause—that the phenomenon of 'colonization,' as we knew it in recent centuries, is definitively concluded" (5).

47. Soravia, "Ascesa e declino dell'orientalismo scientifico in Italia" 279. See also Giacomo Carretto's history of the Istituto per l'Oriente: "The Italy that had undertaken the Ethiopian project and was on the threshold of the Reconquest of Libya when the Istituto per l'Oriente was born saw that Orient as both exotic and familiar, distant, different, and ready to be included in its own world. Distance permitted the Italian to feel himself, without a conscious racism, to be the big brother in good faith of an 'Oriental' from West Africa. The founders and the continuers of the Istituto were the bearers of a 'refined' version of this tendency" ("'Sapere' e 'potere': L'Istituto per l'Oriente" 216).

48. María Rosa Menocal, *Ornament of the World* 10–11.

49. An official account of Ethiopia's charges against the Italians can be found in The United Nations War Crimes Commission, *History of the United Nations War Crimes Commission* 189–90.

50. Angelo Del Boca, *Gli italiani in Africa orientale* 3:231–32 and 310.

51. The letter, in Cerulli's Polizia Politica file at the Archivio Centrale dello Stato in Rome, is not dated; the handwritten reply (there was no fair copy of the reply in the file when I examined it) is stamped "Copiato 28 Feb 1938 XVI." Cerulli's communication begins, "Two lines from the epicenter of the cyclone to tell you that, notwithstanding difficulties both foreseen and not foreseeable, we are working to bring matters toward that systemization that is a necessity for the Nation" ("Due righe dall'epicentro di questo ciclone per dirLe che, nonostante le difficoltà previste e quelle non prevedibili, stiamo lavorando per avviare le cose verso quella sistemazione che è una necessità pel Paese"). Cerulli speaks in general terms about the difficulty of creating order in the colony, and in more specific terms about the necessity of preventing those "eliminated" from the colony from finding "a sympathetic atmosphere" ("un ambiente di impietosimento") in Rome. In his closing paragraph he states: "I am engaging Menapace" ("Sto impiegando Menapace"). Ermanno Menapace is best known for the undercover role he played in a plot to bring down the anarchist and antifascist activist Luigi Camillo Berneri in 1929–30.

52. Richard Pankhurst, "Italian Fascist War Crimes in Italy" footnote 65, page 139.

53. Cerulli's name, initially included on the list of war crimes suspects, had been dropped because it was believed that he was then employed by the U.N. Secretariat and that "extensive inquiries" into his character must have been made before he was offered that position. Therefore he was listed as a witness rather than a suspect. The rumor of his employment by the U.N., however, proved to be false. See Pankhurst, "Italian Fascist War Crimes in Italy" 127–28.

54. Teruzzi to Mussolini, cited in Angelo Del Boca, *Gli italiani in Africa orientale* 3:309; Hugh Stonehewer-Bird, cited in Pankhurst, "The Secret History of the Italian Fascist Occupation of Ethiopia" 72.

55. Cited in Sbacchi, *Ethiopia Under Mussolini* 57. For a more negative assessment of Amedeo, see Pankhurst, "The Secret History of the Italian Fascist Occupation of Ethiopia" 70–71.

Cerulli may indeed—though this is pure speculation—have compared the scion to his memories of the uncle, Luigi Amedeo, with whom he undertook the heroic journey into the African interior decades earlier, thus exacerbating the tension between the two men. In a thoroughly pragmatic relation to a colonial conference in 1943 (one year after Amedeo, the nephew, died, and ten years after the death of Luigi Amedeo) he recommends the region of Adama (near Harar) for agricultural development first and foremost for a sentimental reason: it was from here that the expedition led by Luigi Amedeo to the border of Italian Somalia departed. "And so this glorious memory, once again, has come to guide the new venture of the organization created by the ardent activity of the August Prince" ("La colonizzazione del Harar" 153).

56. Silvio Labella, "Milizia eroica," in *Ad Amedeo Savoia Aosta omaggio di aeropoesie guerriere* 2.

57. Cerulli, "Giuliano Cora e l'Etiopia" 7.

58. Cerulli, *Nuove ricerche sul Libro della Scala e la conoscenza dell'Islam in Occidente* 322.

59. Dipesh Chakrabarty, *Provincializing Europe* 4.

60. Michele Amari, *Carteggio*, March 4, 1849, 1:548 and July 16, 1849, 1:581.

61. See Emily Apter, "Global *Translatio*" and *The Translation Zone* 41–64.

CHAPTER 6

1. For a reading of Bédier's anti-German bias, see Nykrog, "A Warrior Scholar at the Collège de France." On the *Roland* in the context of the Spanish epic tradition, see Ramón Menéndez Pidal, *La Chanson de Roland y el neotradicionalismo*. For a reading of the *Roland*'s historical contingency, see Sharon Kinoshita's "Pagans Are Wrong and Christians Are Right" (in *Medieval Boundaries*, 15–45), an attentive metaphilological study which considers the text in relation to contemporary history on the one hand and the intertextual web in which modern philologists encounter it on the other.

2. Emilio García Gómez, *Silla del Moro* 10.

3. Ibid. 35.

4. Ibid. 79.

5. Ibid. 81.

6. Ibid. 80.

7. S. M. Stern, *Hispano-Arabic Strophic Poetry* 131.

8. S. M. Stern, "Les vers finaux en espagnol dans les muwaššahs hispano-hé-braïques."

9. S.M. Stern, "Un muwaššah arabe avec terminaison espagnole."

10. Emilio García Gómez, "Veinticuatro jaryas romances en muwaššahas árabes" 59 and 60.

11. For the highlights in the *al-Andalus* kharja polemic, see S. M. Stern, "Les vers finaux en espagnol dans les muwaššahs hispano-hébraïques"; Stern, "Un muwaššah arabe avec terminaison espagnole"; Emilio García Gómez, "Mas sobre las 'jaryas' romances en 'muwaššahas' hebreas"; García, "Veinticuatro jaryas romances en muwaššahas arabes"; "Miscelanea internacional sobre las jaryas mozarabes"; García, "La muwaššaha de Ibn Baqi de Cordoba *maa laday / sabrun mu'iinu* con jarya romance"; García, "Dos nuevas jaryas romances (XXV y XXVI) en muwaššahas árabes"; García, "La lírica hispano-árabe y la aparición de la lírica románica"; S. M. Stern, "Four Famous Muwaššahs from Ibn Busra's Anthology"; García, "Los textos y los problemas de la casida zejelesca"; García, "A propósito del libro de K. Heger sobre las jaryas"; García, "La 'ley de Mussafia' se aplica a la poesía estrófica arabigoandaluza"; García, "Estudio del 'Dar at-tiraz'"; Joan Corominas, "El Nuevo Abencuzman"; García, "Hacia un 'refranero' arabigoanaluz: Los refranes poéticos de Ben Saraf (texto inédito)"; García, "Un poema paremiológico de Hilli (s. XIV) en 'kan wa-kan'"; García, "Métrica de la moaxaja y métrica española"; Francisco Corriente, "Acento y cantidad en la fonología del hispano-árabe"; García, "'Poetas en libertad condicional'"; García, "Sobre una propuesta inglesa de correcciones al texto de Ben Quzman"; Ulf Haxen, "The Mu'arada Concept and Its Musico-Rhythmical Implications"; and Ángel Ramírez Calvente (alias of Emilio García Gómez), "Jarchas, moaxajas, zejeles I," "Jarchas, moaxajas, zejeles II," "Jarchas, moaxajas, zejeles III," and "Jarchas, moaxajas, zejeles IV."

12. García Gómez, "Veinticuatro jaryas romances en muwaššahas árabes" 58.

13. See, for instance, García Gómez, "Veinticuatro jaryas romances en muwaššahas árabes," especially 67–68; "La 'ley de Mussafia' se aplica a la poesía estrófica arabigoanda-luza"; and "Métrica de la moaxaja y métrica española."

14. García Gómez, "A propósito del libro de K. Heger sobre las jaryas" 459. It is typical of García's testy territorialism that this gesture of openness is instantly shut down: in this passage he is critiquing incompetent kharja scholarship and warning those without competency specific to the kharjas to stay off the field.

15. Ramírez Calvente, "Jarchas, moaxajas, zejeles I" 273 and 279.

16. See Ramírez Calvente, "Jarchas, moaxajas, zejeles II," "Jarchas, moaxajas, zejeles III," and "Jarchas, moaxajas, zejeles IV."

17. García Gómez, "Sobre una propuesta inglesa de correcciones al texto de Ben Quzman."

18. Ramírez Calvente, "Jarchas, moaxajas, zejeles II."

19. In the second of the articles he published under the name of Ramírez Calvente, for instance, García refers to his own scholarship on pages 151, 152, 153, 154, 155, 156, 157, 158, 159, 162, 164, 167, 174, and 175.

20. For the *Corónica* kharja debate, see the following articles: Helen Boreland, "Ambiguity—and Troubadour Influence?—in a Thirteenth-Century Kharja"; Samuel G. Armistead, "Some Recent Developments in Kharja Scholarship"; Alan Jones, "Sunbeams from Cucumbers?"; Keith Whinnom, "The Mamma of the Kharjas"; Samuel G. Armistead, "Speed or Bacon?"; James T. Monroe, "Pedir peras al olmo?"; Samuel G. Armistead and James T. Monroe, "Albas, Mammas, and Code-Switching in the Kharjas"; Alan Jones, "Eppur si muove"; Samuel G. Armistead and James T. Monroe, "Beached Whales and Roaring Mice"; Richard Hitchcock, "The Interpretation of Romance Words in Arabic Texts"; Samuel G. Armistead, "Pet Theories and Paper Tigers"; James T. Monroe, "A Sounding Brass and Tinkling Cymbal"; Dorothy Clotelle Clarke, "The Prosody of the Hargas"; María Rosa Menocal, "Bottom of the Ninth"; James T. Monroe, "Maimonides on the Mozarabic Lyric"; Mary Jane Kelley, "Virgins Misconceived"; Otto Zwartjes, "La alternancia de código como recurso estilístico en las xarja-s andalusies"; Anthony P. Esposito, "Dismemberment of Things Past"; Francisco A. Marcos-Marin, "Aproximación cuantitativa al estudio de las jarchas"; Gene W. DuBois, "Blown up in the Mine Field"; and Alvaro Galmes de Fuentes, "De nuevo sobre el significado de las jarchas mozárabes." A quick scan of this list of titles reveals one difference, frivolous but amusing, between the *Andalus* and *Corónica* kharja polemics: the relatively whimsical titles given to many of the interventions by American and British scholars.

21. In the first of the Ramírez Calvente articles, for instance, García describes the development of kharja scholarship in Spain and cites the "disciples of J. Ribera," Ramón Menéndez Pidal and Dámaso Alonso, as those who contributed to the field in a way that Stern, because of his lack of competence, could not ("Jarchas, moaxajas, zejeles I" 279). Stern "wrote his first texts for this Review in French," García writes, "and they tell me that he did not speak Spanish, though he read it and possibly could understand the spoken language as well" ("Jarchas, moaxajas, zejeles I, note 9, p. 279).

22. Alan Jones, "Sunbeams from Cucumbers?" 43.

23. Ibid. See also Jones, "Eppur si muove." The title Jones gave to this article—citing the line that Galileo murmured when obliged by the Inquisition to deny his earlier conclusion that the earth rotated around the sun: "and yet, it *does* move"—conveys effectively a sense of the drama that surrounded the debate.

24. Monroe, "Pedir peras al olmo?" 133. Monroe cites S. M. Stern as the exemplar of this sort of modesty.

25. Armistead and Monroe, "Albas, Mammas, and Code-Switching in the Kharjas."

26. Menocal, "Bottom of the Ninth" 37. When reading Menocal's affirmation of the importance of new *critical* strategies to our readings of the medieval literary record, we should remember the conversion narrative which begins her seminal book, *The Arabic Role in Medieval Literary History.* The importance of Arab culture to Spanish history—not

merely as the semantic bedrock of the Spanish language, but as the foundation of Spanish culture—has informed Menocal's work throughout her career. She does not see the acquisition of languages as inimical to cutting-edge theoretical scholarship; the ecumenical nature of her literary scholarship sets her apart from the majority of her peers.

27. Erich Auerbach, *Literary Language and Its Public in Late Latin Antiquity and in the Middle Ages* 11.

28. Stern, "Un muwaššah arabe avec terminaison espagnole" 216 and 218.

29. I use the text of al-Aʿma al-Tutili's muwashshaha edited by James Monroe (*Hispano-Arabic Poetry* 248–51).

30. See Emilio García Gómez, *Las jarchas romances* 138–39; J. M. Sola-Solé, *Corpus de poesía mozárabe* 164; Monroe, *Hispano-Arabic Poetry* 250; Álvaro Galmés de Fuentes, *Las jarchas mozárabes* 92; Otto Zwartjes, *Love Songs from al-Andalus* 239.

31. Alan Jones, *Romance* Kharjas *in Andalusian Arabic* Muwaššah *Poetry* 77–81. I have taken liberties with Jones's redaction. I have converted Jones's transcription to the ALA-LC system of Romanization; I have transliterated the *hamzat al-wasl* with the apostrophe normally used for the *hamzat al-qatʿ* in order to make it more visible as a discrete letter; and I have transcribed the superscript *fatha* in the first line of the second redaction as a lowercase *a*. I have also suppressed the second two manuscript witnesses to the third redaction of the poem, taken from the *Jaysh al-tawshih*, which survives in three manuscripts. There are, I should note, multiple differences between the version of the *Jaysh al-tawshih* I include here and those other two manuscript versions.

32. For descriptions of the manuscripts, see Jones, *Romance* Kharjas *in Andalusian Arabic* Muwaššah *Poetry* 13–16.

33. Ibid. 83.

34. Two Christians, Adulphus and John, were executed almost thirty years earlier, in 822; these executions are typically seen as prelude to the events of the 850s. For a timeline of the executions along with contemporary events relevant to the episode, see Jessica A. Coope, *The Martyrs of Córdoba* xv–xvii.

35. My account of the events in ninth-century Cordoba relies on two recent monographs on the episode—Kenneth Baxter Wolf, *Christian Martyrs in Muslim Spain*; Coope, *The Martyrs of Córdoba*—as well as chapters in broader historical works (Norman Daniel, "The Martyrs of Cordoba," in *The Arabs and Mediaeval Europe* 23–48; Richard Hitchcock, "The Case of Córdoba in the Ninth Century," in *Mozarabs in Medieval and Early Modern Spain* 25–39) and article-length studies (James Waltz, "The Significance of the Voluntary Martyrs of Ninth-Century Córdoba"; Janina M. Safran, "Identity and Differentiation in Ninth-Century al-Andalus"). Two particularly useful works on the sources for historical study have appeared in the last half century: Edward P. Colbert, *The Martyrs of Córdoba* and Dominique Millet-Gérard's *Chrétiens Mozarabes et culture islamique*. Other works consulted will be cited in the course of the discussion.

36. Kenneth Baxter Wolf has pointed out that, although most scholars assume that Eulogius stood at the center of the storm, he in fact had very limited contact with most of those who died (*Christian Martyrs in Muslim Spain* 62–74). Alvarus's role in the affair

seemed to be limited to polemicist. On the absence of documentation of the episode in Arabic-language records, see Safran, "Identity and Differentiation in Ninth-Century al-Andalus."

37. See the "Praefatio" to book III of Eulogius's "Memoriale Sanctorum" (*Corpus Scriptorum Muzarabicorum* 2:438–39), and Wolf's discussion of the shape of Eulogius's narrative (*Christian Martyrs in Muslim Spain* 59–60).

38. Alvarus (or, possibly, an annotator or glossator) explains the purpose of the treatise thus in the introduction: "Hic liber ideo luminosus indiculus dicitur quia luminose que sequenda sunt docet et apertis indiciis hostem eclesie, que homnis uitare Christianitas debet, hostendit" ("This book is called 'Luminosus Indiculus'—'illuminating little register'—because it teaches in an illuminating way those matters which follow and demonstrates with open evidence the enemy of the church, which all Christianity ought to shun"; *Corpus Scriptorum Muzarabicorum* 1:272). For a thorough summary of the contents of the treatise, see Colbert, *The Martyrs of Córdoba* 266–304.

39. Coope, *The Martyrs of Córdoba* xiii.

40. The closing sentence of the treatise (immediately following the passage on Arabic poetics quoted above) reads, "Multa et alia erant que nostre huic expositjoni exiberent firmitatem, immo que ipsam patule in lucem producerent" ("There are many other things which demonstrate the truth of our argument, or rather which bring that truth out openly into the light"). The editor, Juan Gil, explains that a copyist left a note in the margin of the surviving manuscript reading, "quam exponimus" ("which we set forth"; this may also represent catchwords, the opening words of the following page [see Colbert, *The Martyrs of Córdoba* 302]). Gil concludes that "without doubt, therefore, we possess a mutilated copy of the original book" (*Corpus Scriptorum Muzarabicorum* 1:315, l. 64n).

41. *Corpus Scriptorum Muzarabicorum* 1:315. I thank Dwight Reynolds for alerting me to the intricacies and difficulties of this passage. At his request I first tried my hand at translating it; a number of people—Suzanne Akbari, Jill Ross, David Townsend, and Brian Stock—shared their thoughts with us concerning its difficulties. Dwight and I are currently working on a collaborative project on Alvarus's statements on (Arabic and Latin) poetics.

42. See Dwight Reynolds, "Arab Musical Influence on Medieval Europe." In this brief passage, note not only the mini-calque *constringo* (a Latin term translating the Arabic *rawiy*) but also the repurposing of the Latin phrase more commonly written "per cola et commata." Alvarus here uses the terms *commata* and *cola*, both Latinized Greek words which designate the proto-punctuation used to facilitate reading of scripture, to describe the hemistiches of Arabic verse.

43. *Corpus Scriptorum Muzarabicorum* 331–32. The passage cited is from the "Vita Eulogi."

44. See Alvarus, "Vita Eulogi" (*Corpus Scriptorum Muzarabicorum* 1:335–36).

45. The passage quoted is from the "Vita Eulogi" (*Corpus Scriptorum Muzarabicorum* 1:333).

46. *Corpus Scriptorum Muzarabicorum* 1:346.

47. On the manuscript transmission of Alvarus's writings, see the editor of the modern edition, Juan Gil, in *Corpus Scriptorum Muzarabicorum* 1:143–44; Jenaro Artiles, "El codice visigotico de Alvaro Cordobes" (who dates the manuscript to the eleventh rather than the tenth century); Sage, *Paul Albar of Cordoba* 221–23; and Colbert, *The Martyrs of Córdoba* 148, footnote 1.

48. *Corpus Scriptorum Muzarabicorum* 1:314. My thanks to Elizabeth Bergman for reading through this passage with me, and sharing her insights concerning early Arabic prose rhetoric reflected in Alvarus's Latin.

Colbert's translation of this sentence differs at several points from mine; see *The Martyrs of Córdoba* 300. Simonet's translation passes silently over numerous difficulties (*Historia de los Mozárabes de España* 1:369–70).

49. Colbert proposes the delightful translation "thousand fables" rather than "Milesian tales," which—given the ambiguous reading of the single extant manuscript, "fabellis milesuis"; "Milesiis" is Gil's emendation—is a possible, if unlikely, interpretation. (Colbert presumably read the "suis" tagged on to the end of "fabellis mil[l]e" as a possessive pronoun referring to the Arabs, which is awkward [we have just seen "eorum" referring to the Arabs] but not, for Alvarus, impossibly awkward.) Ibn al-Nadim (d. 995 or 998) referred to the *Thousand and One Nights* using a Persian title meaning "a thousand stories," *Hazar Afsan* (see below, Chapter 7). Nevertheless I have accepted Gil's emended text as the more plausible reading.

50. See Allen Cabaniss, "Paulus Albarus of Muslim Cordova" 110, note 25.

51. *Previdentes* here means "storing up" or "providing for"; Alvarus's *prenotantes* is more ambiguous in meaning. The verb means "to mark or note before or in front"; "to entitle" or give a name to a book; "to predict" (Lewis and Short, *A Latin Dictionary* s.v. praenoto). Presumably Alvarus means simply "notantes," noting down, and has tacked on the prefix *pre-* to balance pre*videntes*. More interesting, he may here be using the verb with a double meaning: he may accuse contemporary Christians both of using the name of Muhammad in written statements, and also of praying, in the manner of the Muslims, with open hands ("illis solitum uice eorum nostris manibus").

52. The rhetorical device of repeating words that sound the same (homonyms or near homonyms) is called *tajnis* (or, when the words are derived from the same etymological root, *ishtiqaq*) and may take various forms, including paranomosia, punning, homonyny, and alliteration. For a discussion of these devices in particular during the Abbasid era—specifically, in a work written shortly after Alvarus's death, the *Kitab al-Badi'* of Ibn al-Mu'tazz (written A.H. 274/887–88 C.E.)—see Suzanne P. Stetkevych, "Toward a Redefinition of 'Badi'' Poetry."

53. On the use of this device during the Abbasid era in particular, see J. D. Latham, "Ibn al-Muqaffa' and Early Abbasid Prose" 62–64.

54. In this final section—two pages in the modern edition—Alvarus uses the expression *id est* once (313, line 17); he uses the verbs *video* (page 313, line 7) and *iubeo* (page 314, line 2) in the passive, which requires him to use forms of the verb *to be*. The verb does appear in the final sentence, which may be a later interpolation inserted because the

remainder of the text is missing: "Multa et alia erant . . . " ("And there were many other things . . . "). Again in the final section, Alvarus uses Latin verbs that parallel the Arabic *wujida*, which means "is found" and is used in Arabic where the existential sense of the verb *to be* is required: *invenitur* (314, line 44); *inveniatur* (314, line 54); *repperitur* (313, line 15; 315, line 1). Elsewhere in his writings, including other sections of this treatise, Alvarus uses the Latin verb *to be* as frequently as any other writer of Latin prose.

55. See Hitchcock, "The Case of Córdoba in the Ninth Century" (*Mozarabs in Medieval and Early Modern Spain* 25–39), esp. 26–27.

56. On Ziryab, see Dwight Reynolds, "Music" 64–65 and Owen Wright, "Music in Muslim Spain" 556–59.

57. On Alvarus's biography, see Sage, *Paul Albar of Cordoba* 1–42; Coope, *The Martyrs of Córdoba* 38–39; and Cabaniss, "Paulus Albarus of Cordoba."

58. For an edition of Hafs's translation of the Psalms, see Marie-Thérèse Urvoy, *Le Psautier mozarabe de Hafs le Goth*. On the dating of the text, see ibid. iv–v and D. M. Dunlop, "Hafs b. Albar—The Last of the Goths?" and "Sobre Hafs ibn Albar al-Quti al-Qurtubi."

59. Hitchcock discusses a number of episodes suggesting the linguistic complexity of ninth-century Cordoba, including Christians who presented testimony in Arabic and Muslim judges who received testimony in Romance, in *Mozarabs in Medieval and Early Modern Spain* 34–39.

60. The precise word used by the modern editor of Alvarus's works, Juan Gil, is the Latin *nebulo*; he also termed the manuscript "tam pretios[us] quam corrupt[us] cod[ex]" ("as precious as it is corrupt"; *Corpus Scriptorum Muzarabicorum* 1:143).

61. On the manuscript history, see Urvoy, *Le Psaultier mozarabe de Hafs le Goth* iv–v. On David Colville, who wrote the transcription of the text, see D. M. Dunlop, "David Colville, a Successor of Michael Scot." Colville also created the partial transcription that allows us to understand the shape of the edition of the Qur'an commissioned by Egidio da Viterbo in 1518—in Arabic, with Latin transcription, translation, and commentary—also lost in the Escorial fire. See Thomas Burman's discussion of Colville's transcription: *Reading the Qur'an in Latin Christendom* 150–51.

62. Marie-Thérèse Urvoy, "Note de philologie mozarabe" 236.

63. See, for instance, Otto Zwartjes's exemplary study, *Love Songs from al-Andalus*, which studies the kharjas in Arabic, Hebrew, and Romance in the context of the literary traditions of each of those languages and examines the question of their influence on subsequent lyric poetry in a wide range of Romance languages. Zwartjes discusses the skepticism of Spanish philologists regarding the "negative attitudes towards the handling of Romance texts of earlier scholars" in the context of his survey of modern editions of the kharjas (77).

64. García Gómez, Review of S. D. Goitein, *Jew and Arabs* 467.

65. García Gómez, "Veinticuatro jaryas romances en muwaššahas árabes" 62; emphasis added.

66. Leo Spitzer, *Linguistics and Literary History* v.

67. Ibid. 4.

68. For Spitzer's references to the "inner click" in this essay, see ibid. 6–7, 27 and 28.

69. Ibid. 19–20.

70. Ibid. 26 and 27.

71. Ibid. 24–25.

72. See—in addition to the passages cited and discussed above—the debate on Christian rhetoric in the letters between Alvarus and John of Seville (Epistolae I–VI), especially *Corpus Scriptorum Muzarabicorm* 1:154–55 and 168–71; and the odd insistence on using the term *metricus* to refer to his poems in the text of the poems themselves (see, e.g., *Corpus Scriptorum Muzarabicorum* 1:344 [Carmen Philomel], v. 1; 1:345 [Item alium filomelaicum carmen eiusdem], v. 10; 1:348, v. 12; 1:349, v. 4).

CHAPTER 7

1. Machiavelli, *Discorsi sopra la prima deca di Tito Livio* 1:285.

2. For a study of variance in the early manuscripts that do exist, see David Pinault, *Story-Telling Techniques in the Arabian Nights*.

3. Apter, "Global *Translatio*" 256.

4. Other important returns to philology include the special issue of the journal *Comparative Literature Studies* on the state of philology in 1990. Barbara Johnson contributed an article to this issue that I have found provocative and useful to my argument, although Johnson draws a conclusion quite different from my own. She opposes philological reading practices to "aesthetic intuitionism" ("Philology" 28); I have worked in this study to demonstrate the central importance of the inductive leap (though not of aestheticism) to the philological reading.

Another productive postmodern reconsideration of philological reading practices, Hans Ulrich Gumbrecht's *The Powers of Philology*, appeared in 2003 (the year before the posthumous publication of Said's lectures in book form). In this study, Gumbrecht represents the classical philologist's effort to know and honor textual difference as a desire for textual presence that is never quite fulfilled and, in its inchoateness, ultimately productive.

My short list of recent returns to philology, of course, does not include the important intradisciplinary reconsiderations of philological practice that have appeared in monographs and journals of medieval studies, most notably the special issue of *Speculum* on the new philology (vol. 65, no. 1 [1990]); *The Future of the Middle Ages: Medieval Literature in the 1990s* (ed. William D. Paden); and *Medievalism and the Modernist Temper* (ed. R. Howard Bloch and Stephen G. Nichols). A more recent article by Sarah Kay ("The New Philology") provides a useful survey of these and subsequent reconsiderations of medieval philology from both a North American and European perspective.

See, finally, Lee Patterson's "The Return to Philology," which triangulates its reconsideration of the discipline by making reference to de Man's essay "The Return to Philology" and the republication in book form of the essays from *Comparative Literature Studies* (*On Philology*).

5. Paul de Man, *The Resistance to Theory* 24.

6. Said, *Humanism and Democratic Criticism* 68. It is worth noting, in the context of my discussion of the ramifications of philological practice during the nineteenth century, that the practice of *ijtihad* is intimately associated with a short list of nineteenth- and early twentieth-century figures who, while the word *fundamentalism* cannot be applied to them, yet served as a touchstone for some twentieth-century Islamic fundamentalist movements: Ibn ʿAbd al-Wahhab (1703–92), Jamal al-Din al-Afghani (1838/9–97), Rashid Rida (1865–1935), and Muhammad ʿAbdu (d. 1905). Although each had a distinct perspective on *ijtihad*, all called for a reinvigorated relationship to the scriptural foundations of belief in order to correct corrupt readings of scripture and revitalize a community of believers.

7. See Said, *Humanism and Democratic Criticism* 70. It is, of course, true that Said's notion of philology emphasizes the historical uniqueness of the contemporary reading of the text rather than the historical moment of its production. His is, to a certain degree, a presentist perception of philological practice. I do not think I do his argument a disservice by using his comments to demonstrate the relevance of our readings even of premodern texts to contemporary lived reality.

8. Al-Masʿudi, another tenth-century author, refers to the book as *Alf layla;* the title *Alf layla wa-layla* is first attested only during the twelfth century. See Reynolds, "*A Thousand and One Nights*" 271.

9. Ibn al-Nadim, *al-Fihrist* 475–76; *The Fihrist*, trans. Bayard Dodge, 2:713–14. The translation cited is Dodge's; the elucidation in brackets is my own.

10. See Todorov's essay "Narrative-Men."

11. For the therapeutic reading of Shahrazad's role in the text, see Bruno Bettelheim (*The Uses of Enchantment* 85–90) and Fedwa Malti-Douglas, for whom it is manipulation by modern novelists that allows Shahrazad to speak and articulate her role as heroine ("Shahrazad Feminist").

12. *The Arabian Nights*, trans. Haddawy, 134; Mahdi, ed., *The Thousand and One Nights* 201. I cite Haddawy's translation.

13. Alfred Tennyson, "Recollections of the Arabian Nights" (*The Poems of Tennyson* 1:226).

14. Beverly Heisner, *Hollywood Art* 45; see Cooperson's wonderful discussion in "The Monstrous Births of Aladdin," especially 273 (where this passage is cited).

15. For al-Tabari's account of the downfall of the Barmakids, see *The ʿAbbasid Caliphate in Equilibrium* 201–30, and footnote 297, pp. 201–2, for bibliographical references to other historians' accounts. For the tales about the affair between Jaʿfar and ʿAbbasa in particular, see 214–16, and footnote 731, p. 215 for bibliographic references to other historical sources and modern discussions. Hugh Kennedy gives an overview of historical explanations of Harun al-Rashid's massacre of the Barmakids in *The Early Abbasid Caliphate*, 127–29. Cooperson's summary of the historical accounts is particularly relevant to my argument in this chapter: "The Monstrous Births of 'Aladdin'" 274–75.

On women and power in the caliphal family in Abbasid Baghdad as reflected in the historical accounts of the downfall of the Barmakids, see Tayeb el-Hibri, *Reinterpreting Islamic Historiography* 42–44.

16. Menéndez Pidal, *La Chanson de Roland y el neotradicionalismo* 14. Pidal's response to Joseph Bédier's intervention in theories of manuscript editing is intriguing in light of the themes of this book. Menéndez critiqued Bédier's isolation of the *Chanson de Roland* from the transnational tradition which generated it and insisted that it should be read in continuity with the Spanish epics that (like the *Roland*) commemorated battles between Christian and Muslim armies in the Iberian peninsula.

17. Ibn al-Nadim, *al-Fihrist* 475; *The Fihrist*, trans. Dodge, 2:713. I cite Bayard Dodge's translation.

18. On imaginative narrative in Abbasid Baghdad, see H. T. Norris, "Fables and Legends." On the complexity of medieval Arab views toward storytelling, see Seeger Bonebakker, "Some Medieval Views" and Reynolds, "Popular Prose in the Post-Classical Period" 252–54.

19. See William Granara, "Nostalgia, Arab Nationalism, and the Andalusian Chronotope."

20. Pinault, *Story-Telling Techniques in the Arabian Nights* 86–99.

21. Mahdi, "From History to Fiction."

22. Sercambi retells the *Thousand and One Nights* frame tale in novella 84 of Renier's edition (294–99). For Bosone da Gubbio's retelling of the tale of Yunan and Duban, see *L'Avventuroso Ciciliano* 264–66.

23. Ibn al-Nadim mentions the tale of Sindbad al-Hakim; see *al-Fihrist* 476 and *The Fihrist*, trans. Dodge, 715. The early Arabic version does not survive, although the Spanish translation seems to be a close translation of a thirteenth-century Arabic version. For an overview of the Sindbad tradition, see Domenico Comparetti, *Researches Regarding the Book of Sindibad;* Killis Campbell, "A Study of the Romance of the Seven Sages" and the introduction to his edition of an English version of the work, *The Seven Sages of Rome*; and W. A. Clouston's introduction to his edition of *The Book of Sindibad*. For modern editions of various medieval versions of the text, see *Syntipas* (Greek); Johannis de Alta Silva, *Dolopathos* (Latin); Gaston Paris, *Deux rédactions du Roman des Sept Sages de Rome* (French); *El Libro de los Engaños* (Spanish); Adolf Mussafia, ed., *Beiträge zur Litteratur der Sieben Weisen Meister* (parallel German, Latin, and French versions). For modern editions of the particularly rich Italian tradition see *Il libro dei Sette Savi di Roma*, ed. Alessandro d'Ancona (a late thirteenth-or early fourteenth-century manuscript); *Il libro dei Sette Savi di Roma*, ed. Antonio Cappelli (a fourteenth-century manuscript); *Eine Italianische Prosaversion der Sieben Weisen Meister* (a late fourteenth-century manuscript); *Il libro de' Sette Savi di Roma*, ed. F. Roediger (a late fourteenth- or early fifteenth-century manuscript); *Storia di Stefano* (a mid-fifteenth-century manuscript); Chiara Bozzoli, "*Storia favolosa di Stefano*" (a fifteenth-century manuscript); and *Amabile di Continentia* (a fifteenth-century manuscript).

24. Pinault, *Story-Telling Techniques in the Arabian Nights* 45.

25. Antoine Galland, *Les mille et une nuits* 1:19–20.

26. This text has been edited (*El libro de los engaños*) and translated into English (*The Book of the Wiles of Women*).

27. Here I am paraphrasing a passage from Marshall Hodgson's manifesto-like introduction to his unfinished work on world history, edited and published following his death by Edmund Burke: "We have known for a long time that 'the Crusades brought Europe knowledge of a more advanced culture' than her own. Is it enough to point out the specific items Europe learned, without attempting to set the European and Near Eastern cultures objectively side by side in a single history, where we could see not only what details Europe got, but also what she failed to accept; and more important, in what ways both developed in common?" (*Rethinking World History* 36–37).

28. Luigi Pirandello, *Sei personaggi in cerca d'autore* 59–60. The stepdaughter's rendition of the song from *Chu-Chin-Chow* does not appear in the English translation of the play.

29. *Chu-Chin-Chow* (music by Frederic Norton; book and lyrics by Oscar Asche) had a five-year run in London, from 1916 until 1921. It was made into an equally successful film (1934), directed by Walter Forde and starring George Robey and Anna May Wong.

30. On the relation between Galland's Ali Baba and independent tales in the Arabic tradition, see Aboubakr Chraïbi, "Galland's 'Ali Baba' and Other Arabic Versions."

31. Lane, *Arabian Nights' Entertainments*, note 28, p. 1023.

32. John Payne, *The Book of the Thousand Nights and One Night* 9:331. It is impossible to exaggerate the contempt which Payne expressed for Harun, whom he described as a vicious and ruthless ruler on a par with the Borgias. His vituperation of Harun is interwoven with his celebration of Harun's Baghdad and his account of the rise and fall of the Barmakids, and it makes for a riveting read (see *The Thousand Nights* 9:317–67).

33. Richard Burton, *The Book of the Thousand Nights and a Night* 3:3700 and 3701.

34. *The 1001 Arabian Nights* (1959) was written by Ted Allen and Pete Burness and directed by Jack Kinney.

35. *The Thief of Bagdad* represents a variation on this power dynamic. Jaffar is retainer to Ahmad, Harun al-Rashid's grandson, sultan of Bagdad. He schemes to marry not Ahmad's daughter but the daughter of the sultan of Basra—the ineffectual patron figure.

36. Again, Korda's *Thief of Bagdad* differs from the *1001 Arabian Nights* and *Aladdin* in its relatively critical view of the weak sultan of Basra, who suffers an ignominious end as the price for his frivolity and selfishness: Jaffar orchestrates his murder by one of the mechanical toys that are the sultan's weakness.

37. No fewer than five directors (credited and uncredited) took a stab at directing the project, only to be dismissed by Korda because they didn't agree with his vision for the film. On Korda's oversight of the direction of the project, see Charles Drazin, *Korda* 206–9; Paul Tabori, *Alexander Korda* 210–14; Karol Kulik, *Alexander Korda* 224–26.

38. Korda insisted on lavish sets for his 1940 "Bagdad," and viewers have criticized him (with good reason) for emphasizing the Technicolor splendor of the backdrops and stage dressings and stiffing the actors, who drift like wraiths in their "Arabian" gauzes

through sets that have much more reality than do they. See Kulik, *Alexander Korda* 243 and the *Variety* review, published on January 1, 1940, for critiques of the film.

39. Kulik, *Alexander Korda* 232; Tabori, *Alexander Korda* 216; Charles Drazin, *Korda* 221. June Duprez and Miles Malleson, cast members from *The Thief of Bagdad*, also acted in *The Lion Has Wings*, and Michael Powell worked as a director on both projects.

Korda would make another propaganda film in the United States following *The Thief of Bagdad*: *That Hamilton Woman* (1941). And in 1941 he stood trial before a Senate committee on charges of producing films with the intention of inciting the American public to enter Europe's war (see Kulik, *Alexander Korda* 250–53 and Drazin, *Korda* 237–42 and, on the Senate Interstate Commerce Committee's investigation of antiwar films before the United States' entrance into the war, John Whiteclay Chambers, "The Movies and the Antiwar Debate in America"). When that committee's work was suspended and the charges were dropped, the Senate Foreign Relations Committee picked up the crusade against Korda, investigating him now on the suspicion that he was a British intelligence agent. His hearing was scheduled for December 12, 1941; when the Japanese bombed Pearl Harbor on December 7, the matter was dropped (see Kulik, *Alexander Korda* 250–53 and Drazin, *Korda* 237–42).

Drazin reports a delightful anecdote that illustrates, better than any other I have read, the fascination with Korda as at once a Hollywood mogul and a possible intelligence agent moving with inscrutable European aplomb through a landscape of hazard and uncertainty. On September 3, 1939, after Britain declared war on Germany, an air-raid warning sent the cast and crew of *Thief* to a concrete bunker where they hunkered—in costume—to wait it out. One of the crew members remembers Korda smoking a cigar; "with Merle Oberon [whom he had recently married] holding on to his arm and crying next to him, he took a deep breath and sent a perfect smoke ring into the air" (219).

40. On the shooting schedule see Drazin, *Korda* 212 and Kulik, *Alexander Korda* 240.

41. The bumbling sultan of Basra would rather play with his life-size mechanical toys than face his public. And even Ahmad, at the outset of the movie, is out of touch with the people of his city, Bagdad; his escapades in the movie, of course, teach him to engage more closely with his public.

42. In films made both before and after the 1940 *Thief of Bagdad* and based (often very loosely) on the story of Ali Baba, Abu Hasan plays a role similar in many respects to Jaffar's: see the 1934 *Chu-Chin-Chow*, directed by Walter Forde; the 1937 *Popeye Meets Ali Baba's 40 Thieves*, directed by Dave Fleischer; and the 1979 Bollywood Ali Baba, *Ali Baba aur 40 Chor*, directed by Umesh Mehra and L. Faiziev. Abu Hasan's name appears to be a simplification of the rather more phonetically challenging Khawaja Husain from the print version of "Ali Baba."

43. Kulik, *Alexander Korda* 253–61.

44. Pio Rajna, *Le fonti dell'Orlando Furioso* 451–52.

45. Drazin, *Korda* 16.

46. On Korda's use of Technicolor techniques, see Richard Rickitt, *Special Effects* 22 and 49.

47. Payne wrote, with palpable disgust, "This prince [Harun al-Rashid] is undoubtedly the hero of 'The Thousand and One Nights'; no other name occurs with a quarter of the same frequency and upon no other character is bestowed such wholesale laudation" (*The Thousand Nights and One Night* 9:319–20).

48. See the Christian Broker's Tale and the Jewish Physician's Tale.

49. *The Arabian Nights*, trans. Haddawy, 220; Mahdi (ed.), *The Thousand and One Nights* 295. I cite Haddawy's translation.

# BIBLIOGRAPHY

Aarsleff, Hans. "Scholarship and Ideology: Joseph Bédier's Critique of Romantic Medievalism." In *Historical Studies and Literary Criticism*, ed. Jerome J. McGann, 93–113. Madison: University of Wisconsin Press, 1985.

Abbott, Nabia. "A Ninth-Century Fragment of the 'Thousand Nights.'" In *The Arabian Nights Reader*, ed. Ulrich Marzolph, 21–82. Detroit: Wayne State University Press, 2006.

Abdel-Halim, Mohamed. *Antoine Galland: Sa vie et son œuvre*. Paris: Nizet, 1964.

'Abdel-Malek, Anouar. "Orientalism in Crisis." *Diogenes* 44 (1963): 103–40.

*Achim von Arnim und die ihm nahe Standen*. Ed. Reinhold Steig and Herman Grimm. 3 vols. Stuttgart: J. G. Cotta, 1894–1913.

Agius, Dionisius A. Review of *A Contribution to Arabic Lexical Dialectology*, by Al-Miklem Malti. *Bulletin (British Society for Middle Eastern Studies)* 17 (1990): 171–80.

Akbari, Suzanne Conklin. "Between Diaspora and Conquest: Norman Assimilation in Petrus Alfonsi's *Disciplina Clericalis* and Marie de France's *Fables*." In *Cultural Diversity in the British Middle Ages: Archipelago, Island, England*, ed. Jeffrey Jerome Cohen. New York: Palgrave Macmillan, 2007.

*Alf layla wa-layla*. Ed. Muhsin Mahdi. 2 vols. Leiden: Brill, 1984.

Ali, Muhsin Jassim. "The Growth of Scholarly Interest in the *Arabian Nights*." In *The Arabian Nights Reader*, ed. Ulrich Marzolph, 1–20. Detroit: Wayne State University Press, 2006.

———. *Scheherazade in England: A Study of Nineteenth-Century English Criticism of the Arabian Nights*. Washington, D.C.: Three Continents Press, 1981.

Allen, Roger. "An Analysis of 'The Tale of the Three Apples.'" In *The Arabian Nights Reader*, ed. Ulrich Marzolph, 239–48. Detroit: Wayne State University Press, 2006.

*Amabile di Continentia*. Ed. Augusto Cesari. Bologna: Romagnoli-Dall'Acqua, 1896.

Amari, Michele. *Carteggio di Michele Amari, raccolto e postillato coll'elogio di lui, letto nell'Accademia della Crusca*. 3 vols. Turin: Roux Frassati, 1896.

———. *Description de Palerme au milieu du xᵉ siècle de l'ère vulgaire, par Ebn-Hauqal*. Paris: Imprimerie Royale, 1845.

———. *Diari e appunti autobiografici inediti*. Ed. Carmela Castiglione Trovato. Naples: Edizioni Scientifiche Italiane, 1981.

————. *Le epigrafi arabiche di Sicilia*. Ed. Francesco Gabrieli. Palermo: Flaccovio, 1971.

————. *Storia dei musulmani di Sicilia*. Ed. Carlos Alfonso Nallino. 3 vols. Catania: R. Prampolini, 1933–39.

Andrés, Juan. *Dell'origine, de' progressi, e dello stato attuale d'ogni letteratura*. 8 vols. Parma: Stamperia Reale, 1785–1822.

Apter, Emily. "Global *Translatio:* The 'Invention' of Comparative Literature, Istanbul, 1933." *Critical Inquiry* 29 (2003): 253–81.

————. "Saidian Humanism." *Boundary* 2 (2004): 35–53.

————. *The Translation Zone: A New Comparative Literature*. Princeton, N.J.: Princeton University Press, 2006.

Aquilina, Joseph. "Systems of Maltese Orthography." In *Papers in Maltese Linguistics*. Valletta, Malta: University of Malta Press, 1961.

*The Arabian Nights*. Trans. Husain Haddawy. New York: Norton, 1990.

*The Arabian Nights II: Sinbad and Other Popular Stories*. Trans. Husain Haddawy. New York: Norton, 1995.

*The Arabian Nights' Entertainments—Or the Thousand and One Nights*. Trans. Edward William Lane. New York: Tudor Publishing, 1927.

Arberry, A. J. *Oriental Essays: Portraits of Seven Scholars*. London: Allen & Unwin, 1960.

Armistead, Samuel G. "Pet Theories and Paper Tigers: Trouble with the Kharjas." *La Corónica* 14 (1985): 55–70.

————. "Some Recent Developments in Kharja Scholarship." *La Corónica* 8 (1980): 199–203.

————. "Speed or Bacon? Further Meditations on Professor Alan Jones' 'Sunbeams.'" *La Corónica* 10 (1982): 148–55.

Armistead, Samuel G., and James T. Monroe. "Albas, Mammas, and Code-Switching in the Kharjas: A Reply to Keith Whinnom." *La Corónica* 11 (1983): 174–207.

————. "Beached Whales and Roaring Mice: Additional Remarks on Hispano-Arabic Strophic Poetry." *La Corónica* 13 (1985): 206–42.

Artiles, Jenaro. "El codice visigotico de Alvaro Cordobes." *Revista de la Biblioteca, Archivo y Museo del Ayuntamiento de Madrid* 9 (1932): 201–19.

Asín Palacios, Miguel. "El Averroísmo teológico de Santo Tomás de Aquino." In *Homenaje á D. Francisco Codera*, 271–331. Zaragoza: Mariano Escar, 1904.

————. *Dante e l'Islam: L'escatologia islamica nella* Divina Commedia. Trans. Roberto Rossi Testa and Younis Tawfik. Parma: Nuova Pratiche Editrice, 1994.

————. *La escatología musulmana en la* Divina Comedia. Madrid: Estanislao Maestre, 1919.

————. *La escatología musulmana en la* Divina Comedia. 2nd ed. Madrid: Estanislao Maestre, 1943.

————. Introduction. *Disertaciones y opúsculos*, 1:xv–cxvi. By Julián Ribera y Tarragó. Madrid: Estanislao Maestre, 1928.

————. *Islam and the Divine Comedy*. Trans. and abridged by Harold Sutherland. London: Frank Cass, 1926.

Auerbach, Erich. *Literary Language and Its Public in Late Latin Antiquity and in the Middle Ages.* 1965. Rpt., Princeton, N.J.: Princeton University Press, 1993.

———. *Mimesis: The Representation of Reality in Western Literature.* Garden City, N.Y.: Doubleday Anchor Books, 1953.

Aurell, Jaume. "Le médiévale espagnol au XXe siècle: de l'isolation à la modernisation." *Cahiers de civilisation médiévale* 48 (2005): 201–18.

Averroes. *Averroes' Middle Commentary on Aristotle's* Poetics. Trans. Charles E. Butterworth. Princeton, N.J.: Princeton University Press, 1986.

———. *Talkhis kitab Aristutalis fi al-shi'r.* Ed. Muhammad Salim Salim. Cairo: n.p., 1971.

Baldinetti, Anna. *Orientalismo e colonialismo: La ricerca di consenso in Egitto per l'impresa di Libia.* Rome: Istituto per l'Oriente C. A. Nallino, 1997.

Baldoli, Claudia. "The 'Northern Dominator' and the Mare Nostrum: Fascist Italy's 'Cultural War' in Malta." *Modern Italy* 13 (2008): 5–20.

Barbieri, Giovanni Maria. *Dell'origine della poesia rimata.* Modena: Società Tipografica, 1790.

Barth, John. *The Friday Book: Essays and Other Nonfiction.* New York: Putnam's Sons, 1984.

Beattie, James. *Dissertations moral and critical.* London: Strahan and Cadell, 1783.

Bédier, Joseph. *Études critiques.* Paris: Armand Colin, 1903.

———. *Les fabliaux: Études de littérature populaire et d'histoire littéraire du moyen âge.* 3rd ed. Paris: Champion, 1911.

———. *Les légendes épiques: Recherches sur la formation des chansons de geste.* 3 vols. Paris: Champion, 1912.

———. *La tradition manuscrite du Lai de l'Ombre: Réflexion sur l'art d'éditer les anciens textes.* Paris: Champion, 1929.

Bencheikh, Jamel Eddine. "The Tale of 'Ali b. Bakkar and Shams al-Nahar." In *The Arabian Nights Reader*, ed. Ulrich Marzolph, 249–64. Detroit: Wayne State University Press, 2006.

Benvenuto da Imola. *Comentum super Dantis Aldigherij Comoediam.* The Dartmouth Dante Project. May 2007. http://dante.dartmouth.edu/.

Bertoni, Giulio. "L' 'Istituto di Filologia Romanza di Roma.' " *Cultura neolatina* 1 (1941): 5–13.

Bettelheim, Bruno. *The Uses of Enchantment: The Meaning and Importance of Fairy Tales.* New York: 1967.

Bisaha, Nancy. "Petrarch's Vision of the Muslim and Byzantine East." *Speculum* 76 (2001): 284–314.

Bloch, R. Howard. "New Philology and Old French." *Speculum* 65 (1990): 38–58.

Bloch, R. Howard, and Stephen G. Nichols, eds. *Medievalism and the Modernist Temper.* Baltimore: Johns Hopkins University Press, 1996.

Bodenham, C. H. L. "Petrarch and the Poetry of the Arabs." *Romanische Forschungen* 94 (1982): 167–78.

Boggess, William F. "Aristotle's *Poetics* in the Fourteenth Century." *Studies in Philology* 67 (1970): 278–94.

———. "Hermannus Alemannus' Latin Anthology of Arabic Poetry." *Journal of the American Oriental Society* 88 (1968): 657–70.

———. "Hermannus Alemannus's Rhetorical Translations." *Viator* 2 (1971): 227–50.

Bonavia, Carmel G. "Mikiel Anton Vassalli: A Bibliography." *Journal of Maltese Studies* 23–24 (1993): 230–36.

Bonebakker, Seeger A. "*Nihil obstat* in Storytelling?" In The Thousand and One Nights *in Arabic Literature and Society*, ed. Richard G. Hovannisian and Georges Sabagh, 56–77. Cambridge: Cambridge University Press, 1997.

———. "Some Medieval Views on Fantastic Stories." *Quaderni di studi arabi* 10 (1992): 21–43.

Bonello, V., B. Fiorentini, and L. Schiavone. *Echi del Risorgimento a Malta*. Milan: Cisalpino-Goliardica, 1982.

*The Book of the Wiles of Women*. Trans. John Esten Keller. Chapel Hill: University of North Carolina Press, 1956.

Boreland, Helen. "Ambiguity—and Troubadour Influence?—in a Thirteenth-Century Kharja." *La Corónica* 5 (1977): 77–84.

Borg, Alexander. "Language." In *Malta: Culture and Identity*, ed. Henry Frendo and Oliver Friggieri, 27–50. Malta: Ministry of Youth and the Arts, 1994.

Bosone da Gubbio. *L'Avventuroso Ciciliano*. Ed. G. F. Nott. Milan: Giovanni Silvestri, 1834.

Bozzoli, Chiara. "*Storia favolosa di Stefano:* Edizione critica di una versione italiana inedita del *Libro dei Sette Savi*." In *Carte romanze, Serie 2: Testi e studi italiani*, ed. Alfonso d'Agostino, 41–128. Bologna: Cisalpino, 1999.

Braudel, Fernand. *The Mediterranean and the Mediterranean World in the Age of Philip II*. Trans. Sian Reynolds. Berkeley: University of California Press, 1972.

Brincat, Joseph M. "La caccia alla fenice: Glossari e vocabolari del maltese dal seicento all'ottocento tra mitomania, nazionalismo ed etimologia." In *Lessicografia dialettale ricordando Paolo Zolli*, ed. Francesco Bruni and Carla Marcato, 439–46. Rome and Padua: Antenore, 2006.

———. "Languages and Varieties in Use in Malta Today: Maltese, English, Italian, Maltese English and Maltaliano." In *Rethinking Languages in Contact: The Case of Italian*, ed. Anna Laura Lepschy and Arturo Tosi, 152–59. London: Legenda, 2006.

———. *Malta: Una storia linguistica*. Recco, Italy: Le mani, 2003.

Brown, Catherine. "The Relics of Menéndez Pidal: Mourning and Melancholia in Hispanomedieval Studies." *La Corónica* 24 (1995): 15–41.

Burde, Mark. "Francisque Michel, Joseph Bédier, and the Epic Discovery of the First Edition of the Song of Roland (1837)." *Exemplaria* 16 (2004): 1–42.

Burman, Thomas. *Reading the Qur'an in Latin Christendom, 1140–1560*. Philadelphia: University of Pennsylvania Press, 2007.

Burnett, Charles. "Learned Knowledge of Arabic Poetry, Rhymed Prose, and Didactic Verse from Petrus Alfonsi to Petrarch." In *Poetry and Philosophy in the Middle Ages: A Festschrift for Peter Dronke*, ed. John Marebon, 29–53. Leiden: Brill, 2001.

———. "Master Theodore, Frederick II's Philosopher." In *Federico II e le nuove culture: Atti del XXXI Convegno Storico Internazionale,* 225–85. Spoleto: Centro Italiano di Studi sull'Alto Medioevo, 1995.

———. "Petrarch and Averroes: An Episode in the History of Poetics." In *The Medieval Mind: Hispanic Studies in Honour of Alan Deyermond,* ed. Ian MacPherson and Ralph Penny, 49–56. Woodbridge, England: Tamesis, 1997.

———. "The 'Sons of Averroes with the Emperor Frederick' and the Transmission of the Philosophical Works by Ibn Rushd." In *Averroes and the Aristotelian Tradition: Sources, Constitution, and Reception of the Philosophy of Ibn Rushd (1126–1198),* ed. Gerhard Endress and Jan A. Aertsen, 259–99. Leiden: Brill, 1999.

Burton, Richard, trans. *The Book of the Thousand Nights and a Night.* 3 vols. New York: Heritage Press, 1962.

Byatt, A. S. "Narrate or Die." *New York Times Magazine,* April 18, 1999, 104–7.

Byron, George Gordon. *The Complete Poetical Works,* ed. Jerome J. McGann. 7 vols. Oxford: Clarendon Press, 1980–93.

Cabaniss, Allen. "Paulus Albarus of Muslim Cordova." *Church History* 22 (1953): 99–112.

Caesar, Michael, ed. *Dante: The Critical Heritage.* London and New York: Routledge, 1989.

Caetani, Leone. "Lettera di L. Caetani a Giorgio Levi Della Vida." Accademia dei Lincei. November 2007. http://www.lincei-celebrazioni.it/icaetani_lett_della_vida.html.

Calhoun, David B. *Princeton Seminary.* 2 vols. Edinburgh and Carlisle, Pa.: The Banner of Truth Trust, 1994.

Campbell, Killis. *The Seven Sages of Rome.* Boston: Ginn, 1907.

———. "A Study of the Romance of the Seven Sages with Special Reference to the Middle English Versions." *PMLA* 14 (1899): 1–107.

Candido, Salvatore. "Francesco Crispi scrittore e giornalista a Malta (1853–1854)." *Rassegna storica del Risorgimento* 81 (1994): 179–223.

Cantera Burgos, Francisco. "Los estudios orientales en la España actual." *Oriente Moderno* 35 (1955): 236–47.

Carretto, Giacomo E. " 'Sapere' e 'potere': L'Istituto per l'Oriente (1921–1943)." *Annali della Facoltà di Scienze Politiche* 9 (1982–83): 209–30.

Cassar Pullicino, Guze. "M. A. Vassalli in 1798–1799." *Journal of Maltese Studies* 23–24 (1993): 80–89.

Cassola, Arnold. *Francesco Vella (1793–1868): An Unsung Protagonist of Maltese Language Development.* Sliema, Malta: Minima, 2003.

———. *Il Mezzo Vocabolario maltese-italiano del '700.* Valletta, Malta: Said, 1996.

———. "On the Meaning of Gueri in Petrus Caxaro's Cantilena." *Melita Historica* 8 (1983): 315–17.

Castro, Américo. *La realidad histórica de España.* 3rd ed. Mexico City: Editorial Porrua, 1966.

Cerquiglini, Bernard. *In Praise of the Variant: A Critical History of Philology.* Trans. Betsy Wing. Baltimore and London: Johns Hopkins University Press, 1999.

Cerulli, Enrico. "Les arabes et l'unité méditerranéenne. Relation présentée le 8 juin 1950 au Centre d'Études de Politique Étrangère à Paris." Ms. Accademia dei Lincei (Rome).

———. "La colonizazzione del Harar." *Rassegna economica dell'Africa Italiana* 6 (1943): 149–62.

———. "Dante e l'Islam." *Al-Andalus* 21 (1957): 229–53.

———. *Etiopia Occidentale (Dalla Scioa alla frontiera del Sudan): Note del viaggio, 1927–28.* 2 vols. Rome: Sindicato Italiano Arti Grafiche, 1930–33.

———. *Etiopi in Palestina: Storia della comunità etiopica di Gerusalemme.* 2 vols. Rome: Libreria dello Stato, 1943.

———. "La fine del colonialismo." *Ulisse* 28–29 (1959): 1551–59.

———. "Giuliano Cora e l'Etiopia." *Rivista di Studi Politici Internazionali* 36 (1969): 1–7.

———. "L'Islam nell'Africa Orientale." In *Conferenze e letture del Centro Studi per il Vicino Oriente* 1:74–93. Rome: Reale Accademia d'Italia, 1941.

———. *Il "Libro della scala" e la questione delle fonti arabo-spagnole della* Divina Commedia. Vatican City: Biblioteca Apostolica Vaticana, 1949.

———. *Il libro etiopico dei miracoli di Maria e le sue fonti nelle letterature del medio evo latino.* Rome: Bardi, 1943.

———. "Nuove idee nell'Etiopia e nuova letteratura amarica." *Oriente moderno* 6 (1926): 167–73.

———. "Nuove pubblicazioni in lingua amarica." *Oriente moderno* 12 (1932): 306–10.

———. "Nuove pubblicazioni in linguaggi etiopici." *Oriente moderno* 7 (1927): 354–57.

———. *Nuove ricerche sul Libro della Scala e la conoscenza dell'Islam in Occidente.* Vatican City: Biblioteca Apostolica Vaticana, 1972.

———. "Nuovi libri pubblicati in Etiopia." *Oriente moderno* 12 (1932): 170–75.

———. "Petrarca e gli arabi." *Rivista di cultura classica e medioevale* 7 (1965): 331–36.

———. "Pubblicazioni recenti dei musulmani e dei cristiani dell'Etiopia." *Oriente moderno* 8 (1929): 429–32.

———. "La questione del Califfato in rapporto alle nostre Colonie di diretto dominio: Relazione di Enrico Cerulli al Convegno Nazionale Coloniale a Napoli, 26–28 aprile 1917." Naples: Trani, 1917.

———. "I rapporti italo-abissini nel dopo-guerra." Convegno nazionale coloniale per il dopoguerra delle colonie, Rome, January 15–18, 1919.

———. "Rassegna periodica di pubblicazioni in lingue etiopiche fatte in Etiopia." *Oriente moderno* 13 (1933): 58–64.

———. "Recenti pubblicazioni abissine in amarico." *Oriente moderno* 6 (1926): 555–57.

Chakrabarty, Dipesh. *Provincializing Europe: Postcolonial Thought and Historical Difference.* Princeton, N.J.: Princeton University Press, 2000.

Chambers, John Whiteclay. "The Movies and the Antiwar Debate in America." *Film and History* 36 (2006): 44–57.

Chesterton, G. K. *The Spice of Life and Other Essays.* Ed. Dorothy Collins. Beaconsonfield, England: Darwen Finlayson, 1964.

Chraïbi, Aboubakr. "Galland's 'Ali Baba' and Other Arabic Versions." In *The Arabian Nights in Transnational Perspective*, ed. Ulrich Marzolph, 3–15. Detroit: Wayne State University Press, 2007.

———. "Notes et commentaires sur l'édition des *Milles et une nuit* de M. Mahdi, Leyde, 1984." *Studia islamica* 72 (1990): 172–87.

Ciccarelli, Andrea. "Dante and Italian Culture from the Risorgimento to World War I." *Dante Studies* 119 (2001): 125–54.

Cifoletti, Guido. *La lingua franca mediterranea*. Padua: Unipress, 1989.

Clarke, Dorothy Clotelle. "The Prosody of the Hargas." *La Corónica* 16 (1988): 55–75.

Clouston, W. A., ed. and trans. *The Book of Sindibad*. Privately printed, 1884.

Codera, Francisco. *Decadencia y desaparición de los Almorávides en España*. Zaragoza: Comas Hermanos, 1899.

Colbert, Edward P. *The Martyrs of Córdoba (850–859): A Study of the Sources*. Washington, D.C.: Catholic University of America Press, 1962.

Coleridge, Samuel Taylor. *Collected Letters of Samuel Taylor Coleridge*. Computer file. Charlottesville, Va.: InteLex Corporation, 2002.

Comparetti, Domenico. *Researches Respecting the Book of Sindibad*. Trans. H. C. Coote. London: Stock, 1882.

Conde, José Antonio. *Historia de la dominación de los Árabes en España*. Barcelona: Imprenta y Librería Española, 1844.

"Una conferenza di Taha Husein su I. Guidi, C. A. Nallino, D. Santillana e altri orientalisti italiani che insegnarono in Egitto." *Oriente moderno* 28 (1948): 103–7.

Consolo, Vincenzo. *Reading and Writing the Mediterranean*. Ed. Norma Bouchard and Massimo Lollini. Toronto: University of Toronto Press, 2006.

Coope, Jessica A. *The Martyrs of Córdoba: Community and Family Conflict in an Age of Mass Conversion*. Lincoln: University of Nebraska Press, 1995.

Cooperson, Michael. "The Monstrous Births of 'Aladdin.'" In *The Arabian Nights Reader*, ed. Ulrich Marzolph, 265–82. Detroit: Wayne State University Press, 2006.

Corbellari, Alain. "Joseph Bédier, Philologist and Writer." In *Medievalism and the Modernist Temper*, ed. R. Howard Bloch and Stephen G. Nichols, 269–85. Baltimore: Johns Hopkins University Press, 1996.

Cornish, Alison. "'Not like an Arab': Poetry and Astronomy in the Episode of Idalogos in Boccaccio's *Filocolo*." *Annali d'Italianistica* 23 (2005): 55–67.

Corominas, Joan. "El Nuevo Abencuzman." *Al-Andalus* 36 (1971): 241–54.

*Corpus Scriptorum Muzarabicorum*. Ed. Juan Gil. 2 vols. Madrid: Instituto Antonio de Nebrija, 1973.

Corriente, Francisco. "Acento y cantidad en la fonología del hispano-árabe. Observaciones estadísticas en torno a la naturaleza del sistema métrico de la poesía popular andalusi." *Al-Andalus* 41 (1976): 1–14.

Corti, Maria. "La 'Commedia' di Dante e l'oltretomba islamico." *Belfagor* 50 (1995): 300–314.

———. *Dante a un nuovo crocevia*. Florence: Libreria Commissionaria Sansoni, 1982.

————. *La felicità mentale: Nuove prospettive per Cavalcanti e Dante.* Turin: Einaudi, 1983.

Cremona, Joseph. "Acciocch' ognuno le possa intendere: The Use of Italian as a Lingua Franca on the Barbary Coast of the Seventeenth Century. Evidence from the English." *Journal of Anglo-Italian Studies* [Malta] 5 (1997): 52–69.

————. "Français et italien au XVIIe siècle." In *Actes du XXIe Congrès international de linguistique et de philologie romane,* ed. Annick Englebert et al., 3:135–43. Tübingen: Niemeyer, 2000.

————. "Geografia linguistica e 'lingua franca' del Mediterraneo." In *Carlo Napoli e il Mediterraneo. Atti del Convegno internazionale svoltosi dall' 11 al 13 gennaio 2001,* ed. Giuseppe Galasso and Aurelio Musi, 289–304. Naples: Società napoletana di storia patria, 2001.

————. "Histoire linguistique externe de l'italien au Maghreb." In *Romanische Sprachgeschichte/Histoire linguistique de la Romania,* ed. Gerhardt Ernst et al., 1:961–66. Berlin: Walter de Gruyter, 2003.

————. "Italian-based Lingua Francas around the Mediterranean." In *Multilingualism in Italy: Past and Present,* ed. Anna Laura Lepschy and Arturo Tosi, 24–30. Oxford: Legenda, 2002.

————. "L'italiano in Tunisi." In *Italiano e dialetti nel tempo: Saggi di grammatica per Giulio C. Lepschy,* ed. Paola Beninci et al., 85–97. Rome: Bulzoni, 1996.

————. "La lingua d'Italia nell'Africa settentrionale." In *La lingua d'Italia: Usi pubblici e istituzionali,* ed. Gabriella Alfieri and Arnold Cassola, 34–36. Roma: Bulzoni, 1998.

Curtis, Georgina Pell. *The Interdependence of Literature.* London: Herder, 1917.

Cusa, Salvatore. *I diplomi greci ed arabi di Sicilia.* 2 vols. Palermo: Stabilimento Tipografico Lao, 1868.

————. *La Palma nella poesia, nella scienza e nella storia siciliana.* Palermo: Bruno Leopardi, 1998.

Dainotto, Roberto M. *Europe (in Theory).* Durham, N.C.: Duke University Press, 2007.

Daniel, Norman. *The Arabs and Mediaeval Europe.* 2nd ed. London and New York: Longman; Beirut: Librairie du Liban, 1979.

————. *Islam and the West: The Making of an Image.* Edinburgh: University Press, 1960.

d'Autun, Jean Quintin. *The Earliest Description of Malta (Lyons 1536).* Trans. Horatio C. R. Vella. Malta: Debono, 1980.

De Cesare, Raffaele. *La fine di un regno.* Citta di Castello: Lapi, 1908.

de Fabrizio, Angelo. "Il 'Mirag' di Maometto esposto da un frate del secolo XV." *Giornale storico della letteratura italiana* 49 (1907): 299–313.

De Gubernatis, Angelo. *Matériaux pour servir à l'histoire des études orientales en Italie.* Paris: Ernest Leroux, 1876.

Del Boca, Angelo. *Gli italiani in Africa orientale.* 4 vols. Milan: Mondadori, 1992.

De Man, Paul. *The Resistance to Theory.* Minneapolis: University of Minnesota Press, 1986.

de Simone, Adalgisa. "Salvatore Cusa arabista siciliano del XIX secolo." In *La conoscenza dell'Asia e dell'Africa in Italia nei secoli XVIII e XIX,* ed. Ugo Marazzi, 1:593–617. Naples: Istituto Universitario Orientale, 1984.

Dessoulavy, C. L. Review of A. Cremona, *Mikiel Anton Vassalli U minijietu*. *Bulletin of the School of Oriental Studies* 9 (1938): 812–14.

*Dizionario dei siciliani illustri*. Palermo: F. Ciuni Libraio, 1939.

*Documents on Italian War Crimes Submitted to the United Nations War Crimes Commission by the Imperial Ethiopian Government*. Volume 1: Italian Telegrams and Circulars. Addis Ababa: Ministry of Justice, 1949.

Drake, Nathan. *Literary Hours; or, Sketches Critical, Narrative, and Poetical*. 3 vols. London: Cadell and Davies, 1804.

Drazin, Charles. *Korda: Britain's Only Movie Mogul*. London: Sidgwick and Jackson, 2002.

DuBois, Gene W. "Blown up in the Mine Field: The 'Monoculturalist' Debate." *La Corónica* 29 (2000): 231–34.

Duggan, Christopher. *Francesco Crispi, 1818–1901: From Nation to Nationalism*. Oxford: Oxford University Press, 2002.

Dunlop, D. M. "David Colville, a Successor of Michael Scot." *Bulletin of Hispanic Studies* 28 (1951): 38–42.

———. "Hafs b. Albar—The Last of the Goths?" *Journal of the Royal Asiatic Society of Great Britain and Ireland* (1954): 136–51.

———. "Sobre Hafs ibn Albar al-Quti al-Qurtubi." *Al-Andalus* 20 (1955): 211–13.

*Encyclopédie ou Dictionnaire raisonné des sciences, des arts et de métiers*. The ARTFL Project at the University of Chicago. October 2007. http://www.lib.uchicago.edu/efts/ARTFL/projects/encyc/.

*Enrico Cerulli: Inventario dei manoscritti Cerulli etiopici*. Ed. Osvaldo Raineri. Città del Vaticano: Biblioteca Apostolica Vaticana, 2004.

Esposito, Anthony P. "Dismemberment of Things Past: Fixing the Jarchas." *La Corónica* 24 (1995): 4–14.

*A Faithful Sea: Religious Cultures and Identities in the Mediterranean, 1250–1750*. Ed. Adnan A. Husain and Katherine E. Fleming. Oxford, England: Oneworld Publications, 2007.

Al-Farabi. *Catálogo de las ciencias*. Ed. Angel González Palencia. Madrid: Estanislao Maestre, 1932.

Fernández y González, Francisco. *Estado social y político de los Mudéjares de Castilla, considerados en sí mismos y respecto de la civilización española*. Madrid: Joaquin Muñoz, 1866.

Filese, Teobaldo. *Trasformazione e fine del colonialismo*. Rome: Istituto italiano per l'Africa, 1955.

Forster, E. M. *Aspects of the Novel and Related Writings*. New York: Holmes & Meier, 1974.

Foscolo, Ugo. Review of *Dante; with a new Italian Commentary* by G. Baglioli, Paris, 1818, and *The Vision of Dante*, trans. Reverend H. F. Cary, London, 1818. *Edinburgh Review* 58 (February 1818): 453–74.

———. Review of *Osservazioni intorno alla questione sopra la originalità del Poema di Dante*, by F. Cancellieri. *Edinburgh Review* 60 (September 1818): 317–51.

Frantzen, Allen J. *Desire for Origins: New Language, Old English, and Teaching the Tradition*. New Brunswick, N.J., and London: Rutgers University Press, 1990.

Freller, Thomas. "'Adversus Infideles': Some Notes on the Cavalier's Tour, the Fleet of the Order of St. John, and the Maltese Corsairs." *Journal of Early Modern History* 4 (2000): 405–30.

Frendo, Henry. "National Identity." In *Malta: Culture and Identity*, ed. Henry Frendo and Oliver Friggieri, 1–25. Malta: Ministry of Youth and the Arts, 1994.

———. *Party Politics in a Fortress Colony: The Maltese Experience*. Valletta, Malta: Midsea Books, 1979.

Friggieri, Albert, and Thomas Freller. *Malta: The Bulwark of Europe. Hieronymus Megiser's Propugnaculum Europae. The first comprehensive German description of 16th century Malta*. Malta: Gutenberg, 1998.

Friggieri, Oliver. "Dun Karm, the National Poet of Malta: A Lyrical Interpretation of Life and Citizenship." *Neohelicon* 22 (1995): 157–67.

———. *Storia della letteratura maltese*. Milazzo, Italy: Spes, 1986.

Friggieri, Oliver, and Carmelo Psaila. *Il-Poeziji Migbura*. Valletta, Malta: Klabb Kotba Maltin, 1980.

Gabrieli, Francesco. "Apology for Orientalism." *Diogenes* 50 (1965): 128–36.

———. *Orientalisti del Novecento*. Rome: Istituto per l'Oriente, 1993.

———. *Pagine di diario*. Rome: Edizioni dell'Elefante, 2000.

———. "Il Petrarca e gli arabi." *Rivista di cultura classica e medioevale* 7 (1965): 487–94.

———. "Gli studi orientali." In *Cinquant'anni di vita intellettuale italiana*, ed. Carlo Antoni and Raffaele Mattioli, 2:91–111. Naples: Edizioni Scientifiche Italiane, 1950.

Galmes de Fuentes, Alvaro. *Las jarchas mozárabes: forma y significado*. Barcelona: Crítica, Grijalbo Mondadori, 1994.

———. "De nuevo sobre el significado de las jarchas mozárabes." *La Corónica* 29 (2000): 239–51.

Galoppini, Enrico. *Il fascismo e l'Islam*. Parma: Veltro, 2001.

———. "L'oggetto misterioso: L'immagine dell'Islàm nell'Italia tra le due guerre mondiali." *Africana: Rivista di studi extraeuropei*, 2005. January 2007. http://www.estovest .net/storia/immagine_islam.html.

García Gómez, Emilio. "A propósito del libro de K. Heger sobre las jaryas. Descifre de la jarya de Schirmann." *Al-Andalus* 26 (1961): 453–65.

———. "Don Miguel Asín y el pensamiento islámico." *Boletín de la Real Academia Española* 51 (1971): 383–412.

———. "Dos nuevas jaryas romances (XXV y XXVI) en muwaššahas árabes (ms. G. S. Colin)." *Al-Andalus* 19 (1954): 369–91.

———. "Estudio del 'Dar at-tiraz.'" *Al-Andalus* 27 (1962): 21–104.

———. "Hacia un 'refranero' arabigoandaluz: Los refranes poéticos de Ben Saraf (texto inédito)." *Al-Andalus* 36 (1971): 255–328.

———. *Las jarchas romances de la serie árabe en su marco: Edición en caracteres latinos, versión española en calco rítmico y estudio de 43 moaxajas andaluzas*. Madrid: Alianza Editorial, 1990.

———. "La 'ley de Mussafia' se aplica a la poesía estrófica arabigoandaluza." *Al-Andalus* 27 (1962): 1–20.

———. "La lírica hispano-árabe y la aparición de la lírica románica." *Al-Andalus* 21 (1956): 303–33.

———. "Mas sobre las 'jaryas' romances en 'muwaššahas' hebreas." *Al-Andalus* 14 (1949): 409–17.

———. "Métrica de la moaxaja y métrica española. Aplicación de un nuevo método de medición completa al 'Gais' de Ben al-Hatib." *Al-Andalus* 39 (1974): 1–255.

———. "La muwaššaha de Ibn Baqi de Cordoba *maa laday / sabrun mu'iinu* con jarya romance." *Al-Andalus* 19 (1954): 43–52.

———. "Un poema paremiológico de Hilli (s. XIV) en 'kan wa-kan' con unas observaciones sobre esta forma poética." *Al-Andalus* 36 (1971): 329–72.

———. "'Poetas en libertad condicional.'" *Al-Andalus* 42 (1977): 471–72.

———. Review of S. D. Goitein, *Jews and Arabs: Their Contacts throughout the Ages. Al-Andalus* 20 (1955): 467–69.

———. *Silla del Moro y nuevas escenas andaluzas.* Buenos Aires: Espasa-Calpe, 1954.

———. "Sobre una propuesta inglesa de correcciones al texto de Ben Quzman." *Al-Andalus* 43 (1978): 1–50.

———. "Los textos y los problemas de la casida zejelesca." *Al-Andalus* 26 (1961): 253–321.

———. "Veinticuatro jaryas romances en muwaššahas árabes (ms. G. S. Colin)." *Al-Andalus* 17 (1952): 57–127.

Gaunt, Simon, and Julian Weiss. "Cultural Traffic in the Medieval Romance World." *Journal of Romance Studies* 4 (2004) : 1–11.

Gayangos, Pascual de. *The History of the Mohammedan Dynasties in Spain.* 2 vols. London: The Oriental Translation Fund, 1840.

Giarrizzo, Giuseppe. *Cultura e economia nella Sicilia del '700.* Caltanissetta and Rome: Salvatore Sciascia, 1992.

Gibb, H. A. R. "Literature." In *The Legacy of Islam*, ed. Thomas Arnold and Alfred Guillaume, 180–209. Oxford: Clarendon Press, 1931.

Glick, Thomas F. *From Muslim Fortress to Christian Castle: Social and Cultural Change in Medieval Spain.* Manchester and New York: Manchester University Press, 1995.

Goitein, S. D. *A Mediterranean Society: The Jewish Communities of the Arab World as Portrayed in the Documents of the Cairo Geniza.* 6 vols. Berkeley: University of California Press, 1967–88.

Gottheil, Richard. "Two Forged Antiques." *Journal of the American Oriental Society* 33 (1913): 306–12.

Graham, John M. "National Identity and the Politics of Publishing the Troubadours." In *Medievalism and the Modernist Temper*, ed. R. Howard Bloch and Stephen G. Nichols, 57–94. Baltimore: Johns Hopkins University Press, 1996.

Grafton, Anthony. *Defenders of the Text: The Traditions of Scholarship in an Age of Science, 1450–1800.* Cambridge, Mass.: Harvard University Press, 1991.

Granara, William. "Nostalgia, Arab Nationalism, and the Andalusian Chronotope in the

Evolution of the Modern Arabic Novel." *Journal of Arabic Literature* 36 (2005): 57–73.

Grech, P. "A Portrait of Dun Karm." In *Dun Karm: Poet of Malta* 1–52. Cambridge: Cambridge University Press, 1961.

Greene, Molly. *A Shared World: Christians and Muslims in the Early Modern Mediterranean*. Princeton, N.J.: Princeton University Press, 2000.

Gregorio, Rosario. *Discorsi intorno alla Sicilia*. Palermo: Stamperia Reale, 1831.

———. *Rerum arabicarum quae ad historiam Siculam spectant ampla collectio*. Palermo: Ex regio typographeo, 1790.

Grotzfeld, Heinz. "The Age of the Galland Manuscript of the *Nights*." In *The Arabian Nights Reader*, ed. Ulrich Marzolph, 105–21. Detroit: Wayne State University Press, 2006.

———. "The Manuscript Tradition of the Arabian Nights." In *The Arabian Nights Encyclopedia,* ed. Ulrich Marzolph and Richard van Leeuwen, 1:17–21. Santa Barbara, Calif.: ABC-CLIO, 2004.

Guidi, Michelangelo. *Aspetti e problemi del mondo islamico*. Rome: Istituto Nazionale di Cultura Fascista, 1937.

Gumbrecht, Hans Ulrich. "A Philological Invention of Modernism: Menéndez Pidal, García Lorca, and the Harlem Renaissance." In *The Future of the Middle Ages: Medieval Literature in the 1990s*, ed. William D. Paden, 32–49. Gainesville: University Press of Florida, 1994.

———. *The Powers of Philology: Dynamics of Textual Scholarship*. Urbana and Chicago: University of Illinois Press, 2003.

Hanotaux, Gabriel, and Muhammad Abduh. *L'Europe et l'Islam*. Cairo: Imprimerie Jean Politis, 1905.

Hardison, O. B. "The Place of Averroes' Commentary on the *Poetics* in the History of Medieval Criticism." In *Medieval and Renaissance Studies: Proceedings of the Southeastern Institute of Medieval and Renaissance Studies, Summer, 1968*, ed. John L. Lievsay, 57–81. Durham, N.C.: Duke University Press, 1970.

Haskins, Charles Homer. *Studies in the History of Mediaeval Science*. New York: Ungar, 1924.

Haxen, Ulf. "The Mu'arada Concept and Its Musico-Rhythmical Implications: A Preliminary Clue." *Al-Andalus* 43 (1978): 113–24.

Heath, Peter. "Romance as Genre in the *Thousand and One Nights*." In *The Arabian Nights Reader*, ed. Ulrich Marzolph, 170–225. Detroit: Wayne State University Press, 2006.

Heisner, Beverly. *Hollywood Art: Art Direction in the Days of the Great Studios*. Jefferson, N.C., and London: McFarland, 1990.

Hermannus Alemannus. *De arte poetica*. In William de Moerbeka, *De arte poetica*, ed. Lorenzo Minio-Paluello, 40–74. Aristoteles Latinus 33. 2nd ed. Brussels and Paris: Desclée de Brouwer, 1968.

El-Hibri, Tayeb. *Reinterpreting Islamic Historiography*. Cambridge: Cambridge University Press, 1999.

Hitchcock, Richard. "The Interpretation of Romance Words in Arabic Texts: Theory and Practice." *La Corónica* 13 (1985): 243–54.

———. "Interpreting 'Romance' Kharjas." In *Studies on the Muwaššah and the* Kharja, ed. Alan Jones and Richard Hitchcock, 49–59. Oxford, England: Ithaca Press, 1991.

———. *Mozarabs in Medieval and Early Modern Spain*. Aldershot, England, and Burlington, Vt.: Ashgate, 2008.

Hodge, A. A. *Outlines of Theology*. 1879. Rpt., Grand Rapids, Mich.: Zondervan Publishing House, 1972.

Hodgson, Marshall. *Rethinking World History: Essays on Europe, Islam, and World History*. Ed. Edmund Burke III. Cambridge: Cambridge University Press, 1993.

Hole, Richard. *Remarks on the Arabian Nights Entertainments; in which the Origin of Sindbad's Voyages, and Other Oriental Fictions, is Particularly Considered*. London: Cadell and Davies, 1797.

Hopkins, Gerard Manley. *The Journals and Papers of Gerard Manley Hopkins*. Ed. Humphry House and Graham Storey. London: Oxford University Press, 1959.

Horden, Peregrine, and Nicholas Purcell. *The Corrupting Sea: A Study of Mediterranean History*. Oxford, England, and Malden, Mass.: Blackwell, 2000.

Hourani, Albert. *Islam in European Thought*. Cambridge: Cambridge University Press, 1991.

Hull, Geoffrey. *The Malta Language Question: A Case History in Cultural Imperialism*. Valletta, Malta: Said International, 1993.

Hult, David. "Gaston Paris and the Invention of Courtly Love." In *Medievalism and the Modernist Temper*, ed. R. Howard Bloch and Stephen G. Nichols, 192–224. Baltimore: Johns Hopkins University Press, 1996.

———. "Reading It Right: The Ideology of Text Editing." *Romanic Review* 1988 (79): 74–88.

Husayn, Taha. *The Days*. Trans. E. H. Paxton, Hilary Wayment, and Kenneth Cragg. Cairo: The American University in Cairo Press, 1997.

Ibn al-Nadim. *Al-Fihrist*. Ed. Yusuf Ali Tawil. Beirut: Dar al-Kutub al-'Ilmiyya, 1996.

———. *The Fihrist*. Trans. Bayard Dodge. 2 vols. New York and London: Columbia University Press, 1970.

Irwin, Robert. *The Arabian Nights: A Companion*. London: Allen Lane, 1994.

———. "The Arabian Nights in Film Adaptations." In *The Arabian Nights Encyclopedia*, ed. Ulrich Marzolph and Richard van Leeuwen, 1:22–25. Santa Barbara, Calif.: ABC-CLIO, 2004.

———. *For Lust of Knowing: The Orientalists and Their Enemies*. London and New York: Allen Lane, 2006.

———. "*A Thousand and One Nights* at the Movies." *Middle Eastern Literatures* 7 (2004): 223–33.

*Eine Italianische Prosaversion der Sieben Weisen Meister*. Ed. Hermann Varnhagen. Berlin: Weidmannsche, 1881.

Johannis de Alta Silva. *Dolopathos sive de Rege et Septem Sapientibus*. Ed. Hermann Oesterley. London: Trübner, 1878.

Johns, Jeremy. *Arabic Administration in Norman Sicily: The Royal Diwan*. Cambridge: Cambridge University Press, 2002.

Johnson, Barbara. "Philology: What Is at Stake?" *Comparative Literature Studies* 27 (1990): 26–29.

Jones, Alan. "Eppur si muove." *La Corónica* 12 (1983): 45–70.

———. *Romance* Kharjas *in Andalusian Arabic* Muwaššah *Poetry: A Palaeographical Analysis*. London and Atlantic Highlands, N.J.: Ithaca Press, 1988.

———. "Sunbeams from Cucumbers? An Arabist's Assessment of the State of Kharja Studies." *La Corónica* 10 (1981): 38–53.

Karm, Dun. *Dun Karm: Poet of Malta*. Trans. A. J. Arberry. Cambridge: Cambridge University Press, 1961.

Kay, Sarah. "The New Philology." *New Medieval Literatures* 3 (1999): 295–326.

Keddie, Nikki R. *Sayyid Jamal al-Din "al-Afghani": A Political Biography*. Berkeley and Los Angeles: University of California Press, 1972.

Keenan, Patrick Joseph. *Report upon the educational system of Malta*. Dublin: Alexander Thom, 1879.

Kelley, Mary Jane. "Virgins Misconceived: Poetic Voice in the Mozarabic Kharjas." *La Corónica* 19 (1991): 1–23.

Kennedy, Hugh. *The Early Abbasid Caliphate: A Political History*. London: Croom Helm, 1981.

Kennedy, Philip F. "The Muslim Sources of Dante?" In *The Arab Influence in Medieval Europe*, ed. Dionisius A. Agius and Richard Hitchcock, 63–82. Reading, England: Ithaca Press, 1994.

Kerr, Malcolm. *Islamic Reform: The Political and Legal Theories of Muhammad 'Abduh and Rashid Rida*. Berkeley and Los Angeles: University of California Press, 1966.

Kinoshita, Sharon. *Medieval Boundaries: Rethinking Difference in Old French Literature*. Philadelphia: University of Pennsylvania Press, 2006.

Kirkham, Victoria, and María Rosa Menocal. "Reflections on the 'Arabic' World: Boccaccio's Ninth Stories." *Stanford Italian Review* 7 (1987): 95–110.

Kontje, Todd. *German Orientalisms*. Ann Arbor: University of Michigan Press, 2004.

Kulik, Karol. *Alexander Korda: The Man Who Could Work Miracles*. New Rochelle, N.Y.: Arlington House Publishers, 1975.

Labella, Silvio et al. *Ad Amedeo Savoia Aosta omaggio di aeropoesie guerriere offerto dagli aeropoeti futuristi Silvio Labella, Renato Di Nicola, Vanda Macrini, Giovanni Menichino, Gino Celli, Tullio Previtera, A. Chiocchio del Gruppo romano futurista Gondar*. Rome: Edizioni futuriste di *Poesia*, 1942.

Lane, Edward William, trans. *Arabian Nights' Entertainments; or, the Thousand and One Nights*. New York: Tudor Publishing, 1927.

Lanza, Pietro. *Degli Arabi e del loro soggiorno in Sicilia*. Palermo: Pedone e Muratori, 1832.

Latham, J. D. "Ibn al-Muqaffa' and Early Abbasid Prose." In *The Cambridge History of Arabic Literature: Abbasid Belles-Lettres*, ed. Julia Ashtiany, T. M. Johnstone, J. D. Latham, R. B. Serjeant, and G. Rex Smith, 48–77. Cambridge: Cambridge University Press, 1990.

Lee, A. C. *The Decameron: Its Sources and Analogues.* New York: Haskell House, 1966.

Leopardi, Giacomo. *Opere.* Ed. Giovanni Getto. Milan: Mursia, 1975.

Levi Della Vida, Giorgio. "Carlo Alfonso Nallino." In Carlo Alfonso Nallino, *Raccolta di scritti editi e inediti,* ed. Maria Nallino, 6:408–34. Rome: Istituto per l'Oriente, 1948.

———. *Fantasmi ritrovati.* Ed. M. G. Amadasi Guzzo and F. Tessitore. Naples: Liguori, 2004.

———. "Nuova luce sulle fonti islamiche della *Divina Commedia.*" *Al-Andalus* 14 (1949): 377–407.

Lewis, Charlton T., and Charles Short. *A Latin Dictionary.* Tufts University. February 2008. http://www.perseus.tufts.edu/cgi-bin/resolveform?lang = Latin.

*Il libro dei Sette Savi di Roma.* Ed. Alessandro d'Ancona. Pisa: Nistri, 1864.

*Il libro dei Sette Savi di Roma.* Ed. Antonio Cappelli. Bologna: Gaetano Romagnoli, 1865.

*Il libro de' Sette Savi di Roma.* Ed. F. Roediger. Florence: Libreria Dante, 1883.

*El Libro de los Engaños.* Ed. John Esten Keller. Chapel Hill: University of North Carolina Press, 1953.

Lockman, Zachary. *Contending Visions of the Middle East: The History and Politics of Orientalism.* Cambridge and New York: Cambridge University Press, 2004.

Lowe, Lisa. *Critical Terrains: French and British Orientalisms.* Ithaca, N.Y.: Cornell University Press, 1991.

Machiavelli, Niccolò. *Discorsi sopra la prima deca di Tito Livio.* Ed. Francesco Bausi. 2 vols. Rome: Salerno, 2001.

Mai, Angelo. *Epistolario.* Ed. Gianni Gervasoni. 2 vols. Florence: Felice Le Monnier, 1954.

Mahdi, Muhsin. "From History to Fiction: The Tale Told by the King's Steward in *The Thousand and One Nights.*" In The Thousand and One Nights *in Arabic Literature and Society,* ed. Richard G. Hovannisian and Georges Sabagh, 78–105. Cambridge: Cambridge University Press, 1997.

———. "The Sources of Galland's *Nuits.*" In *The Arabian Nights Reader,* ed. Ulrich Marzolph, 122–36. Detroit: Wayne State University Press, 2006.

———. *The Thousand and One Nights.* Leiden: Brill, 1995.

———, ed. *The Thousand and One Nights.* Leiden: Brill, 1984.

Mallette, Karla. "Beyond Mimesis: Aristotle's *Poetics* in the Medieval Mediterranean." *PMLA* 124 (2009): 583–91.

———. "Dante as Poet of Exile and Resistance." In *Dante's New Life in Twentieth-Century Literature: Modern Intertextual Appropriation of Dante,* ed. Massimo Ciavolella and Gianluca Rizzo, forthcoming.

———. *The Kingdom of Sicily, 1100–1250: A Literary History.* Philadelphia: University of Pennsylvania Press, 2005.

———. "Muhammad in Hell." *Dante Studies* 125 (2007): 207–24.

———. "Orientalism and the Nineteenth Century Nationalist: Michele Amari, Ernest Renan, and 1848." *Romanic Review* 96 (2005): 233–52.

Malta. Debates of the Council of Government of Malta in the session 1880–81. Vol. V, 7 December 1880 to 19 May 1881, sittings no. 1 to 20. Malta: Government Printing Office, 1881.

———. Reports of the Commissioners appointed to inquire into the Affairs of the State of Malta. Part II, continuation of Parliament Paper no. 141, 1837–38.

The Malta Royal Commission, 1931. Minutes of Evidence. Malta: Government Printing Office, 1931.

Malti-Douglas, Fedwa. "Shahrazad Feminist." In *The Arabian Nights Reader*, ed. Ulrich Marzolph, 347–64. Detroit: Wayne State University Press, 2006.

Marcos-Marin, Francisco A. "Aproximación cuantitativa al estudio de las jarchas en muwaxahas árabes." *La Corónica* 24 (1995): 124–52.

Marín, Manuela. "Arabistas en España: Un asunto de familia." *Al-Qantara* 13 (1992): 379–93.

Martin, Laura. "'Eskimo Words for Snow': A Case Study in the Genesis and Decay of an Anthropological Example." *American Anthropologist* n.s. 88 (1986): 418–23.

Martorana, Carmelo. *Notizie storiche dei saraceni siciliani*. 2 vols. Palermo: Pedone e Muratori, 1832–33.

Matar, Hisham. *In the Country of Men*. New York: Dial Press, 2006.

Mazzotta, Giuseppe. *The Worlds of Petrarch*. Durham, N.C.: Duke University Press, 1993.

Melman, Billie. *Women's Orients: English Women and the Middle East, 1718–1918*. Ann Arbor: University of Michigan Press, 1992.

Menéndez Pidal, Ramón. *La Chanson de Roland y el neotradicionalismo*. Madrid: Espasa-Calpe, 1959.

Menocal, María Rosa. "An Andalusianist's Last Sigh." *La Corónica* 24 (1996): 179–89.

———. *The Arabic Role in Medieval Literary History: A Forgotten Heritage*. Philadelphia: University of Pennsylvania Press, 1987.

———. "Bottom of the Ninth: Bases Loaded." *La Corónica* 17 (1988): 32–40.

———. *The Ornament of the World: How Muslims, Jews, and Christians Created a Culture of Tolerance in Medieval Spain*. Boston: Little, Brown, 2002.

———. *Shards of Love: Exile and the Origins of the Lyric*. Durham, N.C.: Duke University Press, 1994.

*Les Mille et une nuits*. Trans. Antoine Galland. 3 vols. Paris: Flammarion, 2004.

Millet-Gérard, Dominique. *Chrétiens Mozarabes et culture islamique dans l'Espagne des VIIIᵉ–IXᵉ siècles*. Paris: Études Augustiniennes, 1984.

Miquel, André. "*The Thousand and One Nights* in Arabic Literature and Society." In The Thousand and One Nights *in Arabic Literature and Society*, ed. Richard G. Hovannisian and Georges Sabagh, 6–13. Cambridge: Cambridge University Press, 1997.

Mira, Giuseppe M. *Bibliografia siciliana ovvero Gran dizionario bibliografico delle opere edite e inedite, antiche e moderni di autori siciliani o di argomento siciliano stampate in Sicilia e fuori*. 2 vols. Palermo: G. B. Gaudiano, 1875.

"Miscelanea internacional sobre las jaryas mozarabes. I: S. M. Stern, Some textual notes on the romance jaryas. II: Juan Corominas, Para la interpretacion de las jaryas recien halladas (ms. G.S. Colin). III: I. S. Révah, Note sur le mot "matrana" (Garcia Gomez, jaryas nos. XVII et XIX)." *Al-Andalus* 18 (1953): 133–48.

Monneret de Villard, Ugo. *Lo studio dell'Islam in Europa nel XII e nel XIII secolo*. Vatican City: Biblioteca Apostolica Vaticana, 1944.

Monroe, James T. *Hispano-Arabic Poetry: A Student Anthology*. Berkeley: University of California Press, 1974.

———. *Islam and the Arabs in Spanish Scholarship: Sixteenth Century to the Present*. Leiden: Brill, 1970.

———. "Maimonides on the Mozarabic Lyric." *La Corónica* 17 (1988–89): 18–32.

———. "Pedir peras al olmo? On Medieval Arabs and Modern Arabists." *La Corónica* 10 (1982): 121–47.

———. "A Sounding Brass and Tinkling Cymbal: Al-Halil in Andalus: Two Notes on the Muwaššaha." *La Corónica* 15 (1987): 252–58.

Morso, Salvatore. *Descrizione di Palermo antico ricavata sugli autori sincroni e i monumenti de' tempi*. Palermo: Lorenzo Dato, 1827.

Mortillaro, Vincenzo. *Lettera del Marchese Vincenzo Mortillaro*. Palermo: P. Pensante, 1868.

———. *Opere*. Vol. 8. Palermo: Pietro Pensante, 1861.

———. *Reminiscenze de' miei tempi*. Palermo: Pietro Pensante, 1865.

———. *La storia, gli scrittori e le monete dell'epoca arabo-sicula*. In *Opere* 3:243–26. Palermo: Oretea, 1846.

Mottahedeh, Roy P. "'Aja'ib in *The Thousand and One Nights*." In The Thousand and One Nights *in Arabic Literature and Society*, ed. Richard G. Hovannisian and Georges Sabagh, 29–39. Cambridge: Cambridge University Press, 1997.

Muhammad 'Abdu. *The Theology of Unity*. Trans. Ishaq Musa'ad and Kenneth Cragg. New York: Books for Libraries, 1980.

Müller-Sievers, Helmut. "Reading Evidence: Textual Criticism as Science in the Nineteenth Century." *The Germanic Review* 76 (2001): 162–71.

———. "Reading Without Interpreting: German Textual Criticism and the Case of George Büchner." *Modern Philology* 103 (2006): 498–518.

Muñoz Sendino, José. *La Escala de Mahoma: Traducción del árabe al castellano, latín y francés, ordenada por Alfonso X el Sabio*. Madrid: Ministerio de Asuntos Exteriores, 1949.

Mussafia, Adolf, ed. *Beiträge zur Litteratur der Sieben Weisen Meister*. Vienna: K. Gerold's Sohn, 1868.

Nafisi, Azar. *Reading Lolita in Tehran: A Memoir in Books*. New York: Random House, 2003.

Nallino, Carlo Alfonso. "I principali risultati del viaggio di Enrico Cerulli nell'Etiopia Occidentale nel 1927–1928." *Oriente moderno* 13 (1933): 430–36.

———. Review of *La escatología musulmana en la* Divina Comedia, by Miguel Asín Palacios. *Rivista degli studi orientali* 3 (1919–21): 800–819.

Nardi, Bruno. *Dal 'Convivio' alla 'Commedia': Sei saggi danteschi*. 1960. Rome: Borromini, 1992.

———. *Dante e la cultura medievale*. Bari: Laterza, 1949.

———. *Saggi di filosofia dantesca*. Florence: La Nuova Italia, 1967.

Nelson, Deborah. "Gaston Paris in Context: His Predecessors and His Legacy." *Studies in Medievalism* 2 (1983): 53–66.

Nichols, Stephen G. "Introduction: Philology in a Manuscript Culture." *Speculum* 65 (1990): 1–10.

Nietzsche, Friedrich. *Werke*. 9 vols. Ed. Giorgio Colli and Mazzino Montinari. Berlin and New York: Walter de Gruyter, 1982.

Norris, H. T. "Fables and Legends." In *The Cambridge History of Arabic Literature: Abbasid Belles-Lettres*, ed. Julia Ashtiany, T. M. Johnstone, J. D. Latham, R. B. Serjeant, and G. Rex Smith, 136–45. Cambridge: Cambridge University Press, 1990.

"Il nostro programma." *Oriente Moderno* 1 (1921–22): 1–2.

Nykrog, Per. "A Warrior Scholar at the Collège de France: Joseph Bédier." In *Medievalism and the Modernist Temper*, ed. R. Howard Bloch and Stephen G. Nichols, 286–307. Baltimore: Johns Hopkins University Press, 1996.

*On Philology*. Ed. Jan. Ziolkowski. University Park, Pa.: Pennsylvania State University Press, 1990.

*The Oxford English Dictionary*. Ed. J. A. Simpson and E. S. C. Weiner. 20 vols. Oxford: Clarendon Press; New York: Oxford University Press, 1989.

Ouyang, Wen-Chin. "Whose Story Is It? Sinbad the Sailor in Literature and Film." *Middle Eastern Literatures* 7 (2004): 133–47.

Pace, Paul. *The Language Question 1920–1934. A Critical Edition of the Relevant Documents*. 4 vols. M.A. thesis, Royal University of Malta, 1975.

Paden, William D., ed. *The Future of the Middle Ages: Medieval Literature in the 1990s*. Gainesville: University Press of Florida, 1994

Pankhurst, Richard. "Italian Fascist War Crimes in Ethiopia: A History of Their Discussion, from the League of Nations to the United Nations (1936–1949)." *Northeast African Studies* 6 (1999): 83–140.

———. "The Secret History of the Italian Fascist Occupation of Ethiopia—1935–1941." *African Quarterly* 16 (1977): 35–86.

Paris, Gaston. "La Chanson de Roland et la nationalité française." In *La Poésie du Moyen Âge: Leçons et lectures*, 87–118. Paris: Hachette, 1903.

———. *Deux rédactions du Roman des Sept Sages de Rome*. Paris: Firmin Didot, 1876.

Pasquali, Giorgio. *Storia della tradizione e critica del testo*. Florence: Felice le Monnier, 1952.

Patterson, Lee. "The Return to Philology." In *The Past and Future of Medieval Studies*, ed. John van Egen, 231–44. Notre Dame: University of Notre Dame Press, 1994.

Payne, John, trans. *The Book of the Thousand Nights and One Night*. 9 vols. London: privately printed, 1914.

Peck, Jeffrey M. " 'In the Beginning was the Word': Germany and the Origins of German Studies." In *Medievalism and the Modernist Temper*, ed. R. Howard Bloch and Stephen G. Nichols, 127–47. Baltimore: Johns Hopkins University Press, 1996.

Petrarch, Francesco. *Canzoniere*. Ed. Gianfranco Contini and Daniele Ponchirole. Turin: Einaudi, 1966.

———. "Invective Contra Medicum." In *Opere Latine di Francesco Petrarca*, ed. Antonietta Bufano, 2:818–981. Turin: Unione Tipografico-Editrice Torinese, 1975.

———. *Letters of Old Age*. Trans. Aldo S. Bernardo, Saul Levin, and Reta A. Bernardo. 2 vols. Baltimore and London: Johns Hopkins University Press, 1992.

———. *Letters on Familiar Matters*. Trans. Aldo S. Bernardo. 2 vols. Baltimore and London: Johns Hopkins University Press, 1985.

———. *Le "Senili" secondo l'edizione Basilea 1581*. Ed. Marziano Guglielminetti. Savigliano, Italy: l'Artistica Editrice, 2006.

Petrusewicz, Marta. *Come il Meridione divenne una questione: Rappresentazioni del Sud prima e dopo il Quarantotto*. Catanzaro, Italy: Rubbettino, 1998.

Pickens, Rupert T. "The Future of Old French Studies in America: The 'Old' Philology and the Crisis of the 'New.'" In *The Future of the Middle Ages: Medieval Literature in the 1990s*, ed. William D. Paden, 53–86. Gainesville: University Press of Florida, 1994.

Pinault, David. *Story-Telling Techniques in the Arabian Nights*. Leiden: Brill, 1992.

Pirandello, Luigi. *Sei personaggi in cerca d'autore*. In *Maschere nude*, 1:31–116. Milan: Mondadori, 1958.

Pirenne, Henri. *Muhammad and Charlemagne*. Trans. Bernard Miall. New York: Barnes & Noble, 1939.

Poe, Edgar Allan. *The Complete Works of Edgar Allan Poe*. Ed. James A. Harrison. 17 vols. New York: Society of English and French Literature, 1902.

Preto, Paolo. "Una lunga storia di falsi e falsari." *Mediterranea: Ricerche storiche* 3 (2006): 11–38.

*The Princeton Theology 1812–1921: Scripture, Science, and Theological Method from Archibald Alexander to Benjamin Breckinridge Warfield*. Ed. Mark A. Noll. Grand Rapids, Mich.: Baker Book House, 1983.

Rajna, Pio. *Le fonti dell'Orlando Furioso*. Florence: Sansoni, 1900.

Ramírez Caliente, Ángel. "Jarchas, moaxajas, zejeles I." *Al-Andalus* 39 (1974): 273–99.

———. "Jarchas, moaxajas, zejeles II." *Al-Andalus* 41 (1976): 147–78.

———. "Jarchas, moaxajas, zejeles III." *Al-Andalus* 41 (1976): 385–408.

———. "Jarchas, moaxajas, zejeles IV." *Al-Andalus* 43 (1978): 173–80.

Reeve, J. J. "My Personal Experience with the Higher Criticism." In *The Fundamentals: A Testimony to the Truth* 3:98–118. Chicago: Testimony Publishing Company, n.d..

Reid, Donald Malcolm. "Cairo University and the Orientalists." *International Journal of Middle East Studies* 19 (1987): 51–76.

Renan, Ernest. *Averroès et l'Averroïsme*. In *Œuvres complètes*, ed. Henriette Psichari, 3:11–374. Paris: Calmann-Lévy, 1949.

———. *De la part des peuples sémitiques dans l'histoire de la civilisation. Discours d'ouverture du cours de langues hébraïque, chaldaïque, et syriaque au Collège de France*. Paris: Michel Lévy Frères, 1862.

———. *Œuvres complètes*. 10 vols. Paris: Calmann-Lévy, 1947–61.

*Rethinking the Mediterranean*. Ed. W. V. Harris. Oxford: Oxford University Press, 2005.

Reynolds, Dwight. "Arab Musical Influence on Medieval Europe: A Reassessment." In *A Sea of Languages: Literature and Culture in the Pre-Modern Mediterranean*, ed. Suzanne Akbari and Karla Mallette, forthcoming.

———. "Music." In *Cambridge History of Arabic Literature: The Literature of al-Andalus*, ed. María Rosa Menocal, Raymond P. Scheindlin, and Michael Sells, 60–82. Cambridge: Cambridge University Press, 2000.

———. "Popular Prose in the Post-Classical Period." In *Cambridge History of Arabic Literature: Arabic Literature in the Post-Classical Period,* ed. Roger Allen and D. S. Richards, 245–69. Cambridge: Cambridge University Press, 2006.

———. "*A Thousand and One Nights:* A History of the Text and Its Reception." In *Cambridge History of Arabic Literature: Arabic Literature in the Post-Classical Period*, ed. Roger Allen and D. S. Richards, 270–91. Cambridge: Cambridge University Press, 2006.

Ribera y Tarragó, Julián. *Disertaciones y opúsculos.* 2 vols. Madrid: Estanislao Maestre, 1928.

Ricci, Lanfranco. "Enrico Cerulli." *Atti della Accademia Nazionale dei Lincei* 44 (1989): 103–13.

Rickitt, Richard. *Special Effects: The History and Technique.* New York: Billboard Books, 2000.

Rivetta, Pietro Silvio. *Il Centauro Maltese ovvero Mostruosità Linguistiche nell'Isola dei Cavalieri.* Milan: Ceschina, 1940.

Rivinius, Karl Josef. *Das Collegium Sinicum zu Neapel und seine Umwandlung in ein Orientalisches Institut: Ein Beitrag zu seiner Geschichte.* Sankt Augustin, Germany: Institut Monumenta Serica, 2004.

Robinson, Cynthia and Leyla Rouhi, ed. *Under the Influence: Questioning the Comparative in Medieval Castille.* Leiden: Brill, 2005.

Rodinson, Maxime. "Dante et l'Islam d'après des travaux récents." *Revue de l'histoire de religion* 140 (1951): 203–36.

Rossetti, Gabriele. *La vita mia.* Lanciano: R. Carabba, 1910.

Safran, Janina M. "Identity and Differentiation in Ninth-Century al-Andalus." *Speculum* 76 (2001): 573–98.

Sage, Carleton M. *Paul Albar of Cordoba: Studies on His Life and Writings.* Washington, D.C.: The Catholic University of America Press, 1943.

Said, Edward. *Humanism and Democratic Criticism.* New York: Columbia University Press, 2004.

Savoia, Luigi Amedeo di. *La esplorazione dello Uabi-Uebi Scebeli dalle sue sorgenti nella Etiopia meridionale alla Somalia italiana (1928–29).* Milan: Mondadori, 1932.

Sbacchi, Alberto. *Ethiopia Under Mussolini: Fascism and the Colonial Experience.* London: Zed Books, 1985.

———. "Italy and the Treatment of the Ethiopian Aristocracy." *International Journal of African Historical Studies* 10 (1977): 209–41.

Schmidt, P. L. "Lachmann's Method: On the History of a Misunderstanding." In *The Uses of Greek and Latin: Historical Essays*, ed. A. C. Dionisotti and Anthony Grafton, 227–36. London: Warburg Institute, University of London, 1988.

Scinà, Domenico, and Adelaide Baviera Albanese. *L'arabica impostura.* Palermo: Sellerio, 1978.

Scott, Walter. *The Life of Napoleon Bonaparte, Emperor of the French.* 9 vols. Paris: A. and W. Galignani, 1827.

Scrofani, Saverio. *Della dominazione degli stranieri in Sicilia.* Paris: Boucher, 1824.

Sercambi, Giovanni. *Novelle inedite.* Ed. Rodolfo Renier. Bologna: Forni, 1971.

Sessona, Anna Zambelli. "The Rewriting of *The Arabian Nights* by Imil Habibi." *Middle Eastern Literatures* 5 (2002): 29–48.

Simmons, Clare A. "'Iron-Worded Proof': Victorian Identity and the Old English Language." *Studies in Medievalism* 4 (1992): 202–13.

Simonet, Francisco Javier. *Glosario de voces ibéricas y Latinas usadas entre los mozárabes.* Madrid: Establecimiento Tipográfico de Fortanet, 1888.

Sola-Solé, Josep M. *Corpus de poesía mozárabe: las harga-s andalusies.* Barcelona: Ediciones Hispam, 1973.

Soravia, Bruna. "Ascesa e declino dell'orientalismo scientifico in Italia." In *Il mondo visto dall'Italia,* ed. Agostino Giovagnoli and Giorgio Del Zanna, 271–86. Milan: Guerini, 2004.

Spaggiari, William. "La 'minzogna saracina': Giuseppe Vella e la contraffazione dei codici arabo-siculi nel giudizio di Antonio Panizzi." *Bibliofilia: Rivista di Storia del Libro e di Bibliografia* 99 (1997): 271–306.

Spitzer, Leo. *Linguistics and Literary History: Essays in Stylistics.* Princeton, N.J.: Princeton University Press, 1948.

Stern, S. M. "Four Famous muwaššaḥs from Ibn Busra's Anthology." *Al-Andalus* 23 (1958): 339–69.

———. *Hispano-Arabic Strophic Poetry.* Oxford: Clarendon Press, 1974.

———. "Un muwaššaḥ arabe avec terminaison espagnole." *Al-Andalus* 14 (1949): 214–18.

———. "Les vers finaux en espagnol dans les muwaššaḥs hispano-hébraïques. Une contribution à l'histoire du muwaššaḥ et à l'étude du vieux dialecte espagnol 'mozarabe.'" *Al-Andalus* 13 (1948): 300–343.

Stetkevych, Suzanne P. "Toward a Redefinition of 'Badi'' Poetry." *Journal of Arabic Literature* 12 (1981): 1–29.

Stone, Gregory B. *Dante's Pluralism and the Islamic Philosophy of Religion.* New York: Palgrave Macmillan, 2006.

*Storia di Stefano, Figliuolo d'un Imperatore di Roma.* Ed. Pio Rajna. Bologna: Gaetano Romagnoli, 1880.

Strika, Vincenzo. "C. A. Nallino e l'impresa libica." *Quaderni di studi arabi* 2 (1984): 9–20.

*Gli studi sul vicino oriente in Italia dal 1921 al 1970.* 2 vols. Pubblicazioni dell'Istituto per l'Oriente 63. Rome: Istituto per l'Oriente, 1971.

*Syntipas.* Ed. Jean-François Boissonade. Paris: G. Doyen, 1828.

Al-Tabari. *The 'Abbasid Caliphate in Equilibrium.* Trans. C. E. Bosworth. *The History of al-Tabari,* vol. 30. Albany: State University of New York Press, 1989.

Tabori, Paul. *Alexander Korda.* London: Oldbourne, 1959.

Tamrat, Taddesse. "Enrico Cerulli (1898–1988): In Appreciation of His Great Ethiopian Scholarship." *Journal of Ethiopian Studies* (Addis Ababa) 23 (1990): 85–92.

Tennyson, Alfred. *The Poems of Tennyson.* Ed. Christopher Ricks. 3 vols. Berkeley and Los Angeles: University of California Press, 1987.

Tessitore, Fulvio. *Schizzi e schegge di storiografia arabo-islamica italiana.* Bari, Italy: Palomar, 1995.

Thackeray, W. M. *Irish Sketch Book and Notes of a Journey from Cornhill to Grand Cairo.* London: Smith, Elder & Co., 1870.

Timpanaro, Sebastiano. "Angelo Mai." In *Aspetti e figure della cultura ottocentesca*, 225–71. Pisa: Nistri-Lischi, 1980.

———. *The Genesis of Lachmann's Method.* Ed. and trans. Glenn W. Most. Chicago and London: University of Chicago Press, 2005.

Todd, H. A. "Gaston Paris: Romance Philologist and Member of the French Academy." *PMLA* 12 (1897): 341–54.

Todorov, Tzvetan. "Narrative Men." In *The Arabian Nights Reader*, ed. Ulrich Marzolph, 226–38. Detroit: Wayne State University Press, 2006.

Uitti, Karl. "Philology." In *The Johns Hopkins Guide to Literary Theory and Criticism*, ed. Michael Groden and Martin Kreiswirth, 567–73. Baltimore: Johns Hopkins University Press, 1994.

United Nations War Crimes Commission. *History of the United Nations War Crimes Commission and the Development of the Laws of War.* London: His Majesty's Stationery Office, 1948.

Urvoy, Dominique. *Ibn Rushd, Averroes.* Trans. Olivia Stewart. London and New York: Routledge, 1991.

Urvoy, Marie-Thérèse. "Note de philologie mozarabe." *Arabica* 36 (1989): 235–36.

———. *Le Psautier mozarabe de Hafs le Goth.* Toulouse: Presses Universitaires du Mirail, 1994.

Valerga, Pietro. *Il divano di ʿOmar Ben-al Fàreʾd tradotto e paragonato col canzoniere del Petrarca.* Florence: Cellini, 1874.

Vannucci, Atto. "Dei recenti studj sulla antica civiltà arabica e della storia dei musulmani in Sicilia di Michele Amari." *Archivio storico italiano* n.s. 3 (1856): 131–70.

Varvaro, Pietro. "Giuseppe Vella e i suoi falsi codici arabi con un documento inedito." *Archivio storico siciliano* n.s. 30 (1905): 321–32.

Vassalli, Mikiel Anton. *Grammatica della Lingua Maltese.* 2nd ed. Malta: Stampata per l'autore, 1827.

———. *Lexicon.* Ed. Frans Sammut. Malta: Mitbugh fil-Marsa Press, 2002.

Voll, John O. "Fundamentalism in the Sunni Arab World: Egypt and the Sudan." In *Fundamentalisms Observed*, ed. Martin E. Marty and R. Scott Appleby, 345–402.

Wacks, David. *Framing Iberia: Maqamat and Frametale Narratives in Medieval Spain.* Leiden: Brill, 2007.

Walther, Wiebke. "Modern Arabic Literature and the Arabian Nights." In *The Arabian Nights Encyclopedia,* ed. Ulrich Marzolph and Richard van Leeuwen, 1:54–61. Santa Barbara, Calif.: ABC-CLIO, 2004.

Waltz, James. "The Significance of the Voluntary Martyrs of Ninth-Century Córdoba." *Muslim World* 60 (1970): 143–59, 226–36.

Wansbrough, John. "Diplomatica Siciliana." *Bulletin of the School of Oriental and African Studies* 1 (1984): 10–21.

———. *Lingua Franca in the Mediterranean*. Surrey, England: Curzon, 1996.

———. "Mamluk Letter of 877/1473." *Bulletin of the School of African and Oriental Studies* 24 (1961): 200–213.

Warren, Michelle. "'Au commencement était l'île': The Colonial Formation of Joseph Bédier's *Chanson de Roland*." In *Postcolonial Approaches to the European Middle Ages*, ed. Ananya Jahanara Kabir and Deanne Williams, 205–26. Cambridge: Cambridge University Press, 2005.

Waugh, Evelyn. *The Essays, Articles and Reviews of Evelyn Waugh*. Ed. Donat Gallagher. London: Methuen, 1983.

———. *Waugh in Abyssinia*. London: Methuen, 1984.

Weinberg, Bernard. *A History of Literary Criticism in the Italian Renaissance*. 2 vols. Chicago: University of Chicago Press, 1961.

Wettinger, Godfrey. *The Arabs in Malta*. Reprinted from *Malta: Studies of Its Heritage and History*, 87–104. Malta: Mid-Med Bank, 1986.

Wettinger, Godfrey, and M. Fsadni. *Peter Caxaro's Cantilena: A Poem in Medieval Maltese*. Malta: Lux Press, 1968.

Whinnom, Keith. "The Mamma of the Kharjas or Some Doubts Concerning Arabists and Romanists." *La Corónica* 11 (1982): 11–17.

Wilkins, Ernest H. "The Genealogy of the Genealogical Trees of the 'Genealogia Deorum.'" *Modern Philology* 23 (1925): 61–65.

William de Moerbeke. *De arte poetica*. Ed. Lorenzo Minio-Paluello. Aristoteles Latinus 33. 2nd ed. Brussels and Paris: Desclée de Brouwer, 1968.

Wolf, Kenneth Baxter. *Christian Martyrs in Muslim Spain*. Cambridge: Cambridge University Press, 1988.

Wright, Owen. "Music in Muslim Spain." In *The Legacy of Muslim Spain*, ed. Salma Khadra Jayyusi, 555–80. Leiden: Brill, 1992.

Zapperi, Robert. "La 'fortuna' di un avventuriero: Saverio Scrofani e i suoi biografi." *Rassegna Storico del Risorgimento* 49 (1962): 447–84.

Zwartjes, Otto. "La alternancia de código como recurso estilístico en las xarja-s andalusies." *La Corónica* 22 (1994): 1–51.

———. *Love Songs from al-Andalus: History, Structure and Meaning of the* Kharja. Leiden: Brill, 1997.

Zwemer, Samuel Marinus. "Editorial." *The Moslem World* 1 (1911): 1–4.

# INDEX

ACKNOWLEDGMENTS

WHILE WRITING THIS book I led a life even more nomadic than most academics', and I begin this manifesto of gratitude by thanking the fellow travelers whose friendship and support meant a great deal to me through those years, especially Suzanne Akbari, Massimo Ciavolella, Diana Fuller, María Rosa Menocal, Bill Granara, and Brian Stock. While thinking about the book, I benefited greatly from discussions at the University of California Humanities Research Institute project on the medieval and early modern Mediterranean, convened by Brian Catlos and Sharon Kinoshita, and at the National Endowment for the Humanities seminar in Barcelona on the medieval Mediterranean, also organized by Sharon and Brian. I have given invited lectures on this material and received valuable comments in response at the Department of Humanities and the Center for Arab-American Studies at the University of Michigan, Dearborn; the Department of Romance Languages and Literatures at the University of Michigan, Ann Arbor; the Humanities Center at Harvard University; the Center for Middle East Studies at the University of California at Berkeley; and the American University of Beirut. Grants from the American University of Beirut and Miami University supported the research that went into the book.

Alberto Varvaro read the chapters on Sicilian historiography and on Enrico Cerulli and corrected a number of errors. Jim Turner read an early draft of my pages on the history of philology and gave me useful advice. Peter Williams and Jim Hanges talked to me about the history of fundamentalism, and George Hoffman read an early version of the first chapter and contributed his own insights into fundamentalism. I benefited from hearing Roberto Dainotto's assessment of Michele Amari's monumental work on Muslim Sicily, while his own pages on Amari (in *Europe [in Theory]*) were in press. A number of Maltese scholars offered me tutorials in the Maltese language and Maltese history: Joseph Brincat, Charles Dalli, Oliver Friggieri, Gloria Lauri Lucente, Simon Mercieca, Immanuel Mifsud, and Dominic Senec. Maria Pina di Simone at the Archivi Centrali dello Stato helped me to track down the letter in Enrico Cerulli's Polizia Politica file. Gianfranco Fiaccadori, a scholar of the languages of East Africa, spoke to me about Cerulli's scholarship and career. Mia Fuller read parts of the chapter on Cerulli in draft and shared with me the discovery of Cerulli's late-career reappraisal of his colonial experience. Bill Granara offered a useful response to an early draft of my reading of the *Thousand and One Nights*. Dwight Reynolds first steered me toward the problematic passage from Alvarus's "Indiculus Luminosus" discussed in Chapter 6, and Elizabeth Bergman humored me by reading Alvarus's Latin with an Arabist's eye. I received invaluable assistance from librarians at the Archivi Centrali dello Stato, the Accademia dei Lincei, the Biblioteca di studi meridionali Giustino Fortunato, the Istituto per l'Oriente, the Biblioteca di storia moderna e contemporanea, the Istituto Italiano per l'Africa e l'Oriente, and the Biblioteca Nazionale in Rome; the library of the Università degli Studi di Napoli "l'Orientale" and the Biblioteca Nazionale in Naples; the Biblioteca comunale tenente Filippo Testa in Formia; and the Melitensia library at the University of Malta. Without the thoughtful advice of this small army of specialists, this would have been a much poorer book than it is; the errors that remain, of course, are my own.

I am especially grateful for the support and interest of Jerry Singerman and the University of Pennsylvania Press. I received very insightful reports from anonymous readers when the book was in press; I owe thanks to both of those readers (one of whom, Chris Chism, is—on her own initiative—no longer anonymous) and apologies where due for the astute advice I failed to follow.

When I first formulated the thesis of this book and wrote the first tentative prospectus describing it, I was living in Beirut and teaching a course at the American University on modern epic literature. We began the semester by reading selections from the *Thousand and One Nights*, and my students encouraged me to see Scheherazade as a heroine in a truly epic struggle: the effort to resist oppressive leadership in order to articulate a national consciousness with its roots in popular sentiment. If my view of Scheherazade has grown darker since then, it is no fault of the students at AUB, who defied my expectations by proposing a vibrant and hopeful reading of her as a model for resistance against long odds.

Portions of this book have appeared in earlier publications and are reprinted with the permission of the original publishers: material included in Chapter 3 appeared in *California Italian Studies* and *Romanic Review*; sections of Chapter 6 appeared in *New Literary History*.